DATE DUE

DE 08 '95			

Conditional Love

Conditional Love

Parents' Attitudes Toward Handicapped Children

Meira Weiss

BERGIN & GARVEY
Westport, Connecticut • London

Library of Congress Cataloging-in-Publication Data

Weiss, Meira.
   Conditional love : parent's attitudes toward handicapped children
/ Meira Weiss.
     p.   cm.
   Includes bibliographical references and index.
   ISBN 0-89789-324-7 (alk. paper)
   1. Parents of handicapped children—Israel—Attitudes—
Longitudinal studies. I. Title.
HQ759.913.W45 1994
306.874—dc20   92-39123

British Library Cataloguing in Publication Data is available.

Library of Congress Catalog Card Number: 92-39123
ISBN: 0-89789-324-7

First published in 1994

Bergin & Garvey, 88 Post Road West, Westport, CT 06881
An imprint of Greenwood Publishing Group, Inc.

Printed in the United States of America

The paper used in this book complies with the
Permanent Paper Standard issued by the National
Information Standards Organization (Z39.48-1984).

10 9 8 7 6 5 4 3 2 1

Contents

Contents

Preface

This is an account of how a child's appearance determines his or her parents' terms of affection. It explores practices of abandonment, dehumanization, territorial seclusion and abuse to which Israeli parents subject their appearance-impaired children. The harsh descriptions contained in the following pages perhaps demand some form of preparatory frame-of-reference, a set of epistemological propositions to prepare the ground for ethnography that touches upon some of our cultural premises which we take most for granted. My point of departure is that parenthood is anything other than "natural"; rather, it is constructed through a matrix of images, meanings, sentiments and practices that are everywhere socially and culturally produced. My search after this "cultural pragmatics" of parenthood will entail the deconstruction of its "poetics"—namely, the myth of bonding and so-called "motherly love." Alongside this deconstruction, it will offer an analysis of what seems to me a universal aspect of behavior—the significance given to "body image" and how it determines the acceptance/abandonment of the child. This book, then, can also be read as an analysis of the biopolitics of falling in love with your child.

Conventional ethical concerns demand that the anthroplogist constantly be neutral and uncommited (cf. Hastrup and Elsass, 1990). The unconventional nature of this ethnography, however, has put me in a double bind, demanding that I be both neutral and committed at the same time. Thus, while I continued to observe and document the harsh sights of child abuse with professional neutrality, my growing commitment toward these children motivated continuation of the fieldwork. Whenever I encountered parental behavior that could be termed abusive in the eyes of the law, I immediately informed the proper authorities. However, this "abusive behavior" raises further questions, on a deeper anthropological and philosophical level, and it is these questions that led to the writing of this book.

Keeping neutral was often a difficult task. It is also reflected in my use of the plural form ("we") throughout the body of the text. This use may seem artificial to some, but it can best be understood as conveying the voice of an anthropologist in professional distress. It is the outgrowth of the double bind of neutrality and commitment. Hence the use of "we" should not be considered as a form of detached voice, but rather as an attempt at distancing oneself from a scene to which one feels too attached. Only in the preface and the conclusion do I use the personal "I" freely, and only in the last part of the conclusion (the "reflections") do I offer an ethical perspective based on value judgements.

Nancy Scheper-Hughes (1992)[1] studied maternal practices in Brazil, where child death is widespread and results in a delayed attachment to infants, as well as a disposition to "abandon" children who are born "passive, sick, convulsed or ugly." Interestingly, she contends that she must establish, in her book, "some basis for empathy, for a shared understanding of sentiments and practices that seem so very different from our own and therefore so profoundly disturbing" (Scheper-Hughes, 1992, p. 340). I cannot share Scheper-Hughes standpoint. The set of parental practices described here remain profoundly disturbing, though perhaps not so very different from our own. They are disturbing by nature, and no rhetorical manipulation is attempted in order to conceal it. The particular set of ecological constraints found in Brazil serves as a materialistic explanation, as well as justification, of the "death without weeping" described by Scheper-Hughes. However, the set of parental patterns of behavior portrayed here was found to occur amid parents of different ethnic origin, social standing, education and occupational status. The ghost of "cultural materialism," therefore, could not be invoked, and my findings had to be construed through a different perspective. Perhaps it is best that I now give a concise articulation of the dicourses in which I find myself a party—both the lay and scientific discourse on bonding, on the one hand, and the feminist discourse on parenthood (and especially motherhood), on the other. It is against these two cultural paradigms that the ensuing ethnography is set, and together they form the material for the synthesis and critique this enthnography offers.

THE MYTH OF BONDING, THE FEMINIST DISCOURSE, AND BODY IMAGE

"Bonding" is commonly understood by social scientists, psychologists, physicians and lay men alike to consist of the natural, regular process of "falling in love" with one's child just after birth. It is "that process through which the mother and the child come together and the child realizes that that's the mother it was born out of and the mother makes the outward realization that that is her child" (a midwife quoted in Arney, 1985, p. 156). Notwithstanding the obvious observation that such "realizations" indeed take place, what interests me here is the definition of that process as being regular, natural, and furthermore, "motherly."

These assumptions regarding the nature of bonding and its universal existence have been accepted uncritically, despite various methodological flaws and scientific problems involved in the research. Evidence for bonding are derived from two sources: ethnological research and quasi-experimental human research (see, e.g., Klaus and Kennell, 1976; Wilson, 1975; Klaus et al., 1972; Schaffer, 1977; Lytton, 1980). These sources perhaps take their conceptual point of departure from Darwin's (1896, p. 563) conviction that the feeling of the mother for her child is "a maternal instinct," leading women to show "greater tenderness and less selfishness" and display "these qualities towards her infants in an eminent degree." For a methodological and conceptual critique of the various studies of animal birth practices, postnatal separation and adoption, the reader is referred to Arney (1985, Chapter 5). This ethnological "evidence," however, only comprised part of the case. It was to join forces with the interest of the medical profession (especially obstetrics) in extending its reach beyond birth to the early postnatal period of "adjustment." "Bonding" facilitated a new synthesis of mother and baby as a unit of interest, following the division of the unit that occurred with the earlier discovery of the fetus. It extended the obstetrical domain outside the hospital and into the family. Furthermore, it provided both direct and indirect justification for necessary social "reforms" and policies, such as legally forcing reluctant parents to take home their appearance-impaired newborns (as in Israel, for example). More generally, it served to resurrect old arguments justifying certain social practices, clothing them in a new scientific rhetoric. For bonding is perhaps first and foremost a theory that lends legitimacy to the notion that women are the only appropriate attendants for children. It is, in the phrasing of Marxist feminists that we shall examine later, an ideological justification for keeping women in the home with their children, hence perpetuating their inequality in the labor market.

"Motherly love" is one of the most prominent commonplace expressions found behind the ideology of bonding. The two are, in fact, mutually dependent; if "motherly love" is uncritically accepted, then "bonding" necessarily follows. However, while "bonding" has lent itself "scientific" definition in the discourse of psychology, ethnology and obstetrics, "motherly love" has remained beyond the reach of "scientific analysis." Below is a rather brief discussion of the invention of motherly love, followed by the ambivalent view that feminists take of it.

Elizabeth Badinter (1981) argues that motherly love is a bourgeois invention, discovered as recently as the 19th century. Viviana Zelizer (1985) found that until the 19th century in the Western world, children were valued by their parents only as workers. Only in the late 19th century did children begin to be valued for their emotional or intrinsic worth; at that point, they became "priceless." For very poor women, the emotional bonding that is taken fo granted by the middle and upper classes may be, even today, an unaffordable luxury (cf. Boswell, 1988; Fuchs, 1984, 1992; Scheper-Hughes, 1992). Numerous historical accounts of children who were so expendable that they were not named until it was clear they would survive their first year (Aries, 1962) support this claim. Indeed, the history of childhood is more characterized by beating, neglect, abuse, abandonment, and even infanticide (cf. de Mause, 1974; Scrimshaw, 1984)—not to mention the common practice of wet-nursing, which may be referred to as little more than a public license to kill unwanted and excess babies, or other notorious social practices such as foundling homes, baby "pap" and the common use of laudanum syrup and other narcotic "pacifiers"—than by romantic "motherly love." Thus the modern invention of mother love goes along not only with the rise of the modern bourgeois nuclear family but also with a demographic transition involving a precipitous decline in infant mortality and female fertility. As Nancy Scheper-Hughes (1992, p. 401) puts it, "modern notions of mother love derive from a new reproductive strategy": to give birth to few infants and to "invest heavily in each one from birth onward."

Having drawn this critical description, we now come to the feminist notions of mother love. These notions fall into two opposing camps. The first succumbs to the radical, ideological interpretation which regards "mother love," as well as bonding theory, as prejudiced against women interested in pursuing a life in which children are not a woman's *raison d'etre* or her exclusive focus of attention. "Mother love" here stands for woman's traditional role in childcare, which constitutes a major source of women's subordination. Tiger and Fox (1974, p. 110), for instance, assert that this role has entailed "the male control of females for sex and dominance, and the female use of the male for impregnation and protection."

The second, opposite feminist view of mother love stems from what Sayers (1982) has called "biological essentialism." Alice Rossi, for instance, who first recommended that sexual equality would only be achieved by getting women and men to participate equally in looking after children (Rossi, 1964), later declared that the traditional division of childcare between the sexes is ordained by biologically determined differences. Biology has rendered women better able than men to care for children (Rossi, 1977). Rossi further implied that oxytocin uniformly makes women maternal towards their children, and that this lactation hormone results in an "innate predisposition in the mother to relate intensely to the infant" (Rossi, 1977, p. 24). It would be wrong, then, for women to ignore their "true nature"; they can achieve equality only by celebrating their unique "feminine virtues." In the same vein, Helen Lewis (1976) urges women to value their traditional role in childcare, a role which she says is devalued only because we live in an exploitative society.

The feminist theories of the "biological essentialism" type are in fact based on a certain conception of human (and maternal) nature. Among the theories proposing essential, or universal, womanly scripts are Sara Ruddick's (1983) "maternal thinking," Nancy Chodorow's (1978) "feminine personality," and Carol Gilligan's (1982) "womanly ethos"—all of which, on closer examination, can be found to be both culturally and historically bound. Chodorow's, for instance, is a brand of "psychological essentialism" arguing that the emotional bond between mother and daughter does not lead to the development of strong ego boundaries, but to identification and mergence. This is reversed in the case of boys, who further distance themselves from their mothers through the oedipal and adolescent stages. This sex difference perpetuates itself when women recreate their early experience of childcaring, a function that men (as a result of their childrearing) are ill-equipped to fulfill.

My own findings challenge both the "scientific" conception of maternal "bonding" and those cultural feminists who argue for a singular, essentialist conception of a "womanly" ethic and ethos of maternal responsiveness, attentiveness, and caring labor. Indeed, these two conceptions are interconnected, as the reductionist form of the latter can be seen in the clinical literature on maternal "bonding" understood as a universal maternal script.

The significance attached by the parents I observed to the external appearance of their child points to an alternative course of analysis. Generally speaking, I will argue that a child's impaired appearance differs from the normal body image that we hold. Note that my use of the term "body image" differs from that of conventional psychological terminology. In the absence of a better word, I use it to denote the overall pattern of cognition, the "gestalt," the species-specific internal representation applying to the human body's contours.

It is this particular difference between impaired appearance and body image which is capable of producing a cognitive dissonance powerful enough to disrupt the "order of things." The congenitally deformed infant challenges the tentative and fragile symbolic boundaries between human and non-human, natural and supernatural, normal and abnormal. Such infants may not fit into a specific category and can be viewed with reserve or revulsion as a source of pollution, disorder, and danger. This can result in stigmatization of the appearance-impaired child as a "non-person," and lead to his/her rejection.

This book can therefore be read as yet another contribution to the growing corpus of "sociologies of embodiment" (Turner 1991). It "re-discovers" the body not only through some abstract, theoretical viewpoint—be it psychological, sociological, or feminist—but also as the phenomenological key to the pragmatics of parenting: the criterion by which we decide to fall in love with our child.

NOTES

1. The Hebrew edition of my book was published in 1991-1992, before the appearance of Scheper-Hughes' book, which only became available at the editing stage in production of the English edition of my book. Nevertheless, due to the great significance of Scheper-Hughes' work, I have made reference to it here.

Introduction

PARENTING: CHALLENGING A MYTH

Among the public at large and professionals in the field it is generally
thought that parents accept their children unconditionally, that they nat-
urally and instinctively bestow on their children endless loving care,[1] and
that parents' love of their children is universal and independent of cultural
affiliation, the child's behavior, or pressures of environment. I challenge
these assumptions.

Do parents always accept their children? Are there situations in which
they do not? How are parental bonds formed? Are they self-evident? Do
they assume varying intensities? Are they automatic, or conditional upon
some examination? Under what circumstances do parents tend to reject
their children, and under what circumstances do they tend to accept them?

In this book I shall examine these questions with reference to abnormal
children in Israel.

Are there difficulties in the cognitive location of the handicapped child?
What significance do parents attribute to the external appearance of their
children? How does a handicapped child appear in her parents' eyes? What
sort of image does she evoke? Who is permitted to enter the territorial
bounds of the family? In what ways is a handicapped child isolated from
the family territory, and in what ways is she included? Do handicapped
children have separate and special rooms or places in the house? What varieties of responsibility do parents assume with respect to their handicapped
children? Can a parent reject a child from the home and yet evince a sense
of responsibility towards her?

These queries lead us to wonder about the essential nature of the most
fundamental human bond and make us realize how tenuous this bond might
be in certain situations.

PARENTING AND BODY IMAGE

This book examines the interrelation of two main topics: the significance of parenting and the significance of body image in social relations.

The significance of parenting is examined in terms of its connection with the body; and the significance of the body is examined in terms of parental relations. Moreover, we shall see that both parenting and body image are social constructs, and that the significance attributed to both is societal and cultural, not personal. We are born into a world in which the significance of parenting and the significance of the body has already been constructed for us.

Throughout the book I shall examine the importance of the child's body in the formation, maintenance, and breakdown of parental bonds. Is it important to be good-looking in order to be pleasing to one's parents? What happens if a person is not good-looking? What does it mean to be good-looking? Is having beauty as defined by the parents' aesthetic criteria a precondition for love and formation of parental bonds? What other aspects of the body are important in the formation of bonds? What prior assumptions regarding the human body are refuted when one comes into close contact with physical abnormality?

ATTITUDES TOWARDS HANDICAPPED CHILDREN

How we relate to deformed and abnormal children has been a subject of discussion primarily for psychologists, sociologists, and social workers. This book approaches several basic assumptions from a different angle than what is generally found in the literature and accepted by the public.

Some experts view parents of an abnormal child as bereaved parents and as such interpret the parents' behavior as "working out their grief" over the death of the normal child who should have been born to them (cf., for example, Solnit and Stark, 1961). These and other scholars view the behavior of a fatally sick child as "advance mourning" for the child before he has died.[2] Such mourning is comprised of a series of responses including: shock, despair, blame, anger, bitterness, and adjustment to the condition. Literature with a psychoanalytic bent stresses the parents' use of defense mechanisms such as: denial, projection, displacement, and intellectualization,[3] and maintains that these mechanisms help parents cope with fears stemming from the birth of a handicapped child and serve to protect their ego structure.

I am opposed to automatically transferring findings, concepts, and analytical methods from studies of bereavement to cases of abnormal children, both because studies of bereavement leave something to be desired in their value judgments, and because relying on these studies is likely to lead to fundamental errors, which I have mentioned elsewhere (Weiss, 1989),[4] being transferred to the field of research on abnormal children. Thus the object of this study is to understand how we relate to handicapped children, without being bound by prior value judgments or expecting stereotypes to be transferred from one area to another. The data that I have gathered over an extended period show that the ideas and assertions that prevail in sociological and psychological studies must be re-examined.

Earlier studies have also asked what factors underlie parental behavior towards handicapped children. Some experts specify the impact of the child's sex, his behavior, and the type, severity, and visibility of his handicap. Others relate to the cause of the handicap (genetic or environmental), the extent to which the defect can be repaired, the estimated time schedule of the repair, the anticipated impediment due to the defect, special treatment necessary, the attendant threat to life, and the circumstances in which a person comes to have the defect or handicap.[5]

Some experts have attributed the parents' behavior to social and cultural factors. These experts classified subgroups in the population according to such variables as education, occupation, religion, or ethnic affiliation,[6] but did not reach a general consensus on the relative importance of these factors in determining the way parents relate to a sick, deformed, or handicapped child.

The shortcomings of their analysis of the ethnic factor are particularly evident. These researchers do not separate ethnic affiliation from other variables generally associated with it, such as: class, education, or living conditions.[7] It also seems that their distinction between "Ashkenazi" (or "Western") Jewish families and "Eastern Jews" is not based on a solid empirical foundation,[8] but rather reflects stereotypical thinking drawn from the researcher's daily life. In this book, in contrast to the existing studies, I shall not get into the dichotomy of "Eastern" vs. "Western" but shall simply note the parent's country of origin.

Moreover, while other studies generally predefine the abnormal child according to medical assessments, this book defines the abnormal child as whomever is viewed as abnormal by his parents. These are some of the differences between this study and other studies dealing directly with attitudes towards abnormal persons.

The last matter I wish to stress in this regard pertains to my research method. I have based my studies on actual observation of parental behavior, whereas most other researchers have based their work on laboratory experiments and interviews. Thus, their findings regarding the essence of parental behavior towards children are based on answers supplied by the parents to questions specifically addressed to them; this method, which encourages adherence to accepted myths, obstructs one from seeing parental behavior towards children as it is in actual fact.

The literature dealing directly with attitudes towards abnormal children, reviewed above, was not helpful in explaining my findings and in many instances has actually been refuted by my study.

The data which I gathered, however, have revealed the relevance of other issues that ostensibly do not appear to be directly related to parental relations towards abnormal children. For example, the importance of aesthetic considerations in social relations, stigmatization, body image, body boundaries, and territorial behavior.

RESEARCH METHOD

My study[9] is based primarily on observations made in the daytime and nighttime, as well as interviews with parents of children hospitalized in three hospitals in different parts of Israel.[10] To understand the primal relationship between parent and child I observed mothers[11] in the labor rooms and maternity wards of two hospitals, newborns in two hospital wards, and premature babies in two wards. To understand the relationship between a parent and a disabled or ill child, after a primary relationship has been formed, I also observed children's wards in three hospitals. In addition, I made occasional visits to children's emergency rooms, general emergency rooms, an orthopedic ward and a burn-treatment ward.[12]

The data were collected over the course of six years.[13] Aside from my observations of and interviews with parents, I also collected material based on interviews with the medical staff, welfare workers, and social workers associated with the hospitals and the communities in which the subjects observed resided. Interviews with the medical staff were used to provide information about the medical condition of the patients. The interviews were supplemented by medical data and descriptions of the medical history in the patients' files.

To understand other facts such as the parents' social setting or the sort of help that the parents received from neighbors or relatives, I made house visits to 200 parents either for a one-time interview or for more extended observation. (These 200 families were selected from the families with whom initial contact was made in the hospital, some by way of liaisons from the hospital.)

Data collection was assisted by many faculty and students, without whose help all the raw material that went into the making of this book could not have been obtained.

The decision to run the study in three hospitals, not one, stemmed from my desire to preclude the possibility of alternate explanations for the parents' behavior, such as the particular policy of the hospital's director or the head nurse, or the particular type of population served by the given hospital.

Central Hospital is a large, centrally located hospital of long standing that serves a secular as well as ultra-orthodox population, Jews as well as Arabs. The hospital provides other hospitals with consultation services and specialized medical treatment; thus it serves a population residing in various parts of the country. Southern Hospital and Northern Hospital are situated in the southern and northern parts of the country, respectively. Both are relatively small hospitals serving only the local population. The maternity ward of Southern Hospital has rooming-in.

The psychological and sociological studies of the subjects concerning us frequently used laboratory experiments[14] and structured interviews, mostly one-time meetings held in the parents' home; but "none of the existing studies of the reactions of adults to children of varying degrees of attractiveness used direct observation of adult-child interactions" (Hildebrandt, 1982, p. 196). Even studies based on interviews reflect a partial severance from real life situations; for example, researchers who examined the behavior of parents towards crippled children[15] did not generally observe actual interactions with such children. Some researchers asked parents to evaluate their interactions by answering questions about the amount of time they devote to their children. In other words, the subjects were requested to report verbally not only on their attitude towards their handicapped children, but also on supposedly factual data pertaining to their behavior towards their children.

I have attempted to overcome the shortcomings of existing research by my study which is based on observation of the actual behavior of parents towards their children and does not rely on verbal testimony after the fact. In my opinion the use of interviews should be restricted to examining verbal expression. When, in contrast, the objective is to examine factual data pertaining to behavior which is not verbal (such as stroking or touching), there is no point in questioning the subject and asking him to report on his behavior towards his children. To know how much time a parent devotes to a handicapped child and how he spends that time one should, in my opinion, observe the parties directly. Also when the purpose is to examine the stands parents take towards handicapped children, one cannot make do with holding an interview in the parents' home. I agree with A. O. Ross, who says, "We do not know to what extent the verbal proclamations of mothers actually match their true feelings" (Ross, p. 1964). By running the study in the hospital, the researcher cannot simply take parents' statements at face value, since in this setting the parents are required to choose in actual fact among a number of alternatives—whether to touch or not to touch their baby, to kiss or not to kiss him, to take their child home or to leave him in the hospital; whether to sing him a lullaby; or whether to wish he were dead.

Also, when studies based on interviews speak of rejection, they do so in a vague manner without relating to actual behavior. Observing an individual in the hospital provides an opportunity to dwell on behavioral manifestations during all hours of the day and night, to observe non-verbal patterns of behavior and messages transmitted by means of ostensibly similar patterns of behavior, and to compare word with deed. The research method, the field of research, and the great length of time devoted to data collection made it possible to follow up on a considerable number of families over the course of several years. Thus I could focus on dynamic aspects of behavior and explain what brought about the changes in the parents' behavior.

Initially my preference of the hospital over other locations (such as the observee's house) as the primary setting for observation and making contact with the families stemmed from considerations of technical convenience. Retrospectively, however, this choice proved to have other advantages. Those hospitals in which I made my observations in most cases let parents spend many hours of the day, and sometimes the entire day and night, with their newborns in order to give their children parental attention and sometimes even certain kinds of nursing care. Thus I was able to observe far more parents for many more hours than would have been feasible had the observing been done in the home. Moreover, since most mothers give birth in the hospital and any child might come to the hospital, I was able to include in my study children who suffered from a variety of disabilities or illnesses: children with protracted illnesses and passing illnesses; children of families belonging to different ethnic groups, nationalities, and socio-economic classes and living in different parts of Israel.

Observing subjects in the hospital in addition to the home was helpful in two other ways. Because there are so many strangers in the hospital, my presence was less obvious there than it would have been in the home; The hospital setting made it more difficult for parents to disguise behavior that is considered unacceptable and that expresses hostility towards their children; at home certain behavior can be hidden even from other family members, but in the hospital everything the patient does is subject to surveillance day and night.

Countering these points, it must be said that observing parents in an unfamiliar setting, surrounded by strangers and with their behavior exposed to others, raised the question whether, insofar as the hospital was not a natural setting, findings based on hospital observation could be generalized to other settings. Therefore it was also important to make observations in the home. Retrospectively, having observed subjects in the hospital as well as in the home, I see that this concern was unfounded. Most parents feel quite comfortable in the hospital after a fairly short time, both because of giving personal signs of identification to the place, making it familiar and personal, and because of socially adjusting to other people being present and to having many eyes fixed on their behavior. In general it seems that there is no single "natural" setting for parent-child relationships. These relationships find expression in a variety of settings, all of which are natural.

I would like to elucidate several more points regarding my methods; for example, how I obtained entry to the hospital wards, how my official capacity was defined, how I presented myself to the subjects and the staff, and how even the hospital staff itself was kept from knowing who were the subjects involved in the study.

I obtained entry into the hospital with the assistance of certain members of the hospital staff: nurses, doctors, and social workers. In each ward I had at least one contact who knew about the study, introduced me to the ward and its set-up, presented the various families and their problems, explained medical problems and let me be present during the contact's conversations with the subjects. In general I enjoyed tremendous assistance. Yet, I also needed a measure of independence, which was likely to suffer occasionally due to attempts by some of the contacts to find out "what I saw today" and to steer me in directions which they felt were important. Therefore, I took the following measures: meetings with contacts were restricted primarily to the beginning of the observation period; observation days and times were varied; and an attempt was made to set observation times that would allow maximum freedom of action; I did my best not to stand out. Only a few of the hospital staff were aware that the study was being made.

Presenting myself to the subjects was simply and easy. I did not have a clearly defined position and generally did not introduce myself, unless explicitly asked. I was simply one of the many strangers—students, residents, and parents—milling around the ward. The situation was no different even when I wore a gown, as the nursing staff sometimes requested me to do. Only on relatively rare occasions was I asked to explain my presence. In such situations, the conversation often ran as follows:

SUBJECT: What are you doing here? Are you a doctor?
OBSERVER: No. I'm doing a study.
SUBJECT: What about?
OBSERVER: Ways of making improvements.
SUBJECT: In what area?
OBSERVER: That is just what I want to find out from you.
SUBJECT: How can I be of assistance?

The last matter I must elucidate is how details pertaining to the subjects were concealed. This was especially important because I had given explicit assurances that everything pertaining to identification of the subjects would remain confidential as a precondition for my being permitted to hold observations, and because of my sense of basic ethical duty. Therefore I changed the names of subjects and details that were not relevant to my main claims.

Every attempt was made to prevent identification of the hospitals in which the observations were made, the names of the wards and the names of the subjects, so that even people working in the hospital would not be able to identify the doctors and nurses whom I quoted or the children whom I described in the book.

THE STRUCTURE OF THIS BOOK

Each chapter presents one main assertion. Each assertion is based on information culled from all the cases. Thus study is based on observation of 1,450 cases, of which 1,288 involved parents of abnormal or ill children, and 162 involved pregnant women who either had a healthy child or a still-birth.[16] This covers all the cases in the wards during the period of study. The claims made in the book are illustrated by detailed descriptions of 43 representative cases, less detailed descriptions of dozens of other cases, and general statistical analyses.[17]

In this book I try to show that the way parents view their responsibility towards their children and their willingness for territorial closeness or distance from their children are responses that stem from the children's external appearance as perceived and interpreted by the parents. Parents tend to accept their children when the latter satisfy the parent's aesthetic criteria, as determined by their culture and social circle; parents tend to reject their children when the latter do not match the parents' criteria of beauty. Moreover, the child's looks have a great impact on his image as either a "person" or a "non-person," and hence also a great impact on behavior towards him. Thus, external appearance relates to image, and image relates to behavior. This assertion is discussed in various chapters of the book.

In Chapter 1, I discuss the importance of aesthetics and looks in parent-child relations. I maintain that the parents' response is influenced by the external appearance of their children. This applies to normal as well as abnormal children. In this chapter we meet a number of mothers of normal children who subject their babies to an external examination as soon as they are born. Only those children who pass the examination and measure up to their mother's criteria of beauty are taken into the family and accepted by their mother. The criteria of beauty include order and proportion among the parts of the body. The children who do not pass the test are generally those who have a deformity or something abnormal about their looks.

In Chapter 2, I investigate the nature of the threat presented by the body of the abnormal child and by his abnormality which leads to his rejection. It appears that a child is rejected when there are difficulties in determining his cognitive location. In such contexts he does not measure up to the accepted image of a "person" and he is perceived and labeled as a "non-person" (by use of such appellations as "monster," "*wahaj*" (monster), "unicorn," etc.). Labeling a child as a "non-person" is especially significant since it paves the way to "legitimized" violence against him.

Thus a lack of aesthetics is viewed as a threat to basic order: we have a vision of how a "person" should look and we reject those individuals whose external appearance affronts our basic image of a "person."

In Chapter 3, I examine whether parental response is direct or indirect. We see that parents respond to the body image of their child (i.e., to the way they perceive his body) and not to the child's body itself. An image is comprised of two components: cognitive and visual. In Chapter 3, I focus on the visual image, i.e., on the distinction between external appearance as it is in fact and the way in which it is interpreted or perceived in the mind. This concept is illustrated primarily via a discussion of the behavior of parents of children with Down's syndrome or cancer.

In Chapter 4, we see that parents reject their children in contexts which produce the feeling that their children's body boundaries have been violated and that, by a sort of contagion, their own body boundaries are threatened as well. This is illustrated by the behavior of parents of children connected to medical apparatuses or children with unusual openings in their bodies, children whose heads have been shaved, or children who emit a foul odor. We also meet parents who are bothered by having to deal with excretions of older children, obesity in children, or drastic swelling of part or all of the body. My findings show that such situations cause parents to feel that there has been a violation of the body boundaries of their children, and subsequently also of themselves.

In Chapters 5 and 6, I relate to two dimensions of parental behavior towards children: accepting responsibility for the child's life and willingness to spend time and live with him in a common territory. In Chapter 5 we see that the territorial behavior towards handicapped children is different from that towards normal children. My findings reveal that a deformed child who is not defined as a "person" is not granted the right to be present in the family territory with equal status to that of other members of the family. This chapter describes the various ways in which territorial isolation is achieved within the home.

In Chapter 6, I maintain that every parent must make a decision regarding the type of responsibility he has for his child, a decision which expresses either acceptance or rejection of his child. Perceptions of parental responsibility range from absolute acceptance of responsibility in every regard to total rejection attesting the complete absence of responsibility and rejection of the child from the parent's world. This rejection of responsibility also manifests itself in violence towards the child or in making demands of others that will assure the child's death. Here, too, casting off responsibility is a result of the interpretation give the external appearance or body image of the child.

Each chapter can be viewed as an independent unit, or as a continuation of previous chapters. For example, the first chapter brings out the importance of the external appearance of the child in determining parental behavior towards him, as brought out in greater detail in the subsequent chapters. Yet this chapter also examines several general questions, such as: is it important to be good-looking? What is the place of aesthetics in social behavior? What does it mean to be beautiful? Similarly, Chapter 5, which deals with the general question of the social construct of the home and the importance of disability in this construct, also is a continuation of previous chapters in that it shows the various ways of actually locating the disabled child and brings out the connection between the nature of the child's location and the nature of the interpretation given his condition and appearance.

The book ends with a presentation of the conclusions that follow from my study and from putting to test the basic, primal assumptions that we make about the essence of mankind, the human body, and parenting.

I conclude with some personal reflections.

NOTES

1. For example, Parsons, in Halsey, 1967, p. 395; Goffman, 1963, pp. 29–77, p. 48; Spock, 1957.

2. Cf., for example, Waechter, 1977; MacKeith, 1973; Solnit and Stark, 1961; Engel, 1961a, 1961b; Peretz, 1970; Clifford, 1969; Kennel, Slyter, and Klaus, 1970; Bruckner, 1954; Daniels and Berg, 1968.

3. Cf., for example, Ross, 1964; Mandelbaum and Wheeler, 1960; Solnit and Stark, 1961.

4. Experts on children with disabilities or diseases assume either openly or covertly that there are "successful solutions," "effective ways of coping," "adjustment," "rehabilitation," or "constructive and adaptive behavior" (Zeider and Marom, 1980, for example); and that, on the other hand, there are also "ineffective patterns of coping," "unsuccessful solutions," and "deficient adjustment and rehabilitation."

5. For example, cf. Titze, 1962; Waechter, 1977; Offord and Aponte, 1967; Ross, 1964; Easson, 1966; Titze and Gomperz, 1962; Clifford, 1969; Tudor, 1979; Denhoff, 1960; MacGregor et al., 1953, Mercer, 1974.

6. For example, cf. Gourevitch, 1973, p. 25; Binger et al., 1969; Friedman, 1964; Yudkin, 1967; Leiken and Hassakis, 1973, p. 51; Gardner, 1959; Zuk, Miller, et al., 1961, 1963; Jordan, 1968; Shurka and Florian, 1983; Florian

and Shurka, 1981; Weller et al., 1974; Palgi, 1962; Mundel, Palgi, Pinkus, and Greenberger, 1969; Chieger, 1966; Rofeh, Almagor, and Yaffa, 1980.

7. This can be illustrated by a review of studies on attitudes towards invalids in Israel. Most researchers maintain that Eastern Jews tend to have more negative attitudes towards invalids than Western Jews. According to Florian and Katz (1983), however, one should be wary of drawing such a conclusion, since alternative reasons can be offered to account for the differences in attitude, such as religiosity, educational attainment, gender of the person holding the attitude, contact with the invalid, cause of the disability, structure of the family (traditional vs. modern), etc. Thus, according to Florian and Katz (1983) we may conclude that the attitudes towards the invalid in Israel do not stem from a single variable, such as cultural background, religion, or ethnic affiliation, but from the interaction of a number of variables relating to cultural, ethnic, and religious norms. In addition, a review of the literature on this question often shows reliance on unfounded studies and superficial generalizations, and therefore many of the findings of these studies must be viewed with reservation.

8. In this regard I agree with Florian and Katz that the "Eastern Jews" should not necessarily be viewed as a homogeneous group.

9. This book is based on research done for my doctorate, written under the direction of two anthropologists, Prof. Moshe Shokeid and Prof. Shlomo Deshen, at Tel Aviv University. The data collection and doctorate were completed in 1986.

10. The real names of the hospitals are not given, a precondition for being permitted to undertake the study. No names or any other details that might expose the subjects or hospital staff involved have been disclosed.

11. The fathers wre generally not present in the delivery room, since in "difficult" births the fathers were generally asked to leave. Moreover, during the years the data was collected (the late 1980's), it was not customary in all hospitals in Israel for fathers to be present in the delivery room.

12. At the time the study was made husbands were not yet routinely allowed in delivery rooms. Nor was there a uniform policy, either in the delivery rooms or in the newborn and children's wards, regarding whether or not parents should be informed of a suspected illness or a defect discovered in their child.

13. During the first few years observations were held three days a week, eight to ten hours each day, and two evenings per week. Once every two weeks all day Saturday was spent observing subjects. In subsequent years the number of observation hours was reduced.

14. For example, Ross and Salvia, 1975; Marwit, Marwit and Walker, 1978; Kehle, Bramble and Mason, 1974; Adams and Cohen, 1976; Hildebrandt and Fitzgerald, 1978, 1981.

15. Cf., for example, Florian, 1977B; Weller et al., 1974; Florian and

Shurka, 2981; Shurka and Florian, 1983.

16. The problems, disabilities, and diseases described in the book include: premature babies, uncertain sex, anacephalous, macrocephalous, spina bifida, hydrocephalous, Down's syndrome, retardation, Klinefelter's syndrome, Turner's syndrome, cleft palate, harelip with or without cleft palate, bone deformation and limping, Hirschsprung's disease, heart defects (blue babies and non-blue babies), hemangioma, severe facial distortion, blindness or severe vision impairment after prolonged incubation, burns, cancer, celiac, diabetes, kidney disease, tracheostomy, colostomy, coma, diseases and infections such as diarrhea, tonsilitis, pneumonitis, and brain abscess.

See Appendix, Table 1. Each defect or disease is explained in the chapter describing the relevant case.

17. See Appendix, Table 2. In each of the cases presented in the book I mention the following parameters: the pseudonym of the hospital, the ward in which the child was hospitalized, the country of birth, educational level, occupation, age, nationality, and socio-economic status of the parents, the disability affecting the child, what information was supplied to the parents and by whom. The case descriptions are based on quotes and precise notes taken on the words and actions of the family members, without any interpretation added. Terms such as "disabled," "handicapped," "abnormal," etc. are used more or less interchangeably.

1

Beautiful Is Fortunate

Parents React to the Looks of Their Children

Is it important to be beautiful? What is achieved by beauty? In what respects is being beautiful most important? What will happen if I am not beautiful? Will I be deprived of certain things that I would have received had I been beautiful? To what extent is beauty significant in our lives?

What does it mean to be beautiful? Is it having a good-looking body? or a beautiful face? What must there be in a face for it to be beautiful? What must there be in a body?

What does it mean to be unattractive? What must be lacking or deficient in one's external appearance to be perceived as not beautiful? Is the focus on a specific part of the body? The overall perception, the gestalt, of the body? Which perception is important? That of the face? The face and hair? If you change what is ugly, do you become beautiful?

Which is more important, the condition of one's heart or the condition of one's hair? When you want to form social bonds with another person, what do you notice in particular? What you know about the inside of the person's body, including essential organs such as the heart and liver; or the person's hair, which is not at all essential to life? Does the same hierarchy of preferences come into play with respect to the decision to sever a bond? In other words, what is the social significance of the external appearance as opposed to the internal condition of one's body?

What is more important—physical traits or personality traits? My looks, or my personality and achievements? Is the same order of factors operative with respect to forming a bond and with respect to maintaining it? In other words, what importance is attached to external appearance in comparison to other messages that one conveys, such as one's achievements and personality traits?

What is the social significance of beauty? Is the very fact of attributing significance to beauty a matter of culture? Is being beautiful, or "not ugly" of equal importance in all cultures? Do all cultures attribute similar importance to external appearance? Are the criteria of beauty the same in all cultures? Do all cultures attribute similar social importance to the presence or absence of hair as a basis for beauty? What can one conclude about a society or culture from the importance given to aesthetics?

BODY AND PARENTING

The general questions posed above are examined in this book with respect to the relations between parents and children. General questions about external appearance and aesthetics will be considered in conjunction with general questions about parenting. For example: How does the external appearance of our child affect our interaction with him or her? our decisions about him or her? Are the expectations that we have of a good-looking child different from those which we have of a child who is not good-looking? Is their a difference in our behavior towards a child who is beautiful and a child who is not? How are parental bonds formed? Are they immediate? Is their formation a gradual process? Are they automatic, or conditional upon examination? What about continuation of these bonds? Is their continuation self-evident? Is it conditional upon re-examination? Can a parental bond be severed? On what grounds? Is failure to pass parental examination likely to lead to severance of a parental bond, once the bond has been forged? What is the nature of parental examination? What is the role of the body in this examination? What is the role of external appearance? of internal aspects of the body?

We shall try to answer most of these questions in this and following chapters.

HOW ARE THESE QUESTIONS TREATED IN THE LITERATURE?

Since there is no systematic study that deals directly with the affect of a child's external appearance on the behavior of his or her parents, I present several studies that deal with the importance of looks in general.[1]

In the social sciences the subject of attractiveness has generally been neglected (Stone, 1962). It seems this neglect stems from the apprehension that to admit the impact of external appearance on interpersonal relations and decisions might sound like a denial of the basic principles of democracy (Berscheid and Walster, 1974). In literature and the humanities, however, the importance of beauty in interpersonal relations has been stressed since time immemorial. Aristotle wrote that "Beauty is the best of all letters of recommendation." In primitive societies, we read in Linton (1936), attractive individuals are more popular, especially as candidates for marriage.

Lately some socio-psychologists have begun to acknowledge physical attractiveness as a legitimate area of study of interpersonal relations. Nevertheless, most of the existing studies on the subject deal with relations among adults, primarily regarding sexual attraction (Gergen and Gergen, 1981, p. 90).

IMPORTANCE OF THE CHILD'S EXTERNAL APPEARANCE

Can one reach a general consensus on the question of who is a beautiful child and who is not? The experts who have looked into this question related separately to face and to body, and found that adults and children generally agree with one another on the attractiveness of the face and body build of children.[2]

Other studies have focused on the expectations had of children who look different. It was found that there is a tendency to be more sympathetic towards children who are attractive and have an average (mesomorphic) body build than towards children who are unattractive and very fat (endomorphic) or very thin (ectomorphic). It was also found that the stereotype "Beautiful is good" is indeed operative. A beautiful child is expected also to be good; to have both positive personality traits and high scholastic achievement (Clifford and Walster, 1973).

No cultural differences were found with respect to stereotypes of body type; a tendency to have positive expectations of a person with an average body type (mesomorph) was found among adolescents as well as adults, among Westerners as well as Japanese and Mexicans.[3]

An inconsequential number of studies investigate differences in behavior towards children who look different. In general, the findings are that children and adults pay more attention and tend to be closer to children who are attractive and not fat. For example, adults take more pleasure in looking at photographs of attractive children than photographs of less good-looking children (Hildebrandt and Fitzgerald, 1978, 1981).

However, there are also studies that have found that the attractiveness of a child does not affect the expectations had of him or her (Dion, 1972; Kehle, Bramble and Mason, 1974), or that it actually has a negative effect (Dion, 1974; LaVoie and Adams, 1974). Hildebrandt concludes from this that physical attractiveness is of limited impact. She (1982, p. 191) and Middlebrook (1980, p. 121) believe that looks have an impact on the expectations had of a child only, or especially, when one does not have other information about the child's personality, achievements, or behavior. When other information is available about the child, the affect of external appearance disappears or diminishes with time. This claim relates especially to studies that dealt with stereotyped body builds and in which the subjects were shown only pictures of the body without receiving further information about the person. Therefore Hildebrandt (1982, p. 193) maintains that perhaps the especial importance attached to body type in existing studies stems from research methods in which no information was given about the person save for that which concerned his or her body type; had other information been given, perhaps it would have decreased the impact of attractiveness. Indeed, a study dealing with body stereotypes (Young and Avdzej, 1979) shows that physical appearance has less impact than behavior on expectations. Also close acquaintance, according to some researchers, is likely to diminish the impact of attractiveness. Thus external appearance has a greater impact in the first few encounters. Nevertheless, there is no consensus regarding this claim, perhaps because most of these studies of attractiveness included only first impressions.

Similar reservations can be brought with regard to studies of people with defects. There are studies showing that children with an external defect are perceived by adults and children as being less attractive than children whose appearance is normal.[4] Nevertheless, some researchers maintain that the impact of the defect is confined only to initial contact, when the child is not known well (Richardson, Ronald and Kleck, 1974). A close relationship, they believe, with a child who has a defect will bring about a change in the response towards him.

None of the studies of adult reactions to children with varying levels of attractiveness employed direct observation of the actual interactions between adults and children (Hildebrandt, 1982, p. 196). Instead of culling evidence through direct observation, they made do with indirect evidence; generally they devised experiments in which the adults were requested to respond to pictures of the faces or bodies of adults and children. Due to the laboratory procedure used by most of the researchers, each study focused on a narrow aspect and traced it over a relatively short period. Moreover, the studies reviewed examined teachers (Clifford, 1975), children (Dion, 1977), college students (Dion, 1972), or parents who were requested to judge children whom they did not know (Adams and LaVoie, 1975). They did not examine beauty as a factor in the relations between parents and children, since one generally does not consider that aesthetic considerations enter into such relations.

Herein lies the innovation of the present study, for it is based on direct observation of the behavior of parents towards their children. Being interested in the broader aspects of the process, I shall attempt to trace it over time and answer some of the questions left open by earlier studies.

Parents' love towards their children is examined in this book through parental relationships to handicapped children. Many scholars and experts in the field view the relationship of parents to children on a continuum of acceptance-rejection. Various reasons, they claim, exist for rejection of an abnormal child: severity of the defect, technical difficulties anticipated in caring for the child, and duration of the illness.[5] I, on the other hand, maintain that it is the child's external appearance that accounts for his acceptance or rejection by his parents. I shall try to substantiate this claim in the course of this chapter.

I begin with a description of the behavior exhibited by mothers immediately upon giving birth to a normal child. As we shall see, the mothers' remarks generally follow a similar pattern. The moment the child is born, the mother expresses interest in the newborn's sex on the basis of external sex organs. At this point some mothers request to see their babies' sex organs in order to confirm the midwife's proclamation regarding the child's sex, which generally elicits either a response of delight or of disappointment. Let my illustrate my point with responses of new mothers from different ethnic and educational backgrounds:

MOTHER 1 (Israeli born, Polish extraction, college education): Wonderful! ... Show him to me (she looks at his penis) ... Wonderful. I wanted to have a boy so much.

MOTHER 2 (born in Morocco, high-school education): What did I do to deserve another girl? I already have four daughters at home! ... I wanted to have a son ... My father passed away, and I wanted to have a son to name after him.

MOTHER 3 (Israeli born, Hungarian extraction, high-school education): Wonderful, I wanted a girl, ... to name after my mother. Let me see her again [*she gazes at the child*]. I am so glad it's a girl.

Thus we see that the initial response has to do with the child's sex. In this regard I agree with Stone (1962), who asserts that on the first level of contact each of the participants presents himself or herself, without words, by his or her external appearance, which makes clear to the observer how the person is to be addressed. Here the sexual presentation is of great moment. In other words, according to Stone, sex is the component of external appearance that determines the nature of the interaction that will develop and the language of address that will be used.

The next element of the mothers' responses is the same for baby boys as for girls. At this stage, when a connection between external form and normalcy is expressed, mothers begin to examine their babies primarily through their sense of sight. The mothers check their babies' bodies, limb by limb, and make comments on their coloring (skin, hair, eyes), size, weight, number of limbs, their perfection and proportion, number of fingers, amount of hair, and cleanliness.

We shall illustrate this next stage with the remarks of several new mothers, beginning with those we encountered above.

MOTHER 1 (Israeli born, Polish extraction, college education): Is he O.K?

Let me see him ... don't dress him; I want to see him bare.

MOTHER 2 (born in Morocco, high-school education): What a cute girl. She's really big.

MOTHER 3 (Israeli born, Hungarian extraction, high-school education): How much does she weigh? She looks so small to me, ... much smaller than her sisters.

MOTHER 4 (physician, born in Egypt): She looks like a real person. Big and pink.

MOTHER 5 (Russian born, vocational school education): What a gorgeous boy. So nice and pink, and such a bright face.

MOTHER 6 (Israeli born, Yemenite extraction, elementary-school education): Tell me, nurse, will her skin remain the same color even when she grows up? What smooth skin ... so soft and velvety ... And pink cheeks ... a face like a cherub ... sweetie.

MOTHER 7 (Christian Arab, high-school education): Look what lovely dark hair he has, ... a head full of hair.

MOTHER 8 (born in America, high-school education): Look how much hair she has, and it's even blond. Nurse, will her skin color stay the same? Will it not change?

We stress that both admiration and disappointment or fear that the child is not "O.K." are based on external signs, such as an oversized head, no hair, purple color, or limbs with imperfections. For example:

MOTHER 9 (Israeli born of American parents, vocational school education): Is he alright? ... Not missing anything? ... Are all his limbs in place? Are they all intact? ... His eyes are closed. Why doesn't he open them? I want to see what color they are.

MOTHER 10 (born in Morocco, vocational school education): Nurse, is everything O.K. with my baby? Are you sure? Why are his fingers blue?

MOTHER 11 (born in Russia, high-school education): Is she O.K.? How do you know if she's normal? She's not missing anything, is she? Does she have all her fingers? She's not missing any toes, is she?

MOTHER 12 (born in Iraq, university education): Why are her fingers so small and blue? Why are her nails so long? It's not an indication that she has something wrong with her, is it? Nurse, you can tell me the truth ... why is she purple? Is everything alright? Her brothers were all pink.

MOTHER 13 (born in Iraq, high-school education): Look what a pug nose he has, but my husband's nose is actually pretty cute ... I hope it will straighten out in time ... Why is his head so big? Is that normal? ...

MOTHER 14 (born in Poland, a nurse): Why is she so bald? She hardly has a hair on her head! ... Her brother was born with a head full of hair ...

If the baby passes external examination and his or her external appearance satisfies his mother, he or she is considered "O.K.," is called "sweetie," and his or her belonging in the family is indicated by references to the external similarity between him or her and some other member of the family. Thus the mother expresses her acceptance of the child. For example:

MOTHER 15 (Israeli born, Polish extraction, high-school education): Sweetie ... cutie ... you look just like your brothers.

MOTHER 16 (born in Iraq, university education): He looks just like his father ... His father is also dark like this ... and look at his mouth ... dimples in his cheeks and chin ... You certainly are your father's son ...

MOTHER 17 (born in Argentina, high-school education): He looks so much like his brother ... His brother also has a beauty mark on his chin ... sweetie ... cutie.

Later we shall see that if the newborn does not pass the test and his or her external appearance does not match his or her mother's criteria for being good-looking, his or her belonging to the family is not asserted and he or she is generally rejected.

Often the mother's external examination of her child also relates to the baby's cleanliness. In such instances the mothers themselves associate dirtiness with ugliness and cleanliness with beauty and æsthetics. This is illustrated by the remarks and behavior of mothers who lay emphasis on cleanliness as a measure of beauty and who do not distinguish between a clean child and a good-looking one.

MOTHER 18 (born in Tunisia, high-school education): Why is he so dirty? Yucch! He's so ugly ... Nurse, clean him up. Give me a beautiful child ...

MOTHER 19 (born in England, high-school education): What are these marks on his face? ... When will they go away? Will they clear up before we go home?

MOTHER 20 (Israeli born, Bukharan extraction, vocational school education): He's drooling ... Nurse, give me a tissue to wipe his mouth [*she wipes him*]. Well, now. What a beautiful child. Now, my sweet, you're not all dirty with drool.

MOTHER 21 (born in Australia, high-school education): What's this white cream all over his body? Last time I gave birth they brought me the baby after they had cleaned him up. He was such a beautiful child. Nurse, will the ointment remain? Can it be washed off?

MOTHER 22 (Moslem Arab, Master's degree, social worker in a hospital): Yucch, I can't stand dirty babies. A dirty child is the ugliest thing ... My children are beautiful because they are always clean.

The recurring pattern of responses among the hundred mothers observed in this study[6] indicates a high degree of similarity in the behavioral messages conveyed by the mothers, despite differences in their nationality, ethnic background, age, level of education, sex of the newborn, number of children at home, etc.

Thus we see that the first encounter between mother and child includes an external examination of the newborn, in every case with attention drawn to one or another aspect of his or her external appearance. We also observed that the newborn is accepted by his or her mother when his or her external appearance measures up to her aesthetic requirements pertaining to the color of his or her skin, hair, and eyes, his or her size and weight, how many limbs he or she has and how well-formed and properly proportioned these are, how much hair he or she has, and how clean he or she is.

FROM NORMAL TO ABNORMAL

The importance which attaches to external appearance as opposed to the internal condition of the body in shaping social relations, the social significance of that which is manifest as opposed to that which is concealed, and the connection between all these and beauty and aesthetics are themes that will accompany us throughout the chapter.

Thus far I have dealt with healthy children; now I move on to children with physical abnormalities, for the importance of physical appearance is especially pronounced in relating to children with physical defects. Some of the cases I shall discuss involve children whose external appearance is marred, others involve children who suffer from internal diseases or defects. Which has the greater impact on their chances of forming social bonds? Is there a difference in response to people with external as opposed to internal impairments?

The following table presents data on newborns with defects discovered immediately after birth.

Table 1: Newborns, by type of defect and parental reaction[7]

Type of defect Parental reaction	Total		Internal defects without external signs		External defects	
Total	(350)	100.00%	(100)	100%	(250)	100.00%
Abandoned	(178)	50.85%	(7)	7%	(171)	68.4%
Not abandoned	(172)	49.15%	(93)	93%	(79)	31.6%

As we see from Table 1, most of the children suffering external defects were abandoned,[8] even though most of them did not suffer from life-threatening illnesses and in certain cases the defect was only severe aesthetically (for example: a cleft lip, malformation of the bones of the leg, or disproportion among facial features). In contrast, most of the children suffering internal disease were not abandoned even in cases of serious illness, such as heart or kidney disease, where the chance of recovery is slim.[9]

Some of this tendency is illustrated in the first case study, in which we see that parents tend to accept their children even when they have internal defects which may be quite serious but are not manifested by external distortion. Let us look at the way Sara related to her newborn son.

CASE 1 "THE BLACK AND BROKEN HEART"

Sara is 25 years old, born in Israel, of Lithuanian extraction, and has a high-school education. She, a secretary, and her husband, a government clerk, have two children and live in a large city in the northern part of Israel.

Their baby, born in Northern Hospital, had a heart defect and was removed from the delivery room before the mother had a chance to see him. Several hours after delivery, the doctor informed the mother that the baby had a severe heart defect. He gave her a graphic description of the nature of the defect, adding that in the last analysis the child would be able to function normally only if he underwent a series of operations that would span several years and that "the first operation must be done immediately, or else the child will die."

The mother informed the doctor that she did not wish to see her child because she did "not want to become tied to a child with a heart defect." She went on, "He probably looks half dead ... all black. Soon he'll die, and I am afraid of developing bonds with a child who is going to die soon." Several hours later Sara changed her mind: "The other mothers in my room all had their babies brought to them to be nursed, and only I had no baby. I left the room ... I could not stand seeing them nursing their babies and enjoying them ... I found myself wandering around the ward ... near the babies ... standing and crying, afraid to enter."

NURSE [*called to assist the crying woman*]: What's the matter? Why are you crying?

SARA: I'm Sara, the mother of the baby who was transferred to you from the newborn ward. The doctor came by and explained his condition to me. At first I thought I would not come see him at all. They explained to me that he suffers from a broken heart [*she cries*]; that his blood can't circulate and that his heart is becoming black, and that the child himself is all black.

NURSE: Please, I beg you, put on a gown and try to come in and see your baby.

SARA: But I am afraid he will frighten me. A baby with a heart defect ... he must be all black ...

NURSE: You're mistaken. He is the cutest baby here ... and he looks wonderful ... and one more thing—if the operation is successful, the bond between you and your baby will be very important.

SARA [*enters hesitantly, stands beside the incubator and says joyously*]: Look, he really is a lovely, big child. And, looking at him, you can't even tell he has a heart defect. ... Maybe it's all a mistake? How could he have a heart defect if you can't see it? His features are so clear and good-looking. He's such a doll. He really reminds me of his brother when he was a baby.

Sitting herself down beside the incubator, Sara cried a bit and gazed silently at her child. Half an hour later she rose and clasped the nurse's hand warmly, saying, "Thank you so much, I am so grateful to you for helping me come in and look at my child ... he is such a sweet little thing." Thereafter she came by every evening to tend to her baby, who was operated on and was convalescing well.

Like the mothers we encountered earlier in the chapter, Sara subjected her child to an aesthetic examination. The child was rejected when his mother imagined that he would not pass the test because of his color. In other words, Sara's initial rejection of her child, even before laying eyes on him, was due to the color she imagined him to have and not due to his illness. When he measured up to the aesthetic requirements, despite the grave incapacity of his heart, he was called "sweet little thing," was taken into the family by reference to his resemblance to his brother, and was cared for devotedly. Sara's behavior is typical of that of hundreds of parents of children with internal defects either in the heart, kidneys, or urinary system, observed in this study.

Thus far we have seen that parents accept their newborns when the children's external appearance (size, hair, and skin color) meets parental expectations. This applies to healthy newborns as well as children who are born with serious internal defects but who outwardly look fine. Next we shall examine the contexts in which children are rejected. To do so, as the data of this study show, we must focus on children who suffer from external deformities. In the cases which follow we see that among Jew and Arab, religious and secular, highly educated and less educated, when children suffer from undisguised external defects, their parents tend to reject them. When, on the other hand, the children's defects can be disguised, their parents accept them.

CASE 2 "THE CHILD WITH THE TAIL"

Mrs. Meshulam, a 21-year-old native Israeli of Yemenite extraction, is a housewife with 10 years of schooling. She and her husband identify themselves as religious, have another son, and live in a large city in the central part of Israel. Their son, delivered at Central Hospital, was born with spina bifida.[10] The midwife noticed the serious defect the moment the child was born, since part of the membranes of the spinal cord were exposed and protruding. The child cried immediately.

MOTHER: Wonderful, is it a boy or a girl?

MIDWIFE: A boy.

MOTHER: Oh, I'm so happy. I so much wanted a boy. Let me see him.

The midwife cut the umbilical cord and took the child out of the room.

MOTHER: Why is she taking him out? Is there something the matter? He looks O.K. to me.

ANOTHER MIDWIFE: Yes, but he seems to have something on his spine.

MOTHER: Is it serious? Is it crooked? Are they going to operate on him in order to remove the crookedness?

The doctor, who was summoned immediately, brought the father into the delivery room and explained the situation to the parents: "The child has no chance of surviving for more than a few months. We cannot repair such a severe defect. My advice is that you sever contact with the child. He will remain in the hospital, where he will receive the fullest care, and most likely he will die within several months. This is what we advise all parents who have a child born with this problem. It is accepted practice to advise the parents to sever contact."

Heavyhearted, the parents remained silent. Then they whispered to each other and finally came to a decision.

MOTHER [*emphatically*]: We want to see the child.

DOCTOR: I don't think you should. It will be hard for you.

FATHER: We insist.

The nurse brought in the child, who was already dressed and looked very cute.

THE MOTHER: What a doll, ... You look so cute.

FATHER: Really beautiful.

The father began kissing the baby, and the mother immediately joined in.

MOTHER: He is such a lovely child. Your saying that he has a defect and is going to die just doesn't make any sense. I certainly won't cut off contact with him.

FATHER: Exactly. We're going to take him home.

NURSE: O.K., give him to me now so I can diaper him.

MOTHER [*distrustful, suspicious that he will be taken away from her*]: First we want to see just what it is our son has on his back.

NURSE: Maybe tomorrow?

MOTHER: No, right now.

The mother kissed and hugged the baby, then grudgingly handed him over to the nurse. The nurse undressed him and showed the parents his deformity. The parents immediately recoiled as if they had received an electric shock.

MOTHER: Get him out of here. Take him away [*motioning away with her hand*]. What an ugly thing.

The mother fell asleep. For two whole days she did not go see her baby. She told a nurse whom she had befriended in the ward that she had given birth to a "baby with a tail" and that she was not going to let "such an ugly thing" into her house.

Before leaving the hospital, the mother came to the baby ward and said, "I want to see the baby, but only swaddled." The nurse showed her the baby, swaddled, as she had requested. After a moment's hesitation the mother could no longer restrain herself; she took the child out of his bassinet and showered him with loving hugs and kisses. Unexpectedly she felt the protrusion on his back, and again, as if jolted by an electric shock, she recoiled and returned the baby to his bassinet, her face bleak.

MOTHER [*addressing the nurse*]: The moment I touch it I remember what it looks like, that horrible thing on his back, and I feel I am going to faint. How could such an ugly thing have come out of me? a creature with a tail! [*Sighing*] Oh, well. I'll consent to leave him here.

That day the mother was released from the hospital and her child remained there. She never returned to see him.

Like the other mothers we have met, the first thing this woman was interested in was the sex of her child. She was happy to hear that she had had a boy. Next, her interest shifted to his external appearance. She cast a rapid, superficial glance at her child (because he was speedily whisked out of the room), enough to see his body, his hands and feet. The impression she received of a normal child made it hard for her to comprehend how, in her own words, "there could be something wrong with him if it doesn't look like it." The parents did not trust the doctor when he said the newborn had no chance of survival; they believed that the child's prospects of living should find expression in external signs: "It must be something visible." Hence their request to "see the child" and examine him themselves. During the first few moments, when the child's deformity was covered, he was called "cutie" and "beautiful" and was showered with kisses, generally bestowed on good-looking children, as we saw in the previous examples. The parents clearly felt a contradiction between the child's good looks, on the one hand, and his likelihood of dying, on the other. Their momentary decision not to sever contact with the child reflected their perception that the child's external appearance was more important than "what the doctor said." But the rapid reversal in their decision was also founded on the same perception; they were repulsed by the child the moment they saw his deformity as it was, bare and undisguised, or the moment they touched his deformity.

CASE 3 "THE MONSTER WITH THE COSMETIC REPAIR"

The child in this case, born to non-religious parents of European extraction, suffered from spina bifida, like the child in the previous case; but in this case the defect was very slight and curable. Nevertheless, as we shall see, the difference in severity of the defect, and in religiousness and ethnic origin, has no impact on the way the parents relate to their son; they attribute significance only to his external appearance.

Gabi was born in Northern Hospital to 25-year-old parents, native Israelis of German extraction, living in a city in the north, parents also to a three-year-old. The couple have post-secondary education and work as computer programers. Gabi was diagnosed as having spina bifida as soon as he was born. Although the defect looked repulsive, the prognosis for cure was very good. The parents were informed that the child must have an operation, after which he would live and develop normally, but most likely would still have a slight, imperceptible handicap in the lower half of his body. The parents asked to see the defect. The moment the child was brought in and his defect shown them, the mother fainted and the father became white as a sheet. Several hours after delivery the mother announced that she did not want to breast-feed "a monster," saying, "this is a child who one day will be a real monster ... and because of this I don't want to have anything to do with ... this thing." The parents left the hospital, firmly resolved to sever all ties with the baby.

A week later the baby was transferred to a hospital in the center of the country for operation. A social-worker appealed to the parents in an attempt to convince them to take an interest in their child. Here is part of the conversation that took place in the hospital:

SOCIAL WORKER: But chances are the baby will survive ... and even will become healthy.

MOTHER: That's not so.

SOCIAL WORKER: But the head of the department himself said just that to you.

MOTHER: But another doctor told us the child has no chance of surviving.

SOCIAL WORKER: Who said so?

MOTHER: A doctor, a young doctor ...

SOCIAL WORKER: Tell me precisely who told you that. We'll check and you'll see that it's not so.

MOTHER: I really don't recall.

SOCIAL WORKER: Actually, it makes no difference. If one tries hard enough one can almost always find an expert who will give a contradictory opinion. What is important is that the head of the department said the child will recover.

FATHER: We don't believe it. We saw him. That was enough for us. Look, we don't need a deformed child ... we don't need to have anything to do with him ... we're not interested in him ... we have a sound child at home. We don't want to ruin the family.

SOCIAL WORKER [*irately*]: You are driving me out of my mind. It's simply cruel of you ... to bring a child into the world and then throw him away ... A volunteer brought him to B. Hospital to be operated on; she put him, all swaddled up, on a stretcher, and walked off. Everyone thought your child was some sort of discarded package that nobody wanted.

MOTHER [*rather calmly*]: Look, maybe it's sad for you. But from the moment we learned he had a defect ... a tail ... we really do not want him.

SOCIAL WORKER: How can you say such a thing? He's your very own son!

MOTHER: Pardon me, but it seems to me that it is you who do not understand me. Look, he's already no longer my son. For us he does not exist.

FATHER: Exactly. You might as well get it into your head that there's no more point in approaching us. Don't write to us about him, and don't come bother us at home.

Before the operation the parents were called to the hospital to give their consent. They arrived, in a temper, shouting at the top of their lungs, "What do you want from us? ... We told you that we don't want the child ... we don't want to see him ... don't want to sign any papers having to do with him ... " The nurse on duty explained to them that if they refused to sign they would be summoned to court, but that once they signed they would not be bothered any more. Only then did they sign hastily and leave the ward forthwith, without seeing the child. Their hasty departure left those present with a sense that the couple was fleeing.

The operation was performed several days later. During the next six weeks Gabi convalesced from the operation but was unable to move the lower limbs of his body. With physical therapy his mobility improved. He began to develop and turned into a smiling baby, full of life, and winning attention, warmth and love from the nurses in the ward, who named him "Gabi ... after the angel Gabriel," as they explained. During this entire period his parents expressed no interest in him. The hospital staff requested a relative of the family, a nurse in the hospital, to report on Gabi's progress to his parents. Even so, they would not change their position. "I recommend that you not go to the parents until you can bring them something positive in hand ... Only go when you have something you can sell them," the nurse advised. Later, after therapy had produced good results, the parents were summoned to the ward. They arrived, looking insecure, their eyes furtive and their gate slow and hesitant. The medical staff was assembled in the doctor's office. And this is how the story unfolded:

As soon as she entered the room, before the conference even began, the mother said [*with determination, but lacking the self-assuredness of previous times*], "Look, you called us, so we came; but realize that we do not want him ... we don't want a child with a defect."

DOCTOR: Soon you'll see that your child no longer has a defect, and in not so long a time he'll be completely healthy.

MOTHER: There's no such thing. Once a child with a defect, always a child with a defect ... a defect can't be cured.

The staff then began a lengthy conversation. The doctor explained to the parents the nature of the operation and the developmental stages that follow it. The physical therapist reported on the progress in the child's development, and the nurse told about the care he was receiving. The parents sat silently the entire time. It appeared they were going to great effort to remain deaf to the reports being made, not to let the information sink in. Finally the mother broke her silence and said, "You are trying to persuade us ... you're trying to put something over on us."

SOCIAL WORKER: But your child is really so charming and full of life. What a face he has!

MOTHER [*interrupting*]: Maybe before, too, he had a beautiful face, but also a tail like an animal [*getting flustered*].

SOCIAL WORKER: Look, here. The doctor has said he can be circumcised. Will you come to the ceremony?

The parents made no response.

MOTHER [*suddenly, decisively*]: I want to see the child.

The child was brought in, but the parents did not turn their heads in his direction. Even though she knew Gabi was in the room, the mother deliberately looked out the window across from the door. The father did likewise. Icy silence reigned. Taking care not to remove her gaze from the window, the mother shouted, "I want to see where the operation was." The nurse undressed Gabi. Only then did the mother turn and look at the child. Minutely she surveyed the place where the defect had been. Several minutes later she burst out emotionally, "You really can't see anything. You have repaired everything perfectly." She began mumbling to herself, "How can it be? This is the first time I've heard that a defect can be removed ... and such a severe defect, at that ... Now he won't have a defect ... they've fixed him up cosmetically ... they've made him look normal ... just like plastic surgery."

Until that moment the mother had not looked at the child himself, at his body, his face, his eyes. Her gaze had focused only on the place the defect had been. Only after assuring herself of the "correction of the defect" did she take her eyes off the spot and look at the entire child, examine the expression on his face and his eyes, and say joyfully to those present, "Look, the child is looking only at me and my husband, as if he recognizes us ... Look how he resembles my husband."

At that moment the parents burst into tears, the mother crying and laughing. They hugged each other and cried with emotion. "Look," said the social worker, "you will probably have pangs of conscience for having abandoned him. You will have to overcome it, and we would like to alleviate your feeling of guilt. Why don't you take this day as Gabi's birthday? What's been done is in the past, and actually the only thing that's important now is what you do in the future." The mother became very attentive to what was being said. She clasped the social worker's hand warmly and said, "Thank you. I really do feel as if Gabi were born to me today. We shan't abandon him again. He is ours." The mother repeated this last sentence again and again during subsequent meetings.

From that day on the parents came to the hospital daily to feed Gabi and take care of him. Even the extended family came to visit him and play with him. Two weeks later the parents took Gabi home. When they came to get him, the father announced, "We have decided to change his name to Samuel. If a new son has been born to us ... he should have a new name, as well."

The child now needs a small orthopedic device on his legs. Every day his mother takes him to a physical therapy clinic in their city to work on strengthening his muscles, and from time to time he is brought to the hospital for surveillance, check-up, and short courses of treatment. The parents come along, and show great gentleness and concern for their child. Gabi is well dressed and appears to be well cared for. The parents take the numerous trips to the hospital in a good spirit, and when help is offered them they reply, "Thank God, everything is fine. We are managing very well. We don't need any help. The medical treatment Sam needs is just like the medical care any healthy child needs from time to time. It's not too difficult. Isn't this what parents are for?"

This case illustrates the effect on parents of an external deformity in their child. It furthers our argument by refuting frequently offered alternative explanations of parents' behavior, such as the import of the medical information given the parents, the amount of special care anticipated for the child, or the severity of the defect as determined by the doctors. The parents' behavior does not change in the wake of learning that less special care will be needed, or as a result of receiving a favorable report on the child's condition. It changes only in the wake of a change in the external appearance of their child. When they saw his aesthetic deformity, Gabi's parents abandoned him and disclaimed any responsibility for him (saying "he's dead" for them) and turned a deaf ear to the favorable prognosis given by a senior physician. After the aesthetic deformity was completely repaired, the child was looked over the way one might examine goods for sale. Only after having assured themselves of the success of the cosmetic repair, did his parents accept him into the family (by commenting on his resemblance to his father) and give him care and devotion.

With the above case we can begin to discuss a theme which recurs throughout all the cases examined—namely, that there is no unequivocal connection between the severity of the child's defect or illness, as established by the doctors, and the parents' attitude to their child. If we compare the behavior of Gabi's parents to the behavior of parents whose children have internal defects (such as heart or kidney disorders), we see a clear tendency to be more rejecting of a child with an external deformity, even if it is remediable, than of a child with a severe heart or kidney disorder, which has no external manifestation.

Thus far we have encountered cases in which the child's deformity was symptomatic of a disease, and when the deformity was removed the disease was eliminated as well. This, however, is not always the case. Below we shall present cases in which there is a clear distinction between the disease and its aesthetic appearance.

Miriam, for example, born with paralysis (due to spina bifida) and also severely deformed aesthetically, was abandoned at birth. She had an operation which removed the repulsive physical deformity, but left her paralyzed and with a very poor prognosis for recovery. The mother was informed that the physical deformity had been removed. After months of having had absolutely nothing to do with her daughter, the mother arrived, examined her girl's naked body, and having assured herself that the physical defect had been repaired, remained at her daughter's bedside and nursed her with warmth and devotion. In Gabi's case, too, there was a change in the parents' attitude as a result of repairing the child's defect. But unlike Gabi's case, where the cosmetic repair of the aesthetic deformity went hand in hand with curing his defect, in Miriam's case the child remained paralyzed. The only change was that the unsightly deformity had been removed.

There are many examples of rejection of children who, aside from having an unsightly deformity, are to all intents and purposes healthy and have the potential for normal, if not better than normal, development. In this study cases were observed in which normal children born with a cleft lip or lack of proportion in their facial features were abandoned at the hospital even though the prognosis for cure was excellent. Thus, it appears that parents tend to reject their children not necessarily because of the severity of a disease, but because of a situation or context in which the deformity becomes the dominant factor. On the other hand, acceptance of such children is clearly tied to an aesthetic improvement in their appearance, irrespective of the severity of the disease as established by the doctors.

FROM NEWBORN TO CHILD

We have seen that external appearance is important at the stage of forming the bond between parent and child; but is it also important over time?
Does it also account for the severance of such bonds?

We have seen how mothers decide to accept their children in the wake of
successful examination of the newborn's body immediately after birth, while
still in the delivery room. Yet some people maintain that this is obvious, for
what criteria does a mother have to go by in her encounter with an infant
who cannot talk and does not yet evince "good" or "bad" behavior? An
older child, however can transmit other messages besides those conveyed by
his looks. Although we cannot accept such arguments as is (for a mother
certainly can also relate to an internal defect in her child), we shall take
them up by asking: do similar processes of acceptance and rejection take
place at later stages, with respect to older children? We shall see if they do
below.

CASE 4 "THE BALD-HEADED MONSTER WITH SCARS"

This case is instructive about the behavior of a mother towards each of
her three children, and towards the same child in different contexts. Thus
far we have dealt with the behavior of parents towards newborns; in the
present case we shall see that similar patterns of behavior emerge when a
child suffers an injury later on, after a bond has developed between the
parent and the child. This case also helps refute alternative arguments in
the literature that attribute the parents' behavior to familiarity with the
case, to the child's behavior, and to his or her sex.

A 28-year-old couple and their three children, ages six, four, and three,
injured by a fire in their home, were admitted to the surgical ward of Southern Hospital with burns on the face, neck, hands, and feet. The parents were
born in Persia, have an eighth-grade education, and work together in the
same public institution, the mother as a telephone receptionist and the father as a driver. The mother, Batya, recovered in two days; the father
was transferred for hospitalization in another hospital; the children, whose
condition was severe, were placed on respirators.

During this difficult period the mother expressed no apprehension about
scars remaining after the children were cured; her main concern was for
the children's health. During the first stage after the children's recovery
from critical condition, when they were still bed-ridden, the mother tried
to provide them whatever they needed and spend as much time as possible
with them. She read them their favorite stories and answered their questions
patiently. She was present at all their medical treatments, stroking them and

soothing them with loving words. She also assisted actively at mealtimes, patiently feeding them and encouraging them to "eat as much as you can so you will get better." She usually ate with them from the same plate.

At a later stage of treatment, the scars on her children's faces and hands began to protrude and deepen. At the point when looking at the children had become difficult for an outside observer, the mother announced that she was going to commit suicide together with her children because, she said, "I do not want monsters in my house." She called them *"wahaj"* (monsters) and ceased going over to her children and taking an interest in their medical condition.

After conversations with a social worker and psychiatrist, the mother stopped her public suicidal pronouncements. Nevertheless, she almost never stroked or kissed her children any more. During this period she often went around with an envelope of photographs of her children from before the accident. She would take out the photographs at any opportunity, look at them and show them to whomever was interested, saying, "What beautiful children I had ... I would get such attacks of kissing ... I did not stop kissing them ... look how sweet they were."

At that time her sons' mouths tightened up as a result of their burns, barely allowing them to eat normally and making them look repulsive to the casual observer. The mother cut down her contact with the two boys to a minimum. She would bring them their trays, shove the food into their mouths without looking at them, and gesticulate with her hands and make sounds with her throat, showing her disgust and desire to vomit. At this stage the mother stopped eating from her sons' trays but continued to eat from the tray of her little girl, who did not suffer from a drawn-in mouth.

A month later the boys were operated on to widen the corners of their mouths. Even after surgery, their faces were not the most attractive, but the older boy's looks did improve somewhat, while the younger boy's looks became worse. Moreover, the younger boy was no longer able, as in the past, to open his mouth sufficiently to take in the amount of food given him, and therefore food often dribbled out of his mouth. The mother expressed repulsion towards and rejection of the younger son, first by avoiding feeding him. She fed her other two children but expressly refused to feed her younger son, requesting the nurse or another member of the family to do so. She expressed repugnance at the younger son both by her hand motions and by saying, "He disgusts me ... just seeing him makes me want to vomit ... Once he was the most handsome of them all, but now ... he's so dirty ... so ugly." Her rejection of him also manifested itself in denying his requests for attention. Even when the boy broke out in tears the mother did not go to him. The extended family, as well, gave attention only to the other two children. Often the younger son (four years old) would sit by himself while the rest of the family gathered around the other children. He would call them incessantly in a voice hoarse from a tracheostomy (an incision in the wind pipe to allow air in and mucus out), but would be rebuked with words like, "Shut up already ... I'm sick of you." Lastly, the child's rejection found expression in his isolation even during sleeping time. The mother, who generally slept in the same room with her little girl, took her older son into the room with her because he was complaining of nightmares as a result of the accident. Thus the younger son remained alone at night, too.

The relative social isolation of the younger son continued until his second operation to enlarge the opening of his mouth. This time the operation was a success and the child's looks became much less repulsive. At this point, however, the three-year-old girl's hair began falling out, and before long she became bald and repulsive. Her scalp was covered with scars from her burns. The girl then became the focal point for repulsion. "This baldness is horrible," the mother would cry. "You forget what my girl used to look like ... no one remembers what a beautiful girl I once had ... Why does a burn have to take a girl, pretty as an angel, and make her into a bald-headed monster with scars? Why? What sort of fate is this? I can't touch her ... I can't even look at her ... I want to, I try. But I can't." This repulsion from the girl continued until suitable hats were bought for her and later, wigs.

We have observed the behavior of a mother towards children whose faces became scarred and distorted and who became bald as a result of a burn. We see that there are shifts in the mother's response to the same child and in her response from child to child. Rejection of the child does not mount as his health declines; rather, rejection becomes more pronounced as the disfigurement becomes more prominent, with no possibility of disguising the external impairment (scars, balding). The mother also perceives cleanliness as an aesthetic value, for in her eyes dirty children are ugly children.

Batya's case brings out the strength of the impact that children's external appearance has on their parents' behavior and refutes other explanations of the change in behavior, found in the literature. Some scholars claim that repulsion from a person with a deformity only occurs at the outset of contact with that person and lessens with the passage of time. Others maintain that the behavior of the impaired child, more than his external appearance, is what affects the behavior of those around him. Examining Batya's behavior towards each of her children and her behavior towards the same child in different contexts reveals that the mother's behavior changes in the wake of a change in the external appearance of her child, with no connection to the child's behavior or sex. Moreover, there was no gradual lessening of the repulsion as the mother grew more accustomed to the deformity.

Case 5 "Yigal, the scoured boy"

All the cases thus far, including those in which we distinguished between the aesthetic aspect of a defect and the severity of a disease, have dealt with children who had some external deformity. The next case illustrates a clear distinction between the medical assessment of a defect and the parent's assessment. The case deals with a child who was rejected by his mother even though the doctors found him to be healthy. The mother continued to view him as having an impairment due to an external change which was not seen by others as an impairment and did not symptomize any disease.

Yigal, 7 years old, was hospitalized in Central Hospital due to a brain abscess. His parents, 50-year-olds, born in Iraq, live in a city in the central part of Israel and are well-to-do. The hospital staff consider Yigal's mother, Dina, a model mother who gives her son superior care. To help understand the mother's behavior, I cite her own account of the background to her son's hospitalization.

> Yigal was feeling ill ... his head would spin ... he was always tired ... I went from one doctor to another and they all said there was nothing wrong. "Ms., you're imagining things. You're son is one hundred percent normal." At home he stopped breathing repeatedly, but the doctors said, "Ms., have you studied medicine? No. So don't you decide that it's a cessation of breathing." One day I saw he had stopped breathing for a short while. It was then that I decided to have him hospitalized ... I called the emergency medical service and told them to send me an ambulance for someone with heart trouble ... The ambulance came right away, and they hooked him up to a monitor ... In the emergency room they told me, "We must hand it to you, Ms. You saved your son's life." ... They examined him and found he had an abscess on his brain and that he must have an operation to open the abscess.

Throughout the entire period of hospitalization, both before and after the operation, the parents, especially the mother, were present with their son. Yigal's mother tended him, slept at his side, and saw to it that a wheelchair was provided for him so that he would not overexert himself. She would caress him gently and call him names of endearment (always saying "my sweet" when addressing him). Yigal was considered the "most spoiled child in the ward."

Other types of behavior, however, lay hidden behind this devoted care. If we examine several of the opening remarks in my meetings with Yigal and his mother we shall discover several recurrent patterns of behavior. The first example relates to the first moments of my encounter with Yigal and his mother, 7:00 a.m. on the day after the operation, when Yigal was feeling very poorly.

AUTHOR: Good morning. Yigal looks great.

MOTHER: Of course he looks great. I've already given him a bath. He's all clean, so he looks great. Looks so handsome.

The next encounter took place the following day, at 12:00 noon.

AUTHOR: How is Yigal doing?

MOTHER: We were just coming back from the bathroom. I gave him a wonderful bath.

The last meeting took place several days later, late in the evening.

AUTHOR: How are things?

MOTHER [*impatiently*]: I had to leave the bathroom for a moment. Yigal is still there. Will you keep an eye on him?

I went into the bathroom and waited for his mother.

MOTHER [*returning immediately*]: This ward isn't run right. They don't even have a single bath brush.

AUTHOR: Why do you need a bath brush?

The mother pointed to marks of iodine around the operation incision that were showing out from the bandage. The marks were barely visible, in my opinion.

AUTHOR: Those marks can hardly be seen.

MOTHER: What on earth are you saying? They stick out of the bandage ... like smudges of filth, or something ... I tried to scrub off the purple ... but they don't have a bath brush here.

The mother continued scrubbing her son with a piece of scouring pad, which she had taken from the kitchen. The boy was doubled-up from pain but entirely helpless.

AUTHOR: You're hurting Yigal.

MOTHER: O.K., tell me yourself, what can I do? Leave him dirty with this purple stuff? It's the ugliest thing in the world. He'll feel better himself when he's nice and clean.

Note that in the first few encounters with the mother, despite the fact that they took place at different hours of the day, she was always busying herself with Yigal's cleanliness. A record of her behavior shows that the boy was bathed at almost every hour of day. Any dirt, whether from food, sweat, or a mark of iodine, or the like, provided reason for washing him forthwith, the mother herself associating cleanliness with beauty. Yigal had to look "scrubbed clean" at all hours of the day and night. The mother could not bear her son to have the slightest stains of iodine, which she interpreted as filth. Thus, notwithstanding the harsh pain and discomfort Yigal suffered from the process of being cleaned, his mother scrubbed his face and body incessantly and changed his sheets every few hours.

Cleanliness as a condition of beauty also appears in the attitude of mothers to their newborns (cf. the description of the mothers' behavior earlier in this chapter), as well as in Batya's attitude towards her children with burns. Later on we shall see that the same approach emerges in the attitude of parents to seriously ill children, sometimes even at the last moments of their life. Even though their children may be terminally ill, the parents strive ceaselessly to improve their external appearance, often by cleaning their bodies. When the parents can not maintain a clean body appearance, we see clear signs of rejecting their children.

Now I return to my description of the behavior of Yigal's mother. In the previous incidents the mother defined cleanliness as a condition of beauty; the next incident brings out the importance of hair as a determining factor in beauty and in the child's acceptance by his mother.

NURSE: I suggest we remove the bandage from Yigal's head. It is not helping medically and simply is a bother to him. Look how he's sweating.

MOTHER: Under no circumstances do I agree.

[*The nurse leaves and returns two hours later.*]

NURSE: I must treat Yigal's cut. We'll take the bandage off and put it back on when we're done.

The nurse took off the bandage. Yigal's mother, seeing that his head was shaved, shuddered and burst into tears.

NURSE: What's come over you? When you brought him here and he was not even breathing, you didn't cry. When the operation was done, you didn't cry. No one here has ever seen you cry. And now, when everything is O.K., you burst into tears?

MOTHER: Please finish up. I can't bare to see him ... with that stubble on his head ... That's not my boy's face ... He looks like a porcupine ... [*several minutes later*] — Nurse, I'm not feeling well. I think I'll go out for a few minutes.

NURSE [*to the author*]: Strange. Until now she didn't miss a single treatment ... not a single X-ray. She always stayed at his side and said sweetie-pie. But this time she got startled, the first time she saw his shaved head.

Yigal's mother remained outside for over half an hour. She did not come back in until the nurse went out and said, "I've bandaged him up again, although it's a pity on him because he's sweating." The rest of that day the mother did not touch her son (except for necessary contact) or call him the usual pet names she used to give him. Several days later, when Yigal suddenly felt ill and dizzy, his mother took him to the bathroom so that he would "vomit there and not on his bed." After he vomited, she went on with her cleaning routine. "Look," she said to me, "his hair is growing back ... look, I can already shampoo it ...   Now he'll be my Yigal again ... with a face like Yigal ... "

Just as Yigal's mother recoiled from him when he was not "scrubbed clean," so, too, she rejected him when she was forced to see his shaved head, and she made his acceptance conditional on concealing the shaved head or growing a new head of hair. A few days' growth of hair made it possible for her to give her son a shampoo and relate to him "as if he already had hair."

Attributing importance to the length or quantity of hair as a condition of beauty is a theme which recurs among many parents in a variety of contexts. It is especially pronounced in cases of children with severe internal defects, where their chances of survival are slim. As we shall see, parents of such children tend to be accepting of them and care for them with devotion. Nevertheless, they are disturbed, even to the extent of rejecting their children, in settings where their children's aesthetic appearance suffers, especially when their hair falls out or is shaved.

Such was the case with 6-year-old Debby, who came to the hospital with a suspected tumor in her head. X-rays revealed what appeared to be a malignant brain tumor. The prognosis, not at all good, was delivered to the parents in plain words. The parents' reaction was sad and doleful, but restrained. Before the operation, however, when the nurse shaved the girl's head, the mother burst into tears and almost struck the nurse. "What have you done to her?" she shouted. "Did you see what lovely hair she had? ... How could you dare do such a thing ... It's as if you killed her ... Look what a face she has now ... That stubble is unsightly. She looks like a porcupine ... " In this regard the doctor in the ward told me, "We learned a lesson about children who are about to have an operation in the head because of a tumor or a suspected malignancy. We learned not to shave their heads here in the ward, in front of the parents. We take the child out of the ward, with his usual hairdo, and shave him after he has bid farewell to his parents and been kissed good-bye. After the operation we put on a large bandage. The only problem is when the parents are present, unintentionally, when the bandage is taken off; then they get a dreadful shock."

Thus far we have dealt with children who underwent substantial physical changes, changes which could be detected by outsiders as well as parents. Sometimes, however, an outside observer has difficulty discerning changes or distortions in external appearance, while a parent nevertheless perceives an external change that is occurring or that will occur in time. Something in the child's body intimates to him, in no uncertain way, about a present or imminent distortion. Rejection of children with Down's syndrome is a prime example.[11]

The staff of one of the hospitals observed (Central Hospital) decided at the time to inform the parents while the mother was still in the maternity ward if their child had Down's syndrome and, with the assistance of a social worker, pediatrician, and psychologist, to help the parents come to terms with the fact and convince them to take their child home and raise him or her with the rest of their children. This approach proved a disastrous failure. During that period, no parents who were informed while still in the hospital that their children were impaired took their children home. The parents disowned their children with Down's syndrome and often threatened to commit suicide. According to reports of the doctors and nurses in charge of the newborn wards that we observed, save for a very few exceptions to be discussed later, over the past fifteen years not a single parent who knew for certain that her child had Down's syndrome took her child home. In the hospitals under our observation, in almost all cases (111 out of 120) the parents left their children in the hospital, and only in very few cases did they take them home.[12]

CASE 6 "THE MONGOLOID"

Tzviya, a woman of 30, born in Israel of Eastern European extraction, has a college education and lives in a city in the southern part of the country. She delivered her baby in Southern Hospital, which practices rooming-in.

As soon as the baby was born the midwife told her she had had a boy.

TZVIYA: That's so wonderful, it's a boy ... I have two girls at home ... Let me see him.

The nurse showed the mother her son, and Tzviya asked the nurse to let her touch him and hold him. She checked almost every limb of his body and said with pride, "Isn't he lovely? He's more beautiful that either of my daughters at home ... but he looks just like them." Tzviya touched the baby and kissed him and asked that her husband, who was waiting outside, immediately be brought news of the birth of "the loveliest baby in the world."

For the next two days Tzviya's countenance bespoke nothing but joy. She breast-fed her baby, never stopped boasting to one and all about her baby's beautiful face and body, and tended her baby constantly. After those two days Tzviya was called in to the doctor's office. Here is part of the conversation that took place between them.

DOCTOR: This is a bit difficult for me to tell you, but it seems your child is not altogether healthy.

TZVIYA [*laughing*]: Is he lacking vitamins? Come on, doctor, how can a good-looking fellow like him not be healthy?

DOCTOR [*also jokingly*]: He really is a good-looking fellow, your young man. But still we have reasonable suspicion that your son has Down's syndrome.

TZVIYA: What's that?

DOCTOR: It's what is commonly called Mongolism.

TZVIYA: Oh, you mean like this? [*She makes a gesture which is meant to represent a retarded child, sticks out her tongue, and contorts her body. Then, shuddering*] Take him away from me [*crying*] ... Who could believe that a retard like that could have come out of my stomach? ... What have I done? ... For nine months, in my womb, I grew a creature that drools ... and his tongue hangs out?

DOCTOR: Tzviya, look here. He's the same handsome guy you had before. He hasn't changed in these few minutes.

TZVIYA: How could I have touched him ... Why didn't you tell me from the start? ... I shake all over just to think that I hugged him all the time, and nursed him ... and thought about him ... Why didn't you tell me? [*She bursts out in the direction of the doctor, almost hitting him.*]

DOCTOR: Tzviya, you mustn't approach this with any preconceptions. First of all, it is not yet certain that he has Down's syndrome. He has to have many tests, and in about two weeks we'll know what his condition is. Secondly, even such children can be brought up nicely.

TZVIYA: Let those who feel like it raise them. As for me, I won't. I can't [*crying*] ... I must go wash up.

I accompanied Tzviya to the shower. Sobbing, she undressed and threw all her clothing, including her undergarments, into the trash. She began to wash, soaping herself again and again, scrubbing her skin till it seemed about to tear. As she scrubbed, she sobbed, "Why did they let me hug him? ... such cruelty ... they knew he was this way from the start ... Why didn't they keep me from kissing him ... with all that drool of his? ... Now it's stuck to my skin ... and his smell ... stuck to my skin ... Now, until I get it all off ... "

After she finished washing, Tzviya requested me to accompany her to her room, where the baby was in his bassinet. When we entered, her roommates told her the child had been screaming with hunger.

TZVIYA: I don't care. Let him cry. He won't get any milk from me. [*Crying and looking at the baby and addressing the author*] ... You know, now it really looks to me like he is not O.K. How did I fail to notice it earlier? His skin color is wrong. His gaze is strange. It actually gives one the chill. How did I not notice? ... I'll ask the nurse to take him out of here.

Several hours later her husband arrived, and the two conferred with each other. That evening Tzviya announced flatly, "We are not taking the child home ... We have two healthy girls at home, and we do not want to cause them suffering. When they see a child who looks like this, they'll get a fright."

Tzviya informed her immediate family by phone that the child had been ill and had died. The next morning she left the hospital without her baby. Since then the parents have not contacted the hospital and have shown no interest in their child's welfare in any other manner.

Let us try to analyze Tzviya's behavior and relate it to the behavior of other parents of children with Down's syndrome whom I observed.

Some children with Down's syndrome have external indications of their disorder which stand out even to a layman. But at birth many children with Down's syndrome look just like any other newborn, and a non-expert can not discern anything strange or repulsive about them. Such was the case with Tzviya's child. The medical staff, indeed, suspected Down's syndrome from the outset, but Tzviya herself did not sense any problem and treated her child in the same way as the other mothers we met in the beginning of the chapter. First she expressed interest and joy in her child's sex. Then she looked over his external organs, examined his body, and expressed admiration at his beauty. Having passed the external exam, the son was then accepted into the family. Even at the outset of her conversation with the doctor, when she was informed of the suspicion of some disease, she made light of the matter by expressing the commonly held view that "it can't be that such a good-looking fellow has a disease."

Tzviya's attitude towards her son is typical of an attitude observed among many parents of children with Down's syndrome. As long as the parent does not know that his child has Down's syndrome, the child passes the initial external examination, is often perceived by the parent as "cute," and is accepted into the family. Only later, when the parents learn that their child has Down's syndrome, do they generally change their former behavior, explaining their rejection of the child on the grounds that he or she is different in his or her external aspect. Even though there was no actual external change in Tzviya's son, and he was better looking than many normal babies, his parents abandoned him on the grounds that he "looks" frightening because of his retardation. The fear of retardation is so great as to make the actual physical being, the child lying before them, whom they called "cute" just a few minutes earlier, virtually disappear before their very eyes, so that the parents actually no longer behold the real child before them. They see only a retarded child, that is, a child who looks retarded. The frightening external indications of retardation (such as a protruding tongue) are the picture their child conveys to them. Thus, as in the other cases presented in this chapter, here, too, the parents' rejection is based on the argument that there has been a change in the external appearance of their child; in this case, however, there is no direct perception of the impairment, but only a change which is imagined in the parents' minds.

In this chapter we have encountered other examples of parental rejection of their children due to an imagined or anticipated change. Sara, the mother of a child with heart disease, rejected her child even before she saw him because of her imagined perception of him as a dead child whose color was all black. Only after her encounter with the real child did she change her original intention of abandoning him.

Thus far I have described changes in the external appearance of a child that arouse repulsion in his or her parents. First, I presented cases of objective physical changes that anyone could perceive. I described both defects and changes that were not defects, such as changes in color, shaving the head, etc. In addition, I presented cases of subjective physical changes, i.e., changes that the parent imagined and that others did not discern.

Note that up to now, when dealing with physical changes that aroused parents' repulsion, I related to the notion of "body" and "physical changes" in the prevailing sense of the words; i.e., I talked about changes in the organs of the body. In the next few cases I shall deal with children who are connected to various instruments and children who have non-routine openings in their bodies for breathing and removing secretions. These cases illustrate a further set of changes in external appearance which are associated with repulsion.

We begin the discussion of parents' attitude towards children attached to various medical instruments with a description of the attitude towards premature babies. It is evident that mothers of premature babies develop less physical contact with their children than do mothers of children born with normal weight, despite the constant encouragement given them by the medical staff to touch their babies and make contact with them. What is it about a premature baby that puts off his or her parents from forming contact with him or her?

Observation of the parents' attitude toward their premature babies and of their questions to the staff indicates that their pulling back from their newborns is related, first of all, to the size of the baby. "He's small ... its frightening ... I say it is frightening, but actually it is disgusting ... he doesn't even have buttocks ... he's so small." Similar remarks, variations on a theme, are heard recurrently from many parents. Recall that the size of the baby is a matter of concern also for other mothers, for those who have had normal children. But, according to our findings, the attitude toward premature children also includes coping with perceptual problems, especially coping with the child being connected to various types of apparatus.

The premature baby ward has infants in it who were born weighing very little, as well as babies who need intensive care. "Problematic premature babies" are those with serious breathing difficulties. They suffer from cessation of breathing, as evinced by a drop in pulse and a change in color (turning blue), and must be resuscitated by an outside force. Such babies are generally connected to various medical instruments: respirators, oxygen tents, infusions, cardiac monitors, apnoea monitors, etc.[13]

The parents are generally given detailed explanations of the function of the instruments and the reason the baby is connected to the various machines. These explanations are given before they enter the room where the baby is. Yet these explanations, it seems, do not obviate daily queries about the apparatus: "Why is the baby getting an infusion? ... What's that in her nose? ... Why is she connected to that machine? ... How does the machine work? ... How long will she be connected to it? ... How many tubes does she have? ... Why does he have that instrument on his eyes? ... Why is that instrument on his hands? ... " Parents of premature babies also ask about their children's chance of survival. For example, "Does she have a chance of surviving? What if she dies?" But, as we saw in the other cases in this chapter, also with premature babies the attitude of the parents does not necessarily vary in accordance with the severity of the illness. The chance of survival becomes associated with and has an impact on the parents' behavior only when it is translated into an external change, including the number of machines the child is connected to. Even mothers of older children who are connected to a machine often behave in a similar way. The paucity of contact between parent and child is especially noticeable in cases in which the child is in intensive care, where he or she is connected to a large number of machines. Besides the tendency to reject children attached to machines, there is a tendency also to reject children in whose bodies unusual openings have been made for breathing and removing secretions.

CASE 7 "A HOLE IN THE STOMACH"

This case describes the rejection of a baby whose body did not change but whose appearance changed as a result of non-routine openings being made for the elimination of feces.

Liz, a 24-year-old housewife of Moroccan extraction, has a high-school education and lives in a town in the southern part of Israel. In Southern Hospital she gave birth to a baby who appeared to the doctors to be healthy. Liz expressed joy at giving birth to a girl, examined her small body, mumbled words of endearment ("cute little thing," "my beauty"), and constantly caressed and kissed her baby. Several hours after delivery the baby was brought in for breast-feeding. The mother held her close and gazed at her lovingly. When feeding time was over, she did not return the baby to her bassinet, but hugged and kissed her and reluctantly gave in to the nurse's request that she return her child to the nursery.

By the morning after birth the baby's weight dropped sharply, she spat up the milk she nursed, and her stomach became distended. She was transferred to intensive care for a series of tests and X-rays. By the end of the fifth day after birth the baby was diagnosed as having Hirschsprung's disease.[14]

The mother was called in to see the doctor, who explained the nature of the disease to her: "The outer end of the large intestine is very narrow, and before that the intestine is broad and lax, like a funnel, thus creating a blockage in the intestines. The baby is not defecating, and therefore must undergo an operation immediately." The mother showed no reaction to the doctor's words. She left the room and went over to her daughter, a look of disgust on her face.

MOTHER [*to the nurse*]: So, her whole stomach is stuffed up with ca-ca.

NURSE: Yes, the poor thing. It hurts her very much.

The expression on the mother's face softened, but suddenly became harsh again.

MOTHER: But how could so much BM collect in such a small stomach? In the end it'll explode.

NURSE: That's why she's having an operation. To take the feces out. [*Several moments later*] Look what a sweet thing your daughter is. In spite of the pain she's sweet. Why don't you caress her?

The mother tried to stroke her baby's head, but stopped immediately, saying, "I can't. Instead of her head I see her stomach ... and besides, I'm probably bothering her. Her stomach hurts her."

Several hours later the doctors managed to empty the baby's stomach by giving her enemas. The mother, informed that the treatment had been a success, came immediately and said, "Great, she doesn't have a big, swollen stomach any more. All the ca-ca is out. She's so clean ... now she's my beautiful little girl again. She doesn't have that big stomach any more. All done, no more ca-ca in her tummy ... Now she doesn't need an operation ... " The mother picked the baby up and showered her with kisses again. Then she turned to the medical staff and asked, "Well, when can we take her home? I miss her so much ... "

That evening the baby was put in an incubator. It was explained to the mother that putting the baby into an incubator did not mean a turn for the worse in the baby's condition, but simply reflected a desire to take care of her after the difficult enemas. The nurse encouraged Liz to stroke her daughter in the incubator or outside it. But Liz did not even try to stroke her daughter at this point. When the nurse actually took Liz's hand and tried to put it in the incubator, Liz recoiled, saying, "I just can't do it ... it's as if my hand were paralyzed ... as if I were getting an electric shock ... and it won't help her, anyway ... "

Even though Liz would not touch her daughter, she and her husband came to visit their child every day. During this period Liz would not look at her daughter. She obtained her information about the girl's condition from questions which she addressed to the staff and from the information sheet hanging on the incubator.

At the end of the week the doctor informed the parents of the decision to operate within a week, adding that because of a surgical problem it would be decided in the course of the operation whether to take out one end of the intestines through an opening in the stomach, so that the baby could discharge feces only through this opening (colostomy).[15] She would remain in this condition until age one, and then would have another operation to close the opening and return everything to normal.

MOTHER: What do you mean? She'll have a hole in her stomach that the BM will come out of?

DOCTOR: Yes, until she's a year old.

MOTHER [*bursting into tears, she turns to the father*]: I can't take it. I'll leave her in the hospital until she's a year old. Then we'll take her home and care for her ...

DOCTOR: That's impossible.

MOTHER: Look, I'll come here every day. I'll help you with whatever you want. I'll fold laundry. I just can't bear to see the BM coming out ... of her stomach ... I'll want to stroke her on the tummy and suddenly I'll be touching ca-ca ... She'll always be soiled with it ... Such a pity, she could have been so sweet and beautiful.

FATHER: And the smell that she'll have about her all the time!

DOCTOR: A healthy one-year-old also has BM coming out of him all the time ... and he also sometimes smells of his bowel movements.

MOTHER: Yes, but it's not the same. When BM comes out of the rear end it's different. You can gather it up in the diaper.

DOCTOR: Here, too, you gather up the feces.

MOTHER: But it's not the same thing when BM comes out of the stomach. Oh, dear! I remember an elderly man I once knew who had the same thing. His guts came out of his stomach ... oh, no. I actually threw up then. Just imagining such a thing already makes my stomach turn.

The operation took place. Now the parents spend almost the entire day in the ward, but they never touch their child. They help out at various tasks (such as folding laundry), but up to now have refused to take their girl home.

We see that Liz felt a sense of repulsion and disgust when her girl's stomach swelled, and that the distended stomach was associated with filthiness. The mother herself drew a connection between dirtiness and ugliness. Liz was not capable of looking at her daughter's face in order to establish contact with her. The girl's stomach was a perceptual obstacle which made it difficult for the mother to discern other parts of her child's body. Once medical treatment succeeded in emptying the baby's stomach of the accumulated excretion, Liz again expressed warmth and longing towards her child. At that moment, when the child was perceived as clean, healthy, and beautiful, Liz expressed a longing to take the child home, despite the doctor's explanation that an operation, which was independent of the size of the baby's stomach, would be necessary. In contrast, transferring the baby to an incubator and attaching her to various machines was interpreted negatively by the mother, and led to the mother's rejection of her child, notwithstanding the doctor's explanation that this did not indicate a deterioration in the child's health. It must be stressed that rejection of the child set in before the operation to make an opening in the stomach. The parents' expression of disgust and declaration of their intention to leave their child in the hospital did not stem from the actual condition of the child at the time, but from what they imagined would be her condition after the operation.

Behavior similar to that shown by Liz is also found among parents whose children have had openings for breathing made in unusual places such as in the trachea. For example, Yousra's parents, Bedouins whose daughter had a tube inserted in her windpipe to let air out, refused to take their child home on the grounds, among other things, that "never before have we seen a child going around with an open throat ... such an ugly child as that has never been seen in our midst ... she was born pretty, but now she's no longer pretty ... never has such an ugly girl as that been seen in our neighborhood." Thus we see that even when the opening is not associated with excretion of feces, it causes rejection, being associated, as the parents themselves attest, with ugliness.

Parental rejection of their children emerges primarily in the wake of a change in the features of the child's face or body, a change which runs contrary to the parents' concept of beauty. Children are generally rejected when parts of their bodies are deformed, even in the opinion of outsiders (as a result of an impairment or the side-effect of a disease—such as balding, change in skin color, etc.); but at times (although less frequently) children are rejected due to an external change which is imagined or anticipated, even when many outside observers detect no change at all.

The examples presented in this chapter show that children who are rejected by their parents in the context of being perceived as ugly have one or more of the following characteristics: blue skin color, an opening along the spine, a cleft lip, lack of proportion in their facial features, scars on the face or hands, slanted eyes and a tongue which thrusts out, loss of hair or a shaved head, medical apparatus attached to them or openings made in their bodies in unusual places, and dirtiness; and the association of these defects and characteristics with ugliness is made by the parents themselves.

Comparing the attitude of parents toward children with external deformities with the attitude of parents toward children with internal defects reveals that parents are bothered more by external, openly visible defects than by internal or disguised defects. We have seen that parents generally accept their children when others share the opinion that the child does not suffer an external defect. This is true both of healthy children and of children with slight internal defects that do not have external manifestations. Parents are more accepting of these children than of children with external defects that cannot be disguised (such as a cleft lip), even if the defect could be completely cured at some time in the future.

According to the findings of this study, the aesthetic factor assumes importance and significance in other contexts, as well. Retardation, for example, is frightening when it is associated with physical deformity. So, too, dirt or secretions lead to rejection, since they are associated with ugliness. These findings pertain both to newborns and to older children.

The newborns that are rejected because of a deficient external appearance are primarily premature babies, infants suffering from a deformity in a limb or the face, and babies with Down's syndrome. Older children (after the age of weaning) who are rejected because of a deficient external appearance are generally victims of accidents, wounds, or medical treatment, or children with a congenital disorder, including Down's syndrome.

As I have said, the external appearance of children has a decisive impact on the kind of treatment they receives from their parents. One cannot, in my opinion, account for the parents' behavior in terms of alternate factors, such as the child's behavior, the degree of familiarity with him or her, and the additional information supplied about him or her. Even though many parents tend to justify their behavior on the grounds of information given them, the findings of this study clearly indicate that this is not so; the parents do not rely on the official information given them, but rather adapt and modify this information, and selectively take in only certain parts. If we examine the various cases presented (Case 1 and Case 2, for example), we see that the behavior of the parents towards their children does not change in the wake of positive information about their children. Rather, their behavior changes in the wake of a cosmetic repair of the defect or in the wake of a change in their perception of the child's external appearance. Information is important only when the parents translate it into visual terms, not generally intended by the doctors. For example, Sara (Case 1), upon learning of her son's heart defect, through her behavior displays an attitude that something internal must have an external manifestation—an internal defect must find expression in the child's color (black), and a fine external appearance is a sign that everything is normal and acceptable.

Each of the cases presented also refutes other theories advanced in the literature to explain the rejection of children, such as the influence of ethnic or religious background (cf. Case 2 and Case 3), the parents' sex, age, and economic status, the child's place of birth, sex, and age, the severity of the defect from a medical point of view (cf. Cases 3, 4, and 5), functional handicaps entailed by the defect (cf. Case 4), the amount of special care that is anticipated, the information given the parents, the degree of familiarity with the child (cf. Cases 4 and 9) or the child's behavior (cf. Case 4).

The data which I have presented give us pause to wonder about the significance of the body over time, about the senses that guide our behavior, about the significance of one's looks, and about the relationship between aesthetics and order, symmetry and harmony. These were all prominent focal points in the attitudes of mothers to their newborns, with which we opened the chapter. Due to their importance, I stress them once more.

How do physical characteristics affect the formation of social relations between parents and children? Which of the mother's senses come into play during the first moments of encounter with her child? What part of the newborn's body is significant in the bond between her and her parents? Do parents respond to how their child looks on the outside or to what is taking place on the inside?

As we have noticed, the sense of sight is the most prominent; mothers look at their children. Parents attribute marked importance to the external appearance of their child, especially to the following elements:

> well-defined sex
> number of fingers
> hair
> cleanliness
> color ⎫
> size ⎬ of head, fingers, facial features, as well as entire body
> weight ⎭

These essentially reflect the stages of forming a bond.

The first stage, which shapes the subsequent relationship with the child, is to determine the child's sex. If his or her sex is clear, one can form a bond with him or her. One cannot form a bond with a newborn whose sex is uncertain. In the stages that follow the mothers continue to examine the external appearance of their newborns, focusing on indicators such as the amount of hair on the head, skin color, hair color, weight, complexion, eye color, and number of fingers and toes.

Moreover, it is by these criteria of external appearance that the mother classifies her child as "beautiful" or "not beautiful." The good-looking child, whose appearance lives up to the mother's aesthetic requirements, is accepted by the mother; the ugly one, rejected. The parents' behavior not only indicates that what one sees is more important than what takes place inside the body, but also underscores the importance of being good-looking.

What does it mean to be good-looking? What does it mean to be an ugly child with whom one cannot form a bond? An aesthetic appearance is interpreted as a matter of being "normal"; of having a face whose size and color is "normal"; of having a head full of hair (a bald baby is perceived as not beautiful); of having the right proportions, not too big or too small; of not missing anything, and having everything in the right place. Being ugly means having something that is not in proportion, something that does not fit; or having something additional that should not be there (such as a dirty spot on the forehead), or lacking something which should be there; or having something which is not in proper order (blackish instead of pinkish coloring, a crooked back instead of a straight one). Furthermore, although parents pay attention to detail, it seems they also accord significance to the overall form, the gestalt, characterized by perfection of the parts (limbs) and the proportions between them. Thus we see a pronounced connection between aesthetics and an emphasis on order, symmetry, and harmony—perfection of the whole. The literature on the subject also associates aesthetics with qualities of organization and order.

For example, Engler (1990), in his article on physics and beauty, asserts that the classical components of beauty or aesthetics are symmetry, simplicity, order, coherency, unity, elegance, and harmony. These concepts are characterized by regularity, organization, concord, and balance—traits which enable man to compose his view of the world, and without which his world would be chaotic. Perfection gives man a sense of pleasure, which he perceives as beauty.

Danet and Katriel (1990) also associate aesthetics with order. In their article on play and aesthetics in collections, they set forth a fundamental aesthetic principle by which collections are built. Their basic conjecture is that a collection is a means of expressing one's aspiration towards perfection. The article mentions five strategies for reaching this goal: completing a set or series; filling in a gap; creating something pleasurable and harmonious; manipulating objects by size (collecting very large or very small objects); aspiring towards perfect objects (purchasing and maintaining objects in perfect condition, and improving the physical quality of items). Danet and Katriel believe that, like art, building a collection is a secure way of coping with chaos in that it makes order of human experience. Our findings also point to the importance of closure as a fundamental aesthetic principle, and to the importance placed on harmonious appearance in the aspiration to have a child whose looks are perfect, or to improve the physical quality of children by cleaning newborns and youngsters, or to disguise their aesthetic defects. For us, too, sorting by aesthetic principles provides a way of coping with chaos and making order of human experience. This will be the main subject of the next chapter.

Also Yannai deals with the question of beauty. In discussing the "biological basis of beauty" Yannai (1990) tries to explain why it is that beauty holds such pride of place. "Beauty, it would seem, has no evolutionary advantage that could account for its causative effect on man's emotional system, and yet this unexplained emotional response is common to all human cultures. Where does it come from and how does it develop? ... Why has beauty had such a deep impact on us from the dawn of civilization? For Plato it sufficed to explain that beautiful things are considered as such by virtue of the abstract notion of beauty. But we seek to discover whether our attraction to beauty is simply cultural, or whether it also has biological foundations." One answer to this question is advanced by sociobiology; it is suggested that the beautiful is good, i.e., that beauty is what helps us arrive at the correct decision when we are faced with the question of who has the correct features (Amotz Zehavi, in Yannai, 1990). But "natural selection cannot provide us with a convincing explanation ... of why we find beauty in features that are not connected with being strong and healthy, such as large eyes, a small nose, and full, well-shaped lips." Another theory is that the beauty of a woman reminds us of a baby, and "thus, perhaps, love of human beauty is one of the means developed by natural selection to strengthen the bond between parents and their offspring, just as the yellow membrane in the corners of a chick's beak serves to arrest possible aggressive behavior towards it on the part of adult birds." The shortcoming of this theory is that it does not relate to masculine beauty. The last explanation suggest by Yannai perceives beauty as a sign of sexual excitation and a symbol of fertility (Yannai, 1990).

All of the current explanations of our predilection for the beautiful leave something to be desired. In our study, as well, this remains an open question. Is the beautiful also the good? Do parents choose the beautiful because it is a useful criterion in natural selection?

A distinction is often made between practical matters and aesthetic concerns (between cognitive knowledge and experiential perception, Hospers 1969, pp. 4–5). The parents' responses relate primarily to aesthetic values, where beauty is perceived as distinct from other matters. Brinker (1990) notes a similar pattern in modern thought, unlike the approach of the ancient Greeks in which beauty was interwoven with other concepts.

Nevertheless, despite this clear distinction between the beautiful and the practical, we shall see later on that parents draw a connection between the beautiful and the good, the ugly and the bad, and that they use this association as the setting for rejecting a child who is not "good-looking." Thus, we must continue to search for a more persuasive explanation of why beauty is more important than other messages.

In this chapter I did not generally distinguish between the various types of parental response. The next chapters will examine what behavioral patterns are affected by the child's external appearance. Does her or his appearance influence the parents' willingness to have close physical contact with their child? Or does it influence the very willingness to form a bond with her or him? We shall also look at a number of other questions, such as the threat posed by children with external deformities (Chapter 2) or by children attached to a medical apparatus (Chapter 4), which leads to their rejection. We shall also try to understand whether a change in external appearance has a direct effect on the parents' behavior, or whether some sort of mediation is necessary for the external appearance to affect the parents' behavior (Chapter 3).

NOTES

1. I shall speak interchangeably of attractiveness, good looks, beauty, and external appearance.

2. Cf. Cross and Cross, 1971; Dion, 1973; Salvia, Sheare, and Algozzine, 1975; Trnavsky and Bakeman, 1976; La Voie and Andrews, 1976; Langolis and Stephan, 1977, Styczynski and Langolis, 1977; Marwit, Marwit and Walker, 1978; Langolis and Downs, 1979; some researchers report consensus among adults about the attractiveness of newborns and premature babies (Corter et al., 1978; Hildebrandt and Fitzgerald, 1981; 1978).

3. Staffieri, 1968, 1972; Lerner, 1969; Lerner and Korn, 1972; Brenner and Hinsdale, 1978; Staffieri, 1968; Iwawaki and Lerner, 1974, 1976; Lerner and Iwawaki, 1975; Lerner and Pool, 1972.

4. Cf. Richardson et al., 1961; Richman, 1978; Centers and Centers, 1973. This finding is clearly illustrated by the difficulty in finding adoptive parents for a child who has a blemish on his face but does not suffer any physical handicaps (Longacre, 1973).

5. Cf., for example, Zeidel, 1973, p. 59; Waechter, 1977, p. 305; Tudor, 1979, p. 2; Begab, 1963; Lobo and Webb, 1970; Farber, 1959, 1968; Holt, 1958; English, 1971; Oberman, 1968; Palgi, 1962.

6. We observed 100 mothers who delivered normal children. See the preface to the Appendix.

7. The data on which this table is based may be found in the Appendix, Tables 1 and 2.

8. No reliable nation-wide record of the percent of children abandoned in the hospital was made during the years this of study.

9. Cf. Appendix, Table 1. It should be noted that out of a group of 250 children with external defects, 120 of whom had Down's syndrome, 68.4 percent were abandoned; whereas out of the 130 children with external defects but no Down's syndrome, only 46.1 percent were abandoned.

10. Spina bifida: incomplete development of or lack of a certain vertebra, usually in the lower part of the spine. When there is no further defect, it does not cause any disruption to normal functioning of the body. There are cases, however, in which the contents of the spinal column protrude from the affected area, covered with a membrane, thus creating a lump on the

back and causing nervous disorders. When the meninges (membranes enveloping the spinal cord) protrude by themselves, without the spinal cord, the condition is known as *meningocele* and there are no neurological deficiencies, although there is a high risk of secondary infection. When part of the spinal cord protrudes as well, the condition is known as *meningomielocele* and is accompanied by neurological deficiency in proportion to the level of the defect. The objective of operating, generally done immediately after birth, is to reinsert the lump into the vertebrae and to assure that the condition not recur. When medical treatment fails and operating is not feasible, a colostomy may be made (Blake and Wright, 1963, p. 338).

11. Down's syndrome: Mongolism. The most common and easily defined genetic disorder. On the average one out of every 800 infants is born with Down's syndrome. The genetic defect which causes the side-effects of the syndrome falls into one of three types (which I shall not discuss here). The clinical manifestations of Down's syndrome include: congenital mental retardation of varying degrees, accompanied by characteristic physical features and body build. At birth the child is small, often premature, with a round skull, and slanted eyes with an extra fold of skin (*epicanthus*) along the inner edge of the eyelid. The cornea sometimes has white spots, called *Brush Field Spots*, the cheeks are usually flushed, the palate is short and narrow, the nose small and the nasal bridge low. Other characteristics include a large tongue (*macroglossia*), a weak lower lip (*cheilosis*), a receding chin (*microgehia*), and broad folds of skin along the neck. The fingers are short and the palms have only one lateral line, in contrast to normal children's palms, which have two. The feet have an unusually large gap between the big toe and the rest of the toes. Muscle tone is generally weak, often resulting in crossed-eye. In many instances the naval is cleft. Diagnosis of the disorder is relatively easy. Newborns suspected of having Down's syndrome upon external examination are usually given a chromosome test immediately after birth in order to confirm or refute the suspicion. Often children with Down's syndrome also suffer from other illnesses, such as congenital heart disease, leukemia, etc. Children with another defect in addition to Down's syndrome often die young. Even without other defects, however, children with Down's syndrome are prone to complications from secondary infections (Brand-Orban, 1979:43-45).

12. The small number of exceptional parents who took home children with Down's syndrome either did not understand the full import of the defect, interpreted its symptoms as something positive, or knew that some member of the extended family, other than themselves, would care for the child. In recent years, after completion of this study, certain hospitals have been forcing all parents to take their children home, by appealing to the law against child desertion.

13. The mode of operation of each apparatus will be explained as the

need arises.

14. Hirschsprung's disease: a broadening of the large intestine, resulting from a congenital deficiency of parasympathetic nerves generally found at the end segment of the intestine. There, around the rectum and slightly above it, the intestines become narrower as a result of muscle contraction, leading to accumulation of feces and gas above that point and producing the clinical symptoms of the disease. In severe cases symptoms appear by the first few days after birth. The newborn does not excrete feces (*meconium*) during the first 24 hours after birth, his or her stomach becomes distended, and he or she vomits. In less severe cases the disease is discovered at a later age, when the child complains of prolonged constipation accompanied by a distended abdomen. When the disorder cannot be successfully treated using enemas, an operation is performed in which the narrow part of the intestines is removed and the remaining segments are joined together. After the operation the child remains connected to an infusion for several days, and a tube is left in his or her stomach (Brand-Orban, 1979:106-107). Sometimes the operation is performed in several stages, with a colostomy made during the first period.

15. Colostomy: an artificial opening made in the side of the abdomen for excretions from the large intestine, due to birth defects, accidents, or tumors. Unlike the modes of excretion people are born with, in this case there is no control over the stoma and its daily functioning.

2

Of Man and Beast

Defining a Child as a "Non-Person" Paves the Way to His or Her Rejection

What defines a "person"? Must certain criteria be met in order to be considered a human being? If so, what are they? In what contexts is a living being defined as a "person"? Who is called a "non-person"? Is there a two-way street between the status of "person" and that of "non-person"? On what grounds do we determine that the other is a "non-person"?

Is an abnormal person "human"? Or is such a person classified as "non-human"? In what contexts? Who is considered normal? By what criteria do we judge "abnormality"? On what grounds do we determine a person to be abnormal? Are there objective grounds for defining the other as "abnormal"?

Why do we need to define what it means to be human, normal, or abnormal? Does defining the other as a non-person help shun him or her, or make him or her the object of violence? How so?

What do we find threatening about contact with someone who does not fit our image of a "human being"? What do we find threatening about contact with someone "abnormal"? Does the abnormal represent disorder?

How do we interpret the body of the other person? What significance do we attach to it? As an entity that is human? That is beast? How do people determine the cognitive location of the other person? How do they determine the cognitive location of an "abnormal" person? Is there any variation in the way abnormal people are perceived? Are perceptions of the abnormal explained by age, sex, country of origin, length of time in the country, or exposure to other cultural characteristics?

Is defining the other as non-human or as a non-person a socio-cultural concern? Is the individual free to choose whether and how to define the other? Is disability an individual or a social construct? Is there variation or is there a common denominator in the way people relate to the concept of being "human" and the way they use this concept as a basis for violence? These general questions will be examined here in the context of relations between parents and children. For example, we shall investigate whether parents label their child as abnormal.

Most of these questions will be answered in this chapter, and some will concern us in later chapters, as well.

First let us see how these questions are treated in the literature.

LABELING AND STIGMATIZATION

Some of the questions on which this chapter focuses have been discussed in the literature on stigmatization. The Greeks originated the term *stigma* to refer to "bodily signs designed to expose something unusual and bad about the moral status of the signifier. The signs were cut or burnt into the body and advertised that the bearer was a slave, a criminal, or a traitor— a blemished person, ritually polluted, to be avoided, especially in public places" (Goffman, 1963, p. 11; see *American Dictionary*, ed. Morris, 1969, p. 1266 for a similar definition).

There are several types of stigma; some mark defects of the body (physical deformities, diseases), others are blemishes of individual character, and yet a third type are "the tribal stigma of race, nation, and religion, these being stigma that can be transmitted through lineages and equally contaminate all members of a family" (Goffman, 1963, p. 14; cf. also Shneidman, 1976, p. 68). All these types of stigma pertain to a characteristic which discredits the holder (Goffman, 1963, p. 13) and to situations in which the society perceives that the individual is not worthy of social acceptance. Stigmatization is a process by which people are labeled as outsiders (Becker, 1963) and are transferred by rites of transition to the status of "abnormal" (Erikson, 1964). This process ends with the individual being removed from the realm of the human: "By definition, of course, we believe the person with a stigma is not quite human" (Goffman, 1963, p. 15). "We may try to act as if he were a 'non-person,' and not present at all as someone of whom ritual notice is to be taken" (Goffman, 1963, p. 30). Accordingly, normal people "exercise varieties of discrimination, ... construct a stigma theory, an ideology to explain his [the stigmatized person's] inferiority and account for the danger he represents. ... We [normals] tend to impute a wide range of imperfections on the basis of the original one, and at the same time to impute some desirable but undesired attributes, often of a supernatural cast, such as a 'sixth sense'" (Goffman, 1963, pp. 15–16).

Some experts maintain that stigmatization stems from the sense of fear, from the threat that people feel when confronted with someone who is different from them (*Combating Stigma*, 1969). This sort of fear is fear of the unknown; therefore presenting the facts should lead to such fear dissipating and to the stigma being reduced.

Other experts stress that, due to their functional role in the social system, stigmas are not easily changed. This is illustrated by stereotypes about mental illness, which receive continual support, albeit non-directed, from the media and from daily conversation (Scheff, 1966). Since the image of mental illness brings out the contrast between sickness and health, shunning the abnormal person makes it possible to certify the health of the system; thus tolerance of such people would be dysfunctional (Cumming and Cumming, 1955).

The definition of stigma in the literature is particularly unclear. It is hard to say whether experts use the term to refer to an attribute, in and of itself, or to an image associated with the attribute. Another lack of clarity concerns the concept of "non-person." In this chapter I shall investigate whether the abnormal individual becomes a "non-person" according to Goffman's perception of the concept (i.e., whether she or he is treated as if she or he were not present) or according to the anthropological understanding of the concept (i.e., whether she or he exists, but as a non-human entity; cf. M. Harris, 1977, p. 5). The literature does not make clear whether rites of transition to the status of "abnormal" are reversible. I shall examine whether such transition can be two-way, from the status of "abnormal" to "normal" and vice versa.

The threat posed by contact with stigmatized individuals is another subject which has not been clarified sufficiently. For example, Goffman maintains that people avoid contact with individuals whose stigma is visible, but does not explain the reasons for such a reaction. I shall try to explain what it is that people find threatening about contact with a person who has a visible stigma. Why is such a person perceived as dangerous? What is the ideology or theory of stigma that explains the inferiority of the stigmatized person and the threat that she or he poses?

Lastly, in this chapter I shall investigate how labeling and stigmatization occur within the family. Few experts have taken an interest in this process due to their implicit assumption that parents accept their children unconditionally. Goffman (1963), for one, maintains that the discussion of labeling and stigmatization does not concern the family, since all processes of labeling and stigmatization cease to function when dealing with intimate circles, especially the family. He claims that the family does not label its handicapped member, but rather becomes a sort of "protective capsule" and hothouse that prevents the self-belittling definitions of the handicapped child from penetrating the "charmed circle" of his or her family (p. 46). Thus the family demonstrates its acceptance of the child and enables the protected child to appear in a special way (p. 113), and "to see himself as a fully qualified human being, of normal identity" (p. 46). In Goffman's opinion, other family members relate to the handicapped child as if he were normal and, unlike the surrounding society, relate to his personality and not to his defect (1963, pp. 46–113). "There is a popular notion," Goffman says, "that although impersonal contacts between strangers are particularly subject to stereotypical responses, as persons come to be on closer terms with each other this categoric approach recedes and gradually sympathy, understanding, and a realistic assessment of personal qualities takes its place. While a blemish such as a facial disfigurement might put off a stranger, intimates presumably would not be put off by such matters. The area of stigma management, then, might be seen as something that pertains mainly to public life, to contact between strangers or mere acquaintances, to one end of a continuum whose other pole is intimacy. The idea of such a continuum no doubt has some validity" (1963, pp. 68–69).

Such statements have popularly been accepted as self-evident and thus have helped buttress existing myths. But this is a subject which must be investigated; perhaps labeling like that which occurs in society at large also takes place in the home? I shall expose the family setting to open examination of stigmatization and shall explore whether a child might be labeled as abnormal by her or his parents, as well; and if so, how? We shall see whether there are factors that reduce or increase the stigma; whether knowing about a sickness or defect helps reduce the stigma placed on a child, or whether parents resist changing existing stereotypes. Essentially I am proposing a new direction in research, insofar as most studies of stigma in the family have focused on other aspects, such as the attitude of women to mentally ill husbands (Schwartz, 1957; Yarrow et al., 1955), or the willingness of a child who has become abnormal to comply with the image of being "bad" and use this as the raw material for building her or his self-image (Shoham, 1983).

DEHUMANIZATION, VIOLENCE, AND BECOMING A "PERSON"

The general questions presented in the beginning of the chapter will be examined here with respect to relations between parents and abnormal children.

There is no comprehensive anthropological study of parental relations towards abnormal children in different societies. Nevertheless, indirect inferences on the subject may be drawn by reviewing cultural world outlooks with respect to related questions, and by culling the few examples scattered throughout anthropological literature and mentioned mostly with respect to questions other than those concerning us. We have in mind concepts such as "person" and "non-person" and the way these concepts relate to violence and to the individual's aspiration towards meaning and order.

Anthropological literature treats the process of becoming a "person" and the pair of concepts "person" and "non-person" as part of a discussion that also distinguishes other pairs of concepts, such as healthy—sick, alive—dead, body—soul. According to Polunin (1977), modern medicine, which relies on examining many and specific parts of the body and on using sophisticated instruments, views the concept of health as a continuum, not a dichotomy. According to such an approach, there is no fundamental difference between a healthy person and a sick person; and if such a distinction is made, it is arbitrary and does not reflect reality. In contrast, medicine in primitive society relies on general observation of the patient and her or his immediately observable symptoms, and tends to make a much more categorical distinction between a healthy and a sick person. This also applies to distinction between the sexes.

Moreover, in contrast to modern society, in which the person, the self, is defined apart from others, among Africans a person carries with her or him the identity of her or his father and forefathers, and a child is viewed as an extension of the social personhood of her or his parents or as the property of her or his living father (Harris, 1978).

According to the literature, our perception of the essence of a person is unlike that of the Africans (Zahan, 1979, p. 9). In Africa a person is defined in terms of *becoming*; he does not exist as a human entity before certain physical or ritual changes take place in him, making him part of adult society and giving him the status of an adult. Among the Vendas the newborn has no social significance until his first teeth appear; until then he is considered "water" and not a "person." Among the Nuer a child becomes a "person" only when he can tether cattle and herd goats. A new father does not tell others he has a son until his son is six years old (Evans-Pritchard, 1956, p. 146). Only after his sixth birthday does the child become a person in his own right; therefore one does not mourn the death of a child younger than six. Several conditions must be met for a living being to be considered an entity in its own right; until such time his or her human essence is considered nill.

Such ideas are widespread throughout Africa, since among most African peoples pregnancy and birth of themselves do not suffice to assure the individual the status of a human being. The status of a "person" is acquired in stages and is fully conferred only when the individual reaches adulthood, the last stage of his or her life (Zahan, 1979, pp. 9–10). What accounts for such a process of dehumanization? According to the literature, viewing young children as not being part of humanity helps the members of these societies accept with equanimity the extremely high rate of infant mortality which prevails among them.

When a culture defines a newborn as a "non-person" it paves the way for infanticide—historically, the deliberate slaughter of newborns with the consent of their parents, family, or community—and at the same time it dulls the psychological price entailed by such slaughter. Annihilating children who have characteristics that contradict the religious ideas of a certain society (such as twins or children with defects) is not considered a crime in these societies (Roumeguère-Eberhart, 1957, pp. 184–185). Such an attitude is found among the Tonga (Junod, 1927), the Bantu in Southeast Africa (Roumeguère-Eberhart, 1957, p. 187), and the Malayans (Young, 1950). The Masai view a noseless newborn as a devil doomed to bring trouble, and therefore such a child is put to death (MacGregor, 1974, p. 39). The Hausa in northern Nigeria immediately throw children with blemishes into the river, and in Borneo such children have their throats slit. Edgerton (1964) also mentions the practice of putting to death a newborn who is not deemed a "person." Among the Pokot, Edgerton writes, a "real person" is defined by the following criteria: economic efficiency, ability to have intercourse, circumcision, and fertility. A barren woman is not considered a real person, nor is a male who has not yet been circumcised thought to be an adult capable of distinguishing good from evil. Since a hermaphrodite is barren and cannot be circumcised, he is not a "real person," and therefore it is customary to put him to death as soon as he is born.

Such ideas are not characteristic exclusively of African peoples. It was the practice among the ancient Greeks, Romans, and Egyptians to kill children with defects. A child whom the council of elders in Sparta found infirm or disabled would be thrown into a deep ravine (Bakan, 1975, p. 8); and Plato recommended that the chronically ill be put to death (Rae, 1982).

Whiting (1964) has found that the practice of killing female babies was widespread among many societies for centuries (p. 302). The Rajputs of Khalapur, India, attached greater value to sons than to daughters because sons were needed for religious duties. Even at the turn of the century this preference for males found expression in the practice of killing female newborns. The British tried to eradicate the practice; and indeed it did decline, yet it continues to exist in certain areas. Sons receive preferential medical care, and this accounts for the doubly high mortality rate among baby girls (Whiting, 1964, p. 302).

Many examples can be cited of violence directed at "ugly" persons with physical deformities, and we know of infanticide of children who were considered culturally inferior because of certain physical traits such as dark skin. The literature describes two groups from Madagascar who had similar physical characteristics except for skin color, one group being dark, the other fair. Dark-skinned children born into the fair group were put to death, even if their parentage was not in doubt, on the grounds that if they were allowed to live they would become possessed, afflicted with leprosy, thieves, or guilty of illicit sexual intercourse. Even Martin Luther, in the sixteenth century, associated that which is different with that which is evil, and ordered that mentally retarded children be drowned on the grounds that they were the emissaries of Satan (Bakan, 1975, p. 8).

A review of the literature on infanticide shows that children with a distorted appearance reminiscent of the looks of an animal were generally subjected to severe treatment. In Mexico, for example, children who had the "face of an animal" were put to death, whereas babies who had defects but not the "face of an animal" were treated as normal (Whiting, 1964, p. 634). According to Evans-Pritchard (1956), often a defect would call to mind an animal, or some limb of an animal, and generally would be attributed to a blemish in the totem of the sacred animal. "I once met a man," Evans-Pritchard recounts, "with only three toes, stocky and undeveloped, to one of his feet. I was told that his maternal grandmother had the ostrich for totem, and that on the day of her daughter's marriage one of the bridegroom's people ... threw a spear at her mud windscreen. She took the spear dots and on examining it found that part of the shaft was bound with ostrich-skin. When her daughter bore a son he was deformed as I have described. The ostriches—or, rather, the spirit of ostrich—had stamped the likeness of an ostrich on the child" (1956, p. 70).

We can infer from the literature that abnormality in children leads to their being defined as "non-persons" and licenses violence against them. Defects are culturally defined: a child is deemed abnormal according to a certain concept of normality which differs from one society to another and which determines what achievements the child must attain in order to be called a "real person" who is "useful and legitimate" in his or her society.

Another subject which concerns us in this chapter is the desire for order as a basis for parents' rejection or acceptance of their children. The lack of clarity inherent in the abnormal child, the unpreparedness to bear cultural chaos, and mankind's aspiration for order—all these underlie anthropological literature on symbolic analysis. Since anthropological literature on the subject does not relate to abnormality in general or to the handicapped child in particular, I shall present the general principles of symbolic analysis, focusing on its applications to the study of the handicapped child.

The point of departure for symbolic analysis is the individual's desire for order and meaning and a perception of culture as providing the answer to this need of the individual. "Culture, in the sense of the public, standardised values of the community, ... provides in advance some basic categories, a positive pattern in which ideas and values are tidily ordered" (Douglas, 1966, pp. 38–39). Thus, all that a person encounters is put into well-ordered and preexisting categories which enable us to explain our world. On the other hand, every culture provides ways of handling aberrations, i.e., guidelines for relating to entities or situations which are not clearly defined and which are difficult to place in a given category.

Edgerton (1964) illustrates the use of symbolic analysis to explain attitudes towards abnormality. He notes that every society defines its concept of normality and determines the criteria by which a "person" is defined. In general these fundamental principles are not challenged and are viewed as self-evident. Yet there are instances in which these principles are seriously put to the test, such as when babies are born with defects. Then a question of symbolic analysis arises: how should one define a newborn whose characteristics are not clear? For example, in every society a normal person is defined, among other things, as having either male or female sexual organs. What happens when a hermaphrodite is born? American society offers a certain solution: use surgery to change the newborn either to a male or to a female, and then the ambivalence disappears. The Navahos (Hill, 1935) give the hermaphrodite preferential status. The Pokots, in Africa, believe that such a "monster" should be killed since it is not a "real person." Hermaphrodites who survive are given a special name, *Serr*, which means neuter, sexless, a sort of "it" (Edgerton, 1964).

Douglas and Evans-Pritchard give other examples of the way in which symbolic analysis deals with people with impairments. According to Douglas, in African societies that are close to nature a normal person is characterized by his unique form and his tendency to beget children singly. In such societies, the birth of twins or of cripples poses a problem: should such newborns be classified as animal or as man? This problem is resolved, according to Douglas, in two main ways. The tribes of Western Africa follow the general rule that twins should be killed at birth. The Nuer treat abnormal newborns "as baby hippopotamuses, accidentally born to humans and, with this labelling, the appropriate action is clear. They gently lay them in the river where they belong" (Douglas, 1966, p. 39). Douglas (1975, p. 50) uses such concepts as dirt or pollution, defined as something which is not in place, to explain how a handicapped child is viewed by those around her or him. Thus, a being that is an affront to conventional images is perceived as pollution which must be disposed of.

Most anthropologists report only one pattern of behavior towards the abnormal child—that pattern which is openly avowed and culturally accepted. They tend to ignore those attitudes towards handicapped persons that do not follow the accepted pattern, even though we know that abnormal cases that do not obey the general rules can be found in every society, including primitive ones (Edgerton, 1976, pp. 68–73; Meggitt, 1962, p. 219; Scheffler, 1965, p. 112; Matza, 1969, p. 13).

The waverings and indecision of the parents who in the end comply are also not generally reported. This creates the impression that parental response towards handicapped children is automatic. In contrast, Edgerton, who describes a culture that condemns hermaphroditic children to death, seeks and finds parents who do not obey the rules or who hesitate before killing their hermaphroditic children. It is clear from his accounts that parental response is not automatic, and that essentially every parent makes a swift personal decision whether or not to obey the rules of her or his culture and kill her or his child.

In this book I proceed from a point of departure that has characterized much of anthropological research. I also deal with symbolic analysis and stress mankind's need for order, for organizing her or his surroundings, for finding meaning in life. I, too, maintain that encountering an abnormal child somehow affronts our sense of order and creates the need to resolve this lack of clarity by giving the child a certain identity. Yet I shall not confine myself to studying the generally accepted response of the culture, which in most instances concludes with the removal of the abnormal person. I shall explore the full range of options available to a parent in a given culture to respond to the birth of an abnormal child, even if some of these options run counter to the accepted pattern.

Anthropological literature which deals with the concepts of "person" and "non-person" has one other limitation. Such research has focused on only one direction of the process—the development and coming into being of the person—and has not taken any interest in the transition from "person" to "non-person." In this chapter we shall elaborate on the subject in both directions. Previous research has also tended to relate to the development of a "person" in terms of chronological age. Such an approach is also well-suited to psychoanalytic theory, which ties the moral development of a person to her or his chronological age and notes that, until she or he reaches a certain age, a child's conscience is not sufficiently developed for her or him to distinguish between good and bad. In this chapter I shall investigate whether chronological development is indeed so crucial in the question of "person" and "non-person."

We have certain reservations about the tendency of anthropological literature to lay emphasis on the difference between primitive societies and modern society regarding mankind's way of thinking about such notions as sickness and health, life and death, body and soul, person and non-person.

Anthropological analysis leaves much to be desired primarily because some of its assumptions regarding modern society have not been verified; the literature is based mostly on primitive societies, and therefore its conclusions with respect to modern society do not hold. For example, I agree that modern medicine has the tools to rate a person's health according to a place on a continuum of several indices of health, or to rate sexuality according to a place on a continuum of several indices of sexuality. Yet it seems to us that the crucial question is not what data are available for medical diagnosis, but what evidence does the average modern human being use when defining a hermaphrodite or a sick person. For example, if the average person is asked to judge whether a certain individual is a hermaphrodite, does she or he do so by observing that the external sexual organs are not in order, or does she or he rely on various indices of disorder in the internal sexual system, such as hormone level in the blood? Examining the reactions of parents to such disorders sheds light on the data which modern people use in appraising the health of their children.

I shall also examine attitudes towards life and death, and shall ask whether parents in our society view life and death as a clear dichotomy, or whether, like the Africans, they too view it as a continuum. I shall consider whether parents in our society relate to body and soul as an inseparable whole. It is hard for me to accept without scrutiny the statement that in modern society an individual's personality is perceived as being clearly separated from the personality of others, while in African society an individual's personality is perceived as an extension of his family ties. Perhaps, as in African societies, parenting in our society is understood as a sort of expansion of the parent's soul, and hence one should view the child as part of the parent.

Of all the distinctions made in anthropology, the most relevant to our discussion in this chapter is the one between "person" and "non-person." Like other distinctions which I have presented, this one, too, leaves much to be desired primarily because it is based only on primitive society. For example, according to Zahan, "becoming a person" is a subject of concern only in primitive society, whereas in modern society, which Zahan has not examined, people are not perceived in terms of becoming. I shall subject this assumption to scrutiny, examining whether modern parents, like the members of African societies, also relate to their children as "non-persons"; if so, in what situations and with what names and ways of address (such as the use of "hippopotamus" among the Nuer and "*Serr*" among the Pokot)? I do not accept as self-evident the assumption that in modern society people do not need animal metaphors to relate to the abnormal person. Note that many disabilities and symptoms of serious diseases are described in our society by terms that have been borrowed from the animal world. For example, we speak of elephantiasis, having a duck-walk, a harelip, or being pigeon-toed, etc. Animal metaphors also occur in our everyday speech, especially to express something pejorative; for example, we might call someone a "black sheep," a "guinea pig," or an "ass."

Essentially I shall deal with questions concerning the essence of human beings, such as: when does a creature begin to be called a "person"? What changes in a being make one wish to remove that being from the family of mankind? Are the changes reversible? If so, what further changes must occur to restore a being to the family of mankind?

The question of when an entity becomes a human being is at the crux of the modern religio-philosophic controversy on abortion (Atzmon, 1979; Sadan, 1982; Rabbi Frankl, 1979). According to Charny (1980), there are situations in which the modern person defines the other as if she or he were not human, but beast. Moreover, using symbolism and ideology, the mechanism of dehumanization (person as beast) is used to justify depriving the other of life. Barram (1975) maintains that "the common denominator of racial persecution, witch hunt, experimentation on human beings, all 'scientifically' justified, is the devaluation of human life. ... The consequence of the devaluation of human life is always violence, the exploited, the victim." The connection with anti-Semitism and modern racism is striking. The examples presented below are a vivid illustration of how the Jew was viewed as a cockroach, a creepy-crawly, a non-human creature, a satanic, cancer-producing, beastly entity, a poisoning and polluting agent; and of how killing a Jew was seen as the legitimate extermination of a nest of pests and insects.

Bachrach (1979) writes in *Modern Anti-Semitism*:

> The Church isolated the figure of the Jew and put the mark of the Devil on him. ... He is not to be included among the good creatures of this world. ... The Church deprived the Jew of his human likeness. ... The non-Jewish world saw the satanic, ... the non-human, the non-usual, the abnormal in the Jew. ... An unbroken line leads from the ignominy that Christianity placed on the Jew in the primitive era ... to Hitler's death camps in our era. ... There is a connection between the doctrine of degradation and the extermination camps.
>
> In 1933, in a conversation with Bishop Burning, Hitler said: "For 1500 years the Catholic Church looked on the Jews as insects and pests. She banished them to ghettos, etc. Then people understood what Jews are. I am only repeating what was done for 1500 years. ... " "Because they are different, they must be removed." (p. 17).

The previous chapter dealt with the tendency of parents to reject children whose looks are abnormal. In this chapter we examine the nature of the threat inherent in a child's physical abnormality which leads to her being rejected. The central thesis of this chapter is that a child is rejected when she does not meet the accepted image of a "person" and her cognitive location is problematic. We take a closer look at the concept of perceiving the other as a "non-person," including the contexts in which such associations are made. Even now, simply from our discussion of transferring the other from the category of "person" to that of "non-person" and from "non-person" to "person," we see that the birth of a being does not automatically confer on her the title of a "person" and that to be called a "person" she must meet certain criteria.

How does the transition to "non-person" occur? As we shall see, becoming a "non-person" is comprised of two processes which stress the individual's longing for order and meaning. One is the process of destroying boundaries. The message a parent receives from the abnormal external appearance of her child shakes up the parent's own cognitive system, undermines its boundaries, and destroys her images of "child," "body" and "man." The child's abnormality violates the existing order; the parents thus view the child as an uncertain entity which crosses the boundaries of familiar categories. The child is perceived as a monster—half man and half beast, half son and half daughter, or half "retard." The uncertainty regarding the degree of monstrousness or humanness of the child is beyond bearing and makes the parent feel an urgent need to locate the child in her cognitive system.

The other process concerns rebuilding the boundaries of the cognitive system by means of verbal proclamations regarding the child's place in it. Verbal pronouncements about order and tearing down boundaries make it possible to interpret the reality and to restore order. An abnormal child can be located in one's cognitive system in a number of ways. When the abnormality cannot be disguised, the tendency is to locate the child by defining and labeling him or her as a "non-person." Defining him or her in this way is especially significant because it paves the way to treating him or her violently. Thus, even when the parents whom I observed sought the death of their handicapped child, they did not feel like murderers killing a human being, but rather like people who were removing a non-human entity from the midst of mankind. "Legitimate" violence towards someone who is defined as a "non-person" will be discussed later in the chapter. We shall see that parents reject their children and are even violent towards them as a result of their being unwilling to tolerate the cultural chaos that such a child represents. The longing of parents for renewed order is stronger than the natural biological bond between parents and children, as formed in the course of pregnancy and birth.

CASE 8 "THE UNICORN"

A girl suspected of having Turner's syndrome[1] was born in Merkaz Hospital to 35-year-old parents with higher education in the sciences, native Israelis of Eastern European origin, with an older daughter at home.

Let us see how the mother related to her daughter immediately after delivery.

NURSE: You had a girl.

MOTHER: Let me see her.

The nurse shows her the baby.

MOTHER [*horrified*]: Oh, look at her! Get her away. She looks simply frightful.

(The girl has a rectangular sort of face and looks somewhat peculiar.)

Meanwhile the family was waiting outside. They were all well-dressed and, as I discovered later, are highly educated, some of them doctors and nurses. When the rest of the family first saw the girl, they too were shocked by her looks and said, "She really is not O.K."

The evening after the birth the doctor had a talk with the parents. Here is part of his conversation:

DOCTOR: Look, the medical staff suspects your daughter might have Turner's syndrome, but all the tests that we have done today have come out alright and do not confirm our suspicions. [*The parents did not ask what Turner's syndrome is, and so the doctor continued.*] A girl who has Turner's syndrome generally has a rather rectangular face and a large distance between the nipples. She will develop secondary sexual indications, but she does not have ovaries and therefore cannot bear children. You should know that many women suffering from Turner's syndrome have a very high I.Q. Moreover, I must stress that the tests we have done have come out negative, that is, they do not confirm our suspicion of Turner's syndrome.

MOTHER: This is not a girl; it's a unicorn. ... She frightens me. ... She makes me confused. A highly intelligent unicorn!

FATHER: Yes, the first association I had when I saw her was that of a unicorn. She terrifies us.

MOTHER: I insist on being released from the hospital as soon as possible. There's no point in my staying here any number of days. I don't want to wait for the girl's test results. They're irrelevant.

The mother was discharged two days later. On the day she went home the doctor called the parents in for a talk again and explained to them that the numerous tests done thus far had not indicated the "presence of Turner's syndrome or of any other possible disease or disability. Thus, it stands to reason that the girl's looks will improve in time. ... "

MOTHER: But she is horrifying. ... Our family is also behind us. She horrifies them, too. ... She's not O.K. ... There's no point in bringing her up. ... We are simply not going to take her home. ...

The girl remained in the newborn ward for two months. During this time the parents did not even visit her once; but every day or two representatives of the family would come and request that the baby not be given anything to eat and that she be starved.

One day the girl's parents came and demanded to speak with the doctor and nurse in charge. Here is part of their conversation:

FATHER: Why are you feeding her?
NURSE: She's hungry.
FATHER: But why should a creature like this grow?
NURSE: Because she was born.
FATHER: Alright, but there's no point to it. Did you see her?!
NURSE: Yes. She's a girl.
FATHER: Then why feed her?

NURSE: Because she is hungry.

FATHER: You can just not feed her for several hours, and that'll be that.

NURSE: Have you ever seen a hungry child? Have you ever heard how a hungry child cries?

FATHER: So lock her up in a room; then you won't have to hear her crying.

NURSE: Look here, I'm in charge of the newborn ward, and I'm not running a concentration camp here. Take your girl home and starve her yourself if you want. Here she's a girl just like any other, and she'll get food and care just like any other.

FATHER: You can worry about our salvation and her's for the rest of your life. It's not human what you're doing to us. You're ruining an entire family.

DOCTOR [*sitting thunderstruck until now*]: Sir, I want to remind you that so far it is not even clear that your daughter has anything wrong with her. And even if it does turn out that she has Turner's syndrome, she could still reach the highest achievements.

MOTHER: We put it to you in plain language. She is not O.K. We won't take her home. You're afraid of taking the responsibility to act decisively. ... We have several important doctors in our family who are on the board of the hospital and the Ministry of Health. ... Go consult them. ...

NURSE: They, too, would refuse to kill a baby.

After two months in the newborn ward the baby was transferred to the children's ward, where she was classified as an abandoned child. A month later she was put in an institution.

Here we have the case of a baby girl who was born with a slight anomaly in her face. The doctors' suspicions of an internal disease were not confirmed, the girl was proclaimed healthy, yet she was abandoned by her parents. She was not rejected due to fear of the internal disease that the doctors initially suspected she might have; the parents did not relate to that at all. It was the girl's external appearance, as perceived by her parents, that frightened them and led to her being abandoned.

The parents' behavior reveals two processes in operation here. First came a proclamation about disorder and destruction of previously existing boundaries distinguishing between a human infant and "other" entities. The baby girl was perceived as something monstrous: a brainy unicorn. The very process of describing the destruction of boundaries indicates how the newborn was interpreted and given the new status of "beast." Thus, by calling the girl a unicorn, the parents were also taking a step towards rebuilding their cognitive system. It appears that tearing down and rebuilding boundaries are like two sides of the same coin. Defining the girl as a unicorn illustrates the dehumanization process which lays the ground for requesting that she be the victim of violence, and her resemblance to an animal is used to provide justification for her death. Anthropological studies of personhood all focus on becoming a "person" and ignore development in the opposite direction, towards becoming a "non-person";[2] in contrast, the case of the "unicorn" illustrates a process at the end of which the child is viewed as a "non-person" and sheds light on how this process is used to justify violence against someone who is defined as non-human.

Is defining a child as a "non-person" a reversible process? Can such a child be re-defined as a "person"? Are these definitions used differently in different ethnic groups? I shall try to answer these and other questions by what we learn from our encounter with Victor's parents.

CASE 9 "THE MONSTER"

Victor was born in Central Hospital. His parents are production workers, thirty years old, native Israelis of Iranian origin, and have an elementary school education. Victor has two brothers, one five and the other three, both of whom developed normally. Victor was born with a severe deformity: both his legs, from the knee down, were lacking bones. At the birth, Victor's mother gazed pale-faced at the medical staff. "Everyone was in a state of shock because of his legs," she recounted later. "Especially since it was a breach birth, and the first thing I saw were those legs of his ... so horrible."

Early the next morning the father arrived, pale and perspiring, and said he had had nightmares that night in which the baby's legs appeared in all sorts of distorted shapes and blended with "pictures of the Yom Kippur War." "I simply couldn't sleep," he said. "I kept on seeing his [the baby's] legs, like snakes writhing back and forth. ... I saw fire ... legs cast in the field, with blood all over them ... like I saw in the war ... half a leg ... a quarter of a leg ... and then again I saw his [the baby's] legs, writhing like snakes. ... " The father turned to the doctor on duty and asked that the baby's legs be covered, "because I can't bear to see him." The doctor immediately called in the medical staff that had examined Victor during the night and told the parents they could ask "whatever they want." This is how the conversation continued:

FATHER: We have nothing to ask. You should have killed this monster the minute he was born.

MOTHER: It's not yet too late. ... You can still kill him now. ...

DOCTOR: But he is a healthy child in every respect. Except for his legs.

MOTHER: So use his good organs for other children. ... Take out his eyes and give them to someone else. ... Take out his nose, ... and his hands. ... I give you my permission.

SURGEON [*shocked*]: I promise you that after a series of orthopedic operations your child will even be able to walk. His disability can be repaired.

MOTHER [*interrupting*]: It's a pity to waste electricity on this child, ... really a pity, all the electricity. ... I don't want to know what happens with him, what will be with him later ... for me, he's dead. ... I knew from the very beginning that something was wrong with this pregnancy. I should have had an abortion. ... As far as I am concerned, he should not have been born at all. ... We're not taking this monster home. We're going to leave him in the hospital, and that's the end of it ... If you force us to take him home, we'll murder the monster, ... we'll throw him into the wadi [ravine] ... and then we'll commit suicide.

The father nodded his head in consent. It was clear that the mother was expressing a joint decision of the couple not to take Victor home.

That same day Victor's parents informed their extended family, including their parents and children, that their son had died in the hospital. Before the parents left the hospital without the baby, a psychiatrist was called in and certified that the couple were not psychotic. In his opinion the behavior of Victor's parents could be attributed to their being under tremendous tension and to their using a mechanism of denial which, he maintained, was characteristic of their cultural and socio-economic background. In view of the difficulties in raising such a child, the psychiatrist recommended that discharge of the parents without the child be approved, and that arrangements be made to put the infant in an institution. In the wake of the psychiatrist's recommendations, social workers affiliated with the hospital tried to find a foster family or institution for the child. But, since finding a suitable institution or foster family for a child like Victor is extremely difficult, the welfare worker in charge saw "working with the child's parents through the welfare department where the parents reside as the best long-range solution. We must try to arouse the parents' sense of responsibility towards their child; and, in the end, I believe progress will be made with them. At the same time, orthopedic treatment must not be delayed simply for lack of the parents' signature. Therefore, we shall appoint the welfare clerk as guardian." The welfare department in the parents' community, working in parallel, found that the child's parents were "very warm and positive people ... who have built a lovely home for their two older children. ... Now, ever since the birth, they have been staying secluded in their house, as if in mourning. The father has not been shaving, they don't put on lights, the shutters are closed ... but it is worthwhile trying to convince them not to give up the child."

When he was three weeks old, Victor had a circumcision ceremony arranged by the hospital staff. Amidst great excitement, the child was named Victor, that he might be "victorious in overcoming his hard lot." Victor progressed and developed well, and by five weeks of age had become a lovely child, bestowing smiles on those around him and treated with loving warmth by the staff of the ward. The nurses would vie for the privilege of taking him out to stroll in the sun, and would compete in bringing him beautiful clothes and toys to hang over his crib. But his parents remained adamant in their position. When the local welfare worker attempted to obtain the parents' signature for the series of operations he had to undergo, they made it conditional upon the department of social services undertaking never to return the child to them. They also returned the form sent them by the social security administration to inform them of their eligibility for a children's stipend upon Victor's birth.

When Victor turned two months old, the department of social services applied to the courts for authorization to have the child undergo operation without the consent of his parents. The parents were summoned to court, where they declared: "If only the child would die. ... Seeing as he hasn't died until now, perhaps he will do everyone a favor and die on the operating table. ... How do you even have the nerve to summon us here? He's dead for us. ... We've already buried him." The judge, convinced of the intransigence of their decision to abandon the child, authorized the operations to be performed without their consent.

At three months of age, Victor began to undergo a series of X-rays and examinations requiring general anesthesia. Throughout this difficult period the parents showed no sign of interest in their son. In contrast, Victor received wonderfully warm attention from the hospital staff. The nurses showered him with love and care. One of the nurses requested to adopt him as a foster child. Other nurses volunteered to provide round-the-clock surveillance for him and stayed after hours until he awakened from the anesthesia. At that time he also came into the care of a devoted person who did much to stimulate his intellect.

The first operation was performed when Victor was four months old. The parents were informed of the success of the operation on the same day; but even so they expressed no interest in the condition of their son.

When he was five months old, Victor's parents came to visit a relative of the family who had given birth in the same hospital where Victor had been born. They went with her to the newborn ward to see the babies. It was then, while looking at the babies, that the parents suddenly turned to the nurse and asked her in a whisper whether they could please "see Victor." A very emotional meeting ensued. The nurse took Victor out of his crib and laid him in his father's arms. The parents, nurses, and doctors cried for at least half an hour. The head nurse, having been the first to regain composure, began singing Victor's praises. "Look how lovely he is. ... Everyone here loves him. ... It's as if he were our own child. ... Look what smooth skin he has. We simply love to stroke him. ... And look what a smile he has. ... He's more accomplished than other children of his age."

Later on the head nurse said, "I have learned from many years of experience that it doesn't do any harm to 'sell' a child like this to his parents."

Victor, whose legs were covered, smiled constantly, as usual for him. The father, bursting into heart-rending tears, asked, "Nurse, do you think he will forgive us for the past?"

NURSE [*smiling*]: We won't tell him ...

Little by little the parents calmed down. Throughout that week they spent every day at Victor's bedside, fondling him with emotion, kissing him, and sobbing inaudibly.

At the end of the week there was a meeting between the parents, the doctor of the ward, the orthopedist and the social worker. The doctor patiently described "what we plan to correct in the next few operations," and in conclusion explained that "the less good leg will have to be amputated beneath the knee." At that moment the parents became "terribly anxious," in their own words. The mother imagined to herself how the deformity must look: "Like butterflies. Now I suddenly understand that his legs will be like butterflies, ... and that he will be deformed, ... that he will have half a leg. ... That's how I see him in my mind's eye. ... I imagine how I'll be walking down the street with a child who does not have a leg, but has a butterfly, ... a snake. ... This is not a child, it's a real monster, ... a boy with a fluttering butterfly instead of a leg ... that's how I see him. ... Oh, it disgusts me, and it frightens me, ... it puts me into a cold sweat." Then, addressing the doctor, she said, "If that's the way it is, let him die. Why don't you kill him? Why don't you give his eyes to someone who needs them? Why don't you cut off his ears and give them to some other child? It's a pity, all the electricity you are wasting on this monster. ... It's a shame for you to be wasting your time."

DOCTOR [*shocked, trying to cajole her*]: But you are mistaken. Victor is a wonderful boy.

MOTHER: A boy? You call this a boy? With an animal's leg? This is a monster!

Once more, the parents ceased coming to see Victor; and again Victor underwent the operation without his parents. At this point Victor was transferred to the children's ward, and his parents were given daily reports on the tremendous improvement in his external appearance. Then they were faced with an immediate decision: whether to take their child home, or to give him up for adoption.

The parents returned to the hospital once more. There they met their son, his legs in a cast, his face lovely and smiling, as always. Again they dissolved in tears and didn't cease kissing and hugging their son. The social worker was pleased to report that they were "softening up." "The only problem remaining is how to reveal the secret ... since everyone around was told that the child had died, and now we must help them disclose the truth to all those around, especially their family. They have to be advised how to tell their other children that their brother did not die, but is actually alive." At the end of that week, for the first time since Victor's birth, his two brothers came to visit him. The next time he underwent operation, his mother sat by him all night long and throughout most of the day. Over the next two months his mother came to visit him daily, to care for him and feed him patiently. The parents would caress their child, stroking his face and hands. With a smile on their faces they would kiss him and show him much love and gentleness, and would even make sure to bring their two older children to the hospital to amuse Victor by playing with him with toys they had brought from home. Together the parents and Victor weathered a very difficult period, during which the infant underwent seven operations.

The parents brought Victor home when he was eight months old. The shutters were opened wide and the house was brightly lit. The parents' outward appearance had changed; the father was neatly dressed and well-shaven, the mother spruce and smiling. With Victor's homecoming the father also returned to regular work. At home Victor was treated lovingly, as evidenced by devoted daily attention and frequent physical contact with his parents. Nevertheless, at times the parents' former reactions re-emerged. It turns out, as we shall see below, that the parents' rejection surfaced in those instances when they had to look at the child's deformity as it was, not concealed in a cast. Recall, that since Victor was first abandoned they had never seen the deformed leg without a cast; for, when they had returned to see him, his legs had already been put in casts. A week before they took Victor home, as the mother was sitting at her son's side, petting and feeding him, a part of the cast suddenly came loose, revealing his deformed leg with its disfiguring scars. The mother instantly threw down the food and, pale-faced, said, "I'm going to vomit." Then the child reached out his arms, asking his mother to pick him up. This was the mother's response:

MOTHER: Leave me alone, you monster. With the face of a person and the legs of a snake [*letting out a shriek*]. Let me go. ... Get away from me. Why are you clinging to me ... like a jellyfish? [*Breaking down, half crying, half shouting*] Take him from me. ... I'll kill this creature. I'll kill this retard. Yes, he's a retard. He looks like a retard. ... You piece of fly-paper, why have you latched on to me?

Her shrieking and crying gradually turned to a quiet sobbing, a mute lament; several minutes later she walked out. She did not return until the evening, when Victor's legs were again in casts. Then, without saying a word, she began feeding him again, hugging him and singing to him.

The parents exhibited similar behavior also after taking Victor home. The same sort of hysteria returned whenever part of the cast happened to fall off while the child was being cared for. Then the parents would come to the hospital, pale and frightened, and would put Victor down on a table and walk out. "We were so terrified," the father said, "it's truly frightening. ... You must keep it covered all the time. It throws us into a panic. ... We can't keep on going into a fright each time the cast comes loose." Once the medical staff had become convinced of the "parents' inability to face the deformity, and of the importance of putting on an apparatus that would prevent the deformity from being exposed," in the words of the staff, it was suggested to the parents that the plaster casts be replaced by a costly plastic device that would not come apart.

Thus, life continued in Victor's family. The mother returned to work, and during the day Victor was cared for by a woman sent by the welfare service. The social worker summed up the situation as follows, "Anyone who didn't know about it, wouldn't be able to tell that there had been such a tragedy here."

We see that the parents' ethnic background and level of education do not account for the way parents relate to a child suffering an external disability. Despite the difference in origin and level of education between the parents of the "unicorn" and Victor's parents, we see a resemblance in their behavior. Victor, a child with a severe deformity in his legs, was rejected by his parents who, in so doing, associated him in their mind's eye with various beastly monsters.

Here, too, as in the case of the "unicorn," we can distinguish two aspects of the parents' behavior. One is the destruction of existing boundaries. Victor's identity is not clear; he violates the boundaries between one category and another, with the "face of a person and legs of a snake." This creates a feeling in the parents of cultural chaos; it jolts their cognitive system. We have seen that parents cannot manage for long with such a sense of anomaly, since, by presenting an unclear situation, the anomaly poses a threat and hence demands a response.

The other aspect of the parents' behavior is the reconstruction of the boundaries of their cognitive system and the restoration of their former definitions of "person" and "non-person." Relating to Victor as if to an animal not only attests a breach of categories, but also constitutes a step in his cultural relocation. In other words, the interpretation given the deformity, and location of the child in the category of animal are the cultural expression of the feeling of a destruction of boundaries.

Analyzing the behavior of Victor's parents adds several dimensions to our discussion which did not arise in the case of the "unicorn." One prominent message is the importance of disguising the defect and the connection between the absence of such a disguise and transferal of a person to the category of "non-person." Victor is rejected when his deformity is not concealed and his "monstrousness" stands out. When his deformity is concealed he is seen as a person and his parents accept him, but only on condition that his deformity continue to be concealed. Thus, Victor's parents alternately evince two patterns of behavior: rejection of the abnormal, on the one hand, and conditional acceptance of him, on the other.

In the case of the "unicorn" the parents' behavior illustrates perception of a newborn as a "non-person" and ends with rejection of a girl who, as these words are being written, remains an abandoned child. Victor's case, on the other hand, illustrates the transition from perceiving the other as a "non-person," rejecting him, and demanding that he be treated with violence, to viewing him as a human being and relating to him with warmth and love. Thus the behavior of Victor's parents illustrates the essential reversibility and inherent impermanence of locating the other in the category of "person" or "non-person."

Lastly, anthropologists who have dealt with the question of the essence of man have associated the development of the concept of "person" with chronological age in primitive societies; a being is defined as a "non-person" until he or she reaches a certain age. Only after reaching that age is he or she deemed a "person." Analysis of the behavior of Victor's parents illustrates a transition from "non-person" to "person" which is not dependent on age. Victor is classified alternately as human or non-human according to the prominence of his monstrousness, not according to his chronological age.

CASE 10 "A BIT RETARDED"

The inability to come to terms with an uncertain stimulus coming from a child's body image is a central factor in the way Shula, whom we meet next, relates to her retarded daughter.

A well-to-do, 35-year-old couple, both professionals, native Israelis of American extraction, had a second daughter. The girl, outwardly charming, was received with love and devotion by her family. As time went by, the mother began to discern that her daughter was not developing properly. The doctor at the well-baby clinic, to whom the mother turned to express her concern, suspected that "the girl's hearing was not 100 percent, and that she seems to have a slight hearing problem." He also suspected that "she has a very slight defect in her lip." But, the doctor stressed, these were only suspicions. "I can't be sure," he said. "You must wait. Many babies arouse such suspicions and then it turns out to be nothing. Take things easy for the time being." But the mother did not take it easy because, as she said, she "felt that something was different about the girl." When the girl was nine months old her doctor raised the possibility that she had a slight heart defect. The mother immediately went to the cardiology clinic, where the following conversation took place:

DOCTOR [*after thoroughly examining the child*]: Your girl has a slight problem with her heart, but it is not significant. It is nothing to be worried about.

SHULA: So why isn't she developing like other children?

DOCTOR: Because she is retarded.

MOTHER [*bursts out in a fit of frightful screaming that lasts a quarter of an hour*]: What?! Why didn't anyone tell me? ... All the time they spoke about small problems.

DOCTOR: Forgive me. I was sure you knew about it. Her file says, "Retardation suspected immediately upon birth, and confirmed two weeks later." I don't know why nobody told you the truth.

Shula left with her girl and, incapable of driving, took the bus home. That evening Shula told me how she had felt:

> I placed her beside me, like a parcel, and thought: what would happen if I should forget her in the bus? I wanted her to die. I felt absolutely nothing for her. I didn't even look at her. All day long I only thought of how she would die, ... of all sorts of ways of dying. ... All my visions focused around the subject of how she would die. ... Then I thought about her retardation. The doctors had told me that her degree of retardation had not yet been determined, that they had to wait and see the results of more tests. I wished it would be severe retardation, as severely retarded as a person could be. I didn't want her to be on the borderline between a normal child and a retard. The hardest news for me to bear would be that she is "a trifle" retarded. ... I don't know how to cope with something like that, with "a trifle retarded."

The mother repeated her wish that her "girl be severely retarded" in later years, as well. As she explained, "Raising a child who is half retarded is an impossible thing. ... You can't sit on the fence." Throughout the entire period the mother refrained from going to her child except for giving her the most basic, vital care. She explained her emotions as follows:

> I don't love the girl. ... She's beginning to look like a retard. ... I don't feel anything, ... but I am imprisoned with her in the house the whole day long, ... and it's terrible, being with her all day. Then all sorts of thoughts come into my mind. What would be if she wanted to eat, and I didn't feed her? ... or if I were giving her a bath and left her in the tub? It was then that I decided we must put her in an institution. We must get her out of the house, before I begin hating her indiscriminately. ... Money is no problem for us, and we must find the best possible institution.

When the girl reached the age of two, her mother had the following to say:

She looks more and more like a severely retarded child. ... I want
to put her in an institution, but we haven't yet found one. For the
time being, until we can find an institution, we have a wonderful
nanny. We pay her a fortune, and she takes care of the girl and
truly loves her. ... We buy her whatever we can. ... The nanny
takes her for walks and plays with her. ... Sometimes I ask how
things are going and if anything is needed. But generally the
nanny buys whatever is necessary. ... Our older daughter also has
a nanny, but a different one. Apart from her sister. We keep the
two of them separate. ...

Now the girl is three and a half years old, and the mother says:

Now she is three and a half, and she really looks retarded. ...
She keeps on going ... and going ... drooling all the time. ...
I want her to die, but I don't do anything about it. ... I don't
love her, ... she has a nanny who loves her. And I am free. ...
At first, before we had a nanny, it was terrible, ... but now I
feel at ease. I feel a sense of obligation to feed her when she is
hungry, and that's all. ... My husband actually loves her. He feels
attached to her. But he's at work all day and only sees her in the
evening. ... So he doesn't have time to give her much in terms of
emotional development. ... I am still looking for a good institution
for her. Recently we have also begun going on trips. Ever since we
found this nanny, we go on trips and leave the girl with her. ...
Look, she doesn't feel anything. It seems to me that she doesn't
even recognize me. ... So, no matter what, she doesn't even know
whether I love her or not. ... The girl is severely retarded. She
looks at me and doesn't feel anything. She's incapable of feeling
or understanding.

The following picture emerges: Shula had a very charming baby girl,
whom the doctors classified as retarded. Their diagnosis became known to
the mother after she had been caring for the girl for several months. At first
the girl was perceived as a threat, in that she presented an unclear stimulus.
The difficulty, according to explicit remarks of the mother, lay in the fact
that she could not bear a state of disorder. The lack of clarity in marginal
retardation—between a normal child and a retard—was threatening. The
mother found herself in a position of cultural chaos. Her culture did not
give her the tools to come to terms with an uncertain sort of being, and she
felt that she must locate the anomaly. Severe retardation, despite all the
hardships entailed, restores order. Thus, despite the fact that the girl looked
very charming and her retardation was not generally evident, as time went
by the girl began to appear more and more retarded in her mother's eyes,
until finally she looked "severely retarded." The mother's behavior towards

her daughter illustrates the problematic nature of marginal conditions, between the category of "person" and "non-person." We see that a marginal condition is far more problematic than a more extreme condition; and, as in other cases, the parents' behavior expresses the difficulty of coping with such a condition and the need to use cultural tools to remove the abnormal children from their marginal condition and thus locate their anomaly.

CASE 11 "THE TWO-HEADED CHILD"

The two cases that I present below also deal with conditions of uncertainty, this time with regard to sex. In one case, the indefiniteness is not immediately apparent; in the other, it is. Is there a difference in the definition of "person" and the behavior of the parents regarding each of these children?

The first case involves sexual uncertainty which is not visually apparent. The child appears in every way a boy; his sexual uncertainty is associated with his inner organs.

Clara, a 39-year-old Russian-born woman, and her Iraqi husband have four daughters. Clara is an office worker in charge of a staff of other workers, and her husband is a clerk. Both parents have a vocational, tenth-grade education. Due to her age, in the fourth month of her pregnancy Clara was sent to Southern Hospital for amniocentesis.[3] Like other women, Clara was very eager to know the sex of the fetus but was told that the answer was unclear. Six weeks later the test results came in, diagnosing Klinefelter's syndrome.[4] Clara and her husband were immediately called for consultation with an obstetrician-gynecologist and a geneticist. Here is part of their conversation:

GENETICIST: You surely must have realized that the test results are not so good. ... We are dealing here with a genetic disease. On the outside, your son will look in every way a boy. ...

MOTHER [*interrupting him*]: So everything is O.K. What can be the matter? We wanted a boy, and that's what we have.

GENETICIST: For the most part, the disease is manifested by infertility. Internally, he will not function altogether like a man. In addition, about 29 percent of the cases also involve mental retardation. Therefore we suggest that you terminate the pregnancy.

CLARA: But I was just examined here by the ob-gyn two days ago.

DOCTOR: Yes, that's in our records.

CLARA: See what he wrote. He felt my stomach carefully and said that he could feel the baby's head. ... Two weeks ago I also had ultrasound and I saw the baby's body, ... I saw his head. ... Look, I want to talk with my husband about this, ... to confer with him in private.

The couple talked with each other, and an hour later Clara announced her intention of continuing the pregnancy.

GENETICIST: It's your decision. I personally would not risk bringing such a child into the world. Think about it at home, and if you change your minds, let us know.

Clara continued the pregnancy and returned to the hospital for more tests.

Two important aspects of this case emerged in my numerous talks with Clara and her husband. The first was that her understanding of the doctor's words was that she would have a "two-headed child." Despite the doctor's reports that the defect was purely internal, without the slightest indication of any external defect in the head of the fetus, Clara understood a "child with a defect" to be a child with two heads. She saw no possibility of there being an internal defect without some concomitant external monstrosity. On the other, looking normal was proof for her of the absence of any internal defect. According to her perception, there must be an absolute correspondence between external appearance and internal health. She said that her decision had been made in the wake of wavering between two opinions. One was the "prediction of the geneticist," as she put it. Even though his report was based on sophisticated medical tests, Clara related to his medical examination as if it were "a sort of witchcraft," in her own words. "Anyway, how can they know for certain?" she persisted. In contrast, she gave greater credence to the manual examination and the ultrasound test in which she saw the fetus, who "looked perfectly normal" to her. In her opinion a fetus who on the outside looks like a male, and cute, could not have a disability, i.e., could not be a monster. His external male characteristics were the significant thing, were what brought joy after having had four daughters.

When the time came for her to give birth, Clara looked happy, extremely calm, and well in control during labor. During the difficult hours of labor and delivery not once did she say anything that betrayed her fears of a possible defect in her child. Even when asked explicitly about the "history of the pregnancy," she did not mention the results of the amniocentesis. She had only one request, which she repeated again the moment the child started coming out, and that was "to see the boy as soon as he is born." Immediately after the birth, the midwife (aware of the results of the amniocentesis) told Clara, "You had a boy, just as expected." Clara did not take an interest in the baby's condition but just cast a quick glance at him and said joyfully, "Please tell my husband right away."

The next few days Clara's face beamed with joy. She took care of her baby (the hospital had rooming-in), and boasted of her son's good looks and charm to one and all. The day she was discharged from the hospital, she entered the delivery room with her baby in arms and went from one midwife to the next and from doctor to doctor, showing them her baby. When she reached the ob-gyn who had advised her to terminate the pregnancy, she said, "See how wrong you were. If I had listened to you, I would have lost this child. You said I would have some sort of strange child ... maybe with two heads ... and despite it all, I had a perfectly gorgeous boy."

Clara took her son home and cared for him warmly. Every year she sends a photograph of him, well-dressed and being hugged in his mother's arms, to the gynecology ward.

Clara's son was born with Klinefelter's syndrome, a disease which often has no external manifestation until puberty. In this instance the child fit into the mother's definition of a "person," and thus she accepted him.

Clara's behavior illustrates that "what is important is what one sees," as she herself put it. Her sole reliance on her visual sense led her to be incapable of conceiving of an internal defect; for her a defect must have a visual interpretation. These findings refute the claims of many scholars, such as Edgerton (1964) and Polunin (1977), that people in modern society rely on many sophisticated tests when it comes to questions of illness or sexuality. The behavior of Clara and her husband, like that of many other parents I met, indicates that the results of these sophisticated tests often have no impact on the parents. Significance is attributed only to those tests that technically help view the fetus (such as ultrasound). Lastly, Clara's behavior illustrates the transition from perceiving a child as a person to perceiving him as a non-person and the clear association between a defect and monstrousness. According to Clara's understanding, the existence of a defect, even internal, is conditional on there being some external monstrousness, which she describes graphically as "a two-headed creature." On the other hand, the human external appearance of her son (having a single head and clear external sexual characteristics) prevents her from understanding that he has an internal defect.

CASE 12 "A BOY AND GIRL IN ONE"

In this case the sexual uncertainty is external and visible. The child's sex cannot be determined by its external organs.

Zippora, 41 years old, came to Southern Hospital for amniocentesis because of her age. After the test she was told that she would have a girl. Zippora and her husband have a tenth-grade education, are of Syrian extraction, and are considered to have an average income. Zippora is a housewife and her husband a truck driver.

Zippora had a difficult delivery. Immediately afterwards the doctors and nurses looked at the newborn, then at each other, and finally they addressed Zippora. Here is some of what they said:

DOCTOR: Zippora, we are having a big problem identifying the child's sex. Your child seems completely healthy, but it is hard to say, externally, whether it is a boy or a girl.[5]

ZIPPORA [*turning pale*]: What do you mean? They told me it was a girl. ... Let me see her.

DOCTOR: Surely. Her face is really lovely. [*The nurse shows the mother her child.*]

ZIPPORA [*turning pale again; then, starting to tremble and bursting into tears*]: What did I need this pregnancy for? I have three healthy children at home. ... What will I do? What will I tell people on the street when they ask me what I had, a girl or a boy? What'll I tell them? ... [*crying*] ... Can you operate? Maybe you can do an operation or ... several operations, and then everything will be O.K. ... *and then people will know whether it is a boy or a girl* [*her emphasis*]. ... Oh, how disgusting. ...

DOCTOR: I'm sorry, but at the moment I can't give you an authoritative answer.

ZIPPORA: This is the first time I've ever heard of such a creature. ... Did you ever see such a thing, half boy and half girl? ... Its, like, abnormal. ... What did I need this headache for?! ... This thing here, you call this a person? There is no such thing as a person who is half male half female.

Zippora's husband and sister were waiting outside the delivery room. The sister went up to Zippora and congratulated her.

ZIPPORA: Why bother congratulating me? How can you say congratulations when you don't know what was born?

Zippora turned and went back to her room. There she cried for two whole days and refused to see the baby, to nurse him or take care of him.

Zippora's child was found medically healthy, except for the inability to determine its sex according to its external sexual organs. The child's abandonment by his mother was clearly attributed to the lack of clarity regarding its identity ("you don't know what was born"). A "person" according to Zippora is someone whose sex is well-defined by his or her external sex organs. In contrast to the case of Clara, here the lack of definiteness cannot be disguised and is interpreted as monstrousness. Straddling the boundary between male and female is considered absolutely forbidden, especially when there is no possibility of performing an operation that will move the child off the borderline between the sexes and will give him or her a human identity (i.e., either a "boy or a girl," in the mother's words).

Thus far most of the children we have met had external defects, either real or imagined, and were rejected by their parents. We have come to realize that for an external defect to be associated with rejection it must arouse a sense of violation of accepted boundaries. The rejected child constitutes a monstrous entity that cannot be fit into the generally accepted definition of a "person."

CASE 13 "THE LITTLE JAPANESE"

This case will help us examine what happens when a child with an external defect is not associated with the concept of a "non-person."

Asnat, 37 years old and of Yemenite extraction, has an elementary school education and is the mother of three children. She works as a housekeeper, but her husband is unemployed. A fourth son was just born to her in Northern Hospital. She received him with kisses and cries of joy. The child was examined several hours after birth. Despite the fact that on the surface he looked healthy and cute, the doctors suspected Down's syndrome.[6] The mother, who did not know about the possible defect, chanced to hear the morning after the birth that "her baby has something wrong with him." Asnat went to the newborn ward and, after crying steadily for several minutes, requested to "know what's up." The nurses, in a quandary, decided to show Asnat her son. "On the outside he looks healthy," they told the mother. "But, just to be safe, it would be best for you to wait for the doctor and hear first hand whether the child is healthy or whether there might be some problems that are not immediately apparent."

Asnat came to the nursery to inspect her child. Not satisfied with looking at him closely, she asked to hold him in her arms. She proceeded to examine him, touching his face, his hands, and his ears, and then said, "Nurse, tell me the truth. I'm a strong woman. Is my son healthy?"

NURSE: On the outside the child looks O.K. But it is best for you to wait for the doctor, because not every disease can be seen on the outside.

ASNAT [*crying*]: That's it. I knew it. ... Please call the doctor, quickly. I can't take it any more.

Asnat entered the office of the head doctor and related in detail the circumstances that had led her to ask about her child's health. She concluded with the words, "Doctor, I am prepared to give my all. This baby is my entire life. Just tell me everything is alright with him, ... or what can be done to make him healthy immediately."

The next day the following conversation took place between Asnat and the doctor.

DOCTOR: Your child was examined several hours ago. True, he looks completely healthy, but there are several external signs that might point to a certain disease. It is not yet certain that the child indeed has any disease. Blood tests can refute or corroborate our suspicions, and we have sent a blood sample of the baby for analysis. ... Until we receive an answer, the best thing is to be patient and treat the baby as if he were healthy.

Every once in a while, as the doctor was explaining the situation, the mother tried to interrupt and ask him what the disease was. Finally, when he concluded, she asked out loud, "What disease are you talking about?"

DOCTOR: Medically it is known as Down's syndrome.

MOTHER: Just a minute, ... just a minute. What do you mean? Do you mean to say that he's ret. ... [*Unable to finish her words and say "retarded," the mother makes a gesture of bodily distortion, tongue hanging out, eyes rolling towards the ceiling. The doctor does not respond, and the mother continues.*] No, that can't be. We don't have anyone like that in the family ... and besides, he's so cute. Doctor, could it be a mistake? Perhaps it's not my son. After all, you didn't examine him; he was examined by another doctor; you only came in just now.

The doctor advised the mother to come with him to see the baby. Together they went to the baby; the doctor undressed him and showed her in detail the signs that might indicate Down's syndrome. The mother began sobbing quietly, left the ward and headed for her room, in which there were three other women after childbirth.

When Asnat returned to her room, she lay in bed, knitting something for the baby. During nursing time she stroked her baby gently and behaved as if he were perfectly normal. When she finished feeding him she lifted him up, drew him close to her, and showed him to the woman in the next bed, saying, "Tell me the truth, the honest truth, isn't he cute? I think he's gorgeous. Look what beautiful slanted eyes he has. Just like a Japanese! I'm crazy about his almond-shaped eyes. Look, your son also has slanted eyes. His, too, are almond-shaped."

MOTHER: Yes. But your son's eyes are more slanted than my son's; and he really is charming, your son. I'm also crazy about almond-shaped eyes.

ASNAT [*drawing her son close*]: My cutie. You see? Everyone says you're charming. Everyone is jealous of your eyes.

At that moment Asnat got up and, taking her son, walked over to his bassinet. On her way she paused every so often by another bassinet, looked carefully at the baby lying there, and then shifted her glance to her own child, lying in her arms, and said, "All the babies are cute. My son, too, is cute. My son looks like his father." Her comments were made out loud, intended primarily for the nurses passing by. Finally Asnat placed her baby gently in his bassinet, gazed at him once more, and said, "Your eyes really are slanted, just like your father's. ... Your nose and eyes are just like you father's. ... "

Three weeks later Asnat had an appointment to receive the results of her son's chromosome tests. At 10 o'clock she entered the newborn ward, holding her son in her arms and hugging him close to her body. The baby was dressed in a white knit outfit and swaddled in a blue knit blanket decorated with flowers. Asnat opened the door of the ward, smiling, said hello in a low voice, and immediately entered the doctor's office and sat down to wait for the doctor.

NURSE [*entering after her*]: Hello, Asnat. How are you?

ASNAT [*constantly stroking her child*]: Fine. The baby feels fine, he eats well, and he is developing all too fast. He smiles, follows brightly colored toys with his eyes, and is startled by noises. [*Holding the baby up, as if to show him off*] Look at him. ... [*Kissing the baby*] Look how cute he is. He looks like me, doesn't he? He has such a beautiful face, just like a little Japanese.

Then the doctor came in, accompanied by a social worker.

ASNAT: Hello. Look at my boy. He's developing beautifully [*and she quickly repeated the account she had just given the nurse. Her story seems to have been rehearsed at home, since she repeated it in exactly the same words and used language that was more eloquent than usual.*] ... So, doctor, tell me that the test results show that the child is healthy, and then I have no problem.

DOCTOR: I am sorry, but the results show that our suspicions were correct.

ASNAT [*looks at the doctor with no change of expression. Then she shifts her glance from the doctor to the social worker and back to the doctor. Suddenly she throws the baby into the social worker's hands and screams*]: Enough! You have him. I can't take it any more. ... I just don't have the strength for all this. ... I don't have strength for all you people. ... You don't understand anything.

DOCTOR [*consolingly*]: We promise we'll give you help and support bringing up the child. There are institutions and organizations whose purpose is to help care for abnormal children.

ASNAT [*shouting*]: My son is not abnormal. ... You don't seem to understand this. A child who looks like a little Japanese is abnormal?! I don't need your help. I don't want anyone to say that my son is ill or abnormal. ... I'm afraid they'll call him things like "retard." [*This is the first time that Asnat publicly and emphatically uttered the word "retard."*]

Asnat's behavior toward her son is unlike that of most parents, who tend to reject their retarded children in the wake of having associated the child's external differences (such as slanted eyes) with the monstrous image of a "retard." We have dwelled on Asnat's behavior in order to elucidate our claim that a necessary precondition for a parent to reject his or her child is the perception by the parent that the child's external defects constitute a violation of accepted boundaries. Asnat sees her son's differentness, but interprets it in such a way that the anomaly can be fit into the accepted definition of a person. Unlike Shula, who imagined that her girl was "severely retarded" despite the fact that her daughter was pretty and had no outward physical signs of retardation, Asnat perceives her son, who has the characteristic Down's syndrome look, as a "little Japanese," an appellation which she associates with looking different but not with being a "non-person." Hence, she relates to him with warmth.

Asnat's case also illustrates the importance of cultural analysis and the broad spectrum within which individual reactions can fall. Although all the mothers of Down's syndrome children whom I observed, except Asnat and four other mothers, rejected their children, it does not suffice to simply describe the usual pattern of behavior. It is precisely the exceptions that prove the rule. Asnat, too, believed that a child must have some element of the monstrous in him in order to be defined as abnormal and rejected. However, thus far in my review of her case, she has not perceived signs of monstrousness in her child. (Asnat's attitude changed later. The precise ways in which it changed will be examined in the next chapter.)

Thus far I have pointed out two aspects of the same pattern of behavior. The violation of boundaries and the verbal interpretation of the way the child is perceived. Below I shall discuss the significance of the names that parents use to describe their children. My findings show that when the other is defined as "normal" or as a "person," he or she is perceived as having traits generally attributed to humans and is called by names that indicate his or her being included in the family of mankind, such as the terms of endearment used for children: "baby," "sweetie," and "darling." When the other is defined as "abnormal" or "not human," his or her human essence is denied and he or she is perceived as having traits different from those associated with humans—traits usually attributed to plants or animals—and is called by names that attest his or her belonging to "another" family, not that of mankind, such as "porcupine," "vegetable," "monster," "frog," "this thing," "monkey," or "parcel."

A similar pattern of behavior is seen with respect to premature babies. As we noted in Chapter 1, mothers of premature babies often relate to their newborns less closely than mothers of full-term babies. The parents attribute their rejection of their premature children explicitly to the fact that they are small, attached to medical apparatus, might not survive, and are associated with "disgusting things." "In short, they do not look like human beings," as some parents put it. The attitude of parents towards premature babies as "not human beings" also finds expression in the way these parents describe their children.

Let us examine, for example, the remarks of two mothers of premature babies. One of the mothers, who gave birth to premature twins one of whom was diagnosed as having a heart defect that required surgery, said:

You know ... she still doesn't have a name. We call the other baby, who is at home, Esther, after my husband's mother, ... but since the one in the hospital is still sick, ... and she doesn't yet have the look of a "person" ... we haven't yet given her a name. Look, she doesn't look normal, ... she doesn't look like a human being, ... she looks peculiar, ... so she doesn't have a name. ...

The other mother added:

... While I was still pregnant, I planned to name her Shirley, ... but when she was born very prematurely, I was afraid. ... I looked at her and she seemed to me like a little animal, ... not like a baby, ... not like a human being. ... I didn't want to give her a name until she had the shape ... , until I knew that everything was alright. Now that they have told me the baby is going to go home—and she looks wonderful—I can name her with peace of mind.

We see that parents of premature babies in critical condition do not give their children first names. Even in instances where the parents care for their premature baby with devotion, they tend to name her or him only after the child's condition has improved. They do not have an official naming, and if they have already chosen a name, they ignore it and do not address the child by this name. Only after the baby's physical condition has improved, when the parents believe that her or his chances of survival have increased, when she or he is freed of the medical apparatus and a date is set for the child's return home, only then do the parents tend to give her or him a first name and use other terms of endearment towards her or him.

In other words, the transition from defining a child as non-human to defining her or him as human, and vice versa, also finds expression in the forms of address used with respect to the child.

CHAOS, ABNORMALITY, AND "NON-PERSON"

The data which I have presented are instructive about the implicit threat posed by an abnormal child, who is not comprehended in terms of the categories familiar to her or his parents and thus gives them a sense of cultural chaos. The child is on the borderline, "has no clear place where he belongs," according to one of the parents. The first way of coping with this sort of condition is to attempt to restore order. Rebuilding the parents' cognitive system takes place in two ways: parents of children with obvious deformities tend to define their children as "non-persons," whereas parents of children with disguiseable defects tend to accept their children as long as the deviation from normal can be concealed.

Which children were called "non-persons" by their parents? The cases reviewed in this chapter show that children with external defects on the face or limbs, children suffering from sexual uncertainty, and children with Down's syndrome were all perceived as not complying with the accepted image of what constitutes a person. Thus, our findings show that a child is considered a "non-person" when he or she does not have a human form. According to his or her parents' perception, the child's body or body image lacks human shape.

"NON-PERSON" AND STIGMA

How does a child come to be viewed as abnormal by his or her parents? The answer lies in the importance of labeling as one of the interpretive mechanisms in the process of becoming abnormal. The way the child is interpreted determines his or her identity and the type of communication that will be used towards him or her. Analyzing the material presented here in the terms generally used by experts on abnormality shows that there are several interpretive mechanisms, such as: labeling, name-calling, and stigmatization. In the examples we see that a prominent role is played by the names a child is called in the process of turning into a "non-person." In his discussion of stigma, Goffman (1963, p. 15) talks about viewing the abnormal person as a "non-person." Studies of stigma also stress the importance of labeling in the process of becoming abnormal; only someone who has been labeled "abnormal" will be isolated from society. Our findings also reveal that great importance attaches to the interpretation of a change or to the interpretation of the image of a change, as opposed to the dissimilarity itself. The important factor is the interpretation, i.e., the image that accompanies the dissimilarity, the names by which the child is called; this is what determines whether her or his deviation from the norm will be considered legitimate, whether it will be considered positive, or whether it will be stigmatized (or, as one mother put it, "the name makes the man"). Recall Asnat, the mother of a Down's syndrome child, who fought against her son being labeled as a "retard." "I'm afraid they'll call him things like 'retard,'" she said and was angry at the nurses for "publicizing" that her son was retarded and "giving him the name retard, ... so that now everyone looks at him." On the other hand, labeling the Down's syndrome child as a "little Japanese" indicated her refusal to accept the negative label associated with slanted eyes. Labeling in this way enabled the mother to accept her child by viewing him as having a legitimate difference.

In this chapter we encountered another notion found in studies of stigma; namely, that internal defects or essential badness are often attributed to the abnormal person. Studies of stigma also stress the connection between totality and stigma. Once a stigma is placed on a person there is a tendency to generalize it to other areas, as well. There seems to be an implicit assumption that a person with one defect also suffers from other defects (Wright, 1960). "We tend to impute a wide range of imperfections on the basis of the original one," Goffman explains (1963, pp. 15–16).

Our examples also illustrate the connection between totality and stigma. Totality is expressed by the fact that the specific deformity in outer appearance takes over all the components of the personality, even in contexts in which it is irrelevant. In terms of research on abnormality, analysis of the material presented here shows that totality is one of the techniques of interpretation, and that stigmatization is one of the expressions of totality. For example, calling a child an "animal" or a "retard" illustrates the process of stigmatization in that it proclaims the child's identity as a "non-person." One aspect of the connection between totality and stigma has already come up in our discussion of attributing basic badness or perversion to the abnormal person. In addition, once a stigma has been placed on a child and it has been determined that her identity is deficient, then a process of generalizing to other aspects of her personality sets in. For example, take the case of Rina, the 15-year-old daughter of a religious family, growing up in an ultra-Orthodox neighborhood in the central part of Israel. Her right leg was shorter than her left, causing her to limp noticeably. Even though she had "normal intelligence" (as attested by her teacher), her parents maintained that, "in accordance with her physical condition, Rina can not reach high academic achievements." When guests would come visit, the parents would ask Rina to stay in the living room "at least five minutes. And talk to the company, otherwise they'll think you're dumb, as well." It turns out that Rina was put in charge of cooking and cleaning for the entire household. Thus, although Rina had no mental retardation, her parents associated her limping with the image of a retarded, dumb servant.

Our discussion of the interpretation given anomalies also ties in with stigmatization. Viewing a child as entirely abnormal becomes possible when the blemished part of her being takes over all the other components of her identity and creates the image of additional deformed limbs, so that the other interprets her as having an overall abnormal or deficient identity (see the discussion of stigma and totality, above). For example, recall the case of Liz's daughter, who had to have an opening for the excretion of feces made in her stomach (Chapter 1). Liz said that "instead of her head I see her stomach," and was unable to gaze at her daughter's face and form a bond with her. The small child's stomach was a perceptual obstacle in that it took control over the mother's ability to perceive other parts of the child's body.

The literature on stigma helps us understand the change from being identified as a "normal person" to being identified as a "non-person," as an abnormal person; but it does not deal with the change from "non-person" to "person." I would like to point out that the change in identity can go either way.

Disguising a deformity and the implications of such an action illustrate the "non-person" to "person" direction of the process of change in identity. We have seen that disguising a child's deformity makes it possible for his parents to accept him and to relate to him as a healthy child. Concealing the deformity essentially allows the unconcealed aspects of the child's identity to dominate. On the other hand, not concealing the defect causes the defect to dominate. Recall Gabi's mother (Case 3) who deliberately was not interested in seeing her son's face or body, but only focused on his defect and said, "His beautiful face is irrelevant, since he has a tail." Only after realizing that his defect had been repaired did she look at his face and note his resemblance to her husband. Here we see that the face plays a dominant role in forming the "spoiled identity" (Goffman, 1963). A blemish on a child's face, or a defect in some other part of his body which is focused on so as to overshadow the face, makes it difficult for a bond to be formed between the parents and the child.

In Chapter 1 we discussed the importance of external appearance. In this chapter we have seen that an external change in a child causes a change in the parents' attitude towards internal aspects of their child. In other words, the stimulus for parental response to their child does indeed lie in his or her external appearance; yet it is also generally perceived that nothing is purely external, that external appearance attests internal condition and that therefore external deformity indicates mental incapacity. Hence one encounters expressions such as, "He looks like a retard, like a criminal, like an animal." The converse is also true; it is felt that an internal defect must be reflected in an external way.

What is the purpose of labeling? Why do parents need to stigmatize a child with a defect? I maintain that labeling or stigmatization of the abnormal child helps restore order. By identifying their child as abnormal parents enable themselves to reestablish their definitions of normality, of humanness, and thus both the parents and the child obtain a more clearly defined self-image and can be cognitively located in a meaningful and recognized status.

"NON-PERSON," UGLINESS, AND VIOLENCE

Throughout the chapter I have been pointing out the connection between defining the other as a "non-person" and treating her or him with violence. But the definition of a "person" also has to do with her or his attractiveness. There is literature that deals with the rejection of ugly individuals, but there are hardly any studies that deal directly with violence towards children as a result of deformity in their looks; the literature teaches us about such a pattern of behavior only indirectly via the historical and ethnographic data which we can cull from various other contexts. This study shows that lack of attractiveness and violence are clearly related. Children who are perceived as externally deficient (if only because they are dirty, overly skinny, or overly fat) are more subject to violence than children who have internal defects.[7]

On the other hand, we see that ugliness is not directly connected with violence. Defining the other as a "non-person" acts as a mediating factor between the unattractiveness attributed to the other and the response of rejecting such an individual. In other words, I have found that only an external deficiency which is interpreted as a deviation from the usual image of what is human leads to rejection.

"Non-persons" as Social Pollutions

In this chapter we discussed two principal ways of perceiving the abnormal child. One relates to the child as "filth" or as "pollution," terms which many anthropologists define as "something which is out of place." We have seen that children with undisguised external deficiencies are associated in their parents' minds with creatures that are anormal, superhuman, or beastly. This lays the groundwork for shunning the child, since non-human entities which are found in place of human entities "are not in place." Thus they are perceived as "pollutions" that must be shunted aside to their proper place. Rejecting an abnormal child and distancing her or him from the "family of mankind" enables the parents not to change their former set of distinctions between normal and abnormal. They call their child a "non-person" (a unicorn, or a snake), and this enables them to continue holding their former definitions of "person" and "non-person."

The second way of perceiving an abnormal child has to do with disguising his or her abnormality as a precondition for viewing him or her as a "person." This pertains primarily to children who suffer internal defects or external, disguisable defects that do not evoke fanciful associations with a "non-human entity." In such cases, the associations evoked on seeing such a child do not lead to a "violation of boundaries" and do not create a sense of chaos.

The fact that parents may accept a child under such conditions does not, I must stress, indicate a change in their basic stand towards disability. Their previous attitude towards disability as deviating from the usual human image continues to guide their perceptions and behavior. However, concealing the abnormality enables them to view their child as "human" as long as the deformity is still disguised. The moment the abnormality ceases being disguised, the child is again defined as "non-human."[8]

In principle, there is a third way in which the abnormal child can be perceived, although this possibility did not occur among any of the parents observed. Nevertheless, I must relate to it. Namely, such a child could be perceived as a "person" in spite of his or her abnormality. Such acceptance, not contingent upon any change in the child or any concealment of his or her abnormality, entails a fundamental change in the definition of "personhood" and "abnormality" so that in the end someone with a disability is no longer perceived as a non-human entity. For example, if we cast aside our former definitions of "person" and say that a person is any being born of woman, this new definition will also subsume a disabled individual and make it possible to regard him or her as a person. What the former definition considered an anomaly is now included within the scope of the normal, and there is no longer the need to relate to a blemished newborn as a "non-person."[9] Both the second way of perceiving a child (accepting him or her on the condition that his or her abnormality be disguised) and the third way (unconditional acceptance), in the end, amount to the parents perceiving their handicapped child as a "person." The third way, however, does not make viewing the other as a person contingent upon changing the individual, but upon changing the stand taken towards abnormality. With the second approach the parents continue to view their child's defect as a deviation from the usual image of what is human, and thus they express their continued adherence to their former criteria of the essence of a "person," his or her basic traits or external form. We stress again that the last possibility (viewing a deformed person as human) is only theoretical; none of the parents whom I observed changed the generally accepted definition of a "person" to "anyone born of a woman."

NOTES

1. Turner's syndrome: a condition resulting from the absence of one of the sex chromosomes, where instead of 46 chromosomes there are only 45. Clinical indications: externally, a girl with this condition is not sexually developed at puberty, due to her lack of ovaries. The breasts are not full-sized, nor are the sexual organs developed. At birth such girls are shorter than usual, and as they grow their height remains below the third percentile. There are prominent folds of skin on the neck, the hairline in back is low, the ears are large, the lower jaw is small, and the distance between the nipples is unusually broad. A grown woman with the disorder is incapable of bearing children (Brand-Orban, 1979, p. 44). Administering estrogen hormones can lead to the development of secondary sexual indicators, including growth of the uterus; on occasion even regular menstruation is achieved, but, of course, it is not accompanied by ovulation or fertility.

2. Cf., for example, Harris, 1978.

3. Pregnant women over 37 are routinely referred for these tests due to the greater chances of the fetus having Down's syndrome.

4. Klinefelter's syndrome: an abnormal condition in which the male has a total of 47 or more chromosomes. Clinical indications: the condition is usually discovered when a boy reaches the age of puberty. He generally has small, insufficiently developed testicles, enlarged breasts, and retarded development of his secondary sexual system. Sperm production is absent, and therefore such children cannot be fertile. Many children with the condition are mentally retarded. The more additional chromosomes the child has, the more severe his condition. Administering testosterone is helpful in treating the aesthetic defect of enlarged breasts, but sometimes plastic surgery is required to repair this defect (Brand-Orban, 1979, p. 46).

5. Pseudo-hermaphrodism (lack of clarity in external sexual organs): at birth, it is difficult to identify the sex of the newborn on the basis of its sexual organs, since the latter do not have a normal shape. The defect can assume many forms, ranging from resemblance to the female sexual organs to resemblance to the male sexual organs. One of the most common manifestations of this defect is adreno-genital syndrome, due to the male influence of adrenocortical hormones on the development of the female sexual organs and indicated by increased glandular secretion. Thus, instead of producing the necessary steroid hormones, the cortex of the adrenal gland responds by overproduction of male hormones. In female babies suffering from the condition the sexual organs develop abnormally and resemble the male sexual organs, and male babies experience unusually early and accelerated sexual development. The condition is usually treated by administering cortisone, which prevents excessive secretion of male hormones. It should be noted that not all babies born with abnormal sexual organs suffer the adreno-genital syndrome described above. In every case experts recommend that a decision regarding the sex of the baby be reached quickly by means of hormonal tests and examination of the child's anatomy, in order to avoid lack of clarity and transition from sex to sex after weaning (Blake and Wright, 1963).

6. See note 11, Chapter 1.

7. This ties in with our claim regarding the greater tendency to reject children with external defects than children with internal defects, since treating children violently is one of the ways in which they can be rejected.

8. Often a deformity is physically concealed by a plaster cast. Sometimes, however, the disguise may be more abstract; even though there might not be a physical cover hiding the deformity, the parents may manage to not see it, or to not attribute significance to the external difference as being abnormal (as in the case of Asnat).

9. Note that the emotional response is a function of the cognitive perception. Therefore, changes in the emotional response of parents to their children are conditional upon changes in their cognitive perception of their children, i.e., changes in their definition of a "person."

3

Body Image

Parental Responses to the Spoiled Body Image of Their Child

What sort of image do we have of our fellow human being's body? What significance do we attribute to his or her face? to his or her body? How is body image built? If a person is fat, do we respond to his or her shape, or to various significations that we attribute to fatness? In other words, is our attitude towards another person influenced by his or her actual appearance, or by the body image we have of him or her?

What images do diseases convey? What is the visual aspect of a disease? Do various illnesses have characteristic looks? Are the visual images of a sickness and a sick person part of our cultural repertoire, so that when we encounter a given disease we attribute to it the specific form associated with it in our culture? Are diseases seen in accordance with what we know medically about them? Do our visual images change in the wake of a change in our medical understanding?

What beliefs and conceptions are associated with disease? Are these beliefs particular to each individual, or are do they belong to a common cultural repertoire? What characteristics, other than visual, do people attribute to a given sickness or sick person? In other words, what are the cognitive components of the image associated with a sickness? Does the visual component of our image of a disease match its cognitive component? What variation is there in images of diseases? How can this variation be explained? Perhaps by such factors as age, gender, country of origin, or length of time in the country? Perhaps the variation is due to exposure to different cultural presentations? Do people respond to the characteristics attributed to a disease by general consensus, or to the actual external appearance of a specific person afflicted with the disease? Is the image of a disease a cultural and social construct, such that we may argue that people respond to its "collective presentation" and not necessarily to its "objective" characteristics? Moreover, if images are "collective presentations," what do they teach us about our society, our culture, our collective existence?

This chapter attempts to answer some of these questions. Later chapters relate to others.

THE LITERATURE ON BODY IMAGE

The term *body image* relates to the way in which our body appears to us (Schilder, 1950). We each have our own mental image of how we look. This image is more than an exact reflection of our looks; it can closely approach the actual structure of our bodies, or it can be quite far from it (Schilder, 1951). Body image relates to the way individuals perceive their own bodies, including their unconscious fantasies about their bodies (Fisher, 1978, p. 115). Proof of the importance of these fantasies and the image attributed to the body is provided, first of all, by the fact that people claim to feel aches in phantom limbs—limbs that have been amputated. Such hallucinations show that the individual has a "picture" of his or her body, which continues to exist even after it is no longer an accurate representation of his or her body (Fisher, 1978, p. 118).

Some scholars differentiate between external and internal body images; the external body image being a concept that pertains to the form, size, and mass of the body and its various limbs, and the internal body image being a concept that pertains to the form, spatial size, sensation, and functioning of the various organs within the body, their proportions and interrelationships (Dennis, 1980). Many studies compare the external body images of healthy and sick persons. Fisher (1966) compared body images in neurotic and schizophrenic patients. Lukianowicz (1967) found a connection between body image disturbances and personal disorders, but found no connection between body image disturbances and gender, education, or socioeconomic status of the patient.

Some studies have examined the effect of changes in external appearance on body image. Schonfeld (1963), in a study of self-image among adolescents, found that changes in actual outward appearance of the body are likely to bring about drastic changes in body image. Studies have also been made of internal body image, some pertaining to children (Gellert, 1962; Nagy, 1953) and others to adults. Casell (1964) found that men are more aware of their body interiors, whereas women are more aware of their body boundaries. Kaminer et al. (1978) investigated whether there exists a body image of internal organs similar to the body image of external organs, and whether such an internal body image is affected by the subject's state of health.

Schneider (1954) stressed the importance of the image of the heart in shaping body image; since the heart holds a central place in many cultures, it was seen as the most suitable organ to consider in examining internal-organ body image. Researchers on this question conjectured that there is a body image of the heart, and that patients with cardiac disease have a different heart image from healthy individuals. Only the first conjecture was confirmed by the findings of the study. No significant difference was found between the heart image of healthy individuals and of cardiac patients. Most of the subjects perceived the heart as a flexible, elastic organ with bidirectional movement. Both cardiac patients and healthy individuals viewed it as the most important organ in the body, anatomically and symbolically.

The last group of studies I review deals with the connection between body image and adjustment. Schalit (1971) examined how individuals' body images affect their adjustment to high-pressure situations. Using perception of the size of one's body as an index for one's perception of body boundaries, Barr (1982) investigated the connection between the perception of body boundaries and general adjustment among a student population. According to the "accuracy theory," Barr conjectured that the more realistic and accurate a person's assessment of his or her body boundaries, the better his or her adjustment; and the more distorted, either oversized or undersized, his or her body boundaries, the poorer his or her adjustment. The study's main conjecture was not confirmed: no connection was found between accuracy in perception of body boundaries and general ability to adjust. Students whose perceptions of the size of their bodies (hands and facial profiles) were highly accurate showed no difference in adjustment in comparison with students whose assessments were inaccurate.

Related studies have examined the effect of amputating a limb on body image and the connection between the amputee's body image and his or her adjustment to life. Korolik (1972) has investigated the way in which amputating a limb is perceived as an injury to one's body boundaries. Renewing one's perception of body boundaries after the amputation is a necessary precondition for establishing a body image as a distinct entity. It has been found that amputees who have a clearly defined perception of their body boundaries adjust better to living with a prosthesis than amputees without well-defined body boundaries.

Psychological research on body image stresses the importance attached to the way the body is perceived; thus it assists us in focusing on the way in which a disease or a sick individual is perceived, and in understanding the connection between this perception and the objective characteristics of the disease or of the sick person. Since I am also interested in a sociological approach, following Douglas and Calvez (1990), I seek to explain the variance in formation of images in the wake of differences in the cultural location of the parents whom I observed.

The literature dealing with images, perceptions, and beliefs concerning disease presents another angle on research and analysis, relevant to our study. For example, let us consider the literature on social attitudes towards Down's syndrome children. According to the literature, one can reasonably expect people to be repelled by a child suffering Down's syndrome. The characteristic physiognomy of a child with Down's syndrome includes crossed eyes, a fold of skin over the corner of the eye, slanted eyelids, a flat nose, a large tongue, a receding chin, a heavy-set body, and edematous skin. These factors in a Down's syndrome child's external appearance operate to his or her detriment, since the social significance attributed to the face or to disfigurement of the face is greater than that attributed to other parts of the body; the face comes into play in verbal and non-verbal communication, and is perceived as a part of the body symbolizing the individual's identity and uniqueness (Allport, 1967, p. 481). The area surrounding the mouth is of particular importance. A defect in this area arouses aesthetic repulsion (MacGregor, 1974, pp. 7–14). The social importance of the face is underscored by the tendency to draw conclusions regarding the character and talents of one's fellow on the basis of her or his physiognomy. In a study in which subjects were asked to rank by intelligence a variety of individuals on the basis of their pictures, those individuals with full, oval faces, crossed eyes, long noses and eyes, and thick lips were ranked as having the lowest intelligence (Cook, 1939). This finding is especially important with respect to Down's syndrome children, who typically have full cheeks, crossed eyes, and thick lips.

It has been found that body type, in addition to physiognomy, also has an impact on the expectations we form of our fellow (Sheldon, 1940, 1942). People with a mesomorphic (muscular) body build are consistently associated with positive characteristics; whereas people with an endomorphic (heavy set) or ectomorphic (spare) build are associated with negative characteristics (Hildebrandt, 1982). In other words, what is regarded to be the "fat, stocky" build of Down's syndrome children is likely to be perceived as signifying negative characteristics. Thus it seems likely that people would attribute negative stereotypical traits to a child with Down's syndrome before they were to become acquainted with him or her and come to know his or her individual personality. Indeed, in a study by Siperstein and Gottlieb (1977) children with Down's syndrome were ranked by other children as being less attractive. The findings showed that a child with Down's syndrome was perceived as less desirable and was expected to behave in a less acceptable manner than a normal child. In two other studies adults were requested to rank photographs of normal and abnormal children. More negative responses were registered for severely retarded children than for slightly retarded children (English and Pallo, 1971). It turns out that the characteristic appearance of Down's syndrome children leads to the formation of negative stereotypes concerning them even on the part of their parents and teachers.

Even though children with Down's syndrome vary widely in their ability to function (Feuerstein, Rand, and Mintzker, 1984), due to their similarities in physiognomy their parents and others who shape the environment of such children form expectations of development supposedly characteristic of Down's syndrome children. These expectations include limited intellectual and educational capacity, far lower than the actual capabilities of such children. These factors hinder the cognitive development of Down's syndrome children and curtail social interaction with them.

In order to help Down's syndrome children, for the past 15 years experts throughout the world have been suggesting that they be given plastic surgery. In Germany, for one, 67 Down's syndrome children had surgery which included reducing the size of the tongue, elevating the bridge of the nose by silicone implantation, smoothing the epicanthic folds, changing the angle of the eyes, enlarging the chin and stretching the lower, undersized lip, and broadening the jaw muscles by silicone implantation. Not every one of these repairs was made in every child, rather a combination of surgical repairs was decided according to the individual case. Lemperle and Radu (1978) report that all the parents questioned were satisfied by the results and relayed that other people in their children's surroundings also praised the improvement in the children's looks and speech. Belfer (1980), on the other hand, maintains that surgery only helps when there is a good relationship between parents and child, founded on accepting the child as he or she is, with whatever limitations. Ebbin (1980) poses a number of questions: does changing the facial features of Down's syndrome children indeed lessen the prejudice towards them and improve their chances of obtaining employment and education? Is the speech improvement obtained by surgery indeed so significant? Should children have surgery simply because their parents wish it? Is our society so rigid that everyone must fit himself to a model of "normal" looks? Ebbin maintains that plastic surgery is clearly beneficial for individuals with a physical defect (such as a cleft lip); when mental deficiency accompanies the physical defect, each case must be decided on its own merits.

Over the years a number of children from Israel have undergone surgery, generally abroad, to reduce their signs of Down's syndrome. Since these operations were done on the private initiative of the parents and generally were kept secret, I have no data regarding the number of children who underwent surgery, and no studies have been made of the effect of the surgery or the degree of satisfaction derived from it. Cooperation between the German Professor Lemperle and Israeli surgeons led to a turning point, and in February 1982 plastic surgery on Down's syndrome children began being performed in Israel. According to Mintzker (1983), the parents' assessment of the results of surgery were extremely positive. Plastic surgery for Down's syndrome children is a new method of treatment giving rise to expectations of significant changes in the overall functioning of such children.

In the study on which this book is based, we encountered a considerable number[1] of parents of Down's syndrome children over the years and found that they generally reject their children. I shall not rest with establishing the fact of such rejection, but shall try to understand what factors contribute to this reaction. What characteristics and images do parents associate with the concept of retardation? What are the parents' expectations of plastic surgery[2] on their children? Are they interested in a specific change? If so, in what part of the body? Do they have additional expectations from such surgery?

Is the stigma attached to a child after surgery different from that before surgery? The answer to this question brings us back to our theoretical discussion on the reversibility or permanence of stigma. I shall investigate whether parents expressed satisfaction from the surgical results; and if so, what changes in their children contributed to this. Were the children who underwent surgery perceived as normal after their operations? In those cases where the parents were not satisfied by the results of surgery, I shall examine the nature of their unfulfilled expectations.

Another topic discussed by the literature on images and perceptions of diseases pertains to our image of cancer. Many experts maintain that cancer is perceived as a stigmatic disease that leads to social isolation of the patient: friends and family have less direct physical contact with a cancer patient, eye-contact becomes a rare occurrence, and conversations are held at a greater distance. Sometimes cancer patients are neglected by their friends and spouses (Krulik, 1978, pp. 14–15). It has also been found that parents, teachers, and medical staff withdraw emotionally and physically from a child who has cancer (Futterman and Hoffman, 1973; Kaplan et al., 1974; Spinetta, 1974); such a child supposedly presents a threat to his or her environment. Thus, many people view cancer as the leprosy of modern times, a disease involving social stigmatization of the afflicted person and his or her family (Sontag, 1978). The frightening connotation of the word "cancer" in our society has an effect on communication with cancer patients (Quint, 1965). People do not want to speak openly about cancer. It is considered taboo due to its identification with death, with hopelessness, with loss of identity (Feifel, 1973). People are reluctant to reveal the diagnosis to a cancer patient, and when they do tell her or him, they bring various strategies into play to avoid interacting with the patient and thus create a situation of "closed awareness" (Glaser and Strauss, 1964). These patterns of behavior are characteristic not only of the layman, but also of professionals. According to McCollum (1981) most human beings wish to deny death due to their inability to bear the certainty of their own mortality. Encounter with a cancer patient destroys one's fictitious sense of security and awakens the healthy person's fears of his or her own degeneration and death (Burns, 1982, pp. 3–6). In McCollum's opinion (1981), a healthy person is also likely to avoid proximity to a person with cancer because of the fear of contagion. Today, however, cancer is not generally considered a contagious disease, and our fear of it stems primarily from our limited knowledge (Berman and Wandersman, 1990).

Although most research on cancer has focused on emotional responses to the disease, two Israeli scholars have focused on other components of the image it projects. Ben-Sira (1977A, 1977B) has focused on components relevant to preventive behavior: susceptibility, prominence, understanding, and prevention; in other words, the actual chances of an individual's contracting the disease, the degree to which she or he thinks about the disease, and the degree to which she or he thinks that the disease can be prevented. Antonovsky (1971), another person who has investigated the image of cancer, notes that the highly educated, European-born population, who are most informed about cancer and least believe it a fatal disease, view themselves as most vulnerable and tend to do more thinking about the disease.

Relatively little research has been done on the connotations of the word "cancer." In a survey by Horn and Waingrow (1964), 12 percent of the respondents said they would not like to work beside a person with cancer, and 12 percent reported that they believe cancer is incurable. Another survey, which examined the opinion of public health nurses in England on cancer, found that 20 percent of the nurses were pessimistic and viewed the treatment given cancer patients in the hospitals as a waste of time (Davison, 1965). A survey of the opinions of medical and welfare staffs found that cancer is perceived as potent, cruel, unjust, threatening, and debilitating (Padilla, 1972). It has also been found that cancer is perceived as more frightening and stigmatic than poliomyelitis and mental illness (Jenkins and Zyzanski, 1968); that it is associated with death, danger, filth, helplessness, and mystery; and that it is considered to have no way of prevention. Other studies, too, have found that cancer is associated with death (Holland, 1976; Assael et al., 1979, p. 4), both among the medical profession and among laymen. Cancer is also associated with a sense of helplessness and shame (Krant, 1976), great suffering (Smith, 1976, p. 42; Sontag, 1978), and uncontrolled growth (Brauer, 1970). Cancer is also viewed as an enemy, and the struggle against cancer as a fight against the enemy (Sontag, 1978). "We may conclude that cancer is far more than a disease. It is a sort of judgment or punishment" (Assael et al., 1979, p. 4).

Despite advances in medical research and improvements in treatment, alleviation of suffering, and prolongation of life, the beliefs regarding the disease have changed at a much slower rate; doctors, nurses, and patients continue to adhere to their former notions, even though these are controverted by the facts (Burns, 1982, pp. 3–16). People with cancer are considered terminal patients who suffer great pain, even if their disease can be controlled by chemotherapy and despite the fact that many cancer patients are known to die without pain. In contrast, patients with heart disease or severe diabetes are not considered terminal cases.

As we have seen, most experts agree that people respond to the image projected by a disease. However, most research has focused primarily on the image's cognitive aspects (such as one's beliefs), and hardly any studies have related to the visual aspects of a disease. Our study examines and stresses the importance of the connection between these two aspects. Some researchers believe one can bring the image of a disease—a distorted perception of reality—into accord with reality by making the populace better informed; thus, if the public knew more about cancer, they would fear it less. These researchers believe that one needs an image of a disease only when there is no clear medical understanding of the disease, when medical information on it is unreliable, and when no cure has yet been discovered. They conclude that if there were a cure for cancer, we would not relate to our image of the disease but rather to the facts of the disease themselves. The work of Susan Sontag (1978; 1989) reflects this approach in the extreme.

Psychotherapeutic literature touches on the visual aspect of images of diseases. In recent years this literature has taken an interest in the visual metaphors that patients have of their illnesses (Simonton, 1978) and views treatment of the visual metaphor as part of the treatment of the disease. The main thrust of this literature, based on clinical experience and not on empirical research, is its interest in the individual and its assumption that, in treating a specific cancer patient, diagnosis and treatment based solely on the physical aspects of the disease do not suffice; rather, the patient's own images associated with the disease must be identified and made more positive.

In this book I am interested in social and cultural images. Therefore I shall look for the common denominator as well as the variations in the way the sick person's body and disease are perceived, and shall investigate how these perceptions can be associated with various social constructs.

In another study (Weiss, 1988) I examined several questions pertaining to the image of a disease. Six hundred students in sociology, social work, and medicine, ranging in age from 20 to 50, were requested to perform the following tasks:

(1) to draw and describe their perceptions of cancer, heart disease, retardation, and AIDS;
(2) to draw and describe how a person with each of these diseases looks to them;
(3) to draw and describe how the disease is transmitted (etiology);
(4) to draw and describe the precautions that can be taken against con-

tracting the disease;

(5) to write down their first association with each of the diseases.

By way of example, I present some of the patterns of response with respect to AIDS. It turns out that people generally view AIDS as a disease that spreads through the body, unbeknown to the sick person, and that at a certain point it bursts forth and infringes on the patient's body boundaries. The subjects in the study drew openings in the body (holes, open lesions, etc.) through which the body's insides, along with the disease, issued forth. It became clear that the disease was perceived as threatening the bodily integrity of others in the surrounding area and infecting them. An indomitable penetrability is associated with the disease. It was also found that the degeneration of the body and violation of its boundaries is perceived as symbolically paralleling the degeneration of the world and violation of its boundaries.

The subjects made remarks such as: "Just as the disease spreads throughout the body and makes it degenerate, so too it is spreading throughout the world and making the world fall apart. The growth of the virus knows no limits. It is a world-wide plague, beyond boundaries. It is leading to a catastrophe, an inevitable world holocaust. Just as the body boundaries of a person with AIDS are penetrable and indefensible, so too there is no limit to the spread of the disease in the world." What stands out here is the fear of contagion, which does not match what we know about the disease and its means of transmission. It turns out that the steps people take to avoid infection are generally ritual or magical; such as not breathing the air in a room with a person with AIDS, washing one's lips, washing one's hands after touching the bed of a person with AIDS, etc.

In this chapter I examine general questions about the importance of body image with respect to relations between parents and their children. I seek to discover what it is that parents respond to. Is it the actual body of their child, his or her external form, or the image of his or her body which they have formed in their imagination? How do parents picture the body their child? What importance attaches to the body image, external or internal, that parents have of their children when they respond to their children? Does an actual change in a child's appearance necessarily entail a change in the body image associated with the child? Can there be a change in a child's body image without there being a real change in the child himself or herself?

These are some of the questions dealt with in this chapter. I begin with the question of whether the behavior of parents is a direct or indirect response to the looks of their children. Do parents respond to external changes that have taken place in their children, or to the images associated with these external changes?

Our observations show that parents respond to the body image they have formed in their minds, and not to the body as it actually is. To substantiate this claim I present cases illustrative primarily of parental relations towards children either with Down's syndrome or cancer. These cases reveal the gap between the child's external appearance and the image her or his parents associate with her or his body. I begin with cases involving an actual change in the child's looks. I shall consider the stories of some Down's syndrome children whose looks changed in the wake of plastic surgery, and examine whether the change in the children's bodies went along with a change in the images associated with them.

CASE 14 "ONCE A MONGOLOID, ALWAYS A MONGOLOID"

Debby is the Down's syndrome daughter of American-born parents. Her mother is a 42-year-old psychologist, and her father a successful business-man. The couple have three other children—two in the army and one in high school. The parents are Orthodox and since their marriage have lived in the central part of Israel, in a mostly religious neighborhood.

When Debby was born her parents hired live-in help to care for her and live in the same room with her. The girl did not eat with the rest of the family, nor did she pass time with them. The parents maintained that they wanted to send her to an institution as soon as she was born, but that the arrangement they had with their live-in nanny was "more acceptable in a religious neighborhood such as we live in."

When Debby turned six years old her parents learned of the possibility of her having plastic surgery in the United States. Before leaving for the United States they had a conversation with the me, parts of which I cite below:

FATHER: Our relatives in the U.S. sent us a picture of a charming eight-year who you couldn't tell, just looking at her, that she had Down's syn-drome. So we immediately jumped on the idea. We thought that maybe we too could have a bit of surgery done on Debby's nose, a bit on her eyes, a bit on her tongue, and we could get her over the border.

MOTHER: Look, I really want her to have this surgery. Very much so. I don't have any illusions. It won't make a normal child of her, but it will repair the thing that bothers her. I personally am not bothered by anything about her.

AUTHOR: So what does Debby find bothersome?

MOTHER: Her tongue. The fact that her tongue always hangs out, that she's constantly drooling. And her runny nose, and her mouth. Everything about her mouth; her open mouth; the fact that when she eats everybody stares at her. That she makes all sorts of sounds, that she dribbles; everything about the way she eats is obnoxious to others. In short, everything about her is a problem.[3]

FATHER: In general, it's the whole aesthetic question. Perhaps surgery will help all that.

MOTHER: No, it's not a matter of aesthetics; its how she functions. She's got to function well; God will help us.

FATHER: Right. Nothing bothers me; but it bothers her. We must help her repair her face. Fix up the general appearance. Because it gets in the way. Everything gets in the way. It's impossible to look at her this way. Everything gets in the way. Everything must be corrected. Everything's important; it's all related. It's not just her face, or her nose; it's everything all together that's important. I want her to have surgery, and I dream of the moment she'll come to. It'll be the happiest day of my life. A new girl will be born to me. ... As for me, I have great hopes that she'll have a normal face. I need to see a human being in front of me.

MOTHER: Look, I don't have any illusions. I know there's not going to be any dramatic change. But it will be good for her.

FATHER: The operation is like a festive day for us, a special occasion. Right after the operation we're going to move. We bought an apartment in the West Bank and we're going to move there after the operation. That's that. In our new home Debby will be known with her new face, and that's it. It'll be wonderful.

The parents went to the United States for the surgery, without informing their friends and neighbors of the purpose of their trip. The doctors proclaimed the operation a big success, and the girl, in my opinion, was made quite good-looking, with no marked signs of Down's syndrome. The parents, however, were not pleased by the results, as we shall see from the next conversation, which took place immediately after their return to Israel, about two months after the operation.

MOTHER: Immediately after the operation, when they told us that it had gone exceptionally well, we jumped for joy. We called our kids in Israel and told them that, with God's help, everything had gone well and that they should tear up all their old photos of Debby. But about two weeks later we began to fear that our rejoicing had been premature ... and now, to tell the truth, we are quite disappointed. On the conscious level, we did not pin such high hopes on the operation; but deep down inside, we thought it would change everything. That there would be some sort of miracle and our daughter would be reborn to us, a new person. We expected that she would change more significantly ... that there would be a dramatic change in her looks, so much so that everything would be completely concealed.

But things are only partially concealed. There's no significant change. The results are positive, but not dramatic.

FATHER: It only helped about 50 percent. If I had known it was only going to improve things 50 percent, I wouldn't have had the operation done.

MOTHER: I expected the entire shape of her face to change. That she wouldn't have the general look of a Down's syndrome child. [*Quietly*] I expected she would be normal. She really does look much better now, but not normal. That is to say, any child in the playground can immediately tell the difference between himself and her. The operation made each feature, itself, look O.K., but her overall looks are still those of a Mongoloid. Her facial expression immediately reveals that she is different. She still has that peculiar look. You can see she has Down's syndrome. People still give her that inquisitive stare.

AUTHOR: Do they look at her as much as before?

FATHER: Maybe a little less.

MOTHER: That's what you would like to believe, but strangers look at her just the same as before. That's it. So, she won't have any friends, again. Except for other kids of her kind. She won't have any normal friends. That's all. ... Even beforehand I didn't pin too many hopes on the operation; but it's sad. Actually, I think that now she looks even more like a Down's syndrome child than before. [*Bitterly*] The doctors get so excited when they manage to change one little nose or tongue. Well, it's fine for them to have changed it, but now you see her Mongolism laid bare. Now she really looks Mongoloid, but like a Mongoloid with a pretty nose. ... I always knew that once a Mongoloid, always a Mongoloid, and nothing could ever help. But I also thought, irrationally, that maybe somehow she got something plugged up in her brain and that one day the plug would come out and she would stop having that dumb stare, and her horrible looks would no longer frighten me. But now I have no more illusions. The plug is never going to pop out. A Mongoloid will always look like a Mongoloid. A Mongoloid will always look like a retard. And I am not prepared to live with a thing like this at my side. I've had it. I don't even feel pity for her. ... She's some sort of beast of nature. I feel sorry for myself. I feel sorry for my children. Oh, I've had it!

FATHER: Yeah, we just don't have the strength for it any more. We've reached our limit. Before the operation I used to have dreams. Sometimes I dreamed that the operation would make her even more retarded, until she died. ... And sometimes I dreamed that the operation would make her suddenly normal. Either dead or normal. But the operation made her something in the middle. And we just don't have the strength for it.

MOTHER: She's not in the middle. She's Mongoloid.

FATHER: We don't have the strength to begin everything all over again in a new apartment; and at that with a Mongoloid girl.

MOTHER: How naïve we were. We thought we would move after she'd been made normal and we'd have no more problems. Oh, I just can't face it any more.

Two weeks later Debby was institutionalized and her parents moved into their new apartment with their normal children.

From the remarks of Debby's parents before her operation we clearly see the conflict between expressing their deep-seated feelings of rejection towards their daughter and conforming to the myth that does not allow parents to lend expression to such rejection. Despite the parents' attempts to obscure their rejection of their child, our observations show that the Down's syndrome girl was rejected within the walls of her home. The parents were upset by Debby's looks, in their eyes a gaping-mouthed, clinging creature; they looked forward to the operation as a turning point that would put to rest the former creature and give birth to a new person. They did not anticipate specific improvement in one or another detail, since, as the father put it, "it's all related." That they viewed the operation as giving birth to a creature with no past is expressed both by burning their photographs from the past and by moving to a new apartment, where the neighbors would only know Debby as a normal child. The operation was performed and brought about a considerable change in the girl's looks. Nevertheless, her parents were incapable of freeing themselves from the visual image of a Mongoloid that Debby projected to them. Her negative image became more prominent and led to more extreme reactions of rejection on the part of her parents, ultimately ending in her being institutionalized.[4]

The behavior of Debby's parents resembles that of most the parents of Down's syndrome children who had surgery whom we observed. These parents generally did not change the negative image that they associated with their children, even after their children's outward appearances had been transformed considerably. In the families that I observed there were ten Down's syndrome children who underwent plastic surgery either abroad or in Israel (in two hospitals). Prior to surgery, eight of these children were associated with the negative image of a clinging, burdensome retarded child, and their rejection by their parents found expression either through institutionalization or territorial isolation within their own homes. Even after the operations, which were considered successful, this negative image remained and at times became more extreme and the reaction of rejection stronger.

In the minority of cases (two couples), the parents initially associated a positive image with their retarded children. The next case shows how these parent-child relations developed as time went by.

CASE 15 "YOUR DIAGNOSIS KEEPS YOU FROM SEEING THE REAL CHILD"

Ron is the Down's syndrome son of 47-year-old parents, his father Moroccan-born and his mother Polish, both working in education. The couple are Orthodox, live in a city in the southern part of the country, and have two other children, ages 24 and 25.

Immediately after the birth, the doctor told the parents that he suspected their child might have a developmental problem and suggested that they return somewhat later for further examination. The mother, in her own words, was "convinced it was all a lot of nonsense." When Ron was five months old his mother brought him to the hospital for re-examination, at which time the final diagnosis became clear. The doctor informed the mother that her child had Down's syndrome. The mother returned home in a state of "terrible shock," feeling, "how could it be that such a horrible calamity is lying in wait for such a charming baby?" The father, too, felt "a broken man." "How," he asked, "could I have brought such a thing into the world?"

The parents did not accept the doctor's diagnosis, and when Ron was nine months old his mother told me: "I still do not believe it. My feelings are worth more than all their diagnoses. I feel that despite their diagnosis so much can be done with him and he'll develop beautifully. He rolls over beautifully. I work with him day and night, and he really rolls over. If the doctors were right about their diagnosis, would he look like this? Would he roll himself over? He's not simply normal, he's exceptional."

When Ron was one year old his mother brought him to a day-care center and fought for her son's right to be accepted with normal children. In the afternoons, she "teaches him; puts all her energy into the child," as she herself said.

Here I present parts of a conversation that took place between the mother and the psychologist at the city's psychology clinic:

MOTHER: You want to transfer him to a day-care center for retarded children, but I won't let you. The proper setting for Ron is the regular educational system, because Ron is not retarded. That was your mistake. He's the star of the day-care center.

PSYCHOLOGIST: You're an intelligent woman. You must get used to the fact that you have a retarded son. Perhaps he should remain in a regular day-care center, but he has Down's syndrome.

MOTHER: He hasn't got Down's syndrome, and besides, Down's syndrome doesn't mean retarded. Even Feuerstein, in an article in *La'Isha* (a woman's magazine) said there's a Down's syndrome girl who developed more in one year than the average for her age, and that the only thing that disturbs her is the way she looks. She's going to have an operation and then no one will call her retarded any more. Ron isn't retarded either. My husband and I are in education, and we know about child development. Ron is not retarded.

PSYCHOLOGIST: Because you're pulling him up. But the time will come when you'll put more and more into him, and he just won't be pulled up any further. And then you'll be in for a shock.

MOTHER: Everyone says he's not normal, but he's more normal than the lot of them. He's an exceptional boy. He's developed better than all my other children. He's just marvelous. He's ours. All the diagnoses are not worth a cent. Anyone who knows him knows he has good natural intelligence. You psychologists don't know anything. Your diagnosis keeps you from seeing the real child. But I'm his mother, and I see the real child.

PSYCHOLOGIST: You're mistaken. You don't see the real child, either. You, too, see your child through your own diagnosis and refuse to confront reality as it is.

MOTHER: Nonsense. I just started studying special education. It's a pity I didn't know before what I know now. I would have developed him even more.

When Ron was four years old, as the external signs of Down's syndrome became more pronounced, his parents found out that plastic surgery could be done on their child. They consulted their older children, and decided to go ahead.

Here is part of the conversation that took place at the psychology clinic:

FATHER: Our children really want Ron to have plastic surgery. Our older son is very religious. He's embarrassed by Ron; he believes that because of him he's not found a wife. He goes out walking with Ron ... and he's embarrassed.

MOTHER: I pin great hopes on the operation. You'll see—after the operation everything will be O.K. The operation will give Ron a chance to be normal. If his looks change, everyone will see that he's completely normal.

Ron had surgery which made some improvement in his nose and tongue, but was mostly viewed as not having done away with the general Down's features. Nevertheless, the parents, undeterred, arranged for a second operation. "They'll re-operate on his cheeks. The next time will be a success. ... And if it isn't, they can always operate again. We've got plenty of patience. In the end it will succeed. Then everyone will see that we were right," his parents said.

Although the operation did not succeed in removing all the signs of Down's syndrome, his parents did not change their image of him but continued to view him as a normal child and hoped that the next operation would be more successful and would make his looks match the positive image they had of him.

One of the conclusions that can be drawn from the behavior of Ron's parents is that one cannot predict exactly how parents will relate to a child with a defect, since the parents do not react to the anomaly itself, but to their interpretation of the defect, i.e., to the image they associate with it. It is true that in general one learns how to interpret external manifestations. That is, the images associated with certain anomalies are part of an acquired cultural repertoire. Nevertheless, there is variety in the way different parents view an anomaly. Different parents are likely to associate different images with the same external manifestation. Therefore, to understand the behavior of parents of a child with a disability, we must first identify what image they associate with the disability. The difference in image associated with the child has an impact on the nature of the interaction that develops with the child.

In the examples that follow I present a number of cases in which the image associated with the child changed, and I investigate whether a parallel change occurred in the child's body. If there was no concomitant physical change accompanying the change in image, we must proceed to ask what it is that the parents respond to, the body or their image of the body?

First let us recall the behavior of Tzviya, the mother of a child with minimal Down's syndrome facial characteristics, whom we met in Chapter 1. Before Tzviya knew her child had Down's syndrome, she cared for him devotedly; but after learning of his condition she and her husband abandoned their child, even though no change had occurred in the looks of his face. They claimed that he looked severely retarded, that he had a protruding tongue and excessive drooling. In other words, the parents did not respond to their child's actual body, but to the image of his body as it appeared in their own minds. Their attitude towards him changed as a result of a change in their image of his body, and not because of real changes themselves.

The behavior evinced by Tzviya and her husband is typical of that of most of the parents of Down's syndrome children whom I observed; most rejected their children due to their images of a severely retarded child with the typical Mongoloid look. This was true even in cases of children who did not have such a look at all. Only five of the families whom I observed refused initially to give in to the generally accepted image of a mentally retarded person in our society, and attached some other label to their children, such as "little Japanese," to enable them to accept their children. Three of these five couples eventually changed their positive images of their children to the negative images that prevailed among the other parents. The mother of the "little Japanese," for example, gradually changed here attitude from viewing her son as a "cute little Japanese" to viewing him as a "retard," and by the time he was one year old she decided to abandon him.

On her son's first birthday, Asnat, the mother of the "little Japanese," brought her son to the hospital where he had been born and said to the nurse, "O.K., I've become convinced you were right. He really is retarded.

Now I'm in a state of despair. I'm beginning to have awfully frightening dreams. Now he has the look of a Mongoloid. He's dumb. He's really retarded. In the hospital they asked me if I would like him to have plastic surgery, but what for? So they can change the shape of his mouth a bit? Change his eyes a bit? What difference will that make? He's retarded. Now there's no more escaping it. ... Put him in an institution. I'm leaving him in the hospital. Take him from me, and I'll keep what strength I have. ... Now I'm convinced he's retarded. ... How am I so certain? Look, he shows clear signs of it. At first I didn't believe the signs. Now I've discovered them myself. For example, when he sleeps I stand at his side and look at him and think, 'You call this thing here a boy?' He looks more like a giant frog. His whole body's small. His head is small, his hands and feet are small and decimated ... and his eyes look like little fish. ... What made me absolutely sure and confirmed that he's retarded was when he started putting out his tongue like a little snake."

Thus, after a year of struggling against an environment that rejected her young child, Asnat left her "little Japanese" in the hospital and for the next year took no interest in him whatsoever. At the age of two the child was given to a foster family, and later he was put in an institution. The "little Japanese" was abandoned because his mother gave in to the social and visual image of a retard, not because of any real changes that took place in his body; for, according to the testimony of other observers, the signs of Down's syndrome were no more noticeable in him at the age of a year than they were at age two months.[5]

The decisive importance attributed to body image as opposed to the body itself has been illustrated here through the relations of parents to their Down's syndrome children. The behavior of parents of children with cancer, several cases of which I present below, confirms the great importance attached to body image. I shall focus especially on cancer patients whose looks have not been affected; some of them are very normal looking, in spite of their illness.[6] In other words, their abnormality is not visually apparent.

CASE 16 "LOOKING AT HER, YOU CAN'T TELL THAT SHE'S SICK"

Leah, a fifteen-year-old girl, was hospitalized with a cancerous growth. Leah has finely drawn features and large dark eyes that stand out against her pale face. Leah is very concerned about her looks; for example, her nails are carefully manicured and painted with red nail-polish. Leah has five sisters and brothers. Her mother is of Tunisian extraction and her father, Polish.

When we observed Leah she was recuperating from an abdominal operation; she had an 8-inch scar the length of her stomach. The scar was delicately shaped, and the stitches had not yet been removed.

Here is an account of what transpired on the day I made my observations.

At 7:00 a.m. several nurses entered the room. Leah was sleeping in one bed, her mother in the next bed. Neither of them responded when the nurses entered.

Half an hour later, Leah's mother was standing beside her daughter, preparing her a drink of milk mixed with powdered vitamins. She mixed the drink and offered it to her daughter.

LEAH [*drinking a bit, but stopping quite soon*]: I feel nauseous.

MOTHER [*taking the glass*]: Never mind. Take a deep breath. You're not going to vomit. Well ... , if you're going to vomit, you'll vomit. There's nothing we can do. [*The mother gives her daughter a kidney-pan, and Leah grabs hold of it. She breaths deeply and finally puts the kidney-pan down on the bed. Her mother immediately prepares a cup of milk with instant coffee and offers it to Leah.*] Take this and drink it; so at least you'll have something in your stomach this morning. [*Turning to the nurse*] Look, she's taking medicine on an empty stomach. That couldn't be good.

Leah took a bit of the drink, then returned the cup to her mother, who took it and put it down on the bedside table. The mother remained where she was, and Leah sat up in bed, doubled over and leaning on her mother's knees, all the while suffering fierce pain.

NURSE [*to the mother*]: Perhaps I could help you bathe Leah?

MOTHER: That's not necessary. I can manage by myself. I've got everything ready. All we need is to have the bath-tub disinfected. Last time I washed her they hadn't cleaned the tub.

NURSE: I'll clean the tub right away. [*She leaves the room, cleans the tub, then returns. Meanwhile the mother prepares Leah's clothes. Then the mother takes out soap, toothpaste, and moisturizing cream which she brought from home.*]

MOTHER: I brought her moisturizer from home, so she'll smell nice. [*She caresses her daughter on the head and kisses her.*] She's the best. Leah is really something special; what I do for her is nothing. Do you know what a good baby she was ... what a fine girl? ... She's brought us nothing but pleasure.

LEAH [*crying*]: It hurts dreadfully.

MOTHER: What can we do? You know, the disease comes in with a pow, but leaves bit by bit. Don't worry. Everything will be O.K. Little by little it will go away, ... my brave girl ... you've crossed the big sea, and now you're in a small sea. ...

LEAH [*by now in fierce pain*]: The sea I'm in isn't so very small. ...

MOTHER: What can we do about your suffering? Soon you'll get a pain killer, but we really should wait a bit, because you just had a shot for the pain two hours ago. ... Now let's go have a shower.

NURSE: Perhaps we should bring a wheelchair to take her to the shower?

MOTHER: It's not a good idea. Let her walk. It's better for her to move her legs.

Leah tried to stand up, but was unable.

NURSE: Perhaps, all the same, we should use a wheelchair?

MOTHER: O.K. ... We'll get her a physical therapist. She has a cramp in her leg. Here, I'll release it. [*The mother massages her daughter's leg, while her daughter sits on the bed with her legs over the side.*] My darling, my heart's delight, you're wonderful. [*Kissing and caressing Leah*] Everything will be O.K., ... don't you worry.

The nurse, Leah, and her mother all reached the bathroom.

NURSE [*to the mother*]: Come, let me help you.

MOTHER: There's no need. I can manage by myself. I'll be here; so you needn't worry about Leah.

Leah's mother helped her daughter into the tub, supporting her and instructing her to step in, first one foot, then the other. She encouraged her, saying things like, "You can do it." Finally, with great difficulty, Leah managed to get into the bath. After she had seated herself, her mother put in the plug and began filling the tub. The water ran steaming hot.

NURSE: Perhaps we should add some cold water?

MOTHER: No, this is good. Hot water is good.

LEAH: It's dreadfully hot, it's scalding.

MOTHER [*stubbornly*]: Hot water is good ... it'll help you get rid of the disease ... and it will also release the cramp in you leg.

The tub filled, and Leah's mother massaged her daughter's legs in the water. From time to time she rubbed the scar left from the operation.

NURSE: When are they going to remove the stitches?

MOTHER: I don't know. But the place where the incision was made can be washed, and the scar can even be scrubbed.

Then she soaped Leah. Telling her to get up a little, she soaped her rear and said, "Lovely, now you're all clean." .

LEAH [*completely exhausted*]: I have to pee.

MOTHER: Oh, no! Don't pee in the bath. You'll get all dirty again.

NURSE: Never mind, we'll rinse her off afterwards.

MOTHER [*taking a small cup and handing it to Leah*]: O.K., pee in the cup ... but I think you won't be able to.

Leah tried, raised herself somewhat, but could not maintain the position.

MOTHER: O.K., just pee, but don't sit back down in the tub.

The mother immediately let down the water, washed her daughter thoroughly, and laid her down in the neighboring bed, all the while handling her the way one might handle a baby. She wiped her head, face, and scar in a gentle, yet slightly cringing manner, whereas the rest of her body she dried brusquely, without shying away. As she wiped Leah's scar, her daughter complained of "a pain in the side."

MOTHER: That's nothing new. [*Turning to the nurse*] After the operation on her stomach, some of the dirt that was in her stomach came out and caused an infection there, and that's why she has a pain in her side. She's getting antibiotics.

The mother finished wiping Leah, then began dressing her, handling her less delicately and cautiously than she had when dealing with her girl's bare body. For example, when she slipped the sleeve of Leah's blouse into the sleeve of the intravenous device, her motions were swift and rough.

When they returned to their room after the bath, the mother laid Leah down in her bed and, standing beside her daughter, changed the bandage covering her stitches. She removed the old bandage, took disinfectant and cleaned the area with an applicator, then re-bandaged her. While doing this she looked straight at the scar (about 1/3 of an inch wide), which was somewhat red and bleeding a little. Her motions in disinfecting the area were careful and slow, the expression on her face very grave. As she closed the bandage, she said, "Fine. Like this its clean, and neat. I know how to take care of it." Then the mother looked at her daughter's head, especially at a spot that had become completely bald due to her having been bed-ridden for so long, and said, "Look what's doing here. Like a little baby, who spends all the time lying in a crib." Then she stroked the spot and kissed it.

Leah fell asleep, and half an hour later five women, neighbors and relatives, appeared. The women were very close to one another and often got together to chat about personal matters, even before Leah's illness. After discussing the neighborhood news and asking how Leah felt, the conversation moved on to more personal matters. The women drew closer, forming a tight circle, and continued their conversation as follows:

DEBORAH [*an aunt, turning to the mother*]: Where do you sleep?
MOTHER: Right here [*pointing to an armchair next to Leah's bed*].
DEBORAH: So close to Leah?
MOTHER: Yes.
DEBORAH: And where do you eat?
MOTHER: Here [*pointing to a table beside the bed*].
DEBORAH: So close?
MOTHER: Yes.
After several moments of silence the conversation continued:
MOTHER: Why do you ask? Do you, too, think that what Leah has is contagious?

DEBORAH: Maybe so.

MOTHER [*after another silence*]: I also thought about it a lot.

DEBORAH: Our neighbor Cohen, his daughter had cancer and was in the hospital. Once I gave her some pudding and I forgot she was sick and tasted some of the pudding from her spoon. Then the nurse called me and said I had been wrong to do that, that perhaps it is contagious and that it was a bad idea to eat from the same spoon.

LEAH [*an aunt*]: Yes; it's awfully hard to talk about it. Only someone who has been through it can talk about it. Especially since it happens in families where many people have the disease. Then it's certain that it's contagious, ... Actually, who knows?

ZELDA [*a neighbor*]: But the doctors say it's not contagious.

DEBORAH: The doctors don't understand.

ZELDA: So tell me; how does one catch it?

DEBORAH: Why, are you a doctor? ... Maybe its transmitted by germs, ... or through the air. [*Silence.*] Ugh, it really is stuffy in here. [*She gets up and opens the window.*] ... It smells so unpleasant. ... [*Addressing the mother*] Did she always have such an odor?

MOTHER: I don't know. But I, too, have noticed for some time now that she has this odor.

DEBORAH: Did you ask the doctor about it?

MOTHER: Once I did, and he said I was imagining things. That there wasn't any odor.

DEBORAH: What do you mean, imagining things? Every one of us is aware of an odor in here.

ZELDA: Actually, I didn't notice any particular odor.

Indeed, it was impossible to detect any sort of odor being emitted by Leah.

DEBORAH [*to Zelda*]: Look, you haven't been through such a tragedy. You're not sensitive to the smell. Whoever has been through a tragedy like this can smell a person with cancer a mile away.

MOTHER: That's so. I can tell who has cancer by the smell.

Leah mumbled something. Her mother jumped up, went over to her bed and stroked her. Then Leah calmed down, and her mother returned to her guests.

DEBORAH [*to the mother*]: How do the other children receive her [*meaning Leah*]?

MOTHER: How should I know? It seems pretty well, actually. Who knows? Do you think I have the presence of mind to think about them? ... [*She ponders a moment.*] Actually, I always tell my children not to forget to wash their hands after they touch Leah's bed ... although I'm not so strict about it myself, and I often forget. Well, that's the way it is. If it's contagious, then I've caught it already. I'm sure I've been infected.

REBECCA [*a relative*]: It's a real plague, this disease. Sara also has it. ... Maybe the Arabs are putting the microbes into our water?

ZELDA: You're really talking nonsense.

REBECCA: Why? Such things have been heard of before; they wanted to poison us. It was in all the papers, ... so who knows? Look, it's all terribly confusing. If they would say that it's definitely transmitted by microbes, then perhaps one could take precautions; but they're not sure.

DEBORAH: That's what's so terrible about this disease, that they don't know for certain. So, let's say we're careful about Leah. Will that make us safe? Hundreds of people are walking around with this disease, and you can't tell just by looking at them. So how are we to stay away from them? Are we supposed to start being careful of everyone? Go checking the smell of everybody? We'll end up having to stay away from ourselves; end up smelling ourselves.

MOTHER: Well I don't care. I've already got it. Yes, the disease has caught me; I can feel that it's caught me, ... but I don't care. It's my daughter [*sobbing silently*].

ZELDA: But how is the disease transmitted? There are no such things as cancer germs!

MOTHER: Who knows? Perhaps by a curse, ... Don't laugh; I think Bertha ... put a curse on her ... [*pensive for a moment*]. The very worst of it is that I don't know what to do. There my daughter lies, and I, her mother, don't know what to do. ... The cancer goes spreading through her body, and I can't stop it, ... I can't take care of my own daughter.

DEBORAH: Now, don't cry. Things will be better. You've already been through the big sea, and you've gotten out of it.

MOTHER [*crying*]: Since when have we gotten through it? We've just entered it. First we were in a stream, in a river valley. But now it's gotten to be like a big sea. And the sea keeps getting bigger. And I feel I'm drowning in it. I haven't got the strength to keep my head above water.

DEBORAH: Have a good cry. Don't be afraid to cry. That's what we're here for.

MOTHER [*crying*]: It's a good thing I have you, ... because I can't really talk with Moshe [*her husband*]. We're both weak. We're just about falling to pieces from weakness. We're both afraid of the same thing. I never knew a person could be so gripped by fear. ... One weak person can't help another. We both have the same nightmares. And when I begin talking with him, I feel that I'm killing him, too. But you're stronger. You can really listen.

VICTORIA [*a neighbor, of Persian extraction*]: Everyone's in the same boat. But be careful. Cancer—that unspeakable disease—is just lying in wait for the moment you let down your guard, and then it'll get you. You'll see. You must be careful.

DEBORAH [*to Victoria*]: What do you want from her [*the mother*]? You weren't careful, yourself.

MOTHER: When?

VICTORIA [*crying*]: Right. When I was pregnant, the last time, ... we took a trip to Africa. An African safari, ... it was so foolish of us. It's the sort of thing a family from Savyon [*a very wealthy community in Israel*] might do; not for us. ... We saw lots of animals, and I wasn't careful. And then, because of that, he was born this way. Poor thing. [*Victoria's son was born with a harelip.*]

ZELDA: Just because you saw some animals you had a kid like that? Just from looking at something?!

VICTORIA: Yes. It's no joke. Our neighbor Miriam, too—her kid caught the disease my kid had because she saw a movie about blacks and other animals, maybe only a month before he was born.

MOTHER: I understand you. You're not joking. Only someone who hasn't had a tragedy like this can treat it as a laughing matter. Sometimes I even feel that I infected Leah. ... Once I went to visit Cohen's daughter, the one with cancer. I kissed her. Then afterwards Leah got sick, ... It's well known that you can transmit germs to someone else, without becoming sick yourself. It's been medically established.

DEBORAH: I told you, you have to take care.

MOTHER: Now, before I touch my children, after having kissed Leah, I wash my clothes and my body, ... But what can we do? Leah's a poor thing ... poor thing. My girl, and so unfortunate. What can I do?

DEBORAH: Don't despair. You must trust in God. Who knows? What do we know about this cancer here? Maybe one morning she'll suddenly wake up well.

MOTHER: If only it were true. That's all I ever dream about. That this cancer just doesn't exist, ... that it never happened, ... that it's all been a bad dream ... [*thinks a while*] ... Tell me the truth, ... I've thought about it a lot, ... Does Leah look sick to you? Look how beautiful her face is. Maybe she's not sick? Tell me the truth.

DEBORAH: What do we know? Are we God? Maybe you're right. If I were to see her on the street I wouldn't guess that she had the disease—let's not mention it by name.

A long silence ensued. Finally the women rose, went over to the mother one by one and told her to "be strong," and left.

Like other parents, Leah's mother relates to the image of her daughter's sickness. She, too, just like many other mothers of children with cancer, tended her daughter devotedly. At the same time, her behavior shows several elements which we believe are common to the behavior of many other parents in similar situations. Various elements that pertain to the image of the child's disease and are reflected in the mother's behavior: Leah's mother spends a lot of time scrubbing, cleaning, and perfuming her daughter. She perceives the disease as dirt, hence her tendency to scrub and disinfect with boiling hot water that which she perceives as the opening for the disease (i.e., the scar from Leah's abdominal surgery). Furthermore, the mother's image of the sick person is confused due to the discrepancy between the sick person's good looks and her dreadful disease. The mother's behavior points out that she views cancer as contagious and as causing a bad odor, and underscores her desire to avoid intimate contact and thus avoid contamination or the danger of infection.

CASE 17 "HANNAH, THE CONFUSING GIRL"

In this case we encounter additional aspects of the special image associated with cancer patients, such as the connection that is drawn between heredity and contagion.

Hannah, ten years old, suffered from leukemia for four years. A year after Hannah was found to be ill, her mother was discovered to have lung cancer and died one and a half years later. Hannah's parents are of Yemenite extraction. When she was taken ill, her father, a school janitor, was 50 years old, and her mother, a housewife, was 45.

Hannah was often in and out of the hospital. Four years ago, when her disease was discovered, she was surrounded by members of her family day and night. After her mother died, the family's visits diminished from day to day. Only her father and older sister continued to visit her occasionally. When the father came to visit he would often speak to her harshly. A typical visit proceeded as follows:

The father entered the room and, without any expression of warmth or any physical contact, sat down fairly far from his daughter's bed.

FATHER: Well, how are you?

HANNAH: So-so.

FATHER: First you got sick, and then right away it passed to your mother.

HANNAH: You know that cancer is not contagious.

FATHER: But I have facts here. Until you became sick, your Mom was a healthy woman. And just as soon as you got sick, the sickness passed to her.

HANNAH: The doctors have explained to me that my being sick might have hastened Mom's sickness, ... that is, the sickness might have been discovered in her sooner than it would have been if I hadn't been sick. But the doctors and I have a more logical explanation for this than you. She took care of me all the time, and became weaker, and then the sickness that was already in her body got the upper hand, ... but she did not get sick because of catching something from anybody.

FATHER: Both are true. ...

The father went out to the hall and cried silently. Several minutes later Judy, a friend of the deceased mother, who generally visits Hannah once a week, arrived. Judy met the father in the hall and entered Hannah's room with him.

FATHER [*returning to his daughter's bed, looking very harassed and turning to Judy*]: Tell me, Judy, is it contagious, or is it not?

JUDY [*taken aback*]: Is what contagious?

HANNAH: He thinks that I'm giving him my disease.

JUDY: What are you, primitive or something? Don't you know that this disease is not contagious?

FATHER: I have proof that it is contagious.

JUDY: Well, so what's your proof?

FATHER: How is it that Hannah was taken ill with it, and then right away her mother was, too?

JUDY [*hesitatingly*]: Touch wood. You've got the brains of a little baby, ... [*thinking*] ... I'm not saying that you don't have to take care. You do have to be careful, for sure. You have to be careful ... that the virus not get you. Because if it gets you, you're lost. But it's not exactly like, let's say, like the flu.

FATHER: Worse than the flu; it's like the devil. No matter how careful you are, it'll get you. ... I'm afraid, ... always afraid. I look in the mirror and I don't recognize myself. I'm scared to death, ... I'm afraid of my own shadow [*almost in tears*] ... don't laugh. Once I used to recognize my shadow and the shadows of my children; we used to play with shadows when they were young. Now everything's changed. ... It's as if, ... as if I and my shadow are two different people. ... I even had a dream one night that my shadow was laughing at me, ... as if it were a messenger sent by this cancer.

JUDY: Interesting. The mother in the next room also says that.

FATHER: Because someone who's been hit by cancer has proof. Yes, I have proof.

JUDY: Your late wife had it. She took such good care of Hannah. With all her heart, but she suffered when she saw that everyone was afraid Hannah had something contagious. She told me that once, at the clinic, when Hannah's hair fell out, all the other mothers moved away and took their children away from Hannah because they thought she had a contagious disease. Your late wife explained things to them, but it didn't help. She tried not to be offended. She said that from their own point of view, they were

right. They're strangers and don't know each other. Why should they endanger their children? But what offended her the most were her sisters.
They were willing to cook at home, and help loads. But they said, "In our
heads we believe it's not contagious, but in our hearts, that it is. Yes, ...
why should we endanger our children?" And then they told their children
not to eat near Hannah. Just to play it safe. When your late wife's niece
had a new baby ... she went to wish them *mazel tov* ... but when your
niece saw her, she took her baby and ran out of the house. She just left all
her guests and fled, ... and simply refused to show her aunt the baby. It
was simply awful. She was actually in tears when she told me about it. She
said that they thought perhaps the disease is passed by the mother. Maybe
they didn't really *think* it, but they felt it, ... that Hannah would somehow
jinx them by way of her mother ... and that they, too, would have a trouble
like this.

FATHER: Yes, she told me about it ... she really suffered greatly then.

At this point, Rivka, the mother of another child hospitalized in the same
room with Hannah, joined the conversation. Rivka, 35 years old, of Polish
extraction, and an instructor in the university, appeared all the while not
to be listening to the conversation that was taking place in a low voice
among Hannah's relatives. However, as it turns out, she had been taking
in all that was said, and now responded with the following remarks: "Yes.
You're right. There really is a problem, there's no one to talk to about
this. It's sort of taboo. ... My son has cerebral palsy.[7] It affects the way
he moves ... duck-walk, can't control the way he moves ... speaks with a
garbled mix of motions ... but everyone knows he's highly intelligent. ...
Nevertheless my close friends tell me ... to come visit only in the evenings.
... They don't want their children to play with him ... because they're
afraid they'll pick up his way of walking and of talking. ... [*Cynically*]
They're afraid of him ... afraid he'll infect their children. ... Even a friend
of mine, a lecturer at the university, [*cynically*] a well-known brain, as soon
as she became pregnant she began avoiding us, ... in the end she said to
me, 'Let's be frank, every time, after I'm with your son, I have all sorts
of dreadful dreams at night. I have an irrational fear that contact with
your son will have a harmful effect on my baby.' But why talk about a
girlfriend? Even my husband left us ... he was scared to death by the
child." Depressed, Rivka returned to her place at her son's side.

JUDY [*to the father*]: So, listen to that. It doesn't only happen with
cancer. You're not the most pathetic person in the world.

FATHER: Nonsense. How can you compare that to cancer? Her child is
retarded. That's something else.

RIVKA [*the mother of the child with cerebral palsy, calling out from where
she sat*]: My son is not retarded.

FATHER: Yes he is ... that's just what a retarded child looks like ... and he doesn't confuse anyone. But she [*Hannah*] is confusing. She looks like a regular child and who knows what's hiding inside her body. ...

Hannah's father expresses the popular perception, contrary to medical fact, that cancer is an incurable disease. He also identifies "hereditary tendencies" with "contagion." The discussion of contagion raises a number of issues.

Firstly, we note the discrepancy between the scientific perception of the facts and the parent's conception of what the facts or evidence mean. The father believes the doctor's pronouncements are based on irrelevant statistical findings. For him, in contrast, the death of his wife in the wake of his daughter's illness provides clear proof of the fact that cancer is contagious. The lack of clear knowledge concerning the disease, as expressed through the perceived danger of contagion, is also implicit in Judy's remarks and her account of the family's behavior. Judy's adherence to the modern medical perception ("Don't you know that this disease is not contagious?") is not altogether consistent ("I'm not saying that you don't have to take care. You do have to be careful"). The behavior of the relatives also expresses this contradiction between intellectual and emotional perceptions: "In our heads we believe it's not contagious, but in our hearts, that it is." Many other parents expressed similar feelings and, even though they understand the medical notion that cancer is not contagious, nevertheless they take care not to "endanger" other members of the family, as Leah's mother put it.

Hannah's father's subsequent remarks are very important to our discussion of the differences between cancer and retardation. According to the father, a retarded child has a clear image since his handicap corresponds to a specific external appearance; the message emitted by someone with cancer, on the other hand, is one of confused identity. Moreover, this confusion in identity, which stems from the cancer patient having, as it were, two entities latent in himself or herself (i.e., he or she looks well, and yet is sick), affects the parents, who themselves come to feel that they, too, have two identities. This sort of confusion and separation of identities is clearly seen in the way the father relates to his shadow. In the past the father and his shadow were one, and the father's awareness of himself and the lines of his body was reflected in his recognizing the outline of his shadow; whereas now there is a bifurcation between the father and his shadow, the shadow representing the cancer.

The perception of the disease, as revealed by the remarks of Hannah's father, relations, and friends, involves magical concepts. The cases we have reviewed thus far and those we shall encounter later show that similar views are found among all parents, including some with higher education in the sciences.

CASE 18 "NOW THE CANCER IS SPREADING LIKE A WEED"

This case, describing Flora and her family, presents additional aspects of the attitude towards cancer patients.

Flora is a very skinny 14-year-old girl with short black hair. She has a hemorrhaging cancerous growth on her neck. She is bandaged with gauze covering her chin and tied around the lower part of her face. Flora has been bed-ridden of late, due to extreme pain. Her right arm is connected to an intravenous device (IV) through which she is given antibiotics and pain-killers. Her face is swollen (because of steroids) and is called a "moon-face" by the medical staff. Nevertheless, even in her present condition, Flora is considered a good-looking young girl. Her mother is a tall, full-bodied, 50-year-old woman. She dresses in old, patched clothing, but is always clean and pressed. The father, a heavy-set 65-year-old, is dressed in dark, tattered clothes. He generally wears a large gold watch and a gold chain with a *ḥamsa* (medallion in the shape of a hand) around his neck. The parents are from Morocco and speak Hebrew fluently with an eastern accent. Flora has two brothers and two sisters, all vocational school graduates. Her father generally visits her two or three times a week, usually accompanied by one of his children. Her mother stays at her bedside around the clock. She helps her daughter a lot, primarily in activities concerning cleanliness and washing up, so that Flora will "look as good as possible," as she puts it. The family also sees to it that Flora will be "in good spirits and will eat well." The mother covers and bandages the growth with great fastidiousness, sometimes with the assistance of her oldest son. The oldest son generally helps his mother and spends many hours of the day at his sister's side. The behavior of the entire family shows their great devotion to Flora. Several sessions were spent observing the family; they are presented below.

First session

At 7:00 a.m., the room was dark, Flora was sleeping in a bed near the door and was attached to an IV through which she was receiving pain-killers. Her bed was raised slightly and her head was resting on a pillow. Her neck was bandaged with blood-stained gauze. She had a ribbon with a miniature book of psalms tied around her neck. Flora was covered with a blanket so that only her hands showed out. Her palms lay at the side of her body; her fingernails were surprisingly well manicured and painted with dark red polish.

The mother was sleeping in the bed next to her daughter, her face towards the window. Silence reigned in the unlit room.

At 8:30 a.m. the mother left the room to request a sedative. Flora began crying, "It hurts ... so much," and accompanied her cries with hand motions. Occasionally she touched the area of the growth, as if wishing to remove it. Her mother stood at her side, kissing her on the forehead and stroking her hand and hair in an attempt to calm her. "Don't worry," she said, "soon they'll bring you something for the pain ... I know that it hurts you dreadfully ... but what can we do ... soon you won't be in pain." The mother continued stroking Flora, and every so often left the room to ask for a sedative. Suddenly, while the mother was not paying attention, Flora pulled the bandage off the growth and it began to bleed. The mother immediately ran to the nursing station and asked them to stop the bleeding. She returned to Flora and said reproachfully: "I've told you a dozen times already not to touch the area ... look, now it's started bleeding, and I don't know how we're going to stop it." The mother herself removed the bandage from the area of the growth, all the while describing in detail the extensive bleeding, saying things such as, "Oh, no! ... Uggh! ... what'll I do now ... that's all I needed! ... Hell! ... look, it's spreading like a weed."

Flora apologized for having touched the growth, saying, "I didn't do it on purpose; I'm sorry, I really am." The mother responded immediately, "Never mind. We'll prevail over it. We'll stop this bleeding." The mother took care of the bleeding herself. She removed the bandage and mopped up the blood with pads. Then she took a can of powder that stops hemorrhages and sprinkled some on the area. Slowly the hemorrhaging subsided and the mother, assisted by the nurses, took a bandage and bound the area, saying, "At long last."

The growth looks like a cauliflower covered with warts. The bleeding is internal and is very hard to stop. The medical staff finds it hard to look at a growth with "such a horrible appearance." The mother is one of the few people who take care of it devotedly, even though it is hard to take care of and she is disgusted by it.

While treating her daughter, the mother often made many contorted facial expressions and verbalized her actions with references to "this dreadful growth." She personified the growth and referred to it as such repeatedly. Every once in a while she would turn to Flora and say, "My dear ... how you're suffering ... but you'll triumph over it ... we'll show it [*the growth*] what it has coming ... it'll come to a bad end, and you'll come to a good one." Her treatment of the disease is perceived as a battle against the growth and the disease.

Even when the mother was told that her daughter's fate was sealed, she continued to speak of her victory over the growth: "In the end, I'll beat the cancer," she often said. "I, too, had this sickness ... " she said, "I even remember ... I was just Flora's age ... but then it wasn't called cancer. ... I had a sore on my neck, all the way up to my left ear, and I lay in bed, listless. Just like Flora ... and nobody touched me ... except for my great grandmother, who used to give me some sort of special tea. It was very sweet ... and in the end I got well ... and my mother, too, had the same sickness. At age 11 ... she herself told me ... they said it was a hex ... and she recovered, too, ... and so will Flora ... I'll exorcise it ... that growth ... we'll make sure it leaves where it came in from ... and we won't give in to it ... we'll stand fast ... we're a very stubborn family."

When the treatment was done, Flora asked to "see the sore."

MOTHER [*blanching*]: You shouldn't, you shouldn't see the growth now. You'll see it tomorrow, when you look better.

FLORA [*entreating*]: I want to see it. It's my sore.

The mother looked at the doctor, who had just entered the room, and then at the nurse.

NURSE: I actually think Flora should see the sore.

MOTHER [*giving in*]: O.K. [*She brings a mirror.*]

FLORA [*looking at the sore, then turning to her mother*]: Why did you make such a big to-do about it? By the way you were behaving I thought it was much worse.

After the bleeding had subsided, Flora lay in bed in a pool of blood. The mother and nurse proceeded to make the bed while Flora was lying in it. The mother brought a bowl of water and washed her daughter's body, taking especial care when she got to the areas affected by the disease—Flora's neck, around the bandage, and the area of her stomach, where she had a scar from surgery to remove part of her stomach due to a hemorrhaging ulcer. "Here's the scar from your operation," the mother explained, "you really must drink and eat something ... so that the trouble you had before with your stomach doesn't recur." "You must wash up well." The mother continued, "Just so there's no dirt or blood. I can't stand it when she's dirty." The mother finished arranging Flora's bed, then said, "Wonderful, now you're neat and clean." Then she sprayed some perfume on Flora's neck and chest, saying, "At least let her smell good."

The doctor left the room.

FLORA [*to her mother*]: I saw you ask the doctor if the swelling in my face will go down. What did he answer?

MOTHER [*evasively*]: Yes. I don't remember ... I wasn't paying attention ... I was so absorbed in changing the bandage that I didn't really hear. [*Looking at the nurse with an expression of helplessness*] ... Would you like to eat? [*Stroking Flora*] ... don't worry, the swelling will go down and you'll be just like you were before.

The mother and nurse left the room and conversed in the hall.

MOTHER [*to the nurse*]: Look. Appearances are very important to Flora. She's in despair now because she doesn't look good. She thinks she's become ugly, she wants to see herself in the mirror and she sees that she looks like a monster. Her faith has been shaken. She knows precisely what she has. When she came to the ward she was a girl who always took care of her looks. ... Looks are very important to her.

NURSE: They're important to you, too.

MOTHER: That's true. Our personalities are very similar ... we both also like to be clean all the time ... I wash Flora several times a day. It bothers me when Flora has dirt on her body. ... I wash her and wipe the blood stains off her hands. ... It's very important to be clean ... you feel completely different ... feel good ... like a new person.

The mother came back into the room, opened her bag, took out a scented bar of soap that she had brought from home, and prepared to wash Flora again. When she was done, she prepared a cup of cocoa and handed it to Flora with a straw, saying, "Take this, drink something, you must put something in your stomach." Flora took the cup with shaking hands. She tried to drink a bit, but stopped; drank a bit, and stopped.

MOTHER [*encouraging her*]: Wonderful, wonderful. Drink it slowly [*looking at the nurse with satisfaction, as if to say, "Look, I've succeeded"*].

Flora drank some more, but did not finish; then she gave the cup back to her mother.

MOTHER: Very good. Even a bit is something. [*Taking the cup, she puts it on the bedside table and kisses her daughter*] My Flora ... everything will be alright.

At 11:00 a.m. Flora's mother left the room and joined the head nurse, then at the nursing station writing reports.

"Do you remember what my girl was like when she was admitted? Do you remember how good-looking she was? Remember, in the beginning it was only a swelling around her cheek, and then they examined the growth and discovered that it was cancer. ... All that was only one year ago ... look ... now it's spreading like a weed. There's no stopping it. And the pain is so fierce ... but how could it be—there's nothing in her body ... nothing at all ... everything's O.K., ... so what is she dying of? I asked the doctor in the clinic what will be in the end, and he said there's nothing to be done ... but how can it be? Everything's O.K. in her body, so how is it she's going to die? ... Oh, what heartache, what hardship ... [*beating her head with her hand*] what a beautiful girl. ... Who would have believed that only a year ago she used to dance, go to all sorts of after-school activities, ... I spent all I had so my children would have it good and succeed. They should only be healthy ... and look what happened to me."

Several minutes later the mother returned to Flora's room.

Second session

This session, held one week later, describes Flora's death.

At 7:00 a.m. Flora lay in bed, with her mother standing at her side, and next to her Flora's older brother and sister. All of them had spent the whole night at Flora's side. Until now the entire family had been extremely careful not to cry in Flora's presence, but this day, the day of her death, they cried and eulogized her in her very presence, even before she had passed away. They took their leave of her and entreated her to look at them in her last hours.

The mother kissed her daughter, held her hand and drew it close to her breast. Stroking her girl's head, she said, "My angel ... I'm sorry I didn't take you to the ends of the earth. Maybe there they would have found you a cure."

BROTHER [*quietly*]: What do want? You did all you could for Flora. You can get the same medicine in Israel as anywhere else in the world. They didn't find it here, and they wouldn't have found it there.

MOTHER: I don't know ... I'm not sure. I should have taken her. She was such a flower ... such a beautiful girl ... so beloved of everyone ... perhaps we should have done what the Rabbi told us ... perhaps we should have turned to the herbalists. ...

All the while Flora was lying in bed, having trouble breathing. Her face was bandaged with gauze, and she was connected to the IV. Her eyes were half-closed. She did not make a sound. Her mother stood at her side, not letting go. Every once in a while she would rock from foot to foot, shifting her body forwards and back. Pounding her head with both hands, she said, "She's coming to the end ... this growth can't be stopped ... what an ordeal ... one year and my daughter was just finished off ... what a beautiful girl ... remember what she was like before this sickness ... she used to dance and sing, she was so full of life."

Suddenly Flora stopped breathing. Her mother began hitting her and shouting, "Flora, Flora, get up, get up." Flora's breath returned, and she began breathing heavily. Her mother did not let her go, but kept hold of her all the time.

Half an hour later Flora passed away. She lay in a raised bed in a semi-reclining position. Her head was bandaged and her face rested on the pillow. She was covered with a blanket up to her head, and looked as if she were sleeping.

MOTHER [*crying and screaming*]: She's dead ... she's dead ... I don't have my girl any more ... that's what's happened to her ... damn ... what a disease ... call the doctor who took care of her. Let her come and see what came of all her care ... The doctor on night duty assured me she wouldn't survive the night. ... She used to look so lovely, before she got sick!

Flora's father arrived and with him Flora's other brother and sisters.

Standing around her bed, they all wailed out loud. From time to time one of them would approach her and kiss her. The mother, close to the bed, stood sobbing and stroking her girl's head and kissing her. Then she opened Flora's blouse and showed everyone: "Look, here they operated on her several months ago; oh, how I looked after her! Just before she died I washed her and cleaned her. Now she's really clean. Now everything is clean. She, and the sheets. I even changed her bandage. It's a pity I didn't take her abroad, all the same, or to the ends of the earth; there perhaps they would have cured her. I took care of her with such devotion. The entire year I never left her side. All the time, only Flora ... Flora, Flora. I let the house go, let the family go; no one ever saw me. And all for what? None of it was any help. I failed, I couldn't save her ... she suffered so much."

The father began to cry, went up to Flora and kissed her on the forehead, then said, "What a girl she was. We'll cry over her a lot." "Take out the pictures," he asked his daughter who was standing in the room, "so everyone can see what she looked like when she was well." The daughter took out the photographs and they all looked at them and showed them to the staff who were in the room. The pictures showed Flora dancing in a tutu.

FATHER: I never used to do anything around the house. Since Flora took ill, my wife was away from home and I began doing the cooking and cleaning.

MOTHER [*touching the bandage*]: Look, the growth got smaller, but my daughter died. ...

After several moments of silence the mother repeated this sentence again and again.

FATHER [*to the staff*]: Thanks to all the staff that took care of her. Thank you for doing all you could for her.

The mother and son lay their heads on Flora's chest, hoping to hear a heartbeat, then said, "Her heart's not working."

The family remained in the room until Flora's body was taken to the pathology department. Then they went into the adjacent dining-room and continued to sit there.

Time and again they recalled Flora's "good" traits and "how she looked before she got sick." The parents stressed repeatedly how important their children are to them. Then, they began fantasizing about what would have been "if". ...

FATHER: I would rather have been penniless, if only Flora would have survived ... I would have done anything, just to have her live.

MOTHER: I tried so hard to save her. All the time I dreamed that this was all one big nightmare, that we would awaken from it and see that nothing had happened. That we have a beautiful, healthy daughter. But in the end, I failed ... I took care of her like a baby ... she lay like a baby ... not like a developed young lady ... and I took care of her the way she was 14 years ago. ... I felt I was kissing my baby ... my girl died twice ... once, now, and once when she began to be sick and became a baby. ... I've been imagining her death for two months, now. Two months I've been imagining how she'd die ... for two months I've been reconstructing it ... [*To the author*] You know, ... maybe she didn't die twice, maybe she actually came back to me when she was sick ... it was many years since I took care of her this way ... since I stroked a child of mine that way ... but my big girl died ... I had a young lady, and she died. ... Sometimes I didn't know what to do ... look, now they all kissed her ... but that doesn't mean it's what they wanted to do ... lots of times you do what you have to ... lots of times I kissed her to show her that I still love her ... for her sake ... not so much for mine. ... Lots of times I did it to show her brothers and her father that she's our girl and that there still is hope ... so they wouldn't shy away from her. ... Lots of times I kissed her to show the nurses in the ward ... so they would not neglect her ... so they would tend her with all their hearts ... because I, her mother, am watching at her side. ... And sometimes I also kissed her because I really wanted to ... but not the same as I used to kiss her once upon a time, at home ... once, at home, I could just kiss her, straight out of the blue, 'cause I felt like it. Here, the kisses were mingled with fear ... with terror.

A long silence ensued.

FATHER: I would like to know if it's certain that Flora was my daughter. Now, don't get me wrong. I would have given my life for her, but I'm not sure she really was my child.

MOTHER: You always say that and I ask you, what's got into your head? Of course she's our girl.

FATHER: The doctors did an investigation for me; whether I ever had this disease, or if my father or mother were ever sick like Flora. But no one ever had this sickness. In our family, we all have a clean slate. So how is it that this disease descended on Flora, of all people?

MOTHER: The angel of death mills around and strikes someone ... without regard to his family.

FATHER: You're mistaken. The doctors made a study of our families, ... to see if there was ever someone with the disease in our family. ... (That is) ... only families who have had someone with the disease can have others sick with it ... and our families were clean.

OLDER BROTHER: Right. They claim it's hereditary.

MOTHER: Well, if so, then it's O.K., because I had the disease ... and so did my mother.

OLDER BROTHER: So it only passes through the female line?

FATHER: You're talking nonsense. Like primitive people. [*To the mother*] You and your mother are both clean. You didn't have this disease. I've known you since you were 14 years old. You were like a flower ... I think that when you had Flora, everything was all mixed up ... and they took our daughter and gave you Flora instead. Couldn't that be?

MOTHER: You're fantasizing ... you're head's always full of dreams. ... How could that be?

OLDER BROTHER: It's been known to have happened ... we read about a case in the papers.

MOTHER [*to the brother*]: Whose side are you on? I always thought you were on my side ... some help you are ... what's your story? what's happening to you?!

SISTER [*somewhat cynically*]: He's afraid of getting the disease, too. He thinks that if he's not part of our family, he has no chance of getting sick. [*She bursts into tears.*]

BROTHER: That's right, but it didn't affect the way I cared for her ... still, if she isn't my true sister, then I'll be less afraid ... you see. If it's a family thing, it must grab hold of entire families. ... All the time I took care of her, and I knew I had to be sick ... the fear never left me ... why should the growth get only her, and not me?

After several minutes of silence, the brother went up to his mother and father and helped them up from their seats. Together they left the room.

The behavior of Flora's mother sheds light on several matters pertaining to cancer and reactions to it. Like Flora's mother, other parents, too, tend to latch onto certain images of the disease.

The mother whom we observed in this case imagines the growth as a "weed" and as "dirt." She tends the apertures of the growth, the lesions; but the growth is inside the body, where there is something like a "weed" or "dirt" that threatens to burst forth through certain apertures. According to the mother's perception, cleaning the openings will help overcome the disease, which she perceives as filth. The growth is viewed as an entity in its own right, and is referred to in personified form. The disease is also seen as an enemy hiding in the body, and treatment of the disease as a fight against the enemy.

Flora's identity is unclear to her mother. The girl assumes one form, then another. No sooner has the mother adjusted to one form, but another one has emerged. Some of the identities are clear, but many are indistinct and convey dual messages. To begin with, there is no continuity between the Flora of the past—the beautiful girl who used to dance ballet—and the Flora of the present—the cancer-stricken child. The daughter that the parents yearn for, and for whom they mourn even before her death, is the Flora in the tutu. Even the photographs, ready to be displayed to anyone

interested, show the beautiful Flora of the past. This is the beloved girl
with whom they knew how to communicate. The girl they see before them
is not the girl they all know. For the mother, the changes in Flora's identity
take the form of a feeling of the former identity having died, and a new one
having been born. Flora died as a grown girl, and returned as a baby (a
perception which, as we shall see later, enables the mother to maintain her
self-image as someone who is supportive of and caring for her girl). The most
difficult lack of clarity, however, arises due to the existence of two identities
in the present. The double messages Flora sends confuse her parents. Who
is Flora? Is the growth part of Flora, or not? Is she alive or dead? When
Flora is medically considered a live person, she emits messages of death (the
mother imagines her death two months before her physical death). On the
other hand, when she is considered medically dead, she conveys signs of life
(she is perceived as sleeping).

There is also a fear of contagion and a clear association of heredity with
contagion.

CASE 19 "THOSE WHO LOOK HEALTHIEST ARE ACTUALLY SICKEST"

This case involves a family from a different ethnic background. Nevertheless, here, too, we see fear of contagion and heredity being associated
with contagion. Thirteen-year-old Sophie is the daughter of aged parents,
a well-to-do couple, long settled in Israel, of Eastern European origin. Her
family is highly educated; her mother has a doctorate in the sciences, and
one of her sisters a doctorate in social work. Sophie came to the hospital
with a complaint of intense pain all over her body. She was hospitalized
for surveillance in the children's ward on suspicion of a viral disease; but in
two days her family was told she had a cancerous growth that had spread
throughout her body.

Her family, who are especially close to her, sat by her side continually.
Her mother cared for her devotedly and indefatigably. Her sister Miri, a
social worker, 17 years her senior and a mother of four, took leave from
her job in order to devote herself to caring for Sophie. Her sister Ziva also
helped care for her.

After chemotherapy Sophie felt better and was sent home. She left the
hospital in a wheelchair and returned once a week for additional chemotherapy. In four months Sophie was able to walk by herself again. She began
losing her hair slowly and had put on weight as a result of the medication,
but otherwise she looked excellent. Never before had her face looked so
lovely.

My encounters with the family were very intensive. I present a number of
conversations that took place between Sophie's mother, father, and sisters

Miri and Ziva. These conversations span a period of two years, from the day Sophie was first hospitalized, until the present.

The first encounter takes place in the hospital. The family's fear that they are responsible for Sophie having become sick through some sort of magic figures prominently in this conversation.

MIRI: ... Sophie entered the hospital three days ago. Yesterday they called us for a meeting with her doctor, and he told us what she has. ... I couldn't stop crying all night. ... I couldn't believe that such a tragedy could strike our family. ... You know that I'm a psychotherapist, in the oncology ward of B ... Hospital. I'm always working with children who have cancer. I'm afraid Sophie got sick because of me. As I got older I began to believe in magic. ... Two years ago I went to such great effort just to get into the oncology ward ... and ever since, I've been afraid someone in my family would get sick. ... All the years I worked in oncology and met with the families of cancer patients, every day I asked myself: how would I behave if cancer were discovered in a member of my family? ... Every time I lost my patience or was angry at a patient's family, I thought deep inside ... who knows how I would behave in such a situation ... and all the time I was afraid that one day I would be put to the test and they would see how I really would behave. ... And indeed, now Fate has put me to the test. ... I was afraid of this all along, but I never imagined that Sophie would be the sacrifice. ...

Throughout the night, for several minutes at a time, I would have these superstitious thoughts ... that I'm essentially to blame for all this ... that I tempted Fate ... pushing myself into the job ... that I infected her ... then suddenly, when the night was over, I felt a tremendous sense of relief. ... I decided to report to work in the morning and tender my resignation ... to forego severance pay ... to flee from there. ... I suddenly felt that in this way I would solve the problem ... and Sophie would get well. ... Of course, by the time I was sipping my morning coffee, I realized it was all a lot of nonsense.

MOTHER: Today we were told that she'll have chemotherapy. ... The doctors are so frigid ... so pessimistic. ... When we left the doctor's office Miri told me ... she was afraid Sophie would have tremendous hair loss. I got angry at her. What does it matter if she loses her hair? Let it be ... in general ... we're so confused. We don't know what to do ... everyone tells us to try natural medicine ... maybe they're right ... maybe if she gets a diet, everything will clear up.

The second encounter, in the hospital, two months later. We see the fear of the disease being passed through clothing and contact with the staff.

MOTHER: I'm constantly afraid. ... I always brought her clothes from the shop. ... Maybe I brought her something that had been put on before by a woman who was sick ... and that's how she came down with it. ...

MIRI: Don't talk nonsense. Cancer is not contagious ... and you don't have to be afraid about Sophie giving it to anyone else.

MOTHER: Look, here. If it's contagious, that won't make any difference in the way I treat her; but it's important when it comes to your children. ... One tragedy in the family is quite enough. We don't need another.

MIRI: So what are you going to do? Place her in isolation?

MOTHER: Well, it seems that I'm immune [*confusedly*] ... maybe you are, too, ... but take care of your children ... I wouldn't want them to catch it. ... Look, yesterday we went for a checkup at the eye clinic. When the examination was over the doctor signaled to the nurse, and she came in and took the sheets off the couch that Sophie had sat on and threw everything in the laundry basket. Sophie asked her, "Do you change the sheets after every examination? after all, I didn't get them dirty?" And the nurse answered that generally not, but that this time she was putting them in the wash. So, if the nurse and doctor seem to think so, maybe it really is contagious.

The third encounter, in Miri's house, three weeks later. The prominent points include attitudes on the patient's loss of hair, and concealed fear of the family becoming infected by kissing or eating from the same dishes.

MIRI: Mother came today, early in the morning, all pale, and told me that Sophie's hair fell out last night. She got up in the morning and found hair on the pillow ... my heart began to pound incessantly. I could barely breath. It made me so anxious. We're always hit with some new blow ... Mother said it also fills her with anxiety. That so much time has passed since they began chemotherapy, and that she had hoped in Sophie's case her hair wouldn't fall out. We immediately went over to my parent's house to see Sophie. I arrived at their house, ... and saw that Sophie was bloated. Her face was all puffed up, her hands swollen, ... her fingers. ... She wanted to make me a cup of coffee. I let her make me coffee, even though I was terribly afraid. She might spill boiling water on herself! But I let her make the coffee, so she'd feel everything was normal ... but whatever can fall from a person's hand, she dropped. She was in despair. She didn't cry, but she was in despair. "I've no strength at all," she said. Her hair is thin. She woke up in the morning and saw gobs of hair on the pillow, and she took fright. She rubbed on castor oil. But she's got no strength. So when she rubbed on the oil, her nightgown got dirty. ... We went out to buy Sophie a wig ... they tried on the first wig, and it looked really artificial. Especially since her hair is so thin. I tried to crack a joke, and said, "Well, at last you'll look elegant." But Mother said, "No. It looks like a wig. I don't like it. You can tell it's a wig." We bought the wig ... and later I said to Sophie, "Come, have lunch at my house, and we'll live it up." She was awfully glad. We rode off, and only just got home now.

The family gathered in Miri's house for lunch. We report part of what transpired around the table. Sophie was glad to see Opher, Miri's son; and he was glad to see her. Sophie picked him up in her arms and kissed him excitedly, and Opher kissed her back.

MOTHER [*fearful, turning to Sophie*]: No kisses. Opher will get you sick. He's not completely well.

SOPHIE [*to her mother*]: What are you afraid of? I won't infect him.

MIRI [*whispering to her mother*]: Cut it out. Sophie picks it up very well that you're afraid she'll infect Opher, not that he'll infect her.

Without speaking, the mother set the table. Sophie was very hungry. Without waiting for the others, she sat down at the table and quickly finished her portion. Opher sat down to eat next to her.

OPHER: I don't have a fork.

SOPHIE: Take mine. I'm done eating.

MOTHER: Just a minute, I'll get him a fork.

SOPHIE: No. Here, take mine. Don't be afraid, I don't have the plague.

MOTHER [*hastily and with a note of fear in her voice*]: No. No. Don't take her fork ... actually, it doesn't matter whether it's your fork or Sophie's fork, but—take your own fork.

Opher finished eating and asked if he could try on Sophie's wig. Sophie was glad to let him try.

MOTHER [*again with a note of fear*]: Don't let him try on Sophie's wig.

MIRI: Why not?

MOTHER: He'll stretch it out.

MIRI: That's nonsense. Opher's head is much smaller than Sophie's.

SOPHIE: Cut it out, already. [*Addressing her mother*] What are you afraid of? I don't have lice.

The fourth encounter was a meeting between Sophie's mother and the doctor caring for Sophie. We see the discrepancy between the fine external appearance of the patient and the progress of the disease, and the difficulty of relying on external signs.

We present part of the conversation between Sophie's mother and the doctor.

MOTHER: What's more important—how Sophie looks and feels, or what's happening inside her body? ... What's strangest of all is that the person who looks least sick ... most tan ... most healthy ... is actually the sickest. ... Sophie looks so good, and yet she's so sick. ... What are her chances? [*Entreating*] Maybe she's among the 10 percent who recover from the disease?

DOCTOR: The treatment has been helping her; but you must know that she can't be cured.

MOTHER: What does that mean? I was convinced the sickness was receding.

DOCTOR: There's been a temporary remission; but she cannot be cured.

MOTHER: What does that mean? Can she go on living this way 20 years, getting treatment? or is it a short-range ...

DOCTOR: I want you to know that there will come a time when we can no longer keep the disease under control.

MOTHER: In other words, the chemotherapy won't overcome the growth?

DOCTOR: That's correct.

MOTHER: But you said there was a remission.

DOCTOR: Yes. But the remission will come to an end, and we have no control over that.

MOTHER: Will the growth take over?

DOCTOR: Yes.

MOTHER [*turning pale*]: It's something that gives no rest. When we see her she looks wonderful. She laughs, horses around, just like she used to. ... If someone on the outside were to see her, they wouldn't know what she had ... who knows how many years she's been going around with this ... it's terrible to think that maybe she's had it since she was a baby ... tell me doctor. Is there some medical center somewhere in the world where you would recommend taking her? We're prepared to sell all we have to get her the very best care ... we've also written to whomever we could ... all over the world. ... about natural medicine ... is there anything in it?

DOCTOR: I'm sorry to say, but we don't believe in it. ...

The fifth encounter, two months later, in Miri's house. In this encounter we see, among other things, the fear of contagion and its connection with the visual image of the patient.

MIRI: Sophie was at the hospital today for chemotherapy. I was so afraid to go with her ... I'm afraid to be near her ... all the time I'm riddled with fear that I might look O.K., and yet be sick with it. Actually, I know I have it. I'm sure of it ... and when I'm with her, I can't run away from the fact that we're going to die. ... When Sophie gets chemotherapy she has a headache that day and she wants to sleep ... and at home her friends bother her ... so today I wanted to suggest that she come over to my place to rest after the treatment and that in the evening I would bring her home. ... I was about to suggest that she come over ... but suddenly I stopped myself ... and I thought ... where would she sleep in my house? On what bed? I'm afraid ... afraid to have her sleep in our house. ... Today I also went to her doctor so he could explain to me about the disease. He told me that by the time they discover the growth it's already been there for about nine years ... I hardly heard the rest of what he said ... I remembered Sophie when she was small, with her blonds curls. A wonderful little girl. Lately I've found myself longing for Sophie for hours on end, remembering how she looked when she was a baby. She was a beautiful baby. ... Was she sick then, too? I really went into a panic. All the time I look around and imagine that we all have it. ... Do all the people around me have it? ... The doctor also said that it might be that the conditions for the emergence of the cancer existed since she was five and that they waited ... and waited ... until a catalyst came along ... they waited all those years ... the cancer waited ... it's monstrous. ... I look at myself ... my surroundings ... and I don't know who I am ... suddenly I'm afraid that my body ... I don't recognize it ... I'm actually repulsed by myself ... like a yoyo. I look at Sophie, she's indefinable ... and then it transfers to me ... I, too, am incoherent. ...

[*Silence.*]

Suddenly I began to come to the realization that Sophie is going to die quickly. I look at her with a sort of look that knows that she'll die ... but she looks wonderful. If someone were to see her he wouldn't know what she has ... what does she have? They said that the disease is spreading. What does that mean? I try to imagine it ... does it pass through the blood stream? ... All the time I see this cancer growing and growing, ... penetrating deeper and deeper ... does it rot? Is it decay? I actually see a visual image of how it progresses, ... this cancer ... will it fill up her entire body? Will it burst out? Where will it erupt? ... She looks so wonderful. Strangers would never guess her secret ... but I see death ... she has a particular smell. The smell of death ... I kiss her because I must, but I find it disgusting ... she has a sallow color ... perhaps I'm imagining ... she's half dead. ... You can't talk with her about the future ... she's not a complete person. ... I'm afraid of her dying. ... What'll I say to her? ... And what a marvelous baby she was ... I keep on turning back to her picture album ... who would have believed this was a girl without a future? ... Dad is angry at Sophie for kissing everyone on the mouth ... why do you have to kiss on the mouth, he says. ... Sophie's also insulted that the friends of the family don't eat with us. ... Dad says it's because Sophie always eats from the common plate.

The sixth encounter, three months after the previous one. Those present included Sophie's mother and father, and her sister Ziva, ten years older than Sophie. Here we see the feeling expressed that the patient is not a member of the family.

MOTHER: At the clinic they always ask us if there were other cases of cancer in our family.

FATHER: We haven't had any. None of us ever had cancer. ... I'm convinced that Sophie is not my daughter. [*Ziva, Sophie's sister, blanches, and her father continues jocularly*]: Your mother fixed me. I know it. Sophie's not my daughter ... they mixed her up in the hospital. ... [*Everyone laughs, yet the conversation is discomforting.*]

MOTHER: Sometimes I, too, have similar thoughts. If it's a hereditary disease, and no one in our family ever had cancer, how can it have struck her? ... On the other hand, I'm sure that I also had this disease. When I was 15, almost Sophie's age, I remember that I felt sick almost the entire year. But no one did anything about it, no one treated it, and it passed.

FATHER: I can't accept the fact that there's nothing to be done. That's awful. I'm convinced that abroad they know more. We'll take her to the very best place. ...

ZIVA: Here, in Israel, is the very best place ... but I heard there's some sort of possibility of implanting bone marrow from a relative ... maybe we should look into it? On the other hand—no ... I'm really afraid that if it's right, that they changed her in the hospital, then they'll discover it just now; they'll get hold of a donor and discover that we're not related ... and that she doesn't belong to our family.

MOTHER: Nonsense. Sophie looks just like me ... and I also had this disease.

FATHER: I'm convinced that she's getting better. You're pessimists ... it couldn't be that she's going ... I know that she'll be healthy ... just you wait and see.

MOTHER: What crushed me in the talk with the doctor was his saying that there's no connection between how she looks and the way the disease is spreading. Last week I hoped that the fact that she's getting more and more beautiful shows that she's overcoming the disease ... but it turns out that we've nothing to rely on. ... How can it be that the disease is spreading and she's becoming better and better looking?

The seventh encounter, in Ziva's house, one month later, again lends expression to the fear of contagion.

ZIVA: Mother came today, in the afternoon. ... She was so tense and pale. ... They had just come back from treatment, and the doctor had told them that Sophie must have radiation. ... Sophie heard it and went into a terrible depression. Until now she'd believed that she doesn't have cancer. Now she surely understands that she does. ... What so terrible ... is this going back and forth. That's the worst ... that each time some new thing descends on you like a wet blanket ... and each time you have to adjust to another thing ... you've already strained all your resources and it seems to you that you can live with it, that you can walk the tightrope without falling ... and then suddenly something else descends on you, plop. And then you're shaken to the core ... your previous resources are no longer any use ... and you have to develop new ones. And you don't have the strength. Nor do you have the confidence ... it's the lack of confidence. That's the worst. I feel completely undermined. All my defenses have left me ... I'm simply drowned in fear ... I'm completely vulnerable ... like my body has been broken into ... everything's broken into ... [*silence*].

I cry all day ... I'm so sorry for Sophie ... my husband says it's terrible. He looks at Sophie and knows that now she's laughing but that soon she'll no longer be. ... We talk about it ... yesterday I went to her doctor and he told me that its only a short while now ... that we should be prepared ... Sophie is so pathetic ... it's strange. None of us knows how long she's going to live. I could walk out into the street and be run over just like that ... or get a hemorrhage in the brain ... but with Sophie it's different. ... She's got a death sentence hanging over her head ... [*laughing cynically*] ... she's got a contract [*crying*]. ... People always ask, how long? If they say 20 years, let it be. By then maybe they'll discover a cure. But if they say only another few months, it's different. ... The fear just wells up in me ... I'm so scared for Sophie, and myself ... and for my husband ... and my children ... I tremble in fear especially when Sophie doesn't take care to fix her hair and put on her wig ... and then her hair is so thin ... and unkempt ... she comes over and I seethe with anger: why is she going around without her wig? Does she want to broadcast to the whole world about her disease? ... so that everyone will look at her? ... but then afterwards I get angry at myself. Poor thing. Sophie. Let her go around however she wants ... she's about to die and I'm busy with my fears. ... She came over in the afternoon and she was tired ... I suggested that she take a nap ... but all the time I kept thinking, where could she lie down? On P's bed? [*Her son's bed.*] But why should I endanger him? On my bed? But my kids sometimes sleep in my bed. ... Let's say I decided that I was willing to sacrifice myself ... to catch it ... but I'm not prepared to have my children catch it ... and anyway ... we all feel that the worst thing is the responsibility ... having to make decisions about another person's life ... having to force Sophie to go for treatments that they say are also carcinogenic ... what a lousy responsibility to have. ... On the other hand, when I talked about it yesterday with the nurse at the hospital, she told me that actually we have no responsibility. All in all Sophie's condition is as bad as can be. All her options are make-believe. They'll all lead to the same end ... and that's even worse. That we have no responsibility. That we have no choice. No control.

Like Flora's mother, Sophie's relatives, too, try to imagine what cancer looks like. That is, they try to form a concrete image of the internal manifestations of the disease. Yet we see the difficulty inherent in this. Like Flora's parents, Sophie's family thinks about the disease as something that spreads throughout a person, takes control, and bursts out by means of a smell or a sore.

The lack of clarity characterizing the attitude towards Sophie finds expression, first, in the perception of Sophie as a being without a future. The feeling that there is no point investing in Sophie's future is expressed also by the fact that the family put aside plans for buying a new apartment they had begun years earlier.

The attitude towards Sophie, with the message of incoherency that she emits, is characteristic of the attitude towards many cancer patients who are in a stage of remission. The family members experience distinct contradictions between the outward appearances of their loved one and his or her internal condition: between looking healthy on the outside yet harboring disease on the inside, between the external characteristics of a living person and the internal reality of a dying person. Sophie is perceived as a dead person who puts on the appearance of being alive.

This case also highlights the fear of contagion. We note that this fear is one of the prominent features of the image of cancer, and it is also expressed through the doubts voiced regarding Sophie's being truly a member of the family, doubts which were also raised regarding Flora. According to the mothers, contagiousness—or hereditariness—provides the principal evidence that Flora or Sophie belong to the family; whereas for the other relatives of these girls, statements about the sick girls belonging to the family are a threat to the existence of the family. Note that Hannah's father also reacted similarly.

In the last section we saw that heredity is identified with contagion. It seems that the people I observed identify hereditary tendencies with contagion both when dealing with disabilities and retardation as well as with diseases such as cancer. The tendency to perceive heredity as "something contagious within the family" exists among people from various ethnic backgrounds, different levels of education, and different socioeconomic classes. There are also other elements in the way Sophie's relatives behaved that are common to many other families whom I observed, without regard to their ethnic or educational background. Firstly, the members of the family feel they bear a certain responsibility for their daughter having come down with cancer; the mother, through clothing, and the sister Miri, by "magic." Leah's mother also related to her own body as a potential carrier of cancer germs from another cancer patient to her daughter. Secondly, we see a prominent desire to isolate Sophie from other members of the family due to the danger of possible contagion. Another matter implied by the mother's remarks concerns the notion of natural resistance or immunity, a concept which also often appears with regard to retarded children. To understand this concept better, we consider the following incident.

Avram, a 28-year-old living in an ultra-Orthodox neighborhood, came to the local health clinic with his retarded three-year-old daughter. Taking a diaper dripping with urine, he wiped the drool off his daughter's mouth.

NURSE: What are you doing?

FATHER: I can't stand her drooling. It drives me crazy. We're very careful about always wiping up the drool.

NURSE: Are you out of your mind? You take a diaper soaked with pee and put it on your girl's mouth?!

FATHER: What are you getting so upset about?

NURSE: It's full of germs ... filthy ... and besides, it's disgusting ... would you wipe your own mouth with a diaper full of pee?

FATHER: No, ... but don't get so upset. She's immune.

The father's attitude here sheds light on the way many parents use the notion of immunity. When they speak of a person who is immune, they mean someone who is infected. Therefore there is no sense protecting him, because he is immune. Those who need to be protected are the healthy, weak individuals, who are not immune. It seems that in every family there is a sort of consensus regarding which members of the family, in addition to the mother, are allowed to come into contact with the sick person, to be "immunized," to be sacrificed and risk contagion.

CONCLUSION

In Chapter 1 we saw that parents reject children whose external appearance does not meet their aesthetic criteria. In this chapter we have seen that parents' behavior is not a response to the actual bodies of their children, but rather to their images of their children's bodies and to the way they picture their children's external appearance.

Often a change in image goes hand in hand with an actual physical change. The importance of the image is most pronounced in those cases where there is no correlation between the actual physical changes in the child's body and the image associated with the child; in such cases it is easy to see conclusively that the parent's response pertains to his or her image of the child. This is especially clear in the behavior of parents of Down's syndrome children, as described in this chapter.

The importance of the visual image of a disease is brought out by the tendency of parents of children with cancer to draw a physical image of the disease in their minds and to visualize its spread throughout the body.

It should be noted that we are not dealing with a need to understand the inside of the body; the X-ray of a child with cancer is not significant in determining his or her parent's relationship to him or her. In our opinion, the pictorial image of the disease ("how it looks") is a factor of great importance in understanding how people relate to cancer patients.

We also presented cases of cancer patients and Down's syndrome children whose appearances do not exactly belie their conditions, and who represent a fundamental lack of clarity due to their similarity, on the one hand, and their dissimilarity, on the other, to normal persons. The parents of a retarded child are not doomed to live with this threatening lack of clarity regarding the child's identity, since the culture provides them a visual image of a retarded child, which is very different externally from that of a normal child. The child's identity thus appears clear and unequivocal.

Cancer patients, on the other hand, present a threat to the family due to the basic lack of clarity resulting frequently from the fact that the patient's looks appear to contradict what is transpiring within his or her body; moreover, there is no clear culturally determined image (such as in the case of a retarded child) that can be invoked to solve the problem of lack of clarity. Our cultural repertoire of images does not include a clear image of a cancer patient. We have no ready-made association connecting cancer with a certain external appearance. Therefore, contact with a cancer patient does not automatically entail any concrete imagery. The immediate association is of the disease spreading through the body. The only image at the parents' disposal, therefore, is their visual image of the disease, which relates to an abstract notion and does not carry with it any automatic course of action.

These last remarks can help us explain why we do not relate to cancer as we relate to a disease or defect that can be concealed. The findings show that we perceive a disability as a defect that can be disguised only when the image of the disease (or defect) is clearly focused and there is no fear of it spreading and erupting to the outside (as in the case of a heart defect, which is perceived as focusing on one internal organ). The image of cancer, in contrast, is of an abstract, spreading entity, that is likely to erupt to the outside at any moment.

The lack of clarity regarding the image of cancer is expressed by the fact that cancer is not perceived as an external disease, but also it is not a purely internal disease that remains hidden within the body.

Lastly, the confusion regarding the image of the cancer patient and the patterns of behavior towards him or her is expressed by the "infection" attributed to the disease.

Cancer, like retardation, is also associated with dirt. In this case, however, the "dirt" is internal, and the parents, finding it hard to grasp the notion of internal dirt, try to convert their notion of infection from an abstract, intangible notion to something more tangible. They do this primarily through their unceasing search for some sort of opening, some aperture through which the dirt can come out. Sometimes the aperture they seek takes the form of a lesion, whose scar they often scrub mercilessly. Also the smell which is associated with the infection inherent in the image of the cancer patient makes it difficult to view the infection concretely. In contrast to the clinginess associated with the retarded child, which requires, so the parents feel, an unequivocal response of pushing away, the smell associated with the cancer patient is a far more abstract and intangible concept.

Thus, despite certain shared elements, there are also differences between the components of the image of the cancer patient and that of the retarded person, and these differences are what account for the difference in attitude towards them. Retarded children have images which make it possible to put stigmas on them and reject them; cancer patients, in contrast, are perceived as having two contradictory identities (that of the child and that of the cancer), and their images do not enable stigmatization and rejection.

It must be stressed that the lack of clarity regarding the cancer patient does not lie solely in the fact that medicine has no clear conception of the disease; for there are other diseases about which medicine knows far more, and yet the parents' attitudes are not necessarily determined by the medical conceptions of the disease, but by their fantasized associations. For example, often parents have no better an understanding of heart disease than of cancer, yet this disease is clearer to them in their world of associations.

The discussion of retarded children and cancer patients in this chapter can help us relate to a number of questions that remain open from previous chapters. For example, in Chapters 1 and 2 I presented cases of children whose looks were especially abnormal and who were associated with the concept of a "non-person" and thus rejected by their parents. In this chapter we saw that the less prominent a child's abnormality, the harder it is to locate him cognitively and the more distressing the resultant cognitive lack of clarity. The parents are afraid of a child who in most respects is similar to them, but is different from them in a respect that is considered culturally significant. Such a child is more of a borderline case than a monstrous child. The fear of contagion ("fear that we have caught it ... that we are like him") and the threat to the parents' self-image ("who are we?") is more pronounced when the child is only a little bit different from them than when he or she is completely different. This issue will be examined in greater detail in the next chapter.

In Chapter 2 I maintained that situations of lack of clarity are generally resolved by putting a stigma on the child and defining him or her as a "non-person," as being "contaminated." But I did not clarify a number of fundamental questions such as: is there cultural guidance that helps the individual deal with borderline cases? Are there situations in which the individual does not receive such cultural guidance? Is the sense of chaos resolved in every instance? What happens when the parents do not manage to reconstruct their cognitive system and the child remains incomprehensible and continues to violate existing boundaries and images? In this chapter I answered these questions primarily by means of my discussion of retarded children and cancer patients, whose looks do not attest their ailment. For example, we saw that the sense of chaos is resolved in cases of retardation, for here one has cultural guidance which leads to the rejection of the retarded child; but the feeling of chaos remains in the case of a cancer patient.

Lastly, according to the findings presented in this chapter, it is clear that there are also body images of sick persons and images of their diseases. Our repertoire includes images of a disease which are independent of our medical knowledge of the disease. It turns out that there is something common in the way we perceive a disease and in the features that we attribute to it. The image of a disease includes features that are attributed to the disease and that concern its visual aspect—how we see the disease—and its cognitive aspect—our beliefs regarding the disease. Most researchers have focused on the cognitive aspect of the disease, whereas in this chapter I have related to both aspects. Like those researchers who related to the metaphor of the disease, to the beliefs and stereotypes associated with it, here too I stressed the importance of the beliefs pertaining to the etiology and method of transmission of certain diseases, which often contradict medical fact. Our principal innovation here pertains to the importance of the visual image of the disease, that is to the way people perceive diseases and sick people. There is a connection between the two components of the image: the content of the image of a disease relates the perception of the disease to the beliefs held about it.

Thus my findings lay emphasis on aspects of the image of a disease that are different from those stressed in other studies. For example, here I stress the fear of contagion by diseases that are not contagious, or the special smell attributed to a person with cancer that tends to pass also to those around him or her; whereas other studies either disagree about these characteristics or else claim they are negligible.

Discussing the importance of the child's body image also made it possible to extend the concept of body image beyond its prevalent understanding in the literature. Most researchers use the term "body image" to refer to the way people perceive their own bodies. In this chapter I have extended the meaning of this term to include the way people perceive other's bodies. I have found that the way people relate to others, as well as the way they relate to themselves, is influenced by a perceived body image and not the actual bodies of others.

NOTES

1. Our study includes 170 children with Down's syndrome. See Appendix, Table 1.

2. The plastic surgery performed on Down's syndrome children in Israel is described in Wexler et al., 1987. Similar operations were performed on some of the children whom I observed.

3. The fact that the parents say one thing and its opposite will be discussed later on.

4. This finding perhaps matches one of the findings in Wexler et al., 1987. The study found that the more sharply focused the expectations, the more satisfied the Down's syndrome children and their parents were from the results. The more general the expectations, the lower the level of satisfaction from the results of surgery. In other words, if the Down's syndrome child

and his or her parents are of the opinion that "the big tongue and slanted eyes" are the problem, then most likely they will be satisfied by the results of surgery; but if their expectations are that the child "will look better," yet they are unable to define more precisely what changes they are interested in, then the surgery is likely not to live up to their expectations.

5. This datum is different from that generally found among Down's syndrome children, who, the older they get, the more prominent their signs of the syndrome.

6. Most of these patients were at a stage of remission.

7. Cerebral palsy: a type of paralysis subsuming a group of non-degenerative motorial disturbances, stemming from improper functioning of the motorial nerve centers of the brain. The brain defect results in disturbances in the form of partial paralysis, weakness, poor coordination, and other motor disturbances. The damage to the brain occurs before the central nervous system is fully developed, i.e., prenatally or at birth. Most of the children with this disease also suffer from other disturbances such as convulsions, mental retardation, and learning disabilities. There are also serious behaviora; problems and emotional disturbances that can be improved through proper education. The basic disease is not progressive and cannot be treated aside from the supportive treatment that enables the patient to lead as normal a life as possible.

4

The Breached Fortress

Parental Responses to Violation
of Their Children's Body Boundaries

What are our body boundaries? In what contexts do we feel that the line demarking a person's body has been breached?

What is it we find threatening about the violation of another person's body boundaries? What assumptions about the essence of man, woman and the human body are challenged by the violation of body boundaries? These are some of the questions dealt with in this chapter.

First I shall review the treatment of this subject in the literature?[1]

Polhemus (1978, pp. 28, 176–180) discusses the concept of body boundaries. Does a person's body end at her skin? Does the body include one's hair, fingernails, secretions (feces, tears, sweat, urine, hair, fingernail trimmings) and artificial decorations of the body (such as tattoos)? The social aspects of the human body do not necessarily end at the physical boundaries of the body, rather they extend outwards to include one's clothing and ornaments. Fischer (1978), too, maintains that the body and the garments and ornaments on it should not be treated separately, but rather should as a single subject of investigation.

Anthropologists have investigated the concept of body boundaries in different societies. Douglas discusses symbolic aspects of bodily secretions, protection of body boundaries, and societal influences on each of these subjects (1966, pp. 114–128). She maintains that the human body should be viewed as a metaphor for society, as symbolizing or resembling society (1970, pp. 65–81; 1975, pp. 83–89).

Postal (1978) investigates the approach of two different societies towards body boundaries by analyzing the content of their folk tales, myths, and autobiographies. She maintains (p. 123) that the image of body boundaries is central in forming one's identity; it enables the individual to distinguish himself from others in his surroundings, and thus provides the foundation for a sense of identity. There are societies where a change in dress and external appearance expresses a change in identity and status. The name by which a person is called is interpreted as one's "verbal dress." Thus a change in a person's name expresses a change in her identity and status, since a name, just like a garment, delimits the boundaries between the individual and the external world.

The connection between secretions, body boundaries, and identity is discussed by Loudon (1977) in an investigation of whether the body's secretions are part of the body. He maintains that one of the ways a baby begins to be conscious of herself as a separate being is through her secretions, primarily feces. Most people are not at all sensitive to their own body secretions, but find the smells and secretions that come from the bodies of others repulsive.

Loudon relies on the sense of smell as indicative of a person's ability to distinguish himself from others around him. It should be noted, however, that there is no consensus among researchers on the importance of the sense of smell in interpersonal communication in modern society. It is widely held that the sense of smell is more highly developed in primitive societies than in modern ones, and that therefore this sense plays a more prominent role in governing behavior among primitive peoples (Loudon, 1977, p. 164); whereas in modern society the senses of sight and hearing are most significant to verbal and nonverbal communication. Some people maintain that the sense of smell is also important to modern man and woman. Childhood reminiscences, for example, often surface in the form of recollection of specific smells (Loudon, 1977, p. 164). Discussing body secretions raises the question whether body products should be viewed as part of the body, as an extension of the body, or whether they are external to the body? I shall relate to this question by considering how various researchers view the social aspects of a person's hair.

According to Morris (1977, pp. 222–252, pp. 233–234) the basic need of primitive primates to groom one another's fur was transformed by our naked ancestors, becoming in the full of time what we now call "civilized conversation." The prominent crop of hair that remained on a person's head became a treasured possession. Having found no outlet, the mutual cleaning instinct—one of the basic animal instincts—led to the emergence of "professional groomers" such as barbers, hairdressers, cosmeticians, and masseurs (Yavsam Azgad, 1983). Indeed, hair care is a universal practice in every human culture (Adamson, 1972, p. 108).

With respect to the artistic, social, and communicatory significance of African hair styles, Dagon (in Yavsam Azgad, 1983) describes the African practice of men combing their fellow men's hair, and women combing their fellow women's hair. African hair styles are made as a complement to the structure of the body and carry a communicatory message: a fellow tribesman can identify a woman's tribal affiliation, age, number of children, and husband by looking at her hairdo. The practice of scalping, once prevalent among Native North Americans, also carries a communicatory message;

scalping victims serves to deny their humanity by changing them into inanimate objects or animals (*ibid*). Thus hair is not only ornamental, but it also symbolizes one's social status (Adamson, 1972, p. 108). Changes are made in a person's hair to express a ritual transition from one state to another; for example, there are societies in which a bride's head is shaved when she marries and a youth's head is shaved when he is initiated into manhood (Evans-Pritchard, 1956, p. 231).

When a man grows his hair long, some researchers interpret this behavior as indicative of his rebelling against societal control, as in the case of long-haired intellectuals (Hallpike, 1978, pp. 141–142). According to this theory, cutting one's hair is symbolic of belonging to society or consenting to submit to discipline. Thus haircutting equals societal supervision. Cutting a prisoner's or a soldier's hair, for example, symbolizes his duty to submit to discipline.

A different approach is presented by Leach (1958), who developed a theory of hair and body symbolism based on the psychoanalytic thesis that shaving and haircutting should be perceived as an act of castration or as restricting one's sexuality.

There are also anthropological theories that view hair treatment in terms of its relation with the soul (Frazer, 1922, p. 230; Hallpike, 1978, p. 139); hair that is cut in a ritual setting is viewed as part of the individual from whom it has been cut. In rites of transition a prominent place is held by actions in which magical powers are attributed to something cut from the individual, such as blood, hair, or fingernail trimmings (Frazer, 1922). Primitive societies think of man as an entity having various extensions, and the magical practices of these societies often involve a person's hair, fingernail trimmings, blood, secretions, personal names, clothes, footprints, and shadow. All of these, according to Hallpike, symbolize the person from who they have been taken and are considered an extension of the body. In burial rites among the Nuer one must wash and purify not only the deceased, but also the deceased's possessions (Evans-Pritchard, 1956, p. 151).

The multiple significance attributed to the hair on a person's head explains why, in practicing magic, hair symbolizes the entire person. First, it is part of the bodily extensions of the individual. Second, being situated on the head, it is associated with the spirit and the soul. Third, because it never ceases to grow it is a clear symbol of vitality. Thus, due to its physical characteristics, like a person's dress, hair can express changes in social or ritual status (Hallpike, 1978, p. 139).

The question of whether hair is part of the body or an extension of it leads to the general question of extensions. Psychologists involved in rehabilitating amputees after prosthesis have grappled with the question of how artificial limbs should be viewed. Should they be incorporated into the person's body image? Or should they be viewed as tools, or perhaps as bodily extensions? (Thalidomide, 1963.)

In this chapter I shall answer questions such as: how do people react to changes in another person's hair or bodily secretions, to a person being attached to medical instruments, to becoming obese, or to foul odors that come from another person's body? Are all these things viewed as part of the body, as an extension of the body, or as something external to the body? Which of our sensory perceptions is the most important? In what contexts does our sense of sight predominate, and when are our responses guided by smell? Is it true that the sense of smell plays a negligible role in directing the actions of modern woman and man? What significance is attributed to hair? How do we relate to personal names? to clothes? to shadows? Are all these interpreted as symbolizing the person to whom they belong? Are they viewed as external to others? Does the modern individual perceive woman or man as a being with bodily extensions? Do perceptions of body boundaries vary in a way that can be attributed to differences in education, ethnic and national background, residence, or degree of religiosity?

These general questions shall be investigated in this chapter in the context of relations of parents towards ill or physically handicapped children. The literature on parental attitudes towards abnormal children does not relate to violation of body boundaries. Our findings, in contrast, stress the importance of body boundaries.

We shall describe the reactions of various parents to their sense of violation of the body boundaries of their children. This violation of boundaries takes place in a variety of contexts and suggests a change in the child's identity. We shall see that violation of a child's body boundaries intimates to her parents a violation of their own body boundaries, threatening to infect them, too, and thus placing their own identities in danger. According to parents' perceptions, the body boundaries of their children serve to protect the body interior from coming out and prevent external factors from penetrating within. In addition, body boundaries help distinguish between a child and others around him. Thus they are the basis for one's sense of identity and uniqueness; consequently, when they are violated one ceases to be able to discern the individual's unique identity and to distinguish between the individual and others in the person's surroundings.

We begin our discussion by presenting the behavior of Bedouin Arab parents towards their daughter Yousra (previously encountered in Chapter 1), who had an opening for exhalation made in her trachea.

CASE 20 "HER JUICE WILL COME POURING OUT"

Yousra's parents, as we recall, are Bedouin Arabs living in a tribe in the northern part of Israel. They are literate both in Hebrew and Arabic, and have two other children.

Yousra, seven months old at the time of our observations, is a Bedouin baby who was admitted to the children's ward several months earlier due to a severe throat infection. She is a lively child and keeps herself amused. Whenever a visitor enters the room she tries to grab hold of the person's clothing, smiles at the person and puts out her hands, as if requesting to be picked up. She is the favorite of all the parents in the room; they smile at her, play with her, cuddle her, and feed her.

In contrast to the loving attention that she receives from various adults who come to her room, she seldom receives a visit from her parents. When her parents brought her to the hospital four months earlier with severe respiratory problems, they were told that her life was in danger. During the first few days of her hospitalization her parents did not leave her bedside. Even when she was transferred to the respiratory intensive care unit and underwent an operation her parents did not leave the ward, even for the night. Several days later the parents were told that their daughter would be released from the hospital with an open trachea. The parents were given detailed information about caring for their daughter, about the possibility of availing themselves of nearby medical services, and about the need for another operation in several months to close the trachea. The parents, both Hebrew speakers, fully understood the explanation given them by the medical staff, but remarked, "This is the first time we've seen a child going around with an open throat ... it will frighten everyone. ... No one will recognize her. ... It's queer for a girl to go around with something in her throat ... people will think she's retarded ... they'll think she's dead. ... No one will want to play with her ... they'll be afraid of her." After this consultation the parents went home and from that time on ceased visiting their little girl. The Arab social worker, from the same tribe as the parents, was asked to explain to them the importance of not severing their ties with their girl.

After having no contact with their daughter for two months, the parents reluctantly came to the ward ("They did me a favor," the social worker said). The doctor explained to them that their daughter was recovering, developing well, and was the favorite of all the parents and nurses. "We won't force you to take your daughter home," he said. "If it's hard for you, you can leave her here, and stay at her side as you did before. It's important for her that you be here. She looks for you ... especially since you live so close to the hospital."

Nevertheless, the parents only took a momentary glance at their daughter, then returned home. Since then they have come to see her once every two months; each time they place a little toy on her bed, sit down far from her bed, and after a short while leave the ward.

On their last visit the mother tried to explain how she felt: "I am afraid to play with her. ... Even if I want to play with her sometimes, I'm afraid to do so. ... I force myself to forget her."

AUTHOR: But the doctors say she will be healthy. She's improving from day to day. All of us here love her.

MOTHER: So why does she have a hole in her throat? Ever since she has had that hole in her throat she has had the look of death in her eyes. ... It looks like a black hole to me. ... I'm always afraid something will come spilling out of it.

AUTHOR: Nothing can come spilling out. It's just an opening to let in air.

MOTHER: Yes. I understand. But I'm afraid her juice will come pouring out through there ... that she'll vomit from there. ... And besides, no one among us has ever heard of such a thing as a child with a hole in the throat. Never has a child looking like that been see in our midst before. They'll say the Jews slit her throat. She won't ever be able to be like a regular girl. ...

Initially Yousra's parents established a warm and close relationship with their daughter and cared for her with devotion. Their intentions to abandon her and the partial realization of these intentions only emerged in the wake of an opening having been made in her trachea. As with many other parents, the fact that no real change had taken place in their daughter's body did not effect the parents' attitude towards her. They focused on the opening made for exhalation of air—the result of the operation—an opening which aroused their fears that the interior of her body would not remain inside, but would come out. They perceived the opening as enabling the interior of their girl's body to burst out. Thus the opening made them feel that their girl's body boundaries could not protect her body interior; the opening challenged their basic assumption that certain substances and organs are intended to remain internal and must not be allowed out.

CASE 21 "LIKE MACHINES BEING OPERATED BY SOMEONE ELSE"

This case presents another aspect of a child connected to a medical instrument. Margalit, a 35-year-old native Israeli of Eastern European extraction, is a university lecturer and the mother of an 8-year-old son. Her son, having been hospitalized in Southern Hospital as a result of an automobile accident, was hooked up to a monitor and a respirator.[2] Several days after being admitted to the hospital he was transferred from the children's ward to the respiratory intensive care unit. Most of the patients there receive artificial respiration and all are connected to several instruments.

Let us listen to part of a conversation that took place between Margalit and the head nurse, two days after her son had been transferred to intensive care.

Margalit entered the room. Looking confused, she stood there awkwardly, passing a handkerchief from hand to hand.

MARGALIT: I'll go have a talk with the doctors.

NURSE: There's no need to. You just talked to them half an hour ago.

MARGALIT: Still, I want to have a word with them.

NURSE: Why don't you relax? ... All day long you've been going in and out of the ward ... always moving around. ... You've already been told that your son is no longer in critical condition. Look, you can put your hand on him. [*The nurse took Margalit's hand and placed it on her son's hand; but Margalit immediately withdrew her hand from her son's.*]

MARGALIT: I can't stay put. ... Maybe I should make him a cup of tea? or go bring him something?

NURSE: A cup of tea? What for? I can't understand you parents! ... We try to encourage the patients' families to sit and talk with them, and you just don't seem to understand how important it is. Every minute you have something else you want to do, anything else but sit down next to your sick son.

MARGALIT: Intellectually, I understand perfectly well—only I just am not up to it. ...

NURSE: Why do you withdraw from him? Why do you stand so far from his bed? It seems that you force yourself to get close to him, but then a minute later I see that you're drawing away. ... Why can't you look him straight in the eyes?

MARGALIT: You're no better ... you, too, treat the patients as if they weren't human. ...

NURSE: Who, us? What have we done to him?

MARGALIT: You've connected him to so many tubes, and you pumping everything into his body through them. Even your own will. The medical staff forces him to breath when he's not breathing ... forces him to give urine when he's not peeing ... forces him to raise his blood pressure when it's low, and lower it when it's high ... forces food into him when he can't actually eat. ... No one asks him if he wants it or doesn't. ... That's also why the staff can't manage to protect the individuality of its patients, or their privacy ... because the patients actually have no personality, or privacy. ... All the families here claim that the atmosphere in the patients' room reminds them of a factory ... that the patients are like machines being operated by someone else. ... We also feel suddenly ... that our child doesn't belong to the family any more ... maybe he belongs to the medical staff more than to his family. ...

Margalit's remarks shed light on the connection between protecting body boundaries and maintaining a sense of individualism and privacy. When patients are deprived of their privacy by being hooked up to medical instruments, they come to be viewed like objects, so much so that in the eyes of family and staff they are perceived as having lost their humanness. Loss of one's human likeness due to loss of one's individuality and privacy is also related to the setting in the intensive care unit. The medical instruments and the noise made by the various instruments calls to mind the "atmosphere of a factory" and makes parents view their children as machines.

In this connection, we must recall the attitudes of parents of premature babies to their newborns. In Chapter 1 I mentioned the subject of medical instruments and described how mothers of premature babies connected to medical instruments form weaker bonds with their infants than mothers of newborns of normal weight. There are several reasons for the reluctance to have close contact with a premature baby connected to medical instruments. Firstly, the instruments make it harder for the parents to identify their child as a unique individual: "He doesn't look like a person." Many parents make remarks such as, "Everywhere you look, he's hooked up to another machine." The parents of a 5-week-old premature baby said, "You can't see that he's a child. You can't know if he's happy, good-looking, lively. You can't actually know anything about him, because everything's just medical instruments." Such remarks are typical of many of the parents whom I observed.

Furthermore, many parents, immediately upon entering the premature baby ward look at the chart on their child's incubator or on the monitor their baby is connected to, but not at their child. Or perhaps they look at the thermometer, or some other instrument—at anything except their baby. In other words, they ascertain the condition of their baby by studying the instrumentation she is hooked up to, and not by relating directly to their child, to her actual body.

This was also the case with Margalit, whom we have just met. She said, "I look at the monitor constantly, afraid it will beep. ... Yesterday suddenly it started beeping, and I ran to the nurse like a madwoman ... and the nurse said to me, 'Why get so excited? ... Don't you see that your son looks fine? You know your son better than the monitor ... so why get so worked up if the monitor starts beeping?' She's right. But I don't recognize my son now ... with all those tubes ... I don't trust myself. ... At home I know him ... at home I trust myself ... but here I rely on the instruments ... I *have* to look at the monitor. It's as if his heart has come out. I don't know who he is now. At home, when his heart is inside and his hands don't have holes in them, I know him by how he looks on the outside; and I know myself, too. But now, it's as if his heart is on the outside. And he doesn't recognize me now, either."

Later, she added, "His eyes are strange ... like a dark shadow ... black. ... I'm afraid of the new being that looks at me now through my child. ... He gazes at me as if he knows me and at the same time does not know me.

... He scrutinizes me and doesn't take his eyes off me. He doesn't let me get away ... and when I take my eyes off him for a moment he chases after me with his eyes. ... But I don't know him, and I don't understand him. ... I know his body. But is the monitor like his body? Is the monitor part of his body? Is this instrument there instead of his heart? Is he showing me his heart? But I am not accustomed to seeing my boy's heart. What person knows his child's heart? Suddenly people want me to know my child by his heart. I know everything I'm saying sounds really strange. I know I'm an educated woman and I'm supposed to understand all these instruments and accept them; but it's not that simple. I'm constantly imagining all sorts of things. It seems to me that my son's body has been torn apart and that his internal organs are coming out of him. As if, on account of his heart coming out, there's no more boy there; only a heart. And it frightens me [*crying*]. I don't know my boy any more. And I don't even know myself. I'm so confused. ... Maybe this mother ought to introduce herself to her son's heart."

Margalit's behavior, which is similar to that evinced by many other parents, illustrates the feeling of violation of body boundaries and the fear that internal organs, such as the heart, will come out of the body. This makes it necessary to relate to organs that generally lay hidden in the body, and accordingly to relate to the child.

When dealing with children who are not connected to medical instruments, parents look for external indications which they use to interpret, among other things, the medical condition of their child; for example, lips turning black, or cheeks turning pink, as indicating a deterioration or an improvement in their child's condition. But when children are connected to medical instruments, parents reduce (and sometimes altogether eliminate) their reliance on observation of bodily changes in their child as evidence of the child's condition, and instead come to rely on the instruments. This is especially noticeable when dealing with older children whose parents, prior their children's hospitalization, relied on external physical characteristics. In the hospital, the parents' prior indicators for knowing their children cease to be significant, and they come to know their children by the information provided them by the medical instruments. In all the intensive care units I have mentioned—i.e., cardiac, neuro-surgical, recovery wards for post-operative patients (after heart and lung surgery), and respiratory units— the patients are connected to more medical instruments than in regular wards.

In contrast to the practice in regular children's wards, where family members are generally permitted to remain with their children and care for them all hours of the day and night, in most of the intensive care wards parents are not permitted to remain constantly with their children. In intensive care wards family members often sit in the hall or at the entrance to the

ward and continually request permission from the medical staff to come in
and see the patient. But when finally permitted to enter, they generally
come in two at a time and remain for a relatively short period. Even when
they have been waiting all day for permission to enter, if entry is conditional upon only one person coming in at a time the parents sometimes
give up their visit or ask that they be allowed to take another family member in with them. Not only are parents afraid to enter alone; they also
conclude their visits remarkably quickly, even when explicitly permitted
to remain longer (half an hour to an hour) at the patient's side. During their brief stay in the patient's room, parents survey the equipment
in the room and look at the other patients, but generally avoid direct eye
contact with the patient belonging to their own family. In addition, their
insistence on maintaining physical distance from the patient's bed is particularly pronounced. Even when the nurse places chairs for them at the
patient's bedside, they move their chairs back to a distance from which they
cannot reach the patient. Most family members do not touch the patient
and do not address their conversation to her, despite the explicit encouragement of the nursing staff; and some even refrain from entering the patient's
room.

Let us illustrate our point with the remarks exchanged between one of
the nurses and an Egyptian-born mother, who had been waiting the entire
day to see her daughter.

NURSE: Your daughter will not be able to talk with you because of the
tube in her mouth. But she will be able to understand whatever you say to
her.

MOTHER: Oh, no. I don't want to bother her. She probably wants to
rest. I'll wait outside.

We maintain that the reluctance to come into contact with patients in
intensive care units is due primarily to the multiplicity of instruments connected to the patients; and that this instrumentation is what upsets the
parents' perception of their child's body and gives them the feeling of a violation of their child's body boundaries, thus adversely affecting their ability
to relate to their child in the ways to which they are accustomed.

CASE 22 "I KNOW MY CHILD WITHOUT HIS FECES"

This case deals with the sense of a violation of body boundaries that
arises when parents must see the excretions of their grown children, or
when unconventional openings are made for bodily excretions.

Adi, like Margalit in Case 21, is the mother of a ten-year-old who was
injured in an automobile accident. However, unlike Margalit, she is Israeli
born, of Egyptian extraction, has a tenth-grade education, and works as a

seamstress. Due to complications resulting from her son's accident, about one week after his hospitalization in Central Hospital the doctors decided to perform a colostomy[3] for the excretion of feces. Adi reacted with intense repulsion to seeing her son's feces situated "inside his stomach," as she said. Crying, she explained:

"It's horrible, his feces coming out of his stomach that way. It's frightening. I'm always afraid the bag will be too small, or that they won't hook it up right and all the ca-ca will come out and everything will get soiled. It's been years since I've seen my son's B.M. Maybe just for a second, in the toilet. But now they expect me to look at his excretions and report to the doctor if there's anything 'abnormal.' That's what they say. But his B.M. doesn't interest me. I know my boy without his B.M. Is he a baby, or a big boy? I'm all confused. I think about it so much. There's so much time to think here. Now they want me to recognize my son by his B.M. As if they want me to be the mother of a baby again. But now it turns my stomach."

Adi's behavior is typical of that often displayed by many other parents in circumstances where the actual encounter with the feces of grown children or with feces coming out of an unusual opening causes a sense of violation of body boundaries and hints at a change in the child's identity. In such circumstances the parents cease recognizing their children by their external appearance and begin understanding them, as it were, by their excrements. It should be noted that colostomy patients elicit more extreme reactions of repulsion the older they are. Contact with their feces is considered disgusting, especially when dealing with older children, and is generally approached similarly to the excretions of a retarded child.

Saliva dripping from the mouth also contradicts parental assumptions that secretions ought to remain concealed. The data presented in the previous chapter indicate that secretion of saliva also symbolizes a violation of body boundaries.

Like Loudon, I too am concerned with the connection between secretions, body boundaries, and identity. Loudon, however, focuses on the way a person begins to become aware of herself through her secretions; whereas I am interested in the place of bodily secretions in the process by which a person becomes cognizant of her fellow human beings.

Thus far I have discussed two situations in which parents have a sense of violation of their child's body boundaries: when a child is connected to medical instruments, and when parents must concern themselves with their child's secretions. Now I proceed to one more situation in which a child's body boundaries are violated and the child is perceived as having lost her identity: when the child's body, or part of it, swells or becomes abnormally large.

CASE 23 A HEAD "LIKE A BALLOON ABOUT TO BURST"

Haggar is a 6-month-old baby hospitalized in Northern Hospital due to a burn on her leg. In the hospital she contracted a fecal virus causing diarrhea. Her parents are 30 years old, native Israelis of Rumanian extraction. Her mother, a housewife with a college degree, and her father, a shopkeeper with a secondary-school education, have two other children and live in a town in the north of Israel. The mother spends the entire day at her baby's bedside, and the father visits frequently.

Due to loss of liquids, both as a result of the burn and of the diarrhea, the girl had intravenous tubes attached to her head. One morning when the mother awakened, she noticed in alarm that her daughter's head was extremely swollen. The mother's own description of the event follows:

"One morning I got up and saw that my girl's head looked like that of a retard ... big ... and strange. ... I was convinced my little girl was no more; that she had died and that the child I was looking at was some retard; and I started to cry. The doctors tried to calm me. They explained that the bag with the infusion had emptied and filled with air, and that that had caused her head to swell. They said I had nothing to worry about; that the swelling would go down. But meanwhile I called the store where my husband works and told him that our girl was "gone." That it was all over. That our girl was no more. Because that wasn't the head of our girl. Done for. Her head got out of place ... a head full of water. To me it looked like a balloon about to burst and spill everything all over me. I felt as if it was growing and growing, taking up the space for her body. Just a bit more, and it would have entered my body. Yes. It was just growing and growing, never stopping. I took fright. This wasn't my little girl. I couldn't recognize my little girl anymore. She was like a faceless balloon."

The external changes in Haggar's body are perceived as changes in the girl's identity, and the death of the "girl that once was" is described in no uncertain terms: "Our girl has gone ... died ... is no more." The mother mourns the death of her pretty little girl and views the girl lying before her as a being of uncertain identity, a being with no individualism, "a retarded child."

CASE 24 "HE DIDN'T HAVE A FACE; HE WAS JUST A BLOB"

Uri, a 2-year-old, was born to an elderly couple of Moroccan extraction. The parents, both of whom have a vocational education, reside in the south of Israel and have three other children. Uri was hospitalized in Central Hospital in a private room, due to severe burns from his head down to his chest. His mother and father took turns at his bedside, throughout the day and night. Let us describe the mother's behavior as observed in one of our sessions.

The mother lay on her back on Uri's bed, with her child on her stomach, face towards her. The heater and television were on, and the mother was half looking at the television as she told of the occurrences of the past few days:

"Uri was unconscious for at least two days. ... His head swelled up and was all red. It kept on getting more and more swollen; and his body looked smaller and smaller. Still, his head swelled more and more. I didn't know when it would stop; how big this head would get; how much more it would swell up. I was actually afraid his head would tear, that the skin on his head would tear open and everything would burst out ... that all this swelling would spill out. ... His face was distorted. You could hardly recognize him. ... I cried all week long, incessantly; I was hysterical. From Friday, when it happened, until Sunday I didn't eat a bite. I didn't eat at all. I only thought about what would happen ... that maybe he would become retarded ... that he would still have something inside ... would be retarded, or something ... and that he would not be able to function normally. ... Do you see Uri? [*Addressing the author*] You see him now? You see what a sweet boy he is? But you should have seen his face at first! He didn't have a face; he just had a blob. His face was hidden; everything was hidden. I was afraid that this wasn't my boy. He looked like a nightmare, not like a child. ... He's lucky that he's a healthy, well-developed kid and could overcome it. Let me tell you, we didn't believe he'd come through it alive. I've got to hand it to the doctors. The doctors and nurses here are simply marvelous. Thanks to them, Uri is alive. ... His condition is improving now. Now you can recognize him. Even the doctor thought he had made a mistake. The doctor came into the room, looked at Uri's bed, and said, "Whoops, that's not Uri," and left. But I called out to him, "Yes, it is Uri," and we both burst out laughing.

"It was such a pleasure. Now I come here all the time ... because he has a face once more, and he's back to being Uri again, and I'm no longer afraid to look at him. ... But when Uri was still in that serious condition and we couldn't see his face, then I was dreadfully afraid of him. He gave me nightmares ... I was afraid to see him. ... Then his two grandmothers were here more than I. Someone in the hospital even said to me, "What's this? You only come to see him for a couple of hours." Uri's brothers missed him. But I didn't bring them to see him until his face was better and looked like a face. I didn't want them to have a shock and not be able to sleep at night on account of it. What good would it have done for them to come any earlier? They wouldn't have recognized him anyway. He didn't look like Uri. He didn't look like a child at all; but like something else altogether. At first there wasn't a room available for Uri; so they gave us a bed in the corridor for the first three days. Everyone who walked by, even these Arab women, looked at Uri, and I saw how they recoiled; everyone made some comment, like, "poor thing," and all sorts of other remarks. So if strangers felt that way, and could not get close to him, but fled from him, what could you expect of his mother? I was just torn to pieces and couldn't bare to look at his face. I was depressed because of the others around me. I couldn't take it anymore, so I requested that he be transferred urgently to a room."

The extreme swelling of Uri's face gave his mother a feeling of violation of her son's body boundaries and hinted at the loss of his uniqueness. The child looked to her like a "blob," in the mother's words. Uri's mother's behavior, like that of other parents, clearly expresses a sense of the loss of the former identity of her child. Immediately after his burn, "He didn't have a face; he just had a blob. ... He looked like a nightmare." His former identity was hidden. The changes of the child's identity can also be seen in the mother's conversation with the doctor.

Extreme obesity is similar to swelling of the body in that it, too, arouses a sense of the body or part of it threatening to burst out, and the individual loses his uniqueness. The child's loss of uniqueness is attributed to her "loss of form," as various parents put it, and to the permission given, as it were, to the external world to penetrate into the child's body and take over the child's will. To illustrate our point, we cite some remarks made by a hospital orderly of Rumanian extraction, father of a 13-year-old boy who was hospitalized due to a serious infection in his leg. The child is very overweight, and the lack of proportion between his small head and abnormal body dimension is striking.

The father, irate at the medical staff, said, "It's true my son is fat ... he's awfully fat ... he really oozes all over the place ... he doesn't have a body; it's as if everything in him, in his body, is jelly that's just pouring out; as if at any moment he'll overflow onto everyone. But just because of that, it doesn't mean he should be treated this way. ... They treat my son as if he were a guinea pig. ... Look who takes blood from him? They sent some young, inexperienced doctor over here, and until he could get some blood out of him you could practically pass out ... they've gone just a bit too far. I'm an orderly and I know what I'm talking about. They think that because he's so fat they can do whatever they want with him ... that he's not a human being ... that he's a guinea pig ... they think that a person that fat has no feelings ... that they can let students practice on him. ... It doesn't occur to them that taking blood from him is actually twice as hard ... that he suffers ... that he is a person. ... It hurts me terribly. ... Sometimes I feel as if I just can't take all this fat anymore ... and that it'll overflow onto me at any moment ... and sometimes I, too, want to give him a pinch ... [*embarrassedly*] he wouldn't feel it, anyway. But I control myself. We are human, after all."

Thus, obesity joins the conditions discussed above in which a sense of violation of body boundaries is aroused and the individual loses his identity. Below we shall see that shaving children's heads or sudden loss of hair is also associated with such perceptions.

CASE 25 "HER HEAD CAN COME OUT"

Hadar is a two-year-old girl, hospitalized in Central Hospital due to a burn on her leg. Her mother was born in Russia, her father is Israeli-born of Tunisian extraction. The couple have a secondary school education, work as clerks in a government office, and live in the central part of Israel. Due to medical complications, the girl's head had to be shaved so she could be given an infusion through apertures in her head. Let us consider the mother's reaction to having her daughter's head shaved, a reaction similar to that of many other parents in analogous situations:

"Oh, look what they've done to her? ... Oh, dear! See how she looks! This isn't Hadar at all. ... [*Crying*] What have they done to you? It's some other girl, lying there. Not Hadar [*crying, she sits down far from her daughter's bed*]. Look what a beautiful girl I had [*taking a photo out of her bag*] what beautiful hair she had. ... Everyone used to comment on it ... but now they've shaved her head. ... I didn't want them to shave her."

The nurse came over and asked the mother to stroke her child: "She wants you to stroke her and calm her down." The mother approached her child, tried to touch her girl's shaved head, but recoiled as if she had received an electric shock, and said:

"It's really repulsive; those bumps on her head. I never knew she had such bumps on her head. Her head could actually come out. I stroked her head and I felt the glands inside. It's really frightening. What'll happen if her skin tears? After all, the skin on the scalp is very delicate; because there's always hair there. What will happen to it now?"

Like other parents, Hadar's mother attributes great importance to her child's hair and to its being shaved. The mother's remarks and behavior clearly reveal her feeling that her child's body boundaries have been violated and her identity lost. The body that she sees lying in the bed seems to her to be a foreign entity, not identifiable with her child. Like Batya, Hadar's mother also longs for the girl she once had, who, according to the mother's perceptions, is not embodied by the figure lying in front of her; to recall her daughter, she looks at the photos in her purse photos that were taken before her girl was hospitalized. Yigal's mother, whom we met in Chapter 1, also reacted in a similar manner. She cared for her son devotedly, but was repulsed by him when she discovered that his head had been shaved, and said, "I can't bare to see him. ... That's not my boy's face." But later, when Yigal's hair grew back, she said joyfully, "his hair is growing back. . . . Now he'll be my Yigal again ... with a face like Yigal."

The cases I observed show that shaving girls' hair does violence to their uniqueness and identity also because of its association with a reversal in their sexual identity. This is illustrated by the behavior of two mothers who come from different ethnic backgrounds and have different levels of education. Debby's mother[4] is of German background and has a college education; Mira's mother is of Iraqi background and has only a seventh-grade education.

Debby, a six-year-old hospitalized due to a brain tumor, had her hair shaved prior to undergoing surgery. Until then her mother had retained her composure; but upon seeing her daughter's shaved head, she burst out: "What have you done to her? ... It's as if you killed her ... Look what a face she has now." Mira's mother also flew into a passion in reaction to her daughter's head being shaved. Mira and her family were involved in a fatal automobile accident. Mira's sister was killed, her brother became a vegetable, and Mira herself was seriously injured, but was slowly recovering. When Mira's head was shaved prior to brain surgery, her mother burst out at the nurse: "Why did you shave her? ... you've finished off my daughter ... she's no longer Mira ... she looks like a boy ... this isn't a girl, it's a boy."

These and similar cases indicate that shaving a child's hair makes parents feel a lack of framework for their child's face and body, makes them fear that their child's body will come apart and that its internal organs will come out. Shaving a girl's head gives a sense of violation of body boundaries also because it is perceived as symbolizing a change in sexual identity.

Thus far I have discussed cases in which violation of body boundaries is due to changes in a child's body which can be perceived by other people besides the parents (such as being connected to medical instruments). Below we shall see that even when no substantive changes take place in a child's body, parents are likely to feel a keen sense of violation of their child's body boundaries due to a distasteful odor that comes from their child or due to a seeming change in their child's shadow.

The examples of parental behavior towards children emitting foul odors pertain primarily to cases of children with cancer (as described in the conversation between Leah's mother and her girlfriends, presented in the previous chapter):

ZELDA: So tell me; how does one catch it?

DEBORAH: Why, am I a doctor? ... Maybe its transmitted by germs, ... or through the air. [*Silence.*] Ugh, it really is stuffy in here. [*She gets up and opens the window.*] ... It smells so unpleasant. ... [*Addressing the mother*] Did she always have such an odor?

MOTHER: I don't know. But for some time now I, too, have noticed that she has this odor.

DEBORAH: Did you ask the doctor about it?

MOTHER: Once I did, and he said I was imagining things. That there wasn't any odor.

DEBORAH: What do you mean, imagining things? Every one of us is aware of an odor in here.

ZELDA: Actually, I didn't notice any particular odor.

DEBORAH [*to Zelda*]: Look, you haven't been through such a tragedy. You're not sensitive to the smell. Whoever has been through a tragedy like this can smell a person with cancer a mile away.

MOTHER: That's so. I can tell who has cancer by the smell.

DEBORAH: That's what's so terrible about this disease, that they don't know for certain. ... So how are we to stay away then? ... are we supposed to go around checking everybody's smell? We'll end up having to stay away from ourselves; end up smelling ourselves.

MOTHER: Well I don't care. I've already got it. Yes, the disease has caught me; I can feel that it's caught me, ... but I don't care. It's my daughter [*sobbing silently*].

In this case, and in others like it, one of the identifying signs of a cancer patient is the odor that presumably is emitted by her. This odor can also be viewed as a sign of unexpected violation of the patient's body boundaries which poses a threat of contagion to others around her. According to the relative's argument, one cannot take precautions against the odor because it is emitted via invisible openings and is itself invisible and not easily perceived; it cannot be touched and it does not affect external appearance. The relatives feel that the odor bursts out of the patient's body and penetrates their own bodies; as they perceive it, the lines demarking the external limits of their bodies are broken, no longer protect the interior of their bodies, and thus make it possible for the relatives to catch their child's illness. Our discussion of violation of body boundaries, therefore, ties in with our discussion of contagion.

This is illustrated by the conversation between Leah's mother and her friends, in which she intimated that the odor emitted by the sick person acts on the people around the patient, threatening them with contagion: "We'll end up having to stay away from ourselves; end up smelling ourselves." A further example is provided by Sophie's parents, whose behavior provides a much more vivid expression of the feeling that the patient's body and the bodies of her relatives are like breached fortresses, undefended, and that contagion is inevitable.

In the previous chapter we met Sophie, a girl with cancer, and her family. Here I shall present additional aspects of their behavior and excerpts of conversations not presented in the previous chapter. I begin with the fifth encounter, which took place with Miri, Sophie's sister. Miri's words lend prominence to the sense that a cancer patient's body emits an odor that does not remain attached to the patient's body, but rather passes to the patient's relatives, who cannot free themselves of the odor even by washing or spraying on perfume. Miri recounted:

"I was with Sophie all day long. ... There is a certain odor about her. She already had this peculiar odor in the hospital. ... It seems to me that everything stinks from her. ... I took some of her underwear to launder, and my whole washing machine stank. ... I went into the bathroom and I smelled her odor coming off of me. It had stuck to me. ...

"Yesterday, too, I spent the entire day with Sophie. ... I had an invitation to a party in the evening. So I went home, washed up, scrubbed myself. I put on lots of perfume, got dressed nicely, and made up my face. I had put on lotion ... but on the way to the party suddenly I smelled myself ... and I noticed that my body was giving off Sophie's smell. ... Her smell had stuck to me. ... I'm disgusted by myself. ... I know that I, too, am contaminated ... that her affliction has passed to me ... I feel that I, too, already have ... you know. ...

"I haven't changed my perfume for the past 15 years, ... but today, after having Sophie's smell coming out of my body all night long, I went in the morning and bought a different perfume. ... But it doesn't make any difference [*sobbing softly*] ... when the perfume was in the bottle it had a different scent. But when I poured it all over my body, it had the same smell as Sophie. ... My body has Sophie's smell again ... [*crying*] ... the smell of her sickness is coming out of my body again ... like a yo-yo."

Miri's feeling of being like a yo-yo is similar to the sensations had by Hannah's father and Leah's mother.

Now I return to the behavior of Sophie's relatives, to our seventh session, held in the house of Sophie's other sister, Ziva. Ziva said:

"I feel like I'm really shaky ... all my defenses have left me ... I'm simply overwhelmed by fears ... as if someone has broken in ... as if my body has been broken into ... everything is invaded."

Miri responded similarly, saying:

"I don't know who I am ... suddenly I'm afraid of my own body ... I don't recognize it. ... I'm constantly looking around myself and imagining that we're all afflicted ... could it be that all the people around me have it?"

It seems that the smell that bursts forth from the child's body makes his relatives feel as if their own bodies have become vulnerable and no longer recognizable. Often this is due to a feeling of the child's body mixing with that of his relatives and an inability to separate the body boundaries of two beings that suddenly appear as one. Below we shall see that violation of the body boundaries of sick children is associated with violation of the body boundaries of their parents, and that this also applies to extensions of the body such as one's shadow. This is illustrated by Hannah's father's remarks to his friend Judith about contracting cancer from someone who has the disease:[5]

"(It's) worse than the flu; it's like the devil. No matter how careful you are, it'll get you. ... I'm afraid, ... always afraid. I look in the mirror and I don't recognize myself. I'm scared to death, ... I'm afraid of my own shadow [*almost in tears*] ... don't laugh. Once I used to recognize my shadow and the shadows of my children; we used to play with shadows when they were young. Now everything's changed. ... It's as if, ... as if I and my shadow are two different people. ... I even had a dream one night that my shadow was laughing at me, ... as if it were a messenger sent by this cancer. ... And now my shadow no longer has the shape of my body. Her shape, Hannah's, has entered mine, and now there's a big jumble in my shadow. It's mixed, not just my own."

The father's attitude towards his shadow clearly indicates a confusion of identity. In the past the father and his shadow were one being, and the father's recognition of himself and the lines of his body found expression in his being able to identify the outline of his shadow; whereas now the father is estranged from his shadow, which symbolizes the cancer. However the father's inability to recognize his own body also stems from his body boundaries and those of his daughter having been breached, so that one body mingles as it were with the other, and thus necessarily infects the other with cancer. The cancer, via the smell and sometimes via the shadow, symbolizes an intangible and hence threatening violation of body boundaries.

The association between cancer and violation of body boundaries is also related to the image of the disease (see the previous chapter) as an entity which does not focus on a single spot, which flutters around and flows out of the body, always with the aim of breaking out of the sick person's body and entering her relatives' bodies. To wit, recall Miri's description of her sister Sophie, in the previous chapter: "I see this cancer growing and growing," etc.

We have seen that the lack of clarity that Sophie projects immediately gives her relatives a sense of helplessness and insecurity in defining their individuality. (If there could be a dead person with the looks of a live person, "Perhaps we're also dead people putting on the looks of being alive?") Uncertainty as to how they should interpret the changes in Sophie's body gives her relatives a sense of insecurity with respect to their view of their own bodies. Moreover, as in the case of patients attached to medical instruments, here too the familiar external indicators no longer provide a basis for establishing communication, and Sophie's relatives have a hard time finding new indicators that can help them understand the uncertain entity now embodied by Sophie.

Lastly, I must note that the sick person's relatives feel more threatened than strangers by violation of body boundaries and the danger of contagion. This was already observed in the previous chapter, in the discussion of the presumed identity between "heredity" and "contagion" that follows from the remarks of Hannah's, Flora's and Sophie's relatives.

The parental responses in the situations examined were similar, despite differences in the parents' level of education, ethnic or national background, and occupation. The parents whom I observed viewed first names, shadows, smells, and clothes as symbolizing the person to whom they belong by virtue of being extensions of that individual. Thus we see that even modern society views these items as bodily extensions.

Our discussion of body boundaries points towards consensus with such researchers as Polemus and Fischer, who maintain that the social aspects of the human body do not necessarily terminate at the physical boundaries of the human form.

My discussion of body boundaries ties in with my discussion of body image. In the previous chapter I maintained that people react indirectly to their fellow person's body; that people actually react to the way another's body appears to them in their mind's eye. In this chapter I discussed a specific aspect of this claim: the way people respond to the changes in another person's appearance that are associated in their minds with a violation of that person's body boundaries.

BASIC ASSUMPTIONS ON THE ESSENCE OF WOMAN, MAN AND THE HUMAN BODY

Our study implies the existence of several fundamental assumptions regarding the essence of the human body and its boundaries. To begin with, the human body is perceived as having a certain "human likeness," a shape particular to "mankind," which is protected by one's skin and has openings at certain established and accepted places. The body is also pictured as an entity that includes organs and substances that are considered external, and other organs and substances that are considered internal and concealed. The adult human being supposedly recognizes other people by their external appearance, not by their secretions or internal organs. Great importance is attributed to the hair, which protects the human body and indicates a person's sexual identity. Lastly, body boundaries, which attest the similarity of one person's body to another's, also have the role of preserving the individuality of each body and making it possible to identify each person as an independent being.

During an infant's first months her condition is ascertained, among other things, by the quality and quantity of her excretions and food. As the child grows, the interest taken in these factors diminishes, while the interest in external appearance increases. Interest in an adult's excretions is not generally accepted as a basis for acquaintance or relationships. It often happens, however, that in time of illness the situation changes and those caring for the sick person must once more take an interest in his excretions, food, and bathing. Thus a change takes place in the signs and characteristics by which we recognize our fellow person, and in such settings the following become frequently asked questions: How are you feeling? How many bowel movements have you had today? What did you eat?

Another factor relating to violation of body boundaries and lapses in communication stems from the need to know the internal organs of others and to cope with the associations that these evoke. Generally we build communication over time, on the basis of our becoming familiar with the external characteristics of our fellow person. Thus, when we think we know another person, this does not mean that we know or love his intestines, stomach, or appendix. For the most part, we have no need to know the inner recesses of another's body, and we identify others by their external appearance. However, in special circumstances, such as severe illness, the internal organs of a close person's body become involved in the bond between us, even though initially they were not part of the contract of association between us and did not oblige us to know or love them.

The point is well put by Sartre, in the short story "Intimacy":

"Lulu [lying next to her husband] ... heard rumblings: a gurgling stomach, I hate it, I can never tell whether it's his stomach or mine. She closed her eyes; liquids do it, bubbling through packs of soft pipes, everybody has them, ... He loves me, he doesn't love my bowels, if they showed him my appendix in a glass he wouldn't recognize it, he's always feeling me, but if they put the glass in his hands he wouldn't touch it, he wouldn't think, 'that's hers,' you ought to love all of somebody, the esophagus, the liver, the intestines. Maybe we don't love them because we aren't used to them, if we saw them the way we saw our hands and arms maybe we'd love them; the starfish must love each other better than we do. They stretch out on the beach when there's sunlight and they poke out their stomachs to get the air and everybody can see them; I wonder where we could stick ours out, through the navel." (1969, pp. 56–57)

Taking an interest in the insides of an individual reflects a different approach to perception of one's fellow person, an approach which emerges, as I have said, in times of illness. As we have seen, we do not understand the insides of our own bodies, or those of our fellow, due to the lack of a visual image of the body interior. Nevertheless, it should be noted that the process of aging is accompanied by an ever-increasing concern with the internal organs of the body.

It would be interesting to examine other facets relating to the findings of this study, such as data pertaining to body position. We are accustomed to recognizing our fellow adult in an upright position. A change in body position, say horizontal, creates a sense of change in a person's identity. The same applies to nudity. The discomfort of sons at seeing their parents naked is quite pronounced; for sons are not supposed to see what their parents look like beneath their clothing.[6] These examples, taken from other areas, illustrate situations in which the codes by which we perceive our fellow person need to be changed, and this change often disrupts our communication with the person. These examples show the relevance of our discussion in this chapter to the human condition in general. In this book we have met people for whom the foundations of their relations with others have been destroyed. These people are incapable of using their past experience to recognize their loved one in the present according to familiar or expected indicators, and they sense that their loved one's privacy and ownership of his or her own body has been infringed upon. In the end, people who were once close become foreign to them. Ongoing communication is based on assuming continuity—past, present, and future—in the identity of the participants, and when this continuity is broken the communication line is severed. Essentially, one's entire course of life is a continuum of breaking former identities (as when a "little" child becomes "big"). These continual changes often necessitate changes in communication styles. But when a person undergoes radical change (as when a child suffers an impairment), we note a tendency on the part of parents to reject their child's new identity, since it is difficult for them to recognize their child. Changing a name is one of the principal indicators that, in the parents' eyes, a substantial change has taken place in their child.

WHO IS A "PERSON"?

The data presented in this chapter and their interpretation with respect to violation of body boundaries tie in with the concepts developed in Chapter 2. There I claimed that every culture attributes importance to the distinction between "person" and "non-person." I said that in all the societies known to us, none view "being born of woman" as the sole criterion of "personhood"; rather, all have certain other criteria that must be satisfied in order to be considered a "person." Whom, then, do the parents we have met consider a "person"?

It turns out that acknowledging another's humanity and maintaining relations with her depends on the fulfillment of a number of conditions. First, decisive importance attaches to a definite external identity, especially the person's sex; it is impossible to form a bond with a being of uncertain sex.[7] Establishing human communication is a second condition by which the content of another's identity is determined. There is a tendency to avoid close bonds with a being that evokes associations of a "retard" or someone "abnormal." Here pronounced importance attaches to continuity in identity and especially continuity of sexual identification; there is a definite perception that sex cannot be changed.[8] Thus a "person" is defined by his location and form in space and time. A "person" is someone who has a "human likeness" (the form of a human being, or someone associated with an image of the human form) and whose present existence points to continuity with the past and the future; someone with no future is not perceived as a "person."[9] A "person" is also someone whose individuality can be discerned and who has clear boundaries between herself and others, or who is perceived as such. Thus a "non-person" is someone whose form has been defaced, so that he does not have a human likeness or individuality. In the final analysis such a person is called an "invalid," "retard," or "abnormal" person and becomes one of a group of "abnormal persons" whose defects are perceived as total, so that attention is not paid to the variation between individuals within the group. Thus the definition of a "person" and the recognition of a being's individuality are interrelated. This was illustrated by obese children and children attached to medical instruments, whose violation of body boundaries was associated with their being termed "non-persons" and losing their former identity. They were perceived as having lost the likeness of human beings because of having lost their individuality, their rights to their own bodies, their control of their fate.[10] Conferring the identity of a retarded person and denying a person's individuality thus are related to lack of humanness.[11]

Conferral or removal of a first name illustrates the importance of individuality and privacy and the connection between these two notions and human existence. Conferring a name on a child is the verbal interpretation given to one's recognition of the child's identity. In Chapter 2 we encountered various names that indicate a child's belonging to the world of mankind as opposed to other names that deny her human essence ("non-person"). I also mentioned the practice of giving a person a first name. Premature babies, whose lives are in danger—babies who have swollen stomachs, or are small, blue, attached to medical instruments, or have uncertain identities—are not called by first names. When there is an improvement in their condition and their looks, and the parents see a likelihood of taking them home, only then do their parents acknowledge their resemblance to other members of the family and give them first names. Recall that even infants born in normal deliveries are only given first names after they pass external examination and their identity is confirmed on the basis of their resemblance to the family. Conferring a first name on a baby attests his belonging to the family. Yet at the same time it also attests recognition of the child's individuality and the uniqueness of his body, personality, and particular details characterizing him. The name symbolizes communication with the child and parental responsibility towards him or her. In this respect, mention should be made of the instances in the previous chapters in which children's names were changed, thus expressing a change in identity. For example, the change in Gabi's identity from being a "cripple" to being a "baby" was clearly reflected by his former name, Gabi, being removed and a new name, Samuel, being conferred on him. Thus, like Postal (1978), I too hold that body boundaries are of central importance in forming a person's identity, that the image of a person's body boundaries enables us to distinguish the individual from others in the surroundings, and that granting a name is an expression of a person's identity and status.

THE IMPORTANCE OF THE SENSES

What impact do the senses have on the behavior of people in modern society? As we have seen, the sense of sight has a greater impact than other senses on the behavior of a broad spectrum of individuals who differ from one another in ethnic and national affiliation, education, and occupation. Thus, I concur with Simmel (in MacGregor, 1974, p. 32) that the eye, more than other factors, determines a person's responses. I must also stress the importance of our visual image of our fellow person, after that image has undergone certain interpretation, in determining how we relate to others. In contrast, the senses of touch, taste, and sound do not have much impact on behavior. The sense of smell, which many social scientists often overlook, also played a part in this chapter. It turns out that the sense of smell only affects behavior on rare occasions and under particular circumstances (such as with respect to cancer patients). Moreover, unlike the sense of sight, the sense of smell does not lead to a clearly defined response; whereas the sense of sight guides behavior in a clear and unequivocal way. There is a more pronounced tendency to reject a person who is externally deformed than a person who gives off a foul odor but whose external form is not adversely affected.

NOTES

1. Studies examining the connection between perception of body boundaries (as part of the body image) and a person's ability to adjust were presented in the previous chapter. In this chapter I review literature that approaches this subject from a totally different point of view and provides a suitable background for the data presented in the chapter.

2. Monitor: an instrument displaying a record of the electrical function of the heart on screens near the patient and at the nursing station.

3. See note 15, Chapter 1.

4. See my earlier discussion of the mother's remarks and of shaving children's heads, in Chapter 1. There I discussed the general tendency to be repulsed by children with shaved heads, whereas here I offer an explanation of this response that relates shaving a child's head to a sense of violation of body boundaries.

5. Here I go into greater detail on the father's attitude towards his shadow.

6. Cf. Simone de Beauvoir's description of her mother's death (de Beauvoir, 1965).

7. Zippora's case (Case 12), for example.

8. Mira's mother, for example.

9. For example, the inability of Sophie's parents (Case 19) to invest in her future.

10. Margalit, in Case 21, for example.

11. Shula (Case 10) or Moshe (Case 30), for example.

5

Social Construction of the Home:
The Case of Deformity

Territorial Behavior towards Abnormal Children within the Home

How does a person construct her home? What significance does one attribute to one's home? How is space in the home apportioned? By what criteria are divisions made within the home? What significance is attached to various areas of one's residence, such as the living room, kitchen, dining room, or bedroom? How are boundaries marked in the home? How does a person convey messages of territorial ownership? What significance is attached to various objects, such as one's bed, photographs, etc., in one's apartment? What factors assist us in constructing our apportionment of our physical surroundings?

Is deformity one of the factors that helps us derive a construct of our physical surroundings? If so, how?

In this chapter we shall examine these questions by observing territorial behavior of parents towards abnormal children within the home, and by examining how social construction of the home is related to social construction of physical deformity.

Sociology generally accepts that reality is constructed according to social criteria. The significance that we attribute to physical reality, and not only physical reality itself, enables us to find our way around in our world and to understand it. Moreover, we are concerned not only with conferral individual significations, but rather with the socio-cultural common denominator of the meanings that we attribute to physical reality. For us, the social construction of reality (Berger and Luckman, 1966) pertains both to physical deformity, as well as to one's residence; therefore we shall examine the connection between both of these, and shall try to discover how the way in which we perceive physical deformity helps us construct our home. I claim that the prevailing ideas about the significance of a deformity or a disability help determine the significance that is attached to various areas of the home. These significations give rise to expectations regarding the types of activity that are supposed to take place in various areas of the house, the members of the household who are supposed to perform these activities, and the relationships among the members of the household. We shall see that different expectations are had of healthy members of the household than of disabled members, and that the physical surrounding created in the wake of these perceptions of deformity compounds and reinforces them.

SOCIAL CONSTRUCTION OF DISABILITY

We have already seen in previous chapters that attitudes towards disability do not stem only from physical deformity; rather, they are also influenced by the ideas that we have about the disability, the significance that is attributed to it, and the threat inherent in it, even when these things do not necessarily match the "objective reality" or "what the doctors say." The significations and metaphors attributed to deformity are not intrinsic to it. They go beyond the disability itself. We have seen that people react to the images they attribute to illnesses, and not only to the objective characteristics of a given illness. The interpretation that they give a physical deformity helps them locate the deformed person cognitively within certain boundaries as being a "person" or "non-person." We have noticed that there is a common denominator in people's perceptions of deformity, and that individual variations are only in the form of expression, not in the essence of the response. In other words, deformity has not only an individual but also a social construction.

In the professional literature on these questions, Goffman's book, *Stigma* (1963), marks an important development in the interest taken in the social construction of disability. Also of importance is the distinction that medical sociology makes between the physiological progression of a disease and illness as a social construct.

Below we shall see that the way in which parents construe the disabilities of their children finds expression in the children's actual location within the home. We shall see that the home, too, has significance which goes beyond its physical essence. Like disabilities, one's home and surroundings, as well, have a social construction; we tend to attribute various significations to different parts of our living quarters.

Since the literature does not deal directly with the way in which parents construe their living quarters in accordance with the disabilities of their children, I shall review the literature pertaining to social construction of one's home and physical environment in general, and later we shall see how this subject relates to disabilities.

TERRITORIAL BEHAVIOR AND SOCIAL CONSTRUCTION
OF THE PHYSICAL ENVIRONMENT

Animals mark out their own territory; people mark boundaries, draw dividing lines, built walls and fences (Lennard and Lennard, 1977). Humans' territorial behavior assumes a variety of forms: consistently and exclusively sitting in a certain chair or on a certain side of the table (Altman and Haythorn, 1967), apportioning separate parts of a closet (Rosenblatt and Budd, 1975), determining a certain length of time or order of access for using certain places (Altman, 1975).

Studies of the significance of boundaries have shown that boundaries may be actual lines that form a physical separation (Lennard and Lennard, 1977), or intangible and invisible imaginary lines (Lyman and Scott, 1967).

Having a territory with well-defined boundaries enables the individual within that territory to have control over that area or space (Lyman and Scott, 1967; Proschansky, Ittelson and Rivlin, 1967). Territory also provides freedom of behavior and freedom of choice. It creates a boundary between ourselves and others, and thus enables us to safeguard our privacy and to prevent intruders from entering (Altman, 1975; Sebba, 1981, p. 40). Territorial behavior achieves this separation of an individual from others around her by manning or marking a place or object which transmits a message that the given place comes under the ownership of that individual (Altman, 1975).

Much of the research on the subject deals with the significance of territoriality in family life. In Israel, for example, a study was made of the differential use of living quarters by members of a family (Sebba, 1981; Sebba and Churchman, 1986; Shamgar-Handelman and Belkin, 1991). Sebba (1981) maintains that in an urban setting the home provides the only opportunity for the individual to be his own master, to follow his own life-style and to behave without supervision. One's apartment is perceived as a system of areas of control, each member of the family having their own area in which they should be able to preserve their individualism and avoid physical supervision by other members of the family. The territorial allocation of one's apartment and the variables derived from it (the number of partners sharing each area, its size, social composition, and the structure of its barriers) affect the degree of control that the individual has within her territory and the degree of satisfaction she derives from the apartment. "An individual's control over her territory will be greater the fewer the partners who share her territory, the greater the control she exercises over its entrances, the larger the territory which is shared in common, and the more her social status in the family gives her jurisdiction over the territory" (1981, p. 1). The greater an individual's control over her territory, the more likely she is to view herself as owning that territory and to behave in it freely (Sebba and

Churchman, 1986). Shamgar-Handelman and Belkin (1991) also view allocation of territory within the apartment as an index of the family's power structure. According to their findings, parents exercise control over space in the home and children are in a weak position with respect to all that concerns allocation of territory.

The significance attributed to various rooms in an apartment has also been studied. Israeli researchers have shown that the living room is perceived as a showroom and as a center for joint family activities (Shamgar-Handelman and Belkin, 1991). These activities include watching television, receiving guests, and other leisure activities (Sebba, 1981; Yuchtman-Ram, 1974–1975).

Anthropological studies of material culture have shown that the objects that people bring into their homes have cultural significance and help them bring order into their existence and draw distinctions between various categories. (Csikszentmihalyi, Rochberg and Halton, 1981; Appandurai, 1986). In all cultures objects symbolize social location. Some objects, like photographs, also provide a sense of identity and belonging (Csikszentmihalyi, Rochberg and Halton, 1981).

Ownership, privacy, and preventing the entrance of intruders are among the important messages transmitted by means of one's physical environment to potential interactive partners. Thus territorial behavior emphasizes the social construction of a person's territory and brings out the deeper signification, not only the physical characteristics, of the environment within which one lives.

FACTORS AFFECTING SOCIAL CONSTRUCTION OF THE HOME

Some scholars maintain that the various significations attributed to the home are related to the way in which the body is perceived in a given society. They view the home as an extension of the human body (Cooper, 1971). Others (Corti, 1990) explain that there is a complex connection between the social body and the physical body (Douglas, 1975). These studies teach us that the significance which is attributed to the body in a given society and the principle ways in which it is generally divided in that society (right side vs. left side; upper vs. lower halves) are reflected in the physical arrangement of the home.

The Rom gypsies illustrate this principle. A girl who begins having a menstrual cycle must sleep apart from other young girls and when she is menstruating must sleep in a specific part of the house. She is supposed to face the corner and keep her legs tightly crossed.

The above example, cited by Sutherland (1977) shows how the basic division of the body finds expression in the organization of the home and affects social relations among members of the family. The home makes a social and physical demarcation between the activities of those who come in contact with the lower part of the body and are considered contaminated and others who do not have such contact.

Other researchers have discussed ways in which physical organization of the home reflects and is supported primarily by divisions of gender and age. The different expectations regarding the activities and relationships appropriate to men as opposed to women (Franck, 1985) or to various age groups (Shamgar-Handelman and Belkin, 1991) determine the layout of the home and physical environment. It has been found that middle-class sub-urban American homes (Franck) and Israeli homes in a neighborhood of Jerusalem (Shamgar-Handelman and Belkin) support and reinforce age and gender systems and make a demarcation between the activities of men vs. women and adults vs. children. Social distinctions, or different expectations of men vs. women and adults vs. children are translated into physical param-eters, or into physical division and separation. The social significance given the biology and morphology of the body illustrates the biology dichotomy.

In this chapter we shall consider territorial behavior within the family and examine whether territorial behavior towards abnormal children differs from territorial behavior towards normal children. Does the social construc-tion of the home subsume this distinction? Are certain areas of the home apportioned and set aside for family members with disabilities and others intended for normal individuals? Are distinctions made between one area and another according to the types of activities expected from each group? Are certain individuals segregated on the basis of principles of contamina-tion vs. ritual cleanliness attributed to the disabled vs. the normal? We shall examine whether the social segregation stemming from different ex-pectations of the abnormal vs. the normal supports physical segregation of such individuals, and if so, how.

TERRITORIAL BEHAVIOR TOWARDS THE ABNORMAL CHILD

This chapter adds one more level to our understanding of the significance of parenting an abnormal child. In the previous chapters I did not draw a distinction between parents who refused to take home their handicapped child yet did not disown all responsibility for the child, and parents who disavowed responsibility to the extent of calling for their child's death. This and the next chapter are each devoted to a discussion of distinct aspects of parental behavior which stood out in my study: first, the territorial distance (or proximity) that parents have from their children; and second, the willingness or unwillingness of parents to accept responsibility for the fate of their children.

In the course of this chapter we shall observe various forms of locating children within certain boundaries in the home and shall explain the significance of their being placed within these boundaries. We shall try to understand the significance of the territorial allocation made to the child by relating it to the following questions: is the territory assigned to the child located within the home, or far from the home? If it is within the home, is it the children's bedroom, or some small side room? Is it considered general family territory, or servant's quarters? Does it indicate that the child is accorded a different status from other members of the family? What relationship does the abnormal child's territory bear to the territory of other children in the family? or to the parents' territory? Are boundaries marked, and if so, how? Is there neutral turf between one area and another? Or are the areas contiguous? What is the nature of the boundaries between the child's territory and the territories of other family members? Are they thick and rigid, or thin and flexible? Is the child allowed to spend time in common family territories, such as the living room or kitchen, and to participate in general family activities, such as mealtimes and television watching? Does the abnormal child have a special place set aside in the closet for her clothing? Is she forbidden to use certain objects? How much control do handicapped children exercise within the areas assigned to them? Are there areas in which they have exclusive control? What process is used to establish the abnormal child's place within the home?

My information on territorial behavior towards handicapped children was collected through observations combined with interviews held in the homes of two hundred families. My initial contact with most of the parents took place in the hospitals in which their children were hospitalized due to a defect or disease, prior to the period in which I made my observations. For the purposes of this study I chose parents who agreed to be visited at home. Even though the sample thus obtained is not statistically representative, nevertheless it subsumes some important variables in Israeli society. My sample includes Jews (96 percent) and Arabs (4 percent), religiously observant families (5 percent ultra-orthodox) and non-religious. Most of the parents lived in urban environments (98 percent), ranged from age 35 to 50, and subsumed a wide variety of such variables as ethnic background, education, and socio-economic status. Their children suffered from the following defects or diseases: spina bifida, hydrocephalus, Down's syndrome, harelip, cleft palate, other facial distortions, missing or undersized limbs, and heart or kidney disease.

In this chapter I shall focus on describing the various manifestations of territorial isolation illustrative of dynamic or developmental aspects and the changes that took place in the parents' behavior over time. The data will be presented via five specific cases and general summations. The cases chosen represent different categories in terms of national and ethnic affiliation, socio-economic status, education, and religiosity.

TERRITORIAL ISOLATION OF THE ABNORMAL CHILD

Territorial behavior towards the handicapped is different from behavior towards normal persons.

In my observations of the behavior of two hundred families I found that parents tend to reject deformed children within the walls of the home. In the homes of 80 percent of these families one or another pattern of territorial isolation was manifest. Families removed a child from the family territory (such as the kitchen, living room, etc.) or allocated the child a special territory which was not considered appropriate to other members of the family.

Each of the cases that we shall describe in this chapter represents different manifestations of territorial rejection within the home. For example, the child may be prohibited from entering certain rooms which other family members are allowed to enter, or she may be imprisoned in a small room, forbidden to spend time in public areas, or not looked at by others (thus attesting the creation of imaginary walls). The cases which we shall present show that territorial rejection of one's child, in its various manifestations, exists among parents from different countries of origin, with varying levels of education and religiosity, among Arabs and Jews, and in urban and rural families. We shall also look at the process whereby territorial rejection is achieved. We shall see that the cognitive mapping of an abnormal child finds expression in the child's location within certain real boundaries in the territory assigned to her.

We begin by presenting two cases, one from the Arab sector and one from the Orthodox Jewish sector. In the opinion of the welfare authorities, these sectors show a greater tendency than other sectors to care for abnormal children within a family or communal setting.

CASE 26 "THE SERVANT'S QUARTER"

Michal is a 13-year-old Down's syndrome[1] daughter, the oldest child of a religious couple who were born in the United States and live in an ultra-Orthodox neighborhood in the central part of Israel. The father has an advanced education in Jewish rabbinics. Until age 10 Michal lived at home with her family. Ostensibly life ran smoothly, except for when the family received visitors. At such times the mother would keep a firm hold on her daughter to make sure that she not "make a fool of herself." Otherwise, as her father said, they wanted "Michal to be at home all the time, . . . not to go out, . . . Her brothers are embarrassed to go out with her. It's best for her to stay at home, in bed, and draw pictures. Her mother and I both feel uncomfortable out in public with her; you can never tell what she'll do to us, . . . " When she was nine years old, the parents reported, "She began to do dreadful things." For example, her mother told the following story:

"On Friday night, . . . after her father returned from the synagogue, . . . we ate supper, . . . and sang Sabbath table hymns, . . . The lights had already gone out [Orthodox Jews often set their lights to go out automatically on the Sabbath eve] when suddenly we saw a light, . . . and realized that Michal was putting on the light . . . so we shouted at her, 'What, on the Sabbath?!' . . . But she doesn't understand, and continues to put on lights on the Sabbath. We don't know what to do, . . . It's one thing when she makes in her pants every so often . . . or just does something ridiculous, . . . that's tolerable. But desecrating the Sabbath?! In public?! The next day all the neighbors gazed at my husband in synagogue and whispered about him behind his back. When a light is lit all of a sudden in a Jewish home on the Sabbath eve, well, that's not just something you can pass over lightly."

By then Michal's parents knew that it was "imperative to find a way of getting her out of the house, . . . but it's complicated finding . . . because we want an institution where they won't desecrate the Sabbath and they won't eat non-Kosher." So the parents waited, until the fateful Sabbath after which they decided they "could not not take it any longer."

Two days after that Sabbath, the mother described the events of the day in the following words:

"Saturday our neighbor was about to give birth, . . . They called an ambulance, which drove into our neighborhood to take her to the hospital. . . . When we hear an automobile driving on the Sabbath, we immediately know that something has happened. So, I went out to see what it was. What a sight greeted my eyes! There was Michal, hanging on to the door of the ambulance and swinging back and forth, laughing, horsing around and refusing to let go. It was as if she had been possessed by a demon. The ambulance driver was startled, wanted her to get down, and shouted something foul at her, like 'maniac, get out of the way.' But she just clung to the door and rode off with him. . . . Never had there ever been such public desecration of the Sabbath in our community, . . . so . . . the next morning, yesterday that is, we put her in an institution."

When Michal was thirteen years old, her mother filled us in on what had happened in the interim.

"We weren't pleased with the first institution where we sent Michal. So, a month later we switched her to another place, . . . and we kept transferring her from one institution to another, until we finally found the place where she is now. It costs a fortune, and they're not so religious, but she likes it there. We buy her presents and visit her every two weeks, and she comes home on weekends. ... Lately she has preferred to remain in the institution because at home she withdraws into herself all the time. ... When she comes home, Friday she's responsible for doing the cleaning and cooking. She does it very well. She always cleans the house. Saturday night, too, ... when we go out for a walk, she doesn't like to come with us; and then she cleans up and fixes us a light meal for our return. ... Her brothers take advantage of her a bit, and they always wake her up at night. When she's home, we don't get up when the little ones cry. She does. We fixed her a place to sleep in the armchair near the baby's crib. We don't have anywhere else for her; so that's her place. We also gave her the lower shelf in the baby's closet. So that's her corner, and she doesn't interfere elsewhere. Then, when she sleeps in the chair next to the baby, she wakes up as soon as he starts to cry. ... Now, actually, we wouldn't mind if she came home. She gets along well with the little ones and makes things a bit easier on me. Only, now, she doesn't want to come home. And we don't want to force her. Maybe it's because the kids call her Cinderella and treat her like a servant."

Let us examine how Michal's parents behaved towards her prior to transferring her to an institution. One prominent feature was that they kept her away from public areas. Thus, the message their behavior conveyed was that public territory was not to be shared jointly by the parents and their handicapped child. Essentially a similar message, restricting the common territory, was conveyed by keeping the girl imprisoned within the house. Michal's parents expressed the desire that she remain "in the house," when essentially they were isolating their handicapped girl within a certain special area of her own (such as her bed) within the home and were preventing her from having access to other areas. When Michal returned home on vacations, a similar pattern of behavior was repeated, except that in addition to being allocated a special territory, the territory assigned to her attested a certain social position. Michal became in charge of performing servants jobs and was given a servant's territory. She was allotted a shelf in the baby's closet, slept in an "armchair ... next to the baby, that's her place." Sleeping in this place enabled her to be constantly at the baby's beck and call, and freed the parents to take care of their healthy children. Lastly, Michal's presence in the home was conditional. She was permitted in certain territory within the home provided she did not violate the borders of the territory assigned to her. When she invaded forbidden public territory, especially under particular circumstances (such as on the Sabbath) she was removed from the family territory. Accepting her back into this territory was permitted on condition that she remain solely within the special territory assigned to her within the home and perform the menial duties that went along with the territory given her.

CASE 27 "A PRISON AT HOME"

Here we describe the behavior of Moslem Arab parents living in a village in the north of Israel. We shall examine whether the difference in their national affiliation leads to any difference in behavior towards handicapped children.

Sammy and Amira, ages ten and eleven, are Down's syndrome children of a Moslem couple living in a village in the Galilee. Both the parents and the children speak Hebrew as well as Arabic. The children learned Hebrew in an institution for retarded children, where they spent two years. The father has a tenth-grade education, and the mother an elementary-school education. The father earns a living selling cakes baked by the mother. Sammy and Amira have two healthy brothers, ages seven and eight.

Until they were three years old, Sammy and Amira were raised normally. The mother did not realize "what it means to be retarded," as she put it, and treated Sammy "as any firstborn son" and Amira "as any daughter." According to the mother and her neighbors, the mother was always "hugging and kissing" her children and often took them out for a stroll in the neighborhood. When the children were approximately three years old, the mother noticed that "the children began to look peculiar, ... and then I began to understand what it means ... " Little by little the parents' relationship to their children began to change. A neighbor reported, "He [Sammy] would crawl around in the road on all fours, and she wouldn't even notice. She didn't care ... didn't treat them the way she used to ... as if they weren't her children any more. ... If her mother and sister hadn't fed and clothed him, he wouldn't be alive."

In order to establish how Sammy and Amira were treated at the time of this study, I spent five days with the family.[2] Let us observe the parents' interactions with their children over the course of an entire day.

The mother rose at 5:00 a.m., to bake cakes for sale. At about 7:00 a.m., the healthy brothers showed up in the kitchen. The mother, who by then was quite tired, placed two mouth-watering pastries on the table, and the children sat down to eat them. Several minutes later, Sammy and Amira came in. They, too, wanted cookies, and when they were not given any immediately, they tried to grab their brothers' cookies. The mother shouted at them, brandished her towel at them, and finally gave them a good whipping with her towel. Then she threw them two slices of bread, which they ate standing up. Meanwhile the healthy children had finished their pastries, and their mother went with them to help them get dressed. While dressing them, she gave them plenty of hugs and kisses. Sammy and Amira remained in the kitchen, casting long glances at the cookies. The mother returned and, yelling again, motioned to them with her hand to clear out of the kitchen. When they failed to leave, she resorted to whipping them with her towel, until finally they left the kitchen. At about 10:00 a.m., the parents went out to a main street corner, where they sell their baked goods. As soon as they left, Sammy and Amira followed them. The parents shouted at them, and shoved them back inside. Several minutes later, however, after the parents had arrived at the usual place they sell their goods, the children showed up and approached their parents.

MOTHER [*in a tone of despair, addressing the author*]: They cling to us like flypaper. And their mouths are always open and drooling. Everyone is afraid of them.

FATHER: No one will want to buy any food or eat any pastries when they are here.

MOTHER [*to the children*]: Take some pastries and go home.

CHILDREN: We don't want to.

The mother continued offering the children pastries, and the children continued refusing. As the tension rose, the father picked up some stones from the road. The children did not budge. The father began throwing stones at them. Startled, the children began to move aside, but did not head for home. Their father continued throwing stones at them, sometimes hitting them. Only then did the children begin to run for home.

FATHER [*addressing the author*]: It's like this every day. What did I do to deserve them? to have them stick to me like that?

MOTHER: If only they would die, then we'd have some rest from them. . . . We sent them to an institution for retards, but they were thrown out. They were a pain and a nuisance to everyone. They cling to everyone. They've worn everyone out. . . . They're always causing trouble. . . . We sent them to school and thought they would be born again, would stop being demons . . . but it didn't help them, . . . they stayed devils. They weren't reborn as children. . . . I really feel sorry for them, but I also yell at them. . . . They're not normal. . . . Actually, I don't want to dress them or feed them. I have no desire to, but its my duty, . . . if the family doesn't care for them, who will? . . . But actually, what do I care? What do I care if they're sad? I don't feel that they're my children, anyway, . . . I only have two children [the healthy ones].

At 1:00 p.m. we returned home. The two healthy sons returned from school, came into the kitchen, and their mother gave them each a pita filled with meat. Sammy and Amira were sitting in the corner of a room with broken-down walls. After the rest of the family had finished eating, the mother brought Sammy and Amira a pita filled with some scraps of meat. The children ate silently, not uttering a word. At about 4:00 p.m. company arrived, some of them family, others neighbors. The mother immediately took Sammy and Amira to one of the bedrooms and locked the door. Several minutes later she appeared somewhat troubled, went into the kitchen, cut two slices of bread, returned to the room where her children were locked up, and threw them the bread. Then she relocked the door, shouting at them as she did so, "Don't you dare come out, ... " and explaining to me, "They are not permitted to wander around the house, but they don't obey. So they'll get a spanking from their father. They are not allowed into the kitchen, but earlier I saw them go into the kitchen and steal some pastries. They can't be allowed into the kitchen, ... especially the kitchen. ... I made them a table in their own room, and they eat in there. ... I don't like to have my guests see them, ... the company wouldn't want to eat, ... they wouldn't be able to talk freely. ... "

AUTHOR: But Sammy and Amira are such good and quiet children. They don't bother anyone.

MOTHER: But you never can tell what they'll do. They are like ... devils. Not humans. They can't be allowed to walk about freely.

AUTHOR [*as if making a joke*]: So you put them in jail?

MOTHER: The poor things; it's a pity on them, but what else can I do? They have to have a prison at home.

Before continuing any further in my description of Sammy and Amira's treatment by their parents, let me describe the room in which they were kept prisoner. The family was in the process of building their house. The father had been constructing it himself, assisted by his relatives. Most of the rooms had been finished and furnished, and were used as a residence for the family and for receiving relatives. Only two rooms had not yet been tiled or plastered. [Most construction in Israel is done with cinderblock, and finished by plastering the walls and laying terrazzo tiles on the floors.] These two rooms had not yet been connected to the electrical system and are full of building materials; hence the other children in the family were forbidden to enter them. "There are snakes in there, ... and everything is dirty, ... and you could injure yourselves," the mother often warned the others. Yet Sammy and Amira were put precisely into these two rooms, and the table on which they ate there was nothing more than a construction plank that had been tossed into the room.

A month after the events described above, a change took place in the treatment given the children. The extended family got together and reached the conclusion that "something must be done with the children." As their mother told me,

"We have an aunt, ... one of my husband's sisters. She's thirty-five years old, ... and sick, ... so she'll never get married, ... but the poor thing, she loves children. ... My husband's brothers are building her a lovely house, ... the whole family gives her lots of money, more than any of us have; and she will take care of Sammy and Amira. ... Sammy and Amira are going to move in with her, ... and she'll take care of them, ... properly, ... she'll teach them how to clean and cook, ... so they'll be able to do something."

Now the children are cared for by their aunt, who treats them in a warm, motherly way. The aunt, who lives wealthily, is the sole person in charge of the children. The parents take no interest in their welfare and do not even visit them. Nor do Sammy and Amira visit their parents; and essentially they call their aunt Mother.

Thus, the parents' behavior amounts to having excluded their Down's syndrome children from the family territory. Initially they forbade the children to enter certain rooms (such as the kitchen), and prevented them from participating in activities that took place within the family territory (primarily eating together). Another prominent feature in the parents' behavior was their avoidance of spending time with their handicapped children in public areas (the corner where they sold their pastries, or the living room when they were receiving guests). Disassociation with the family also found expression in the children being locked up in a room which was considered unsuitable for other family members to live in. Allocating them this territory reflected the difference in emotional attitude towards Sammy and Amira and their different social location in comparison with the other children in the family.

The family gradually excluded Sammy and Amira from sharing the family territory within the home. The process of their exclusion was accompanied by acts of physical violence, and ultimately resulted in establishing boundaries that separated the abnormal children from their parents and healthy siblings, isolating the abnormal children, and preparing them for servile occupations.

CASE 28 "THE MONSTER'S GHETTO"

This case describes the behavior of Helit's parents, who live in a city in central Israel. The couple, 30 years old, were born in Tripoli and came to Israel at an early age. The father went to elementary school through the fourth grade, and the mother through seventh grade. The father has a partnership driving a truck. Until Helit's birth he was in fine economic condition, able to support his parents and his in-laws. The mother is a housewife, known for being a warm and loving mother towards her two healthy children, ages 5 and 6. The family lives in a one-bedroom apartment without a porch. Earlier they had lost a daughter, who died unexpectedly at the age of 3 months.

Helit's medical record reads: "Helit was born in the eighth month. ... Her condition is 'poor' and her outward appearance abnormal. She has many deformities, asymmetry in half her nose, and internal heart and kidney defects. Her chromosome test is normal, and therefore there is no indication of mental retardation."

Two days after Helit's birth, a representative of the family showed up and said, "The father is having a breakdown and wants an institution [for the child]." A social worker requested to speak with the parents. After repeated requests, she finally met with them two weeks after the birth, after all the tests had been completed. At the meeting the mother did not cease crying. The social worker began the conversation by saying that the nurses call the baby Helit.[3] Later she tried to explain to the parents the necessity of removing the girl from the hospital.

FATHER: Look, things are hard for us. Don't make things worse. We are good parents. My wife is a good mother, ... but I simply don't want this girl in our home ... because she's sick and she looks like a monster. ... She's blue [due to her heart defect], her eyes don't match, she has a big nose, each ear is a different size. ... Anyone who sees her is grossed out. ... [*The mother bursts into tears.*] It's dreadful, ... there's just not way of coming to terms with her condition and the way she looks. ... We don't want this girl.

SOCIAL WORKER: But she is not retarded, and I don't understand how you'll find an institution to take a child who is not retarded. ...

MOTHER: Get us right. We can't bring this girl into our home. I'm prepared to come visit her in the hospital, but not to take her home ... because of the kids at home. We're afraid that the kids will see her and go into shock. Anyway, where could we put her? Our apartment is very small, ... there's no place she could be put where she wouldn't be seen.

SOCIAL WORKER: But you must understand us. ... Perhaps you could take her for now, until some solution is found for her?

MOTHER: But where will we put her? No one will want to share a room with her. We don't have a porch where we could put her, and if we put her in the hall everyone will have to see her. ... We just won't take her home.

The parents returned home but ceased being able to function. The father, who was a partner driving a truck, stopped going to work and simply lay sick in bed, crying constantly. The mother ceased being able to care for her two healthy children. Once a week she would go with the local social worker, who was very supportive of her, to visit Helit. Both parents shut themselves up in their home, drew the blinds and would not admit strangers into the house for fear that Helit might be sent home. The social worker invited them to another meeting and requested that they reconsider the possibility of taking their girl home. "I had become convinced that Helit could not be taken home," she said, "but in the long run she cannot be kept in the hospital. ... The head nurse insists that Helit either be taken home or put into an institution. But institutions are only for retarded children, and Helit isn't retarded. She's developing normally."

Having become increasingly afraid "that the girl will be brought home," the parents fled to the father's family, who gave them much emotional support.

When Helit was half a year old the social worker asked the parents to provide the hospital a form from their health insurance undertaking to pay the girl's hospitalization expenses. The mother said they had not been able to pay their health insurance premiums because, since the girl's birth, her husband had not gone to work and the family was in severe economic straits, and this was also bringing down their parents, who relied on them for sustenance. Two weeks later the social worker again requested the mother to "come take Helit home for a while. ... because the head nurse has put her foot down. She refuses to have Helit remain in the hospital any longer. ... You won't have to become attached to the girl. I promise you that Helit will not remain at home for good, and that I will arrange for her to be taken in an institution as soon as possible." The mother tried to bargain with the social worker, arguing, "What's the hurry? Every day I hope that maybe the girl will show some sign of retardation and then you can put her in an institution. ... A girl with such a face has to be retarded. ... Get it into your head, we can't take her home. What will the neighbors say when they see her all of a sudden?"

At this point the girl's treatment was entrusted to the hospital authorities, whose representative appealed to the police, reported that the girl had been abandoned, and demanded that they intervene. Two days later a telegram was sent informing Helit's parents that the girl would be brought home the following day. On the morrow, early in the morning, Helit was taken out of the hospital, carried by a nurse escorted by a policeman. The policeman arrived at the family's house and, when no one answered the doorbell, placed Helit, completely swaddled, by the door. About two minutes later the door opened and Helit was quickly taken inside. I had come to the house about an hour earlier and watched the parents' behavior.

Very quietly, the father took Helit and said, "Where shall we put her?"

MOTHER: In the living room?

FATHER: That's a problem. How will we watch television?

MOTHER: Maybe we should put her in the kitchen?

FATHER: No, that's impossible. We eat in there.

MOTHER: So let's put her in the hallway. There's no other choice. The kids will play in their own room or else in the living room.

And so, Helit was assigned to the hall. The father removed the light bulb, leaving the hall completely dark so that Helit could not be discerned. "It's a ghetto for monsters," the parents said.

The mother took reasonable care of Helit's physical needs. She was kept clean and free of sores. Nevertheless, approximately every two weeks she is readmitted to the hospital. Whenever Helit is in the hospital (which is quite often) the hall light is put back and the house is opened wide. "We have to breath every once in a while," the father explained. The mother, too, "tries to rest," as she puts it, when Helit is in the hospital, and prefers not to visit the girl. She only comes to the hospital at mealtimes, since the "nurses require me to come at least to feed Helit, ... and they say that they're not a warehouse for storing away children." When she feeds Helit in the hospital, she holds her far from her body and does not look at her. "I don't want to become attached to her," she explained. "It's very hard for me to feed her, ... she's looks revolting, ... but I have to."

Sometimes the mother brings her two healthy sons to the hospital because she "doesn't want to leave them home alone," but they do not go near Helit and only watch television outside the girl's room.

Helit died when she was a year and three days old. Her mother cried. Two months later the parents had a healthy boy. The mother laughed with joy and said, "For me, only the girls come with defects."

The behavior of Helit's parents illustrates, among other things, a desire to remove their girl from the family territory, i.e., to keep her out of the house. By law they were required to bring their girl home, but they only did so on condition that they could make some sort of "ghetto for monsters" within their home. At first, both before Helit was forcefully brought home and afterwards, the parents did not see how they could isolate her physically, in other words how they could place her in a territory that would preclude intimate situations between them and their daughter, where by intimate situations we mean the kind formed through physical contact or even eye contact. Being unable to have physical isolation meant that there would be territories shared by Helit and the rest of the family, a sharing which the parents wished to avoid. Helit's removal from the family territory was finally accomplished by making the territory assigned to her dark, thus essentially turning it into an empty zone "outside of the home," not allowing for contact between the girl and the rest of her family.

Case 29 "A prison with a color T.V."

This case deals with a girl with spina bifida.[4] We shall see whether differences in type of defect, ethnic affiliation, and degree of religiosity lead to a difference in the territorial behavior shown towards this handicapped child.

Simha,[5] a 13-year-old girl, is paralyzed in the lower half of her body and has impaired bladder control due to spina bifida. Most of the time she is hospitalized in a ward specializing in the care of patients with paralysis.

According to the social worker, Simha is "properly developed for her age, chubby, ... used to walk with crutches, but due to lack of motivation has ceased using her crutches and now for the most part gets around by wheelchair. ... She shows environmental retardation, ... dresses slovenly, and lacks the motivation to change her diapers at the appropriate time when in school, so that she comes home wet and smelling, ... therefore she had a permanent catheter inserted.

"Simha's parents are of Hungarian origin. They are Holocaust survivors, 50 and 55 years old, and have an elementary school education. The father does not work due, as he claims, to hypertension. The parents have six children, of which Simha is the second. They describe themselves as religious. Their economic condition is poor. They live in a religious neighborhood in the same large city where Simha's hospital is situated. They have a three-and-a-half-room apartment on the third floor, without the necessary living conditions for a crippled child. At one time they were offered a ground-floor apartment, which would have helped them manage with a crippled girl in the family, but they turned down the offer and sought a larger apartment, even on the third or fourth floor. ... Relations between the parents are good. ... Every four months Simha comes home for vacations of one or two days."

To understand the parents' treatment of Simha, we shall observe what happened when she came home for a short visit. Two days before the projected visit a social worker called the parents' home to tell them that their daughter would be coming home for a two-day break.

SOCIAL WORKER: Hello. I wanted to check whether it's O.K. for Simha to come home Wednesday.

FATHER: I'm sorry, but it's not very convenient.

SOCIAL WORKER: Nevertheless, perhaps you could make a special effort? Simha really wants to come home for a vacation.

FATHER: A vacation? I though she was only going to come for several hours.

SOCIAL WORKER: What we had in mind was for her to come on Wednesday and remain until Friday.

FATHER: That complicates things. How will she get up to the third floor? Our house isn't suitable for her. How will she get up the stairs? ... Maybe we should postpone the whole thing?

SOCIAL WORKER: That would be a pity, because Simha hasn't come home for a visit for three months, and she's longing to see you and her brothers.

FATHER: Look, I get up-tight just thinking about her coming home. She'll make it dreadful. ... It's better for her not come. There's no sense in her coming.

SOCIAL WORKER: Maybe you should talk it over with your wife?

FATHER: Sure, have my wife. Let her do what she wants. [*Signs of disagreement between the parents, and between the parents and children could be detected beneath the surface.*]

MOTHER: Hello, ... Yes. I heard your conversation with my husband. You have to understand him. ... The girl wants to visit us? O.K. Who will come with her? You, together with a volunteer? Then it's fine. We'd be delighted to have her for a visit. I'll start getting things in shape for her right away. The whole house has to be gotten ready for her visit.

SOCIAL WORKER: Can I lend you a hand in any way?

MOTHER: No, thank you. We'll have to fix her a place with a television, and games, ... bring up the folding-bed we keep specially for her in the basement, and we'll have to prepare lots of sweets for her so that she won't bother her brothers. ... It's O.K., don't worry. I'll get the house ready for her.

Simha arrived on Wednesday, escorted by the social worker and myself (I was introduced as a volunteer), for the projected visit. The mother saw us from the window of her apartment and came down to greet us. She hugged her daughter with one arm, but her eyes were directed towards me. The girl reached her cheek forward for a kiss, but the mother had already turned to look behind her.

SOCIAL WORKER: Come, let's get Simha upstairs together. Our volunteer and I will help you.

We went up to the third-floor apartment, and collapsed, winded, in the living room.

SIMHA: Isn't anyone home? Where are the kids? Where's Dad?

MOTHER: Dad's not home, and your brothers are playing downstairs. We've fixed up a nice room for you so you can play there and watch T.V.

SIMHA: I don't want to play by myself. I want to play with my brothers, ... I want to watch television in the living room.

MOTHER [*embarrassed*]: But we put the color T.V. into the bedroom for you, and we brought the black and white one into the living room for us.

SIMHA [*making a face*]: Did you bring up that folding bed for me again?

MOTHER: We don't have room to keep another permanent bed in the house.

SIMHA: O.K., if that's the way it is, then today I want to trade with the kids. They can take the folding bed and the color television, and I'll take their bed.

MOTHER [*exploding*]: What? You'll take their bed?! and they'll sleep in your bed?!! Who do you think you are? Don't you dare say that ever again. Otherwise, it'll be hell here.

SIMHA: I don't care.

MOTHER: So, you've become a princess. It doesn't become you. One might think they treat you better in the hospital! Where else will you get a room with a color television?

SIMHA: It's like a prison with a color T.V.—a princess in prison with a color T.V.

The father came home and said hello to me, the social worker, and the mother. He did not address a word to Simha or even glance in her direction.

FATHER [*to the mother*]: Why is she [Simha] in the living room?

MOTHER: I don't know. It just happened that way, ... She's hungry; I'll go set the table. Call the children upstairs to eat.

FATHER: It'd be better if you fed her first. After she finishes, then we can eat.

MOTHER [*embarrassed by the presence of the social worker and myself*]: She can eat with us.

FATHER: O.K., then I'm not hungry. You go ahead and eat now; I'll eat later.

MOTHER [*addressing us apologetically*]: Look, it's always very difficult when it comes to food. ... We don't have much money, and she always asks for seconds, and it irritates him. So he wants to eat by himself, in peace and quiet.

The father paced around the living room, noticeably agitated. Finally, he went up to Simha and said, "I'm asking you, please don't make a mess in the house. When the children come upstairs, don't bother them. If they want to, they'll play with you. And if they don't, then stay in your room. We'll put the T.V. on for you, we'll bring you as much as you want to eat, in your room. ... The last time you were here, there was an uproar. This time I'm warning you, if you don't behave nicely, we won't bring you home." Simha sat in her wheelchair looking at me and said, "I'll do as I please." Several minutes later I left the apartment.

Like other parents of deformed children, Simha's parents as well show territorial rejection of her. We saw that the parents' attempt to remove Simha from the common family territory found expression in situations that called for sharing territory, such as eating, sitting in the living room, watching television, or playing with one's brothers and sisters. In these situations an attempt was made to isolate her in a separate territory. We also saw that the boundaries set up between Simha and her family found expression not only in an attempt to isolate her physically, but also in building imaginary walls. Simha's father "does not see her"; for him she simply does not exist. These imaginary boundaries are manifest by not looking at Simha, not saying hello to her, and generally avoiding contact with her.

In the behavior of Simha and her parents we see a conflict over the question of belonging in the home. Simha's behavior amounts to an implied declaration that she is part of the home, whereas the message of her parents' behavior is that she is a stranger with no place in the home.

The attitude that Simha is not part of the household finds expression, firstly, in establishing boundaries between the home and the hospital and in viewing Simha as belonging to the hospital, not the home. Her family turned down a housing offer which would have enabled them to take Simha into their home on a permanent basis. They deliberately chose a way of life that suited the healthy and not the handicapped. The father's words underscore his desire to make the boundaries between home and institution more rigid and to prevent any contact between Simha and the home. Even when contact between Simha and the home was forced on the parents, the struggle continued between the two sides. The parents related to Simha's arrival as if it were a visit by a stranger who did not belong to the family, whereas Simha made it clear time and again that she was not a guest coming for a visit, but rather that she should be treated as someone who had come to her own home. The parents' view of Simha as someone who does not belong to the household was also expressed in the way they spoke about having "to get the house ready" to receive her. Later it became clear that preparing the house did not mean getting it ready for a handicapped person to live in it, but rather preparing it for a visit by someone who must be kept in isolation; the preparations for receiving Simha essentially amounted to preparing an isolated territory for her from which she would not be able to leave and enter common territory with her parents.

CASE 30 "THE RAVAGED TERRITORY: 'EITHER THE BOY, OR ME'"

This case enables us to trace changes in the attitude towards a child, ranging from initial acceptance to territorial rejection, ultimately removing him from the home.

Moshe is the third child of Iris and Benjamin, both 32 years old and of Moroccan extraction. The family lives in a six-room apartment. Each child (a 5-year-old son and a 4-year-old daughter) has his or her own bedroom. In addition, each child has his or her own corner in another room, intended as a playroom. Before Moshe's birth, his parents moved out of their bedroom and began sleeping in the living room, and fixed up their bedroom for Moshe. The father painted the room pale green, hung pictures on the walls, put up two green shelves, and stood a crib, painted green, in the corner of the room. The parents put much thought into the arrangement of the room for the expected child. In addition, they also cleared him a corner in the playroom. "Even though it will still be a long time before he plays here," his mother explained, "I want the older children to begin getting used to the idea that this is his area, ... that it already belongs to him. ... "

Two weeks after Moshe's birth his parents, who had been taking care of him devotedly, noticed that "his head is oversized." Indeed, medical examination revealed that he needed immediate surgery, and at age three weeks he had brain surgery.[6] When their child was in the hospital the parents remained at his side constantly. They took an interest in his condition and helped the nurses however they could (by diapering and feeding him, etc.). A week later the baby's condition deteriorated. He began to run a fever and was put on antibiotics. The mother did not quit her son's bedside, but stayed by him day and night. She expressed milk from her breasts and tried to feed him a little of it in the hope that "maybe it will help." The father brought food and clothing to the hospital for the mother, and took care of the other two children who remained at home.

Nevertheless, in spite of the medical care the child received, as time passed his head grew larger and larger. The doctors were divided as to his prognosis, although some of them maintained that "there is a chance that the child will not pull through the illness, and even if he survives, he will apparently be in poor shape intellectually." The father began imagining his child as a "revolting retard," immediately severed all contact with him, and demanded that he be institutionalized. The mother refused. The parents had bitter arguments over the matter. About a week later the father informed his wife: "I'm laying down the line. You'd better make up you mind, ... because it's either me, or the kid. I won't have such a child brought into the house. If he comes in, I'm leaving." Heavy-hearted, the mother decided to bring Moshe back home. The father left home. The mother cared for Moshe; she brought him into his room, and laid him in his crib. His play corner remained strictly reserved for him.

Six months later, Moshe's mother brought him to the hospital with pneumonia. Once more she remained at his side constantly, but from day to day made more comments about his "oversized head." She began to pay less attention to how she dressed and to stare blankly into space, stopped breast-feeding her son, no longer responded to his cries, and did not initiate taking care of him. She kept pictures of her two healthy children in her wallet. Every so often she would take out these photographs and show them off proudly to everyone around.

One morning, while conversing with the mother of another child in the same room, she announced flatly, "With a head like his, it's clear to me, ... that either he'll die, ... or he'll be retarded." Later that day the mother went up to the head nurse and informed her that she was going home "to wash up." Since then she did not reappear in the ward. Two days after her disappearance, one of her brothers showed up with a message that "Mother won't come any more; she can't take it, ... she's been telling everyone that she doesn't have a baby any more, ... that her baby died." The brother requested in the mother's name that the hospital see to finding an institution for the child.

The father returned home. Neither of the parents took any more interest in their son's welfare. They refused to take him home until a suitable institution could be found, saying, "for us he's dead." They made their house look as if Moshe had never been born and had never lived there. All the objects associated with Moshe (his crib, playpen, clothes and toys) were thrown out. His room was repainted and the parents' bed was moved back in.

In time it became clear that the doctors' worse prognosis had been wrong. Moshe lived and developed well, although the size of his head remained abnormal and it was clear that he would need special care. The parents were informed of this, but did not go back on their decision.

The child was transferred to an institution and continued to develop well. The parents did not contact the institution at all, and continued raising their two healthy children with warmth. Three years later the mother called the institution anonymously. She came to the institution, looked at her son, remarked that "his head looks simply dreadful," and did not form any contact with him.[7]

The behavior of the parents, especially the father, conveys the message that they and their son have no common territory. This message was expressed radically by the father when he left home in order to avoid sharing the same territory with his son. In other words, the moment the child was brought home, the home ceased being the territory of the parent. Later we were witness to the destruction of the territory intended for the child within the home, thus signifying his death socially.

In the first few chapters we maintained that a child whose appearance evokes associations of a "non-person" is generally rejected by his parents. In this chapter we have seen some of what this rejection means through descriptions of territorial rejection within the home. A child who is defined as an individual "person" is considered to have the right to territory of his own within the home, where the boundaries between his territory and other territories in the home are not rigid. A child who is perceived as a "person" also has the right to share the common family territory, enjoying the status of a member of the family. When a child is perceived as a "non-person," he is rejected from common family territories.

Examination of parents' territorial behavior towards abnormal children within the home reveals a general tendency to isolate deformed children. Eighty percent of the 200 hundred families that we observed isolated their handicapped children territorially. Various manifestations of territorial isolation were presented in five typical cases.

One expression of territorial isolation took the form of laying down territorial restrictions within the home, as well as assigning the abnormal child a special role in running the household; Michal's religious family assigned her a special area within the home (the corner near the baby), and thereby lent symbolic expression to her status as a servant. Her remaining in the home was conditional upon her willingness to accept the territory assigned to her and the obligations that went along with it.

The second type of territorial isolation which emerged here may be called that of the "prison." This type of isolation is likely to assume various forms, such as locking a child in a room with the family's best television (Simha's case), or in a room which is not considered suitable living quarters for other members of the family (Sammy and Amira's case).

In Simha's case we encountered another way of isolating an abnormal child. Here the isolation was manifest in circumstances requiring joint action within common family territory, such as eating, playing in the living room, or watching television. On these occasions the parents tried to enclose her within her own territory or else set up non-physical barriers and boundaries between the girl and the rest of her family by looking away from her or not greeting her and in general by refraining from contact with her. When Simha's father could not lock his daughter up in an actual room, separated by physical walls, he created an imaginary room. Simha's parents kept their girl within defined boundaries. A striking feature of this case was the struggle for territory, which protects one's identity and establishes one's place socially. Simha was interested in spending time with her parents and brothers in the common family territory, but her parents were interested in separating the family territory from the territory belonging to Simha, the "guest." In so doing they were defending their territory and identity. Social arrangements that separate the healthy from the sick fend off the danger of contagion and the threat to the parents' self-image. A prime illustration of this is the argument between Simha and her mother with respect to switching beds.[8]

Social isolation pertained both in territories that could be shut by doors (Sammy and Amira, Simha) and in open territories, such as halls and corners, that were surrounded by imaginary boundaries. Helit was assigned the hall, an area that was redefined from a well-lit play area to an empty, dark region reserved for the abnormal child. Even in these cases the borders that were established were rigid and impenetrable.

Abnormal children who were defined as "non-persons" were removed from the common family territory; they were permitted to remain at home on condition that they not force their parents to have the degree of intimacy that would follow from sharing the same territory.

We have also seen that parents' territorial behavior towards their children changes as their subjective perception of the degree of their child's normalcy changes. Moshe's parents' behavior reveals a process of gradual exclusion from the family territory, where the child's abandonment clearly stems from the way in which his external appearance is interpreted by the parents and not from the actual state of his health. When Moshe was thought to be normal, he was given a territory of his own, thus expressing his belonging to the family. Later on, when he was considered abnormal (appeared and was called retarded), his territory was destroyed, thus symbolically signifying his death socially and indicates disavowal of responsibility for his life.

We also see that removing a child from the family territory finds expression, among other things, in the child's removal from family photographs.

Situating a child within certain boundaries that in fact create a barrier between her and her family is essentially a technique for preventing intimacy. Similar techniques were described in the previous chapters as well. Parents of children attached to life support systems tend not to touch their children, and sometimes even refrain from looking at them; instead they busy themselves with various other tasks in order to avoid even having to sit beside their children. A buffer region is maintained between the two sides, to prevent one territory from touching the other.

In this respect, recall Tzviya, the mother of a Down's syndrome child, who scrubbed her body in order to obliterate any vestige of contact with her retarded child,[9] and the mothers of children with cancer, who often defended themselves against the "smell" of their children by spraying on perfume or seeing to it that there was a fresh breeze in the room. Even Haggar's mother, on entering her daughter's room, said, "It's so hot in here," then opened the window and added, "now the germs will leave," although her daughter did not have cancer.

We have focused on the isolation of handicapped children, since we found this to be the prevalent pattern of behavior. Nevertheless, despite its theoretical and practical importance, this pattern of behavior has not been described in the literature; but patterns of closeness to handicapped children have been dealt with extensively.

Isolation of handicapped children within the home is especially significant in an urban lifestyle, where the parents generally can not find such alternatives as having their children raised by other members of their community and are supposed to find their own solutions and ways of coping with the care of their children.

The five cases presented in this chapter involve a number of important and diverse characteristics of Israeli society in terms of national origin, ethnic affiliation, socio-economic status, religiosity and level of education; nevertheless, a tendency towards territorial isolation was common to all. We observed territorial isolation of abnormal children on the part of religious and non-religious parents, Jews and Arabs, urban and rural families, parents from different countries of origin and with varying levels of education, and cases where the child's abnormality resulted from deformities, defects, and various diseases. This fact casts doubt on claims advanced in the literature that the parents' behavior is influenced by their national and religious affiliation.

We noted that 20 percent of the two hundred families observed did not evince signs of isolating their handicapped children over the time span of the study's observations. The percentage of parents who did not isolate their handicapped children territorially, however, might be much lower. Firstly, these parents might have isolated their children, except not in the presence of the observer. Secondly, the sample was chosen on the basis of parental consent to visits by the author and other observers who accompanied her. We may reasonably assume that if we had examined a random sample of parents, we would have found that the overall percentage of parents who isolated their children was higher than that found in the group we observed.

With respect to the ability to generalize from the findings presented here, we do not mean to assert that the process we have described is universal and that all parents will always isolate every handicapped child. Even the parents whom we observed isolating their handicapped children did not do so in every social circumstance. Moshe's mother refrained from isolating him for a long time. We simply wish to stress the great potential that exists for reacting in such a manner.

Furthermore, even though the findings presented here provide evidence of a tendency to isolate handicapped children, we have not attempted to quantify this isolation or rate it on a scale of intensity.[10]

This chapter is likely to lay the groundwork for examining the assumption that stigma is attached not only to people (Pfuhl, 1980; Johnes et al., 1984; Ainlay et al., 1986), but also to living areas intended for the handicapped. We saw how parents set apart a room or specific area in their home, gave it a stigmatic social significance (such as a prison, ghetto, servant's quarters, etc.), and had the stigmatized person live there. This ties in with the claim made by Deshen and Deshen (1989) that people stigmatize objects as well as people.

In our discussion of the social construction of disability in previous chapters we saw that, as with the distinctions of gender and age, so too with respect to disability, observable biological differences are transformed to social differences. In this chapter we saw that the biological distinction between the handicapped and the normal, like that between men and women, creates a dichotomy between the patterns of behavior appropriate towards the handicapped and the patterns of behavior appropriate towards normal persons, and that these are translated to the physical surroundings.

We have attempted to describe the connection between abnormality and territorial behavior. Psychologists, sociologists, and social ecologists have discussed each of these concepts separately. We have stressed their interconnection and the resultant theoretical and practical implications.

We have seen that the significations attributed to abnormality help other members of the abnormal person's family build a construction of their home in which they adopt and adhere to notions that contribute to making separations and setting up physical and imaginary boundaries between activities and regions of the home that are intended for abnormal members of the family vs. those intended for normal people.

NOTES

1. See note 11, Chapter 1.

2. Some of the time I was accompanied by the daughter of the family under observation, who was studying in the university and acted as an ad hoc interpreter. The conversations that took place in my presence, however, were primarily in Hebrew.

3. The parents did not give their girl a name; but later, when they took her home, they did not change the way she was called.

4. See note 10, Chapter 1.

5. Simha was named by a nurse in the neonatal ward of the hospital where she was born (since initially her parents had refused to recognize her as their child). Her parents continued to call her by this name.

6. Moshe suffered from hydrocephalus, a condition in which cerebrospinal fluid accumulates in the ventricles of the brain or in the arachnoid spaces on the outer aspect of the brain, due to an obstruction in the passage of the fluid from the region of its secretion to the place it is reabsorbed (generally between the third and fourth ventricles). Sometimes the accumulation of fluid results in excessive secretion.

Clinical indications: the first signs of hydrocephalus appear close to birth or at a later age. When the fonticuli are still open they are wider and tauter than usual, the forehead protrudes, and the whites of the eyes are visible above the upper part of the cornea. The skin over the skull is shiny and the veins protrude. The condition is often accompanied by crossed eye, disquiet, high-pitched shouting, and sometimes retardation of growth. Most patients with the disease are not mentally retarded, unless the condition is prolonged and there is a serious disturbance of the nervous system. Motor ability suffers due to the head's excessive weight.

Treatment: before beginning treatment, each case must be kept under observation for an extended length of time to establish whether or not there is exaggerated and gradual growth of the skull beyond the upper limits of the norm and whether the diagnosis is accurate. This is done by taking photographs with air. The operation generally performed to relieve the pressure involves inserting a bypass catheter from the brain ventricles to the venous blood system or directly to the heart. There may be many complications resulting from the operation's failure and a need for reoperation. Mortality is high when not operated. With operation, 10–15 percent of the cases develop normally. Psychomotor development in the remaining cases is marginal or poorer. (Brand-Orban, 1979, pp. 202–204.)

7. This information was given to the mother.

8. Zippora's parents also avoided putting her down to sleep in a bed used by others. Some researchers claim that the bed is one of the archetypical symbols of family life (Shamgar-Handleman and Belkin, 1991).

9. In my opinion parents' constant scrubbing of their children can be accounted for by a similar explanation.

10. We have not attempted to quantify rejection or compare the intensity of isolation from one family to another in terms of saying that "the isolation in family X is stronger than that in family Y."

6

Parenting and Responsibility

Varieties of Responsibility
towards the Abnormal Child

In the previous chapter I discussed parental relations towards children living with them in the home. Now I proceed to the question of parental relations towards children who are cared for outside the home.

During the six years of this study, I saw that about half (i.e., 50.8 percent) of all the babies who were discovered to have congenital defects were abandoned by their parents,[1] either immediately at birth or at some later stage. The parents of these newborns refused to take their babies home, and for the most part also refused to visit them in the hospital. In some cases the law against child abandonment was invoked and the babies were sent home by force, either in a police van or an ambulance of the hospital.

We have seen, however, that parental responsibility does not amount merely to deciding whether to take their children home or abandon them. There are other ways in which parents evince responsibility towards their children. In this chapter I shall present a variety of forms that parental responsibility can assume.

CASE 31 "GIVE HER A DRUG TO END HER LIFE"

Ayalah, 45 years old, and her husband are a religious couple, born in Poland. They are well-to-do and live in a non-religious urban neighborhood. The couple's fifth daughter, born in Central Hospital, was diagnosed as having Down's syndrome.[2] At first Ayalah cared for her daughter devotedly, showering her with hugs and kisses. Two days after the birth Ayalah was informed that her daughter had been diagnosed as retarded and that the doctors had decided to put her in an incubator due to being underweight. Upon hearing this news Ayalah and her husband held each other by the hand and cried for an hour or more. Towards evening Ayalah requested to have a talk with Dalia, a good friend of hers who was a nurse in the same hospital. Here is part of their conversation:

DALIA: I was so sorry to hear about your girl ... I feel for you. ...

AYALAH: Who would have imagined that such a thing would happen to us ... such a tragedy. ... What causes it?

DALIA: No one knows.

AYALAH: ... I have a favor to ask you. ... We've been friends for a long time ... let's be frank ... there's no point in taking a girl like this and putting her in an incubator. Why put her in intensive care? Why go to such effort? ... I pray that she'll die ... pray to God. ... Maybe you can fix up something? You're a nurse here, after all. Maybe you can see to it that they not take so much care of her, ... after all, you know that children like her die young ... and maybe if they don't try so hard to save her, then that way she won't go on living.

DALIA [*horrified*]: I'm sorry, that's impossible. I understand you, but that can't be done.

AYALAH [*shouting*]: Why not? Why are you putting me under such pressure? Don't you understand that she is a threat to me?

DALIA: I'm not putting pressure on you. Anyway, why are shouting at me? Go shout at the doctors.

And so it was; the next few days Ayalah and her husband asked the doctors to terminate their daughter's life. When Ayalah was released from the hospital, she refused to take her girl home. She told her other children, her family, friends, and neighbors, "I had a girl, but she was weak and small, so she died." "There's no point in my kids knowing that the girl exists," she explained to the author. "She's still in critical condition, and chances are that she'll die soon. So why should they know? Also, I don't want to ruin their futures. ... It might get in the way of their getting married ... and in our circles ... among religious families ... getting married and having children are of paramount importance. ... Also, they might begin to fear that they themselves have something wrong with them, too, ... that there's something in our family, ... in our blood, that's not O.K. ... It could put them into a terrible depression, ... so it was better to tell them she had died. ... It raises fewer questions."

The girl, however, put on weight and grew stronger; and the hospital directors summoned the parents and demanded that they take her home. Here is part of the conversation that ensued between the parents and the doctors:

DOCTOR: Your daughter's weight has improved, she's no longer in critical condition, and she's getting stronger. ... The hospital presses for the release of such children who reach a suitable weight and who are in good health.

FATHER: Look, we told you already that we have four healthy children at home ... and that there's no point in trying to save the girl's life.

DOCTOR: Look, you don't know Down's syndrome children. They are good as gold ... they can take care of themselves ... are capable of doing simple jobs, and mainly, they are a source of great joy to their parents. ...

FATHER: We demand that the girl remain in the hospital until we find a suitable institution. ...

DOCTOR: So, take the girl home, and when you find the right institution, transfer her there.

MOTHER: How can we do such a thing? No one at home even knows she exists. ... We'll do just the opposite. First we'll find an institution, then we'll transfer the girl straight from the hospital to the institution.

FATHER: And besides ... Doctor, if you'll permit ... I have a very personal request ... My wife and I request that you ... give her a drug to end her life.

DOCTOR: ... I'm sorry. I cannot do such a thing.

FATHER: But you must help us.

DOCTOR: You are a religious man, sir. Would you, yourself, be able to give her such a drug?

FATHER [*bursting into tears*]: Forgive me ... God forgive me ... I'm just a ruined man. I have no solution. ... I've thought about it all so much. ... We're not prepared to care for the girl at home. It'll destroy our entire family. But it's also difficult to find an institution ... and even if some place could be found, the prices they demand would simply ruin the family. I'd have to steal things from my own children in order to pay the institution. ... Is that fair? For years I've been saving up for my children ... and now everything will have to go to the institution? Why spend money on an institution? Why invest anything at all in such a girl? Isn't it a waste of money, investing in a creature like this?

DOCTOR: What do your relatives say? You are a religious family, after all.

MOTHER: We don't live close to our family. They don't know anything about the whole affair.

DOCTOR [*to Ayalah*]: How are you feeling? I see you're looking very well.

AYALAH [*well dressed, and very impressive looking*]: I have to look good, [*apologetically*] I have to keep the house running just as before. ... I have four girls and a husband, and I have an obligation to them both as a woman and as a mother. ...

DOCTOR: What do you think about the baby?

AYALAH: I don't want any visual connection with the girl. ... There's no point to it ... she'll surely die in not too long a time ... so there's just no point. Don't you see that she frightens me?

DOCTOR: Actually, her condition is quite good now. ... Incidentally, does she have a name?

MOTHER: No. We didn't give her a name. Why should we?

After great efforts, the parents found a suitable institution. Ayalah and her husband, who as I have mentioned lead a life of observant Jews, put their daughter in an institution run by nuns in Jerusalem. The parents continued to ignore their daughter's existence for years to come. They also hid the fact of her existence from the rest of the family, never visited her, and did not take any interest in her welfare.

Thus, we have seen that when these parents learned that their daughter had Down's syndrome, they totally disclaimed responsibility for her. This found expression in their requests that the doctors put her to death, and in their announcement to the rest of their family, neighbors, and friends that their girl had died. They maintained that there was no point in taking care of a retarded girl within the home or in putting her in an institution that would deprive them of resources which they believed were owed to their healthy children. Their renunciation of responsibility towards their retarded girl also found expression in their unwillingness to invest in her future. The parents' attitude indicated a sense of parental responsibility and obligation only towards healthy children.

CASE 32 "CANCEL THE OPERATION; LIFE AND DEATH ARE IN GOD'S HANDS"

Here I describe the behavior of two couples who met each other in the wake of having given birth to deformed children. I shall describe the behavior of all four individuals, since in this instance the dynamics of their decision-making regarding the fate of their newborns took place among the group of four, not each couple separately.

Galia and Avram are a young couple of Austrian extraction, 25 years old, and have college degrees in the sciences. The couple, who live in a large city in the south of Israel, had a second daughter who, immediately upon birth was diagnosed as having the congenital defect spina bifida.[3] Her head was small and flattened in back, and her face was very distorted. She was immediately transferred to a hospital in the center of the country, and her mother, Galia, remained in Southern Hospital, where she had given birth. Galia shared a double room with a woman by the name of Bracha.

Bracha and her husband Yosi also had a child with spina bifida, but in their case the child had no concomitant distortions in the way he looked. Indeed, their son was actually quite good-looking. Bracha and Yosi are 30 years old, religious Jews, have a vocational education, are of Yemenite extraction, live in a rural area in the southern part of Israel, and have three other children, all healthy. Yosi and Bracha, too, were told immediately after their son's birth that he must have emergency surgery. Accordingly, he too was transferred to Central Hospital, and his mother Bracha remained in Southern Hospital in the same room with Galia. The two mothers, neither of whom had yet seen their babies, looked worried yet tried to reassure each other, saying such things as, "The children will probably come through O.K." While the women remained hospitalized after childbirth, their husbands set off together for Central Hospital, where their children were, and demanded to see the children. Let us describe the fathers' immediate reactions upon seeing their deformed children.

Avram was admitted first into the doctor's office. Upon seeing his daughter he took fright and ran out, crying and sobbing. "It's dreadful," he said to Yosi, "just dreadful. ... She has a bag on her back ... and the face of, of, of I don't know what ... I've never seen anything so dreadful. ... It's good that Galia didn't see her ... how horrid ... simply horrid. ... What causes such a thing to happen?"

Next Yosi, pale and frightened, entered the doctor's office to see his son. Yosi's son, in contrast to Avram's daughter, was a good-looking baby. Smiling broadly, Yosi turned to the medical staff and said, "I don't understand it. The child looks fine and well. ... He's the handsomest of all my children ... he's just wonderful. ... Please explain why he needs an operation at all? What's wrong with him? Maybe you can get by without operating? ... Have you considered it carefully? ... Show me what's the matter with him."

The nurse removed the diaper from the baby's back. Yosi, becoming aware of the defect, immediately recoiled in utter shock, saying, "It's dreadful ... dreadful ... truly dreadful."

Yosi quickly left the room and joined Avram, and the two of them sat and cried. Two hours later the doctor requested to have a talk with the fathers. By the time of this conversation one could already detect the fathers' desire to disclaim responsibility for the lives of their children.

Avram was the first to enter.

DOCTOR: If you don't mind, I would prefer to read the doctors' decision from the paper. [*Reading*] It is the decision of the medical staff that your daughter needs immediate surgery. ...

AVRAM [*interrupting the doctor*]: And what if they don't operate?

DOCTOR: Without an operation your girl will die in a short while. ...

FATHER: And what will her life be like after the operation?

DOCTOR: She will never be completely normal.

FATHER [*paling*]: Is there a risk involved in the operation? What are the chances of her dying on the operating table?

DOCTOR: The survival rate after operation is 25 percent, and the mortality rate during operation is 75 percent.

AVRAM: Could you please give me what you just said in writing?

DOCTOR [*somewhat embarrassed*]: I don't know if it's done, but ... well, O.K., here.

Avram took the slip of paper and requested some time to confer with his wife. He left the room, and Yosi entered immediately after him.

DOCTOR: Your son needs to have an operation ... post haste.

YOSI: After the operation, will my son be 100 percent normal?

DOCTOR: I must tell you the truth ... there is a chance your son will remain paralyzed after the operation ... and he might not be able to control his defecation ... and perhaps, I stress perhaps, he might turn out to have some mental retardation.

YOSI [*trembling all over*]: Oh, no! So why bother with the operation?

DOCTOR: Because there is also a very reasonable chance that your son will grow up and be a perfectly normal child.

YOSI [*after a moment's thought*]: And what if you don't operate on him?

DOCTOR: In such a case the baby will die in several days time.

YOSI [*after a few moments of silence*]: Tell me, doctor, tell me the truth. What would you do in my position?

DOCTOR: I can't make the decision for you.

YOSI: O.K., don't decide for me as a doctor. But if you had a child like this, what would you do? Think as if you were a father, not a doctor.

DOCTOR: It's hard to say. You must decide for yourself.

YOSI [*obviously wavering*]: Maybe the operation can be canceled for the time being? I would like to explain the situation to my wife, and she's still hospitalized in the south.

DOCTOR: But you must decide ... in no more than 36 hours.

Yosi left the room silently and joined Avram. Without saying a word, they left the hospital and set off to see their wives in Southern Hospital and relay the doctor's diagnoses to them.

After spending a sleepless night sitting together, all four parents in the same room, given over to hard thoughts and tears, the parents decided against permitting operations for their children, and thus sealed their children's fate. Let us look at how this difficult decision was made.

AVRAM [*seating himself close to Galia*]: Look, Galia, I've come to a decision. I won't sign a release for the operation ... [*sits in silence*] ... Look, if the doctors say that chances are she'll die in the operation, then if I consent to have her operated on, it's as if I gave permission to murder her, or as if I permitted them to cause her to die in an unnatural way. ...

GALIA [*bursting into tears*]: It's so cruel ... so cruel.

AVRAM: Just think what it'll do to the family. ...

GALIA [*crying*]: Let me think about it.

YOSI [*to Bracha*]: You should also think about it ... think well what it means to raise a child like this in our home. ... Everyone will be afraid to come into our house.

GALIA [*still crying*]: It's so cruel. ...

YOSI: What can anyone do? I don't know. [*Turning to Bracha*] Maybe we should call off the operation? What do you think?

BRACHA: I don't know yet.

YOSI: One thing you should know—they told me that if we sign the release for the operation, it's like agreeing to continue caring for him afterwards, too ... in other words, we'll have to take him home after the operation ... and we'll have to care for him at home. ...

BRACHA: Who told you that?

YOSI: I don't remember ... but they said it. ...

AVRAM: Yes, that makes sense. ... If we consent to the operation its like an irrevocable commitment ... and it doesn't make any difference what the outcome of the operation is, we've already committed ourselves to caring for the girl.

GALIA: Who told you that?

AVRAM: It makes sense.

YOSI: And, in the end if you send a kid like this to an institution it involves a huge financial outlay ... and all that will ruin our three children ... because what it amounts to is that a child like this takes a vast amount of time. And in the end nothing comes of him. And it also takes our time away from our children ... Bracha dear ... you must decide. ... [*Addressing Galia*] Have you made up your minds already?

GALIA [*crying*]: It's dreadfully cruel. I can't just forget about a child that I carried in my womb for nine months ... we should let the doctors do all they possibly can to put her in a condition in which we could take her home.

AVRAM [*gently*]: You must realize what the consequences it will have for Reva [*their two-year-old girl*].

GALIA [*crying incessantly*]: And what do you think the consequences will be for me, if we disown the girl? Have you thought of that? How will we be able to live with ourselves ... and remember, she could be a simply lovely little girl.

AVRAM: She'll never be a lovely little girl. You'd better realize that she'll hardly be able to function. She'll be retarded, really retarded. ... Try to imagine whom you intend to take care of ... and besides, what I'm doing is not called disowning. I think that consenting to the operation would be actually disowning her ... like signing your girl's death warrant with your own hand ... what I'm doing is not called disowning.

GALIA: But without the operation, she'll die for sure.

AVRAM: But it'll be a natural death. God works wonders ... and I won't condemn her to an unnatural death. Life and death are in God's hands, not mine.

GALIA: What's this, you've become religious all of a sudden?

AVRAM: I haven't become religious. But don't blame me; you'd be talking the same way yourself, if you had seen the girl. ... It's easy for you to talk, because you haven't seen her ... but, forgive me, I must tell you that what came out is ... a monster ... a real monster ... you can't imagine what she looks like ... such a creature can't possibly be normal or "lovely." She must be retarded. ... [*Galia continues crying.*]

BRACHA [*in tears*]: It's horrible ... really horrible for us to have to decide such a thing ... really awful. ... [*Addressing Yosi*] I too think that we ought to call off the operation [*sobbing out loud*]. A child like this will cause a crisis in the family ... he'll hurt the kids. ... It's easier for me than for you [*stroking her husband*] ... I didn't see the child and I don't feel tied to him. It's harder for you, because you saw him. ... Do you feel firm about your decision?

YOSI: Yes, but I want to be sure that you really agree, too.

BRACHA: Yes ... we'll decide it this way [*crying*].

AVRAM [*to Galia*]: What about you? Have you made up your mind already?

GALIA: I don't know. [*Shouting*] I don't know. I don't know what to do.

AVRAM: O.K., I'll give you an ultimatum. It's either me or the girl. You'll have to make up your mind. There isn't room for both of us. You'd better realize that if you want the girl, you'll have to give us up, give up me and Reva. So decide. Towards whom do you have a greater commitment— towards us, or towards a girl who'll be retarded. ... You don't owe her anything ... and you'd better realize that a retard like this isn't aware of who's caring for her ... and she won't even notice if you don't care for her ... so make up your mind.

GALIA [*quietly*]: I don't know. You decide.

Galia held her face in her hands and cried. Avram went to the corner of the room and burst into tears again. After half an hour of silence Avram went to the public telephone in the room. In a trembling voice he informed the head doctor: "My wife and I have decided to call off the operation." Galia listened all the while to the phone conversation without reacting, without moving a limb. Avram concluded his conversation and returned to sit by his wife. He hugged her and stroked her arms, and they both cried.

YOSI [*to Bracha*]: Maybe we should call my parents? see what they have to say?

BRACHA: Do whatever you see fit.

Yosi did not call from the telephone in the room, but went out to use a phone in the hall. In the end, however, he decided not to call his parents, and came back into the room several minutes later.

YOSI: I didn't call them. ... I didn't want to cause them pain ... but I know what they would have said if I had told them. ... They too would have agreed that we should call off the operation. ... They would have said: Why should a baby like that suffer? Poor thing. ... Also, they would have said that a baby who is completely paralyzed in the lower half of his body could never have children ... so what would ever come of him? ... I keep on thinking, ... all the time ... that it's so unfair. ... The doctors saw that we had a kid like this ... they should have done what had to be done ... and told us that we had a stillbirth. ... It is they who should make the decision; the doctors; it's their job. ... Parents mustn't be put in such a position ... but they wash their hands of it all, and walk out of the picture. And we, two people, ... who are practically children ourselves, have to make these difficult decisions. ... It's not our job to make this decision here ... so what will we do? ... Before this happened to me, I must have imagined a million times what parents would do in such a situation ... I always said that parents have to take care of their children. That's how I was brought up. We're religious ... but none of that's any help now. ... If we take him ... we'll see him every day and we'll suffer terribly ... we'll blame one another ... we won't know who's to blame for us having a child like this. ... The kids will be afraid, too, that maybe they'll have kids like this ... and we'll be afraid to have more kids because he'll always be there, before our eyes ... and we won't be able to forget. ... That's what happened with our neighbors, the Zahavis, I know. ... Who will take care of him? He'll pee in his pants all his life ... and who will take care of him? Bracha works hard, ... both our mothers are elderly, ... so there isn't anyone to care for him. ... Everything that we've saved up by hard work will go down the drain ... and we'll be a burden on our family ... and what good will come of it in the end? None at all. He's a retarded child, and nothing will come of him. ... Our family would back our decision not to take the child home. I'm sure of it. .... So it's decided. Now I feel better, and I'll go back to the hospital and inform them of our final decision to cancel the operation. ... [*Painfully*] I know I'm actually writing his death warrant, ... but what else can we do?

BRACHA: Don't go there, phone the hospital from here.

YOSI [*hesitatingly*]: You're right. ... I won't go back there ... so they won't be able to force me to take the child and care for him [*crying*]. How horrible.

Several minutes later he went to the telephone, called the hospital, and in tears informed them of their decision to call off the operation.

The next day, early in the morning, Yosi put through another call to the hospital where his son was. The conversation went as follows:

YOSI: Today my son was supposed to have an operation. ... Yesterday I notified you that we cannot consent to the operation ... but I'm terribly anxious ... just wanted to check that you really won't operate.

VOICE ON THE TELEPHONE: Yes. You can rest assured ... we are not operating on him ... you're notification was received.

YOSI: Thank you. I'm really very much reassured.

Yosi and Bracha did not talk about their baby any more. Two days later the child died. His parents gave him a funeral, which was attended by the people of their village, and two months later they erected a tombstone over his grave. Galia and Avram, as well, no longer talked about their girl. They treated each other with gentle concern. A week later they were informed of their girl's death. The couple received the news in silence. They too gave their child a funeral and erected a tombstone. The father didn't shave and wore a yarmulke for a month. "We've been going through a terrible period," Galia said two months later. "In the final analysis, my husband was right and his arguments were rational . ... Every once in a while we're troubled by a sense of guilt ... but we try to overcome it. ... To tell the truth, we felt a sense of relief when she died ... deep down inside, we were even happy. ... But the important thing is that, in the final analysis, we acted properly towards her, as parents. We made a funeral, and put up an expensive stone. The works. ... "

The two couples did not maintain contact with each other after parting ways in the hospital. In both cases the couples' friends and other family members did not know of the parents' refusal to consent to the children's operations. The relatives were told that the babies had been sickly and had died several days later.

We see that despite differences in ethnic background (Austrian vs. Yemenite), education (college vs. vocational), residential area (urban vs. rural), sex of the newborn, and degree of religiosity, both pairs of young parents abandoned their newborns with spina bifida. Both instances involved not only rejection from the family territory, but also renunciation of parental responsibility for the child's life. The newborns suffered serious defects and were due to undergo operations—the only way of their having a chance of survival. The parents' indecision whether or not to consent to the operation is essentially indecision regarding the essence of parental responsibility towards one's children. There are several aspects to this responsibility.

The parents attribute critical importance to the decision regarding the operation, since this decision is perceived especially by the fathers as signifying acceptance of responsibility for the children's lives in the future and as an irrevocable obligation to continue caring for them. Refusing to consent to the operation meant disclaiming responsibility for their children's lives; but both couples found it difficult to admit their responsibility for the death of their children and sought an arrangement that would enable them to stress their not being involved in the children's deaths. One of the ways was the approach taken by Avram and other parents whom I observed.

Avram maintained that he was not willing to accept responsibility for his girl's death, when in actual fact he was not willing to accept responsibility for her life. He decided on a course of action that led to certain death for the newborn, when consenting to the operation would have increased her chances of living. The parents' remarks that the responsibility for the decision ought to lie with the doctors should be viewed in a similar manner. Ostensibly they wished to free themselves of the responsibility for deciding the fate of their children and to pass this responsibility on to the doctors, nurses, and other family members; but a closer examination of their words shows that the parents essentially were not interested in transferring the responsibility for the fate of their children to any other body. After having decided that it would be best if the babies died, they were not prepared to accept any other decision on the part of the doctors. (Remember Yosi's call to the hospital to make sure that the doctors had not overruled his decision.)

In turning to outsiders, and even to each other, the parents sought an arrangement that would present their decisions as the decision of some other body, and thus would release them of responsibility for the death of their children. Yosi's suggestion that he call his parents ostensibly expressed his desire to spread the responsibility for the fate of his child and his need to involve his family in that responsibility. However, due to his fear that social pressure might coerce him to accept a decision contrary to his own, he refrained from actually calling his parents, doing so only in his imagination as part of his efforts to convince himself that the rest of his family would support his decision, due to the child's "infertility." Thus, Yosi used imaginary diffusion of responsibility so that he could avoid viewing himself as the sole person responsible for his child's death.

Another aspect of parental responsibility towards one's children is that deciding the fate of a handicapped child is interpreted as choosing between various parental responsibilities. Yosi and Avram presented their wives with a choice between conflicting obligations. In their opinion, one could not be responsible both for a retarded girl and for the rest of the family. In attempting to persuade his wife to abandon their handicapped girl, Avram plays on her sense of responsibility towards her healthy girl. Avram's behavior reflects the view that parents have an obligation to their healthy children, and not to retarded children "who aren't aware of who's caring for them, anyway." Yosi and Bracha, too, justified their renunciation of responsibility towards their handicapped child on the grounds of their sense of responsibility towards their healthy children. Their renunciation of the values of the social system with which they were inculcated is actually justified on the grounds of an obligation to that system and its values; for they reject a child who does not satisfy the family-oriented values of the system ("he won't be able to have children") and who would impoverish its members. Other family values of the system are invoked to sanction the individual's renunciation of his child and to give him support in his decision by keeping him from feeling that he bears the sole responsibility for the death of his child.

The last aspect of the perception of parental responsibility which we see in this case pertains to rites of mourning. In deciding not to permit the operations, both couples expressed their renunciation of responsibility towards their children as living beings; however they did not cast off their responsibility towards their children in death. They gave them proper funerals and erected tombstones for them. Even though they were not religious, Galia and Avram observed Jewish religious mourning practices. Avram did not shave (a Jewish rite of mourning) and wore a yarmulke (a sign of identification with religious Jews). As Galia summed up the period of mourning, "We acted properly ... as parents."

CASE 33 "DO NOT DO THE OPERATION. EVERYTHING IS IN ALLAH'S HANDS"

This case, which concludes our discussion of total parental disavowal of responsibility for the life of a baby with a defect, describes the behavior of parents whose national affiliation, education, and residence are different from that of the parents I have described thus far.

Ḥitam and her husband are Moslem Arabs, illiterate, 37 years old, and live in an Arab village in central Israel. On her seventh delivery in Northern Hospital, Ḥitam gave birth to a girl with spina bifida.[3] Here is an account of what transpired at the end of the delivery and thereafter.

MIDWIFE: It's O.K., Ḥitam, it's all over. Congratulations, you have a girl.

Suddenly the midwife turned white, removed the baby, and called the doctor. The doctor looked at the infant, placed her on the table and began examining her.

ḤITAM: Oh, it hurts so much. Vey, vey, this girl killed me. I have a girl, but she's killed me with the pain. Vey, vey ... I want to sleep now ... let me sleep ... [closing her eyes].

Having examined the girl, the doctor approached Ḥitam together with the midwife.

MIDWIFE [touching Ḥitam gently]: We want to talk with you.

ḤITAM [smiling]: What is it? I'm tired.

DOCTOR: I'm sorry, but there is something we must tell you. Your baby girl is not quite healthy. She has something seriously the matter with her spinal cord.

ḤITAM [*in alarm*]: What's the matter with her? What's the matter?

DOCTOR: ... It causes paralysis in the legs, and can cause death.

ḤITAM [*in a panicky voice*]: What's the matter with her? What's wrong? Show me. I want to see.

NURSE: That's not advisable ... but we told you about her, because we might have to operate and you'll have to sign.

ḤITAM: What's wrong with her? Show her to me. ...

The midwife brought her the girl.

ḤITAM [*looking at her girl, making a distorted face, and saying in disgust*]: This is a *waḥaj* (devil). [*She didn't touch the child, but sighed, turned her face to the wall, and closed her eyes.*] It's yucky; it frightens me.

DOCTOR [*gently*]: Look, Ḥitam, the child must have an operation. If she does not have the operation, she'll die immediately. You and your husband must decide and sign a form that you consent to the operation.

Ḥitam made no response. The doctor and midwife moved aside. Several minutes later Ḥitam turned her face the other way and called the midwife.

ḤITAM [*to the midwife*]: Do me a favor. I want to speak with the doctor again.

MIDWIFE: O.K. We'll call a pediatric specialist ... to look at your girl.

ḤITAM: And also bring my husband from the village ... tell him to come quickly.

The midwife went to do what Ḥitam had requested. Half an hour later the pediatrician arrived and set about examining the girl.

ḤITAM [*to the nurse*]: Nurse, I want to speak to the doctor.

The doctor came over to Ḥitam.

ḤITAM: Look, doctor ... you've seen the girl ... a *waḥaj* [*crying*]. ... I've heard of such cases before, in our village ... even our family had a *waḥaj* once. ... Thank you very much for caring for kids like these ... but I don't want anyone to operate on the girl ... please don't take care of her ... leave her be ... let her die ... don't do anything ... it's a waste ... trust Allah. ...

DOCTOR: That's just the point. I'm not God. I can't decide not to take care of the girl.

ḤITAM: Exactly. We're not God, so we won't decide. Let God do what's good and what's necessary. Allah is great ... only He knows what is good.

DOCTOR: If we don't come into the picture, if we don't operate, your girl will die.

ḤITAM: Everything is in God's hands; we are but clay. God decides.

DOCTOR: Ḥitam, do you have any other requests to make?

ḤITAM: Yes. I'd like to know why she [*the girl*] looked dark, not pink?

DOCTOR: I don't know.

The doctor left, and the girl was taken to another room.

Ḥitam lay in bed, resting and drinking coffee. An hour later her husband arrived. Ḥitam told him about the great misfortune that had befallen them, and her husband turned pale.

NURSE: Can I get you some coffee, sir?

HUSBAND: Yes, thank you.

NURSE: Would you like to speak with the doctor?

HUSBAND: No thank you, my wife has explained to me ... and I agree with her. ... What's the point of operating? It's a pity for her to suffer ... better not to take care of her ... everything's in the hands of Allah.

NURSE: What about the rest of your family in the village? Have you talked it over with them? Do they know anything about it?

HUSBAND: No. When they called me to the hospital, I understood that something was wrong ... so I didn't even tell them that Ḥitam had already given birth ... I wanted to come and see what's up, first.

ḤITAM: That's good, good.

Four hours later the doctor arrived and informed them of their girl's death. The parents received the news quietly. Several minutes later the father got up from his chair, exchanged a few words with Ḥitam, and went over to the doctor.

HUSBAND [*to the doctor*]: Doctor, my wife requested me to ask something of you. Please don't throw the girl away ... we want to take her back to the village and bury her there.

DOCTOR: I don't know what the procedure is, but I'll see to it that your request is fulfilled.

HUSBAND: Thank you, ... thank you for all your care ... please give all the nurses and doctors here ... our thanks for their care. [*Coming over to Ḥitam and addressing her*] I have to go back, to tell everyone.

ḤITAM: Yes.

HUSBAND: Be prepared, because after we tell them, they'll all come to see you.

ḤITAM: What for?

HUSBAND: You know that's how it is. ...

Towards evening Ḥitam's relatives arrived and told her they were sorry to hear she had had a stillbirth. Ḥitam lay in bed, apathetic, and did not respond to her relatives' attempts to feed her.

As in the previous cases, Ḥitam too refused to consent to an operation on her daughter, and thus disclaimed responsibility for her life. She disagreed with the doctor's view that to remain passive was to be an accessory to the girl's death. To clear herself of responsibility, Hitam appealed to God. "Trust in God," she told the doctor. In other words, she wished not to intervene in the work of creation, where non-intervention meant certain death for her girl. The behavior of Hitam and her husband resembles that of Yosi and Avram and their wives also insofar as they disclaimed responsibility for their child's life, yet as parents felt a responsibility towards the child's body after death.

The cases that I have presented thus far describe extremes of disavowal of parental responsibility for the life of a child who is perceived by her or his parents as a threatening entity. In these cases, territorial rejection or abandonment of children in the hospital is tantamount to a total disavowal of responsibility for their lives. In the cases which follow I shall illustrate other shades of renunciation of responsibility, ranging from total rejection of responsibility to total acceptance of responsibility for one's child and for all that happens to her or him.

CASE 34 "AFTER ALL, SHE'S OUR DAUGHTER"

Gali and her husband are of Polish extraction and have two daughters. Gali is a secretary at the university, and her husband is an assistant professor. When she came to Central Hospital for her third delivery, she was sure that "this time it will be a boy." Nevertheless, she showed no signs of disappointment when the doctor who delivered her told her she had had another girl. The day after the birth, the child was brought to her mother for breast-feeding, at which time the mother noticed "something the matter with the girl." Noting that the baby had a broad neck, narrow eyes, and short fingers, the mother said, "She's not normal . . . she makes a chill run down my spine." Immediately she called the nurse and asked, "What's wrong with my girl? Did the doctors examine her? Did they say anything? I think she's got something wrong with her." Gali refused to rediaper her baby, and asked the nurse to do it. She rushed to the phone to call her husband and, crying and shouting, demanded that he come to the hospital immediately to have a talk with the doctor, because "something's wrong with our girl." When the father arrived at the hospital, his wife's diagnosis was confirmed. It turned out that the girl had been diagnosed as having Down's syndrome at birth, but that the diagnosis had not been passed on to the parents due to "the unpleasantness of passing on such terrible news," as the doctors put it. Gali and her husband were dumbfounded. They tried to find causes for the defect, but could not; their other children were normal and they had no family history of such defects. The father concluded that it must be "an accident, . . . a mistake of nature."

The joy of the birth vanished. Gali refused to nurse her child since, as she put it, she did not want "to form any bonds with her." Her husband also was not interested in seeing the child. Nevertheless, Gali paid a daily visit to her daughter in the nursery. Gali and he refused to take their baby girl home, because they did not want "any ties with the girl," in the mother's own words.

Meanwhile it became clear that the girl also had severe defects (in the heart and lungs) in addition to being retarded. The parents began a search for "the best institution ... the most expensive ... with the best name possible." Having found an institution that met their requirements, in the north of Israel (although the parents live in Tel Aviv), they had the girl transferred directly to the institution, without taking her home.

For the first few weeks both parents visited their girl once a week. Afterwards only Gali went. The father was ashamed of his girl. "The sense of shame really bothers him," Gali told us, "he really cannot bear it ... and if there's someone who didn't know I was expecting, we don't tell them anything about it."

The atmosphere in the home became more and more tense. Gali and her husband blamed each other for the girl's handicap. Their older children asked incessantly, "Where's the new baby? Why isn't she at home?" Gali also had sharp words of reproach against the doctors: "Why didn't they strangle her the moment she came out? Why isn't there a law that would save us the dreadful suffering we have now? ... who knows what the future holds? ... and we're not the only ones! So where is the law? They should have strangled the girl around her neck, should have said she came out dead, and then told the parents." Her husband, too, never stopped wondering, "I just don't understand how I came to have such a pathetic creature, half this and half that ... how this baby has any connection with me."

Nevertheless, the parents continued to lay out vast sums of money for institutional care of their daughter. Gali continued to visit the institution regularly, even though she returned from each visit in tears and suffering. "The more she grew, the harder it was," she said.

After a year, the girl died. Her parents gave her a funeral and buried her in the city in the north of Israel, where the institution was. They also erected an expensive tombstone over her grave. "After all, she's our daughter," Gali said. A year after the girl's death, Gali and her husband had another daughter. Immediately upon birth the doctors examined the baby's neck and eyes. Everyone was delighted. The girl looked healthy. Today, two years later, the father is happy with his little girl, and never mentions the girl that died.

In this case we met a couple who were not willing to take their retarded child home. Yet they did not renounce all responsibility for her life. These parents expressed social responsibility for the fate of their child unaccompanied by any feeling of intimacy towards her.

Shula's case (see Chapter 2) provides another example of accepting responsibility for a handicapped child while trying to avoid intimate contact with her. In Shula's case the mother casts off her responsibility towards her girl only in her dreams. Like many other parents, even though she takes care of her child, in her fantasies she imagines or hopes her child dead; in other words, she has a deep desire to unburden herself of the responsibility for her child's life. In day-to-day reality the mother accepts a certain type of responsibility and bond with her girl. This is a sort of social responsibility towards her daughter (expressed, for example, in finding substitute childcare) devoid of emotional closeness.

CASE 35 "HOME IS FOR THE HEALTHY"

Here I shall describe the behavior of Moshi's mother. As we shall see, in the hospital she cares for her son, prepares food for him, feeds him, and takes him out to walk; but refuses to do all these things for him when he is at home.

Moshi is a six-year-old diabetic boy who is frequently hospitalized in Southern Hospital. The family is on welfare and has seven other children at home. The parents are of Moroccan extraction. The mother comes to visit her son almost every day. She spends several hours at his side, brings him tasty things to eat, and takes him out for short walks on the hospital's grounds. On the rare occasions when the mother cannot pay him a visit, other members of the family are requested to come in her stead. Indeed, the family is very warm and loving towards Moshi.

Moshi is not allowed to eat sweet things. Each of the previous times he was hospitalized, he was released after his condition had improved; but each time he returned to the hospital several days later, in serious condition. Every time the mother brought her son back to the hospital she claimed that she had adhered strictly to his diet and that she did "not understand how the child manages to put things into his mouth ... it's as simple as that ... so I bring him back to the hospital. ... He mustn't be left with me now ... with me he just gets more and more ill. ... "

The following scene illustrates the mother's behavior.

After his rounds, the doctor requested the mother to see him in his office.

DOCTOR: We have examined Moshi. He feels much better. He looks alright ... so you can take him home even this evening, or tomorrow morning. ... I want to remind you once more how important it is to watch Moshi's diet. Here, in the hospital, we kept him to his diet and now his condition is very good ... remember, under no circumstances is he to eat food containing sugar.

MOTHER [*laughing*]: I know, I'm half a doctor by now. But I'm not sure Moshi is really ready to come home yet. In my opinion, he's not completely well yet.

DOCTOR: According to our tests, his condition is good enough for him to be sent home.

MOTHER: I'd prefer it if he stayed here. It's hard to care for him at home. I'm afraid of him at home. ... Understand me, it's strange having a sick person wandering around the house. ...

DOCTOR: I don't understand. In the hospital you care for him marvelously. So take care of him at home, just like you do in the hospital.

MOTHER: There's a very big difference ... it's not the same thing being in the hospital and being at home. ...

DOCTOR: I'm sorry. ...

The mother left the ward and returned two hours later, carrying some corn patties.

MOSHI: Hey, Mom, what did you bring me?

MOTHER: Guess ... [*taking out the corn patties and serving them to Moshi*] corn patties!

MOSHI [*delighted*]: Great. I haven't even tasted a corn patty since I came to the hospital. [*Grabbing the patties, he began to eat, then addressed the author*]: I can tell by the way you're looking at me that you're jealous of my having patties ... are you crazy about them to? Want a taste?

AUTHOR: Sure.

MOTHER [*who at first had not noticed that the author and the nurse were in the room, tries to prevent Moshi from giving me a bite*]: Don't give her ... she'll get your sickness. ...

AUTHOR: Moshi's disease is not contagious.

MOTHER [*trying to prevent me from tasting the patties*]: Maybe, actually, you should eat them later ... all the kids in the room will be jealous of you and want a bite, and you'll have nothing left for yourself. ...

MOSHI [*to the author*]: I want to offer you some ... and I don't care about the other kids. Let them be jealous.

Moshi offered me the patties. I tasted them and discovered that they were exceedingly sweet. I didn't say a word, but Moshi's mother turned pale.

MOTHER: It's just sweet by accident ... I swear to you ... maybe one of the kids added sugar by accident. ...

NURSE: Let me have a taste. [*She takes a bite and immediately cries out*] It's absolutely inconceivable that a mother who knows her child could die from such a quantity sugar should do such a thing to her child!

MOTHER [*silent at first, but then answers softly*]: He won't die from the amount of sugar in the patties ... he'll only pass out . ... and then they won't send him home. ... [*Bursting out*] I can't do it ... I don't have the setup to take care of a sick child ... I can't cook separately for him ... and especially I can't constantly keep an eye on him to make sure that he does not snitch things he's not allowed to have ... but in the hospital I'm prepared to do anything, to be beside him all day long ... everything ... but I can't keep him at home. ... [*Imploringly*] My husband really loves Moshi, because he's the most mischievous of all the children. ... I beg you, please don't tell him ... he mustn't know about this ... and the children mustn't know about this.

NURSE: Throwing your kid into the hospital is no solution.

MOTHER: I'm not throwing him there. I could throw him into an institution ... but I don't want to give away my Moshi forever ... I'm his mother, after all ... I don't want to give him to a hospital for chronic diseases, either ... after all, here the child knows the nurses and doctors, and it's better for him here than at home. ... He needs to be here ... I also explained that to the doctor ... I told him beforehand that he should keep Moshi here. ...

NURSE [*understandingly*]: I have a suggestion to make ... so that you won't have to cook specially for Moshi at home, we'll cook his food in the hospital and bring you everything all prepared. What do you say to that? If we were to see to it he's provided proper nutrition, would you be able to keep him at home?

MOTHER: No. You don't understand, I want to cook for him. I like cooking for him. I put all my love into my cooking.

NURSE: Then maybe you have some idea how we could help you?

MOTHER: The only help you can give me is to arrange for Moshi to be in the hospital.

NURSE: Look, I understand you. You have a lot of children, and it's hard for you with a sick child. But what do you save yourself by having him in the hospital? Even when Moshi is in the hospital you cook for him at home, and you also worry about his not snitching things that he's not allowed to eat from the other children in his room. ... And you bring your children here to play with him, and you have to keep your eyes open all the time to make sure they don't give him something forbidden ... so just do the same thing at home. ...

MOTHER: You don't understand. I don't want to get rid of Moshi. I'm his mother. I love him and I have to take care of him, but not at home. At home I can only care for healthy children, ... home is for the healthy ... Moshi is sick and should be in the hospital. ... I want to take care of Moshi, but only when he's in the hospital ... you don't understand. When there's a sick child in the home it causes terrible fear. I'm afraid of him; he's sick ... I keep on seeing him as if he were dead ... I'm afraid suddenly he'll die ... he confuses me ... he's strange when he's at home ... he's sick, and I only know how to be a mother to healthy children. You can't rely on me.

At home he'll die on me. The hospital is the only place where he will be healthy.

Moshi remained in the hospital for a few more days. Four days later, when his mother was asked again to take him home from the hospital within two days, she made no response. The following morning Moshi fell out of bed. His mother was not with him at the moment, so the nurse ran over to him. As she picked him up off the floor she found all the pills he was supposed to have taken the previous day (3 pills).

NURSE [*shouting*]: Where is that mother?

MOSHI'S MOTHER [*entering the room in a panic*]: What's happened?

NURSE: What's happened?! I found all Moshi's pills under his bed.

MOTHER [*embarrassed*]: Well, I suppose you forgot to give them to him.

NURSE: How dare you say such a thing! True, we always give him his medicine, but yesterday morning you insisted that we give you the pills and that you would give them to Moshi. But instead of ending up in his mouth, the pills found their way to under his bed!

MOTHER: So what if I forgot to give them to him? Why are you yelling at me?

NURSE [*still furious*]: What kind of a mother are you? You know that Moshi must have those pills!

MOTHER: Nothing serious will happen to him if he misses one day. At worst he'll get a bit bloated. People don't die of that in this day and age ... and don't shout at me. You think it's easy for me? ... I have to stay with him in the hospital, day and night ... so I can't hold a regular job ... but I don't care, because he's my beloved boy ... this boy is the light of my life.

NURSE [*softening up*]: So take him home; it'll be easier for you.

MOTHER: You really don't understand a thing. None of you understand anything.

Moshi's mother's behavior is not total territorial rejection; for, even though she rejects Moshi from the family territory, she does not abandon him (as she said, "I'm not throwing him away"). As long as the child is hospitalized, his mother acts with a clear sense of responsibility towards him and expresses her willingness to care for him devotedly, provided he not be sent home.

The son's rejection is couched in terms of practical difficulties; but it turns out that the problem is actually cultural. According to the mother's perceptions, the home is for healthy people and should not include sick individuals such as Moshi. A close analysis of the situation reveals that the mother's behavior is completely consistent. Moshi's mother has him put in the hospital, because only there can she forget that he is sick; when he is hospitalized she cares for him as one would care for a healthy child: she cooks for him, feeds him, and takes him for walks, but she does not give him any special nursing care. In contrast, when he is at home, she is expected to care for him as one does for a sick person; but it is precisely this contact with a sick person that she finds threatening.

CASE 36 "WE WANT TO CHECK WHAT THEY'RE DOING TO OUR GIRL"

This case presents a variation on the theme of the behavior seen in the previous case.

Rita is a seven-year-old diabetic, the daughter of 35-year-old parents who immigrated to Israel from Georgia, U.S.S.R., eight years ago. The mother is a housewife and the father a store owner. Rita has two healthy brothers, ages four and five. Rita is frequently hospitalized in Northern Hospital; often she falls and is bruised or breaks a hand, or gets infections that do not heal. The nurses suspect that the mother has been intentionally infecting her daughter's sores so that she will be kept in the hospital.

One day Rita was brought to the hospital due to complaints of a severe stomach ache. She came with an escort of about twenty relatives. The girl was sent for an X-ray, and was taken there by an orderly, again escorted by her relatives. She returned from the X-ray, with all her relatives. The relatives were laden with baskets of food, packages and bags. After the nurse put Rita in bed, the relatives emptied their baskets, producing vast quantities of food, canned goods, fruits, and bottles of juice. They put all this on Rita's bed, in her bedside table, and under her bed. Her mother took several apples, sandwiches, and a bottle of juice, put them in one of the baskets, and then all the relatives left the room and installed themselves in the hall, near her room.

Later a nurse came into the room. She was immediately followed by all the family, who surrounded Rita's bed on all sides. When the nurse left the room, all the family left after her. This scene was repeated whenever any of the medical staff entered Rita's room. Whenever the staff member left, the family left after her. When the medical staff had to take care of the patients and the members of the family were requested to step out for a moment, they would refuse, saying, "We are afraid something will be done to her ... we want to see what they're doing to the girl ... we're keeping watch to see that they don't do anything to her."

Rita ate very little. Most of the food was consumed by her relatives. After several hours the women took off their shoes and walked barefoot throughout the ward. Even when the relatives were milling around the ward, some of them always stayed with Rita's mother, close by the door to Rita's room, to keep an eye on the comings and goings of the medical staff. The female relatives remained with Rita's mother throughout the night. In the evening they dragged chairs from beside the beds of other patients into the middle of the room and laid themselves down on them. Later at night other relatives, who had not been around during the day, showed up. Each one brought a basket full of food, intended for the visitors, not the patient. The visitors finally departed at ten o'clock at night, leaving only the mother and six of her relatives.

One morning Rita fell out of bed, lost consciousness, and was transferred to intensive care, where she was given an infusion. Several minutes later she regained consciousness but was kept in intensive care for the next day. All her relatives were assembled outside the room. The number of relatives present remained more or less constant, but upon closer examination it became clear that the composition of the group was always changing, one group of relatives relieving another each day.

At the time of the conversation recorded below, Rita's parents were outside the room, accompanied by their relatives. The nurse entered the intensive care room, and Rita's father followed her. (Bringing other relatives into the intensive care room is strictly forbidden.)

NURSE [*adjusting the infusion and explaining to Rita*]: Be sure to keep your arm straight all the time so the infusion won't get blocked.

FATHER: It's hard for her to do that.

NURSE: So hold onto her hand.

FATHER: That's what you're here for.

The nurse made no response. She left the room, followed by Rita's father. An hour later the doctor came into the room. The father followed immediately after him. The doctor examined the girl.

FATHER: The nurse is not keeping a good enough watch on Rita.

DOCTOR: You're right.

The doctor left the room, and with him the father. An hour later the nurse came in, followed by the father. She checked the infusion. Rita had bent her arm, and the nurse straightened it.

FATHER [*to the nurse*]: You're not doing your job properly. You keep on waking the girl up.

NURSE: Kindly leave the room.

FATHER: I won't leave my daughter unattended ... tell me, what sort of nurse are you, anyway?

The father went to the door and called Rita's mother, "Come take over for me."

The next morning Rita returned to her room in the children's ward. Two days later she began having severe diarrhea and was transferred to a separate room. The mother was requested not to leave Rita alone, because she might become dehydrated due to the diarrhea. The mother heard the request, but left the room and joined her relatives.

NURSE [*who had come to check the girl's condition and had found her by herself, addressing the mother*]: Tell me, why are you wandering around the ward and not sitting at your daughter's side?

MOTHER: You get paid a salary and you're supposed to take care of her, not me.

Later in the afternoon two patients of Russian origin were admitted to the ward. Rita's relatives talked with them and toured the ward together. Rita's mother did not take care of her girl or feed her.

NURSE [*who had come again to check Rita's condition, again addressing the mother*]: What shall we do with you? Have you forgotten about your girl altogether?

MOTHER: I'm tired. I didn't come here to take care of my girl. It's enough for me to take care of her at home. Anyway, you're getting paid plenty to take care of her.

Thus, for the next few days the mother was constantly present in the hospital, but essentially spent very little time with her girl.

On the seventh day of Rita's hospitalization in the ward, her mother made friends with two nurses of Georgian origin. She began spending many hours at the nursing station, putting on fingernail polish and talking with the nurses. Every so often she would serve the two Georgian nurses coffee from a thermos brought by her relatives, adding sugar or saccharine according to their taste and always remembering what cake or cookie each one liked to have with her coffee. The mother often fell into conversation with the families of other patients, took an interest in the details of their ailments, and was well versed in the dates each of the patients was admitted or released from the ward. Her pattern of behavior towards the medical staff and her daughter remained as before. For example, consider the following event:

A nurse (not Georgian) entered the room, and Rita's mother ran after her.

RITA: I want a bedpan.

MOTHER [*to the nurse*]: The girl wants a bedpan.

The nurse didn't say a word.

MOTHER [*to the nurse*]: Will you bring Rita a bedpan?

The nurse left, brought back a bedpan, placed it beneath the lower part of Rita's body. After Rita finished, she said, "I'm done peeing."

MOTHER [*to the nurse*]: The girl's finished peeing. Will you take the bedpan?

The nurse took the bedpan and left the room. The mother followed after her. An hour later another nurse, also non-Georgian, came in. The mother followed on her heels.

NURSE [*to the mother*]: Rita has to have an X-ray. You should go with her.

MOTHER: I'm sorry, but it's hard to go with a wheelchair ... that's the orderly's job.

From that moment on, the mother constantly reminded the nurses that "you must call the orderly to come and take Rita." When the orderly arrived, he was joined by the mother and her relatives, loaded down with their baskets. The orderly pushed Rita's wheelchair, while the mother and all her relatives clustered around him.

Two days later the doctor told the mother, "Rita can be sent home."

MOTHER: I won't take Rita home. She's not well. I'll only take home a girl who's well.

DOCTOR: You must take her.

MOTHER: We'll see about that.

Ten o'clock that evening screams were heard from the mother and her relatives. The nurses ran to Rita's room.

MOTHER [*screaming*]: What is this here? You call this a hospital? Why isn't anyone taking care of my daughter? The doctors walked past her bed and said that she can go home ... but look how sick she is ... no one's taking care of my daughter ... see for yourselves what a cut she has.

The mother ripped off Rita's bandages and showed all those present in the room her daughter's cuts. Rita screamed and writhed in pain, and her mother told her, "Shut up, I'm doing this for your own good."

A surgeon who had been summoned to the room examined Rita, rebandaged her, and said irately to the mother, "The last time Rita was in the hospital she had a serious infectious inflammation of the bone due to an open lesion in her hand. We suspect that you've been infecting your daughter's cut. You keep on letting the cut be open ... even though the medical staff has explained to you repeatedly about the danger of it becoming infected."

The following morning the doctor told the mother again, "By this evening you must take Rita out of here, since there is no medical justification for keeping her in the hospital."

Late that afternoon Rita fell out of bed. Her mother was not at her side. She received a bruise on the head and was taken to the emergency room by the nurse on duty. In the emergency room her cut had to be stitched. The mother and about ten relatives came to the emergency room and started yelling loudly, "My daughter cut her head open!" "Again, they're not looking after her properly in the ward," said the mother.

NURSE: Don't yell. Sit down and listen to who's not taking good care of your daughter. Your daughter fell because you weren't at her side. ... You'd better stop shouting and start taking care of her. There's no justification for keeping her here ... take her home.

Rita was taken back to the ward. This time the mother and her relatives entered Rita's room, but refused to communicate with the staff. The mother sat in the room, occupying herself with knitting, filing her fingernails, and talking with her relatives. She sat in a corner far from Rita, in a place where it was impossible for her to keep an eye on her girl. The relatives themselves explained their "retreat from the corridor," as they themselves referred to it, in the following words, "O.K., ... it's not a good idea for them to see us all the time and tell us to take Rita home. This way they'll forget about Rita."

However, the parents' expectations that Rita would remain in the hospital were not fulfilled, and the next morning she was sent home. By the evening of the same day the family (the mother, Rita, and some relatives) were already back in the emergency room. The mother was wearing a fur coat and bedecked with gold jewelry.

MOTHER: Rita has a fever.

NURSE: True, but why bring a girl with a fever to the hospital? It's so cold outside. Couldn't you take care of her at home?

MOTHER: She had a fever, so we brought her here.

Rita was examined and given medicine to reduce her fever. Her fever dropped and the doctor requested that she be taken home.

DOCTOR: There's no reason to bring a girl with the flu to the hospital.

MOTHER: Look how she feels! Is that what you call feeling good? I want you to hospitalize her ... there's no way I can take care of her at home.

DOCTOR: Miss, there are no beds available in the hospital, and there's no medical reason for hospitalizing Rita ... she only has a fever, and you should take care of her at home.

MOTHER: Doctor, I want you to realize that the minute you release her from here, if anything happens to her, it's on your head.

DOCTOR: You're her mother. You're responsible for her.

MOTHER: True, I'm her mother and that's the reason I brought her here. It's my responsibility to notice that my daughter is ill ... and to bring her here. From the moment I bring her here, you're responsible for her and you have to take care of her.

DOCTOR: I'm sorry, but I must discharge her.

MOTHER: On your own responsibility. As for myself, I've done what I had to. I can't take care of a sick child at home. I care for my children only when they're healthy.

The girl remained in the emergency room until the next morning and then was sent home.

As in the previous case, here too the parents' behavior does not show total territorial rejection; rather, it indicates that the parents do accept a certain sort of responsibility. Like Moshi's mother, Rita's parents also refuse to take her home and deliberately subvert her cure in order to keep her hospitalized; but in so doing, according to their own perception, they are not evincing total renunciation of responsibility for her life. Unlike the parents of Victor and the "unicorn," Rita's parents remain in the ward almost around the clock. Nevertheless, one should not be overly impressed by their purely physical presence, but should note the message that their presence conveys. As I have said, the mother is present in the ward most of the time, but is not actually at her daughter's side and refuses to give her any nursing care or other attention (such as helping her eat). When something needs to be done, the family turns to the nursing staff and instructs them to do whatever is necessary. The assignment of roles reveals a notion of allocation of responsibility to which the parents adhere fanatically. Responsibility for taking care of the girl is placed on the nurses. The parents view themselves as responsible for giving orders to the medical staff (the mother instructs the orderly to take her girl for an X-ray, and the nurse to bring her a bedpan), but they do not consider that actually caring for their girl falls within the realm of their own responsibility.

The family gathering also serves to underscore the importance of this division of responsibility. The parents are in charge of overseeing the medical staff, and their relatives are supposed to encourage them not to abandon their watch. So that the relatives can perform their duty, an elaborate system of hosting is required (food, a place to sleep, the ability to go around barefoot) to make the visitors feel at home. The girl's hospitalization is also used as a social happening and for stressing the strength of the bond among family and friends. The fight between the mother and the doctor brings out more sharply the differences of opinion on the essence of responsibility and how responsibility should be divided between the mother and the doctor. It also reveals the cultural perceptions underlying the allocation of responsibility. According to the view expressed here, home is for the healthy, and the mother's role only extends as far as caring for healthy children. Therefore Rita's mother shows willingness to remain with her daughter and oversee the administration of medical care by the medical staff as long as her daughter is in the hospital, but she refuses to care for her daughter and tend to her needs when she is within the family territory.

When the mother notes a sign of sickness, as simple as the flu, she feels she must have her girl hospitalized in the place intended for sick people and absolve herself of responsibility for caring for her girl.

Moshi's and Rita's mothers reflect a territorial dimension of rejection and acceptance. At home they are not mothers to their sick children. However, they are prepared to remain with their children when in the hospital and to help care for them there, each in her own way.

CASE 37 "THE EXPERT"

In this case we shall see yet another way of perceiving responsibility towards one's child. Ayal is a 13-year-old boy with a malignant growth on his right hand. He is hospitalized in Southern Hospital for an operation to remove the growth. His parents are in their forties and are of Rumanian origin. The father comes to visit his son once a week. The father is a factory technician and takes responsibility for running the house whenever Ayal is hospitalized. Ayal has two older brothers, ages 9 and 10, both of whom are healthy. His mother, a tall, broad-shouldered woman, usually wears a faded wool wrap and old clothes.

Ayal and his family are well-known in the ward from previous visits in the hospital. Let us observe his mother's behavior on Ayal's first day in the hospital.

Ayal and his mother enter the ward and walk up to the nurses' counter.

MOTHER [*handing some forms to the nurse*]: Hello. Here we are. I don't believe I know you. Are you new here? Where's Rivka?

NURSE: She's not working here anymore. Come, I'll show you to Ayal's room.

MOTHER: We're used to having Room 12 (a room with two beds). This is the sixth time Ayal has been here.

NURSE: I'm sorry, but Room 12 is taken. You'll have to settle for Room 14 (with 5 beds).

MOTHER: At least let him have his own bed.

NURSE: What do you mean?

MOTHER: Let him have the bed by the window.

NURSE: We'll go see if that bed's available.

They all went to Room 14, but the bed by the window was taken by another boy.

MOTHER [*walking up to the mother of the boy lying by the window*]: Would you mind changing places? We're used to having this bed. This is usually his bed.

MOTHER OF THE OTHER CHILD: I don't mind.

MOTHER: Come, let's make the change quickly. I don't have the patience to wait.

The mother moved the beds herself. Then she opened a suitcase and took out a small pillow and put it on the bed. Afterwards she took out slippers and a housecoat for herself and put them into the bedside table. Finally she sat down beside the bed to wait for the doctor's visit. Half an hour later the doctors came in. One of them she recognized and two of them not.

MOTHER [*sitting next to her son's bed and addressing the doctor whom she recognized in a voice intended for all the doctors to hear*]: Hello, doctor. Do you remember us?

DOCTOR: Yes.

MOTHER: The last time Ayal was here they did not tell us whether the growth was ... or ... [*using Latin medical terms*].

DOCTOR: It's ... [*answering her in Latin. The mother shook her head as if understanding, and the doctor wrote something down in the child's medical record.*]

MOTHER: Have you already found Ayal's previous medical record?

DOCTOR: I don't know. I think it has not yet been requested from the archives.

The doctors left the room. The mother went into the corridor, where she met a nurse whom she recognized from Ayal's previous periods of hospitalization.

MOTHER [*happily*]: Congratulations. I hear you had a child. Last time we were here you were pregnant. I remembered you and brought you a little something. [*Returning to Ayal's room, she takes out a pack of chocolate from her bag and hands it to the nurse, who is somewhat embarrassed.*] If a bed becomes available in room 12, could you please transfer Ayal? Thanks.

NURSE: I'll try, but I can't promise anything. [*She leaves the room.*]

MOTHER [*to Ayal*]: Oh, no! I just remembered that last time we had an armchair. I'll go see if I can find one in one of the other rooms. [*She leaves.*]

The next morning Ayal was taken in for surgery. Then he was hospitalized for post-operative recovery, with a terrible prognosis. He was receiving respiratory care through his trachea and had an infusion. Ayal's mother usually arrived at the hospital at 5:00 a.m., every morning. A typical day proceeded as follows:

His mother entered the ward but, before going to her son's room, went into the staff rest-room to change into what she called her "work clothes." She took off her pants and two of the four sweaters that she usually wore one over the other. Then, over her sweaters, she put on a white robe like the ones worn by the nurses, put on white bobby-socks and slipped her feet into white slippers. Then she came out of the rest-room and greeted the staff with, "Good morning. How did the night go?" Afterwards she walked up to two parents sitting in the corridor and asked after the health of their children, using Latin medical terms. Then she entered the room where the clothing and nursing supplies were stored, took a pair of pajamas, towels, sheets, and shampoo, and placed them all on a bath cart. She pulled the cart down the corridor to her son's room. After a brief interchange (How are you? How was the night?) she helped him down to the bath chair and said to the nurse, who was watching her with admiration, "Well, you too know how to do this all by yourself, without any help, don't you?" She took her son to the bathroom, gave him a shower, then brought him back to his room, wrapped from head to foot. Leaving him in a wheelchair, she prepared him a cup of tea and poured half of it into her own cup. Mother and son drank their tea together. When she had finished her tea, another parent who was caring for his son in the same room asked her to help him, but she refused, saying, "I must take care of my son." Then she took her son off the bath cart and transferred him gently to his bed. She removed the interior part of the cannula (a metal tube inserted in her son's trachea), washed it in hot tap water, placed a clean pad under the cannula, then addressed the head nurse proudly, "Look at this professional job of cleaning the cannula. See how it's done? There's a lot that everyone can learn from me."

The mother generally left the ward at 8:00 p.m., but that night she decided to remain in the ward. "I don't feel sanguine about the night care," she explained to the nurse on duty in the ward during the day. "The last few days, all the effort I have been going to during the day has been going down the drain at night ... and I find Ayal in poor condition in the morning. I must stay here one night and check things out."

At 10 o'clock that night Ayal asked to eat. "I won't let you eat now," his mother said. "I want to see how they feed you."

The nurse came over and began feeding Ayal a bowl of cereal.

MOTHER [*to the nurse*]: Why don't you raise his torso? He'll choke.

The nurse made no response.

MOTHER: Pardon me, but you must prop him up. ... Give me the bowl. I'll hold it for you, and you can lift him up. [*The nurse hands the mother the bowl.*]

MOTHER [*tasting the cereal and bursting out angrily*]: What's wrong with you?! It's boiling hot. Why don't you check how hot the food is before giving it to him? [*The mother demonstrates to the nurse how to check the temperature of the food by letting a few drops of the cereal fall on the back of her hand.*]

NURSE [*to Ayal's mother*]: Maybe you would like to feed Ayal yourself?

MOTHER: That's not my job. I'm here to see to it that you take care of Ayal properly.

The nurse finished feeding Ayal. His mother sat by her son's bed, while the nurse checked the infusion. The mother counted the drops.

MOTHER He's supposed to get 50 drops a minute, and I counted 40.

NURSE: I just counted it now, and Ayal is getting 50 drops.

MOTHER: You're mistaken. I demand that the head nurse come and count the drops, and she'll see whether or not I'm right.

NURSE: Ayal is receiving exactly the number of drops he is supposed to get. So calm down.

MOTHER: You're wrong. And I don't have to calm down. I have to make comments so that you'll work the way you're supposed to. That's what I have to do.

The nurse left the room. The mother adjusted the drip, saying to her son, "Well, I've no other option. They simply won't listen to me."

Half an hour later the mother looked at her watch, left the room, and addressed the nurse: "It seems to me that Ayal should have had his medicine a quarter of an hour ago. . . . Look here, I'm going to lodge a complaint about you tomorrow with the director of the ward. It's a disgrace how you people here on the night shift mistreat the patients."

The mother requested to speak with the doctor on duty and complained to him about the deficient care of the night nurse. The doctor went immediately to check Ayal. He asked all the parents present in the room to leave while he was examining him, but Ayal's mother remained in the room. The doctor asked her too to leave.

MOTHER: Me, too? It seems you don't know who I am. I always remain in the room during the doctors' visits.

DOCTOR: All the same, I'm asking you please to leave.

MOTHER [*leaving reluctantly*]: This is the first time I've been treated this way.

The mother pressed against the door from the outside and, upon hearing a loud noise made by the sides of the bed, charged into the room, caught hold of her son's hand, and said to the doctor in an excited voice, "He'll break the infusion."

DOCTOR: Please leave the room.

The mother left, looking downcast, but while Ayal was being examined by the doctor she approached the room and peeked through the curtain. The doctor finished his examination, left the room, and the mother entered.

AYAL [*yelling at his mother*]: I'm sick of you. You always want to take control of everyone, you're always arguing with everyone; you're always washing me, getting on my nerves, getting on everyone's nerves. That's enough. Go home. At least let me have some peace and quiet at night.

MOTHER: You'd better realize that if I go, I'm not coming here anymore . . . don't you think I'm sick of it, too? I'm only 40 and I look like an old woman. Do you think I enjoy all this? I'm done for, I'm just a wreck.

Your illness and your behavior have done me in. Why on earth do I come here? Why do I put in so much of my time? I have so many other things to do. It's a number of years since I last read a book. ... [*Gently*] You must appreciate what I do for you. I don't owe you anything. I don't owe anyone anything. There are mothers who come here for a few hours, dressed to the hilt, don't dirty themselves, go walking around in their high heels, and run home in the evening to go out to a concert. Twenty people couldn't do for you what I manage to do. [*The mother leaves the room and brings Ayal a cup of tea.*]

AYAL [*his face red with anger*]: I don't want to eat ... don't want to drink.

MOTHER: So don't eat ... but wash up. You'll lie in filth ... you'll stink ... I'm warning you ... as long as you listen to me, I'm willing to go on living like this, sacrificing everything for you ... but if you start acting up, if you don't listen to me, you'll be left alone. I won't come, and you'll be a poor thing. ...

AYAL: I told you that it's better if you don't come.

The mother left the ward and did not show up the next day. The following day she came as usual, put on her work clothes, and greeted the staff with "good morning."

NURSE: Why didn't you come yesterday. Ayal was terribly lonesome for you.

MOTHER: Since when? He doesn't listen to me ... nevermind. He'll learn his lesson.

The mother helped wash her son. Then Ayal fell asleep, and his mother helped the nurse hand out food to the other patients and left Ayal's meal on his bedside table. Afterwards she went into the corridor and poured out her heart to the head nurse, with whom she was friendly. "It's dreadfully hard for me," she cried. "I feel I can't go on anymore ... it's so hard for me to see Ayal this way ... and even when he yells at me so ... until I want him to die." She stopped crying, left the nursing station, sat down beside a mother who was knitting, and tried to learn the stitch she was doing. Later she went back to Ayal's room and found him still asleep. Ayal awoke about an hour later.

MOTHER: You must eat something.

AYAL: I'm not hungry.

His mother sliced up some vegetables for a salad, left the room and sprinkled some paraffin oil on the salad. "O.K., I've put some oil on it," she told Ayal, "to make the salad like what you get at home ... with dressing."

AYAL: Where did you get oil from?

MOTHER: From the kitchen.

She did not tell him she had put on paraffin oil. Ayal ate up all the salad. His mother, very pleased, covered Ayal and took the plates out of the room. Then she made black coffee and offered some to the staff and the other parents.

Hanukkah was to begin that Tuesday night. The day before the doctor had told Ayal's mother that her son's condition required him to be under medical surveillance for at least "a month or two," during which time he would have to come to the hospital for treatment twice a week. The mother told the doctor that she was not interested in taking Ayal home from the hospital and bringing him back as an outpatient. "It's better if he gets ongoing care in the ward," she explained. "Besides, I need all sorts of special equipment for Ayal, and I don't have the necessary conditions for taking care of him at home."

On Tuesday, the first day of Hanukkah, Ayal's mother brought him a pair of pajamas from home when she came to visit.

AYAL: Great. I'm sick and tired of the hospital's pajamas. They always come unbuttoned.

MOTHER: That's not all I've brought. I also brought you loads of Hanukkah presents. Close your eyes and wait 'til you see what Dad has for you. [*His father brought in a television and radio.*]

AYAL [*overjoyed*]: Wow, that's super, . . . but what will the kids at home have?

MOTHER: They agreed to give up the T.V. Don't worry, they can watch at their friends' homes.

Ayal's father plugged in the television and radio.

AYAL [*happily*]: It's really wonderful, but I don't feel good about my brothers at home. Maybe you should bring them here? I miss them dreadfully.

MOTHER: It's hard for healthy kids to be in a hospital . . . and to see their brother in such a condition . . . and I don't want you to see them walking and dancing around, and be jealous of them. But soon you'll be better; and as soon as you're better, we'll bring them here.

FATHER: Ayal, my sweet, I've brought you some clothing to change into, and also some boxes of cookies. . . . [*Laughing*] Since you've been sick I've learned to bake.

AYAL: The nurses are always waiting for your cookies.

FATHER: Who would have imagined that I'd learn to bake?

They all laughed. Then the father turned serious, and with eyes downcast said, "I also brought you a little food from home . . . you like our food, don't you? Grandma sent it to you."

AYAL: Great. I'm sick of the food Mom's been shoving into me here.

MOTHER [*bitterly*]: O.K., go and complain about me; it's a long time since you've complained about me.

FATHER: He didn't mean it. Don't be angry at him. He's only a child, after all.

MOTHER [*sadly*]: Sometimes I forget that he's just a child. [*To her son*] You forgive me for being angry at you, don't you?

Ayal smiled, watching television and listening to the radio simultaneously. Turning serious and sad faced, his father rose and said, "I'm sorry Ayal, but I left the rest of the kids home alone, and I must get back. Be a good boy and feel better." He kissed Ayal on the forehead, touched his wife gently on the shoulder, and left.

The most striking aspect of Ayal's mother's behavior is that she presents herself to the doctors, nurses, and other parents as a "professional." Her "professionalism" finds expression in such actions as changing her street clothes for "work clothes" (as she calls them) that resemble a nurse's uniform, using Latin medical terms, and showing off her talent at administering excellent nursing care. She views herself as part of the medical staff and therefore is astounded that the doctor on night duty should ask her to leave the room. During the day the mother gives what, in her opinion, is thorough and excellent professional nursing care, and is insulted when her ability is not recognized and the responsibility for her son's nursing care is taken away from her. In her view, she is responsible for seeing to it that her son receive the same professional nursing care at night, as well. Therefore she remains in the hospital one night in order to test the staff and supervise their professional behavior. She acts in place of the nurses (doing such things as adjusting the intravenous drip) only when "they don't listen" to her, as she claims. Her confrontation with Ayal can also be understood in these terms. As long as her son let her play the role of the professional she was prepared to "sacrifice herself" and give him good and devoted nursing care. But when he refused to recognize her as having professional authority and would not cooperate with her, then she deserted the fray.

In the course of my observations I encountered many parents who followed a similar pattern of behavior. I often saw that parents who take care of their children with a great sense of devotion and self-sacrifice present themselves as "professionals" and view their children as patients and as a means for them to display their professional expertise. Parents who become "specialists" on their children's handicaps often remember many numbers by heart, such as the measurements of their child's head, chest, etc., use technical medical terms, or refer to the professional literature in the area of their child's handicap. (One such mother said, "I have several voluminous files on the disease.")

Sometimes "professionalism" is also particularly evident among parents of children connected to medical instruments. Those parents who have a more thorough command of the instruments and understand their operation in a "professional way" show greater willingness to spend long periods of time with their children. In this connection, recall Goffman's discussion of turning a stigma into a profession (Goffman, 1963, p. 132).

The last three cases that I have described represent three types of parental responsibility towards a handicapped child. In these cases the child is a threat to her parents only when she is in the family territory; hence she is disowned only within that territory. On the other hand, in the hospital the child is not perceived as a threat to her parents, and therefore her parents show responsibility for her there. The difference between the above cases lies in the type of responsibility the parents assume upon themselves in the hospital. We have seen that some mothers only assume responsibility for motherly care. Some parents believe they must supervise the care given by the professional staff, and others hold that they are responsible for the actual administration of professional care to their children.

We explained earlier that the fact of parents spending time at their child's bedside does not suffice to understand their attitude towards their child; for similar behavior can convey different messages. As we have seen, both Rita's parents and Ayal's parents "bring the home" into the hospital, as they put it; but in so doing, they each convey a different message. Rita's family brought objects and food from home to the hospital, and as a result felt a sense of being at home (as seen in their taking off their shoes, etc.) which enabled them to keep an eye on the medical staff. Ayal's mother, in contrast, felt at home in the hospital; but in this case the mother acted directly for the child's sake in order to make her caring for her son easier on her. These parents brought the home into the hospital; but they were not willing to take their children into their homes (as in the case of Rita) or to have the sick child come in contact with other members of the family (as in the case of Ayal), to the extent that the degree of his belonging to the home comes into question. One begins to suspect that, despite the parents' willingness to empty out their home of certain objects, denying the healthy members of the family of these things, they are not willing to view the handicapped child as part of the healthy family. (In this connection, recall the behavior of Simha's parents, Case 29.)

The parents' responses are classified as showing "acceptance" or "rejection" according to the message their behavior conveys. Behavior is termed "rejective" when it is designed to renounce responsibility for what happens to one's child or to reject her from the family territory. It is termed "accepting" when the message it conveys is one of accepting responsibility for the child's life.

Thus, denying medicine to a child who is deathly ill was not categorized as behavior expressive of rejection, even if it caused the child's death. But deliberately preventing a child from receiving medication, in order to cause a deterioration in his condition so that he would remain in the hospital and not be taken home (Moshi) is a technique of manipulation for rejecting a child. Just as deliberately undermining the process of recovery is significant, so too is a father's refusal to consent to his daughter having an operation on the grounds that he does not want to cause her death, when essentially he is not willing to take responsibility for her life (Avram).

The previous three cases dealt with renunciation of responsibility in special circumstances and presented a concept of responsibility which is tested by territorial considerations. The following case will help us discuss conflicts between various types of responsibility.

CASE 38 "THE RABBI SAID NOT TO DO THE TRANSPLANT"

This case involves a request that a parent give an organ or part of her body. In order to realize her responsibility for her children, a woman is asked to give up the wholeness of her own body, and even to jeopardize her well-being. The mother's behavior in this case also puts to the test her proclamations about her willingness for self-sacrifice. This case, therefore, will help us examine the myth of unbounded parental responsibility towards their children.

Ella, a 15-year-old girl, has chronic kidney disease. She was born in Israel. Her parents are native Israelis of Lithuanian extraction and live in a city in the south. After two years of dialysis, Ella was switched to treatment with an artificial kidney. Her parents were aware of the gravity of the situation and of the danger to her life. They did not leave their sick daughter alone for a moment, but took turns sitting by her side, day and night. In the wake of a further deterioration in her condition, the head of the department suggested a kidney transplant as "the only solution that would enable her to survive." The parents responded gladly. "I'll do anything for her," her mother said, "whatever I'm asked. If I can give her a kidney, I shall. The most important thing is to save her life."

Tests were done on the parents and it was found that the mother had suitable tissue to be a donor. Excitement ran high in the ward over the next few days. The mother talked with the medical staff about the imminent operation all day. On the eve of the operation, Ella and her mother went through preparations for the operation (shaving, enemas, ...). Suddenly the mother requested to consult a rabbi. Her request aroused considerable surprise, since the family was known to be non-religious. Nevertheless, the mother was let out to consult a rabbi. She returned several hours later and asked that the doctors be called in for an urgent conference. In a few minutes several of the senior doctors and nurses had assembled. Then the following conversation ensued:

MOTHER [*excitedly*]: You know I went to consult a rabbi ...

1ST DOCTOR: No. It was my understanding that you went to receive a rabbi's blessing, not to consult a rabbi.

MOTHER: Do you know him? They say he's very famous ... he really does make a good impression. ... I told him about the operation. ... I asked his opinion ... and the rabbi said not to do the transplant ... because the operation will not succeed ... my daughter will reject the kidney. ... That's why I called all of you ... so you'll know that I decided to call off the operation.

1ST DOCTOR [*astounded*]: On what grounds did you decide to call it off?

MOTHER: On the basis of my conversation with the rabbi.

2ND DOCTOR: Are you a religious woman?

MOTHER: No ... [*embarrassed*] ... I don't know. ...

2ND DOCTOR [*assertively*]: This is not child's play. Your decision is going to endanger your daughter's life ... you know how dangerous Ella's condition is. Your decision is rash and irresponsible.

MOTHER: Look, it's a shame for you to waste all your effort. I've thought about it and I've made my decision. It's done and you're not going to change my mind.

HEAD NURSE [*almost in tears*]: We are utterly shocked ... actually hurt ... angry. ... We've become so attached to Ella and we placed such great hopes on this transplant. Besides, [*shouting*] do you know how many doctors and nurses have stayed here through the night on your account the past week? They're all sitting here ... this entire hospital has been standing on its head for the past week ... the entire hospital will be struck dumb when they hear about this ... suddenly she remembers to go and consult a rabbi?! You've known about this transplant for several weeks already.

1ST DOCTOR: We're all very tense. I suggest that we all calm down.

MOTHER: I haven't called off the operation. It's only been postponed a little ... we'll do it a few days later.

NURSE: ... What's gotten into you? Suddenly you're afraid of the operation? Why, we've explained to you about it for weeks.

MOTHER [*apologetically*]: Look, I'm her mother ... I'm the one who always wanted to donate a kidney to her . ... [*Angrily*] Why are all the nurses giving me such looks, as if I were some sort of murderer? ... I'm the one who's going to lose a kidney, not you. I'll remain a half person. I'm scared to death, but I'll get over it. Just give me a few days.

1ST DOCTOR: We won't press you ... we'll do as you like. We'll postpone the operation a few days.

The next day the mother felt "pressure in her chest" and was absent from the ward for several hours in order to have her "heart examined." She returned later, armed with a doctor's note from the local clinic indicating a "suspicion of a slight ulcer in the appendix, which need not restrict activity in any way." The mother was immediately taken in for a second round of extensive testing. The report written upon conclusion of the tests said, "There is nothing to impede performing a kidney transplant operation. ... The suspicion of a slight ulcer does not constitute any illness or impediment."

Nevertheless, the mother informed the staff of her final decision to call off the operation on the grounds that "with a heart defect you don't go and have an operation."

Ella spent the next five years between home and hospital, and continued living with an artificial kidney until a suitable kidney was found for her, donated by a stranger.

We have seen that Ella's parents cared for her with exceptional devotion; they were present at her side all day and night, and answered her every need. When her conditioned worsened and the doctors recommended a kidney transplant as the only way of saving her life, her mother reacted joyfully, announcing her willingness to donate one of her own kidneys. The mother's promise reflects a common myth regarding the "natural guardianship" of parents for their children. But parents are not generally called on to realize this natural guardianship at any price, to face the test of self-sacrifice and to give up an organ to realize their responsibility for their children. Ella's mother was asked to stand this test. Despite knowing that only a kidney transplant could save her daughter's life, she was not prepared to sacrifice part of her own body for her daughter's sake. Instead, she looked for all sorts of tactics to enable her to prevent the transplant without appearing responsible for her daughter's death. She accomplished this by means of the opinions of a rabbi and a doctor. Even though she was not religious, she went to a rabbi for consultation. Moreover, she did it precisely the night before the operation, when there was not sufficient time for a dissenting opinion to be presented. Thus she precluded the possibility of retreating from her decision to cancel the operation. Also her grasping at a non-existent heart defect was designed to provide justification for calling off the transplant.

In the cases we have seen thus far parents have cast off responsibility (totally, or under specific circumstances) with respect to children with whom they could, potentially, have established communication. This is not true in the following case.

CASE 39 "THE VEGETABLE"

This case describes parent-child relationships with a child who has been termed a "vegetable." Despite the parents' difficulties in establishing communication with their child, they nevertheless accept complete responsibility for his life.

Oren, six years old, is the son of a couple of Moroccan extraction, who have an elementary school education and live in an urban neighborhood of blue-collar workers. The parents have two other children, both healthy. Oren developed normally until age one; he sat, crawled, and spoke a little. At age one, after receiving a vaccination, he was diagnosed as having severe brain damage as a result of a reaction to the inoculation. Now, at age six, the child lies down most of the time, is incontinent, is not capable of walking, mumbles inarticulately, claps his hands, eats baby food, and only responds to sharp pain. He is very good-looking, smiles a blank smile most of the time, recognizes his parents, and when they stroke him he responds with catlike motions. The doctors and nurses diagnose his condition as a "vegetable." He is generally cared for at home, but often is brought to the hospital for check-ups. Let us observe his parents' behavior in the hospital on a number of typical days.

Sunday

Oren's mother, very well dressed, sat by her son's side from the morning. She stroked him gently and, as always, took excellent physical care of him, so that he looked clean, satisfied, and smiling. On the child's bedside table there was a flower pot, and above his bed pictures of animals which had been brought from home. Oren was wearing clean, pressed pajamas from home. His mother took a thermos full of food from home out of the bedside table and put it on the table. She didn't stop talking to Oren, asking him questions and answering in his stead (remember that Oren does not understand anything):

"How do you feel? Good, ... don't cry. You're crying because you're hungry. Just a minute and I'll feed you ... yes, now we're going to eat ... but it's hot, so we'll wait a few moments until it cools ... [*feeding him patiently*] ... tasty? Good ... [*Oren finished eating and clapped his hands*] You're clapping your hands? Good [*happily*] that's a sign that you feel good. You love your Mommy, don't you? Yes. Of course. I know you do. And Mommy loves you. Do you want to hear what I did yesterday? [*She proceeds to tell him in detail.*] Oh, look at your fingernails, how long they've grown. Here, let's cut them [*taking out a small pair of scissors and trimming his nails*]. Good. You understand everything ... all you need is to have lots of time devoted to you, and then you come along very well. ... Maybe you want Mommy to tell you a story?" [*She tells him the story of Little Red Riding Hood, asks him questions, answers for him, makes him "laugh" and laughs "with him."*]

Tuesday

Oren's parents and two siblings entered his room. They were all well-dressed. That day they gave Oren a birthday party. The tried to pick him up, brought him a cake with candles and said, "Now Oren will blow out all the candles." The child didn't understand a thing, stared vacantly into the air, and smiled. His mother blew out the candles and said, "Good, Oren."

Wednesday

Oren's mother approached one of the staff and said, "I'm really very upset that some of the doctors and nurses have been calling Oren a 'vegetable.' It's very insulting to us and to Oren.... " She announces that the family will not come for a week. They were planning to visit relatives in the southern part of the country. "But we'll send a postcard," she explained, "so that he won't worry about us."

Thursday, the following week

The family returned from their visit and came "to see Oren," as they put it, "before going home."

MOTHER [*to the nurse*]: Did he ask after us? Did he ask for us? [*Again, remember that Oren understands nothing. Approaching Oren, she says*]: My darling [*and kisses him*], we missed you so much. ... Are you angry at us? Don't be angry ... it was also hard for us. ... We are used to coming every day ... it's become second nature to us ... and if we can't manage to come, then we get up tight. ... Come, sweetie. Let's take you to see television ... so you're not bored.

At the beginning of this chapter I tried to show that renunciation of parental responsibility cannot be attributed to the sort of defect the child has. The present case supports this conclusion. Oren, a boy who understands nothing, does not talk, and is medically determined to be a "vegetable," is treated by his parents as if he were a normal child who understands, talks, worries, and laughs. They do this by answering questions in his stead, speaking for him, "making him laugh," sending him postcards "so that he won't worry," and by taking an interest upon their return in whether he "asked after them." They even hang pictures of animals over his bed "so that he won't be bored."

CASE 40 "DON'T THROW AWAY THE FETUS; I WANT TO TAKE IT FOR BURIAL IN MY VILLAGE"

Fadah, a Moslem Arab woman, mother of five children (two boys and three girls), came to the maternity ward of Northern Hospital because she could not feel the baby. After having been examined, she was told that the fetus had died and that she would have to have an abortion. Let us look at what transpired immediately after the fetus was aborted.

The fetus came out, and the midwife hid it.

FADAH: Show it to me.

MIDWIFE: I don't recommend that you see the fetus. It's rather an unpleasant sight.

FADAH: What was it, a girl or a boy?

MIDWIFE: A girl.

FADAH [*not believing her*]: I know it was a boy. I saw that it was.

MIDWIFE: I'm sorry, but it was a girl.

FADAH: Show me.

The midwife showed her the fetus.

FADAH [*Looks at the fetus and moans*] Why is it such a dark color, not red?

MIDWIFE: Because it died in the womb.

FADAH: Please, I beg of you ... don't throw away the fetus. I want to take it for burial in my village.

Fadah, a Moslem Arab, shows a sense of responsibility towards a stillborn baby, takes an interest in the baby's looks and sex, and wants to give her a funeral. A similar sense of responsibility is also evinced by Rosa, whom we meet next.

Rosa, a young woman of 22, is an ultra-Orthodox Jew of Eastern European extraction, a teacher by profession. She arrived at Central Hospital Saturday morning. The midwife who examined her could not hear any fetal heartbeat.

ROSA: What happened? Is something wrong with the child?

MIDWIFE: I haven't managed to hear any heartbeat, but that doesn't mean anything. Wait a moment and we'll call the doctor.

DOCTOR: I'm sorry to say, but we can't hear any heartbeat. It's very likely that the baby has died in utero.

ROSA: Please, don't seal his fate. Treat the fetus as if it were alive. Maybe you're mistaken. After all, we're only human.

DOCTOR: Rest assured, we'll do the delivery as if everything were in order, down to the last minute. You can be sure of that.

ROSA: Don't say anything to my family. I beg of you. Maybe everything will be all right. God works wonders.

The baby was born, and judging by its appearance, had been dead for several days. The midwife cut the umbilical cord and wrapped up the baby.

ROSA: Nurse, tell me what's going on. He's not crying, is he?

MIDWIFE: I'm sorry, but he's not alive.

Rosa's face remained frozen. She neither cried nor uttered a word, as if she had not taken in what had been told her. Several minutes later she requested to see the baby and took an interest in its sex. The midwife refused to show her the baby, took it into a corner, and gave it to the doctor to be examined.

ROSA [*shouting*]: What are you doing with my baby?

DOCTOR: We're sending him to pathology. Externally the baby looks like everything is in order. We don't know what caused his death. Maybe there are serious internal defects that are difficult to diagnose at the moment.

ROSA: I won't have you touch the body. If he's dead, it's a sign he was supposed to die. That's his fate. God is almighty. There's no need for any examination; the fact is that I already have an older child, in good health—may he live and be well for many years. I know that according to the *Halakhah* (Jewish law) he has to be buried without doing anything to any of his organs.

The doctor tried to explain to her the importance of the examination.

ROSA: O.K., I'll talk with my husband and we'll consult the Rabbi. We'll do whatever he says. But you must promise me not to do anything without my consent.

DOCTOR: I give you my word.

In certain cases parents express responsibility for their child, even when the child is no longer alive or has been found to be a "vegetable"; whereas in other cases parents renounce responsibility for their child even when she is alive and active. Moreover, sometimes parents disclaim responsibility for their child while the child is yet alive, but express parental responsibility for their child's dead body (Avram and Ḥitam in Case 33).

The next two cases, which deal with mothers' behavior towards newborns, illustrate further variations on the theme of parental responsibility.

CASE 41 "BEETHOVEN"

Dina (of Moroccan extraction) and Ya'akov (Rumanian) live in a city in southern Israel. The couple's second daughter was born in the seventh month and weighed only 1 lb. 14 oz. The baby was put in an incubator in an intensive care[4] room of Southern Hospital. Dina came to intensive care about six hours after the birth and said, "My daughter is here." The nurse showed her around the ward and acquainted her with its basic rules (such as washing one's hands and putting on a gown before entering the ward). The mother washed her hands, put on a gown, and followed the nurse into the ward. At the entrance to the room she stopped and looked around with a blank stare. The nurse explained to her what all the instruments connected to her baby do. Little by little she focused her eyes on the instruments, and lastly looked at the newborn lying in the incubator.

NURSE: You can open the windows of the incubator and put your hand in.

The nurse left the room, and Dina remained alone with her child. She stood still and did not open the windows of the incubator or put her hand inside. She paced around the incubator, looked at her baby, and said, "She's so small ... smaller than the palm of my hand ... I'm not used to such a size. ... at home I have an older son who was born at a normal weight." Several minutes later she left the ward.

In the evening both Dina and Ya'akov came to visit their daughter. They put on gowns, washed their hands, and entered the intensive care room of the premature baby ward. Immediately upon entering they looked at the chart hanging on the incubator (registering data on the child's weight, amount of food received, etc.), and did not say a word. Later, the parents each found themselves a place on either side of the incubator and stood there with their hands clasped behind their backs.

DINA: Oh, dear! She's connected to so many tubes. ...

NURSE: You can open the incubator door if you like.

Dina opened the door very cautiously; but she and her husband kept their distance and did not approach the incubator.

NURSE: Why don't you touch the baby?

YA'AKOV: We're afraid to touch her. ...

NURSE: The baby will actually enjoy the feel your hands.

The parents continued standing where they were, hands at their sides, not daring to touch the baby.

DINA [to Ya'akov]: You can put your hand in and stroke the baby.

YA'AKOV: But she's so small. ... Really, it's not a good idea. Let's wait 'til she grows a bit. ... Our hands are cold. ...

NURSE [to Dina]: Maybe you should have a try, all the same?

Dina reached her hand into the incubator, but did not touch her girl. Instead she rested her hand on the diaper in the incubator, then immediately withdrew her hand as if she had touched a hot object.

DINA [to the nurse]: Tell me, how is her condition?

NURSE: She's doing well; she's put on almost an ounce.

Dina turned around, looked at the other babies in the room, and asked how much they weighed. She called her husband's attention to a premature baby that weighed 1 lb. 7 oz. and was attached to a respirator. She mumbled, "When I hear of other children born at such a low weight and in an early stage of pregnancy, then our daughter looks pretty good in comparison. ... It encourages me ... because I really want her to pull through."

Two days later the baby's condition took a turn for the worse. She needed a large amount of oxygen and was given an umbilical infusion. When the sonde was being inserted into the baby's stomach, the doctors discovered necrosis of part of her intestines. They summoned the parents immediately and requested their permission to perform an emergency operation.

DINA [*startled to find that her girl had been put on a respirator*]: Does she have any chance of survival? Is there any point in her suffering? [*breaking into tears*].

DOCTOR: The operation in and of itself is not dangerous. Many babies have survived it; but there is an inherent danger due to the baby's weight and general condition.

PARENTS [*looking at each other and immediately responding*]: O.K., let it be.

The baby was transferred to a hospital in central Israel, where she was to have the operation. She remained there for a month and a half. During this entire period her parents came to visit her twice. Dina was "convinced the girl was about to die," and felt, in her own words, "it's a pity to become attached to her. ... Anyway, if anything happens, they have our phone number ... they'll let us know."

After a month and a half, the baby was sent back to the premature baby ward in the hospital where she was born. The parents were overjoyed and said a "new girl" had been born to them. Dina began spending entire days at her girl's side. She would arrive early in the morning, be present when the girl had her bath, help the nurses (by handing them a diaper, and the like), and talk with her daughter. "My sweet, now you'll feel comfy," she would say to her premature baby. "The nurse will give you a bath and Mommy will feed you and pamper you." After the bath Dina would smile at her girl, stroke her head, and feed her from a bottle. The baby was no longer connected to medical instruments most of the hours of the day. At this point her mother announced, "Well, thank God everything is alright. We've decided to call our girl Dalit." The mother began addressing her girl only as Dalit, and continued to care for her devotedly.

Two days later the doctor informed Dina that "as a result of Dalit having had to receive oxygen, ... and as a result of her initial condition, her eyesight has been affected and work must be done to improve it." Dina was not overly worried. "That's not so terrible," she said, "so we'll have a girl who'll wear glasses. ... So what? ... I know that Dalit has a few problems ... but everything will be O.K., in time. We'll develop her, we'll play her music, and everything will be O.K." By the very next day Dina had already begun working on Dalit's vision. She brought toys and colored objects from home and moved them patiently in front of Dalit's eyes.

A week later Dalit's condition worsened. She developed shortness of breath and a raspy cough (diagnosed as stridulate), and was given vapor treatment and put in a bed with an oxygen tent. Her regular feeding was also suspended and replaced by an infusion.

Dina came to the ward as usual and checked in with the nurse, who informed her of the setback in her daughter's condition. Dina hurried over to her daughter's room and stood by her bed.

DINA [*to the doctor*]: How is she?

DOCTOR: It's not unexpected. After this operation many children develop stridor and need to be treated until the acute condition passes.

DINA: Why isn't she receiving food?

NURSE: For a child with respiratory problems the very act of eating is an exertion and makes the breathing more difficult. Therefore, when things are most acute an infusion is given instead of food.

Dina started crying, turned around immediately and left the ward. She did not come at all the next day and showed up two days later.

NURSE [*to Dina*]: Why didn't you come yesterday?

DINA: What's there to come for? She had already been taken off all the tubes, and I thought I had a girl, then suddenly I got such a blow ... anyway ... what can I do here?

She left the ward forthwith, and again did not show up the following day.

Two days later, upon arriving at the ward, she found that her girl was still connected to the infusion and was still not receiving regular food. She was told that her daughter's condition had deteriorated further. "She had a bit of cyanosis," (turning blue) as the doctors put it, and had to have oxygen again. Dina headed straight for the doctors' office, without entering her daughter's room at all.

DINA: I've come to ask about my daughter.

DOCTOR: Please remind me, what's her name?

DINA: She doesn't have a name anymore. ... You tell me how she is. I see that she's still not receiving food. ... What's going to be with her?. ... How come her condition worsened?

DOCTOR: She wasn't feeling well, she was having trouble breathing; we tested the oxygen level in her blood and concluded that she needed to be given oxygen.

DINA [*twisting up her face*]: I don't like that.

NURSE: What's happened to you? What don't you like?

DINA: What'll be with her eyesight? Surely the oxygen you gave her will make the condition of her eyes worse ... so what will be with her?

NURSE: I tried to give her a low concentration. We have a digital machine that measures the concentration of oxygen, and we are extremely careful to keep the concentration of oxygen below the maximum permissible level.

DINA: How much does she weigh? Why has she not put on weight?

NURSE: That's not important now. After her respiratory problem is solved, then we'll worry about her putting on weight.

DINA: The way things are now, I'm in despair. I've lost hope of her ever pulling through.

NURSE: Why are you talking like that?

DINA: Are there children who have pulled through?

NURSE: Yes, of course. You mustn't lose hope.

DINA: Look, here. There's nothing for me to do here. Call me when I can take care of my girl.

Dina left the ward and did not come to visit for the next few days. Several days later, when the baby's condition had improved and she could be fed orally, Dina was called to the ward. The nurses told her, "We rely on you alone ... there's no one who knows how to feed the girl as well as you." Dina took her girl and fed her in the oxygen tent. She expressed no warmth at having physical contact with her child. When she had finished feeding the girl she left the room. A week later Dalit was taken off the medical instruments. "Great, Dalit's now completely healthy," her mother said joyfully, and once again related to her daughter with warmth and physical contact.

Two weeks later Dalit's parents took their girl home. They treated her as a normal girl until age five months. It was then that they began to come to the realization that their girl was handicapped. "It became more and more apparent to me that she had something wrong," her father said. "I'd take a flashlight and shine it in her eyes, and she would not respond. ... We were alarmed ... so we went to an eye doctor ... and he said that she's totally blind ... and that it was a result of her being in the incubator."

The parents were shocked. "We went to a certain professor ... and he said ... that we should refer her to an institution ... that it was a pity, both for our sake and her's."

The parents wavered for a short while about sending Dalit away from home, then decided that they were all against putting her in an institution. "Even her sister was opposed and said that if Dalit were sent to an institution she herself would run away from home. She would no longer be our daughter ... and the entire family is terrific. Everyone helps out. They take care of her when we have to go out to a wedding ... and even my brother said he was prepared to donate one of his own eyes ... but that's just idle talk."

At age three Dalit went to a regular nursery school, and at age six she "wrote songs and played the piano," as her parents recounted. To understand the parents' relationship towards Dalit at age six, we shall observe a scene in the guest room of their apartment.

All the rooms in their apartment, including the guest room and Dalit's room are wallpapered with colorful patterns and are full of decorative objects. The guest room has a piano and a recorder on which Dalit plays and many pictures of Dalit decorating the walls.

FATHER [*addressing the author*]: What do you think of Dalit? Did you hear how nicely she plays? Isn't she a real genius? Our Beethoven, a real Beethoven [*the father's emphasis*] ... from the moment we learned that she was blind, we had the feeling that she's like Beethoven ... and we've worked at developing her musical talent.

SISTER: She brings us such honor. ... There was a music competition, and she won. ... Here, look at the pictures on the opposite wall ... a photograph of her with the Mayor.

Dalit's mother brought over some pictures of Dalit with her classmates. Showing me the pictures, she asked, "Would you say she's blind? It really doesn't show."

DALIT: Mom, please put on the T.V. There's a program I want to watch now.

MOTHER: O.K. [*Addressing the author*] She watches all the programs.

FATHER: It's interesting. There are few children Dalit's age who read so well. Look what a vast library of Braille books she has ... and how many records she has. ... She's really a very special girl ... she knew all the capitals of the world at age 4 ... the whole family agrees that we have a genius here ... and they see how much we dote on Dalit, and they too are full of love for her.

Dalit was concentrating on viewing the program on the television.

MOTHER [*whispering to the author*]: This morning I looked at her picture and I cried. I wanted to hug her ... whenever someone tells me that she's blind, it affects me badly, then I look at her picture ... she's so cute ... you really can't tell, looking at the picture ... she's really a little beauty ... just you wait and see, you'll be hearing about her in a few years. She'll be a real Beethoven. ...

This case brings out the connection between the extent of the threat posed by the girl and the vacillations in the parents' sense of responsibility towards their child. Again we encounter the same attitude towards premature babies discussed earlier, and the parents' withdrawal from physical contact with a small premature baby attached to medical instruments. They accepted full responsibility for their child only after she was brought back after her operation and conveyed a message of a complete change in identity ("a new child was born to us"). The girl was given a first name only after her condition normalized and she was taken off the medical instruments. But her name is revoked when her condition worsened and she was again connected to life support systems. In the end, after Dalit's parents took her home and she was diagnosed as "blind," her parents accepted full responsibility for her.

CASE 42 "NUMBER ONE AND NUMBER TWO"

This case, which presents fluctuations in the sense of responsibility felt by one mother to her two twins in the wake of changes in their external appearance and the ability to conceal a physical defect, gives further support to our thesis.

Karen is 32 years old, a native Israeli of American extraction, and has a university degree. Karen gave birth to twins in Central Hospital. One of them (whom we shall call Number 1) the doctors found to be a normal girl, slightly underweight. The second had a cleft palate,[5] but the prognosis for its repair was good. The defect was covered with an adhesive bandage so that it was hardly noticeable.

In the scene which follows, Karen had just entered the premature baby ward for the first time and introduced herself.

NURSE: Let's go see your girls.

Karen and the nurse went over to the girls.

MOTHER [*turning pale*]: Oh, my God! What are these creatures? [*Bursting into tears, she requested to sit down*] ... I was so foggy after the birth, that I don't remember exactly what happened.... After I had had two hours to recover they told me that the girls were small, but I never imagined they meant something like this.

NURSE: You have such sweet girls. You can even hold them.

MOTHER: What's there to hold? How can you hold something so small as this? ... I'm not capable of it. I'm afraid ... and what's that bandage on Number 2?

NURSE [*laughing*]: I see you've already given them names: Number 1 and Number 2. How original.

MOTHER [*impatiently*]: Why has she got a bandage on her?

NURSE: The baby has a problem with her palate, but don't worry.

MOTHER: I don't understand.

NURSE: You should go speak to the doctor. He'll explain to you all about it.

The mother began crying, while the nurse called the doctor. The doctor explained what a cleft palate was all about, and concluded by saying, "Don't worry. Everything will shape up, and you won't notice it at all."

Karen did not respond. Over the next few days she came to the premature baby ward every day. She always went over to Number 1 first, and then to Number 2.

Two weeks later the girls were found to be "O.K." and the mother was asked to "get ready to take the girls home in ten days." Karen was overjoyed. She named both her girls, but devoted her attention primarily to Number 1. She asked her husband to bring a camera and to photograph her with the girls, especially with Number 1. She expressed her own milk and brought it to the girls, but took an interest primarily in Number 1's reaction to the milk.

Let us listen to a conversation between Karen and the nurse.

KAREN: Did my girl (Number 1) get the milk I brought her?

NURSE: Of course.

KAREN: What time does she get it ... because I want to see how she responds to it.

NURSE: Rest assured, she eats well.

KAREN [*to her girl*]: Look, you're getting food from your Mommy.

Karen seemed calm the next few days. She began putting her hands into the incubator and touching her girls. She always did this in the same order; first Number 1, then Number 2.

Two days later there was a sharp change in the condition of the girls. Number 1's condition became quite serious. She came down with an acute bronchial infection, her lungs were hardly functioning, and she was put on supporting instruments. When Karen arrived that morning she was told of the turn for the worse in Number 1's condition.

MOTHER [*bursting into tears*]: You can hardly see the child ... only instruments ... this thing is not a baby.

After crying for several hours, the mother began to ignore Number 1. As soon as she entered the room she would approach Number 2 and stand at her side, with her back to Number 1's incubator. When the nurses called her attention to Number 1, she would say, "Look, I'm trying to separate myself from her, so that it won't be so hard for me if she dies ... I hope that at least Becky (Number 2) will survive ... that at least I'll have her."

The mother ceased calling Number 1 by the name she had given her. She tried not to mention the child at all, but when it was absolutely necessary, she referred to her as Number 1. When a new nurse asked whether Number 1 had a name, she was told, "What difference does it make?" Karen no longer brought pictures of Number 1 to the ward. "I think she ripped up all the photographs of her (Number 1) ... she doesn't want any reminder of her," the father said. While initially the mother had hardly paid any attention to Number 2, now her attention was focused on her exclusively.

Let us consider the following development.

Karen entered the room, stood with her back to Number 1, and looked only at Number 2. She looked at the baby's chart (registering the baby's weight and food intake), put her hands into the incubator and stroked her child.

KAREN [*to the nurse*]: I'd like to hold her when she wakes up.

NURSE: O.K.

Karen continued stroking the baby, until she awakened.

MOTHER: May I take her out of the incubator? ... Maybe she should have her diaper changed first.

The nurse changed the baby's diaper, took her temperature, and cleaned some liquid out of her respiratory passages.

MOTHER [*watching the nurse take care of the baby*]: How often do you clean out her respiratory passages?

NURSE: As often as necessary. Generally every three hours.

MOTHER: Tell me, how big was her head at birth?

NURSE: I don't know, but we can find out ... why do you want to know?

MOTHER: I was just curious.

The nurse finished with the baby, swaddled her, and handed her to her mother.

MOTHER [*to her girl*]: My sweet little thing. You don't know me so well yet, but I'm your mother. ... Look, they're fixing up your bed so it'll be nice and clean. ... Shall we tell you a bit about home? I'm so anxious for you to come home already.

Half an hour later she kissed her baby goodbye and left.

A week later there was another change in her children's condition. As she entered the room she was told that the tongue depressor that had been put into Number 2's mouth the day she was born (to prevent her tongue from falling back and choking her) had been taken out that day. The tongue depressor had been held in place by adhesive bandages, thus hiding the lower half of the girl's face. That day the mother set eyes on the girl's defect, undisguised, for the first time.

MOTHER [*approaching Number 2, then running away in alarm*]: Why did you take the tongue depressor out?

NURSE: We wanted to see how the baby would breath without it. So far her breathing has been nice and calm. But if any problems develop, we'll have to put it back.

MOTHER [*crying and screaming*]: It's so dreadful. I never knew she had such a terrible thing. ... How will I manage? How can I bring her home? ... I see. I gave birth to two girls, and now I don't even have one ... I'm getting out of here. I can't stand this place anymore.

The mother did not return for the next two days. On the third day the father came and requested that Number 2 be covered up, otherwise her mother would not come. Only after the baby's face was covered with bandages did the mother agree to come again.

This case, too, illustrates withdrawal from small premature infants and parental interest in external appearance. We see fluctuations in behavior towards two premature baby girls depending on their external appearance, the possibility of concealing defects, their being attached to life support systems, and the image they project.

When Number 2 was covered with bandages, the mother preferred Number 1. When Number 1's condition took a turn for the worse and she had to be put on a large number of life support systems, the mother ignored her and turned to Number 2, whom she accepted only on condition that her defect be concealed. When the girls' condition was determined as good and a date was set for taking them home, the mother accepted responsibility for them, as expressed by her close physical contact with them, giving them names, and photographing them with other members of the family. In this way the mother proclaimed the twins' belonging to the family. Her rejection of responsibility for Number 1 was expressed in an analogous way—denying the child's first name, refraining from close physical contact, and ripping up the child's photographs. Both cases illustrate the connection between the child's external appearance or body image and extreme fluctuations in the parents' sense of responsibility towards the particular child. When the child is seen as a normal child who does not pose a threat to her parents, her parents show complete responsibility towards her, in whatever way. But when the child is viewed in the parents' eyes as a being with a defect that they find threatening, the parents cast off their responsibility for her life.

The last question that I shall try to answer in this chapter concerns the impact of religion. Some researchers maintain that religiosity is a factor in shaping parental attitudes towards deformed children.[6] Even though there are no studies that support this contention unequivocally, nevertheless many professionals in the field (especially doctors, nurses, and social workers) maintain there is a clear difference between the behavior of religious parents and the behavior of non-religious parents. They attribute this difference to the religious person's humanitarian world view, which prepares her to accept unconditionally, as one of God's creatures, any being that she bares. As proof, workers in the field claim that abandonment of children with external defects occurs in non-religious families but not in religious ones.

The findings of our study refute this contention. It turns out that religiosity *per se* does not affect parental behavior towards a child who is considered deformed in her parents' eyes. The operative factor in determining the attitude one will have towards a deformed child is the nature of the social network in which the people live.[7] Abandonment of deformed children is more prominent in a loose-knit social network than in a close-knit social network. The similarity between the patterns of behavior shown by religious Jews and rural Arabs living in closely knit social networks, on the one hand, and Jews (religious and non-religious) and Arabs living in an urban setting in loose-knit social networks, on the other, reinforces our argument.

Religious and non-religious parents showed an equal tendency to disclaim responsibility for a handicapped child. The difference lies only in the **excuses** they give for disclaiming responsibility. When a religious individual has the option, he behaves like a non-religious person and rejects his deformed child; he simply gives a different set of reasons for his behavior.

This study reveals that it is actually the more closely knit social networks that lean strongly towards concealing physical deformities, especially from fellow members of the social network; which shows that here, too, the child is not accepted as is.

Religious families living in a non-religious area behave much the same way as non-religious families. Again the difference is in the justification that they give for their actions. Ayalah and her husband, for example, a religious couple living in a non-religious environment and a loose-knit social network, that does not offer assistance and support, asked the hospital authorities to put their child to death. They presented their request for the girl's death as if it stemmed from an accepted system that stresses family values. Ayalah's reason for requesting that her retarded girl be put to death was the possibility that the child would jeopardize the chances of her healthy children getting married, and "in our circles ... among religious families ... getting married and having children are of paramount importance." Nevertheless, the parents' close adherence to a religious value system did not deter them from entrusting their daughter to the care of a Christian institution.

CASE 43 "DON'T TELL MY FAMILY I GAVE BIRTH"

Marsha is a 42-year-old, ultra-Orthodox mother, born in America and living in an ultra-Orthodox neighborhood. On her eighth delivery she gave birth to a Down's syndrome boy. Let us observe her behavior immediately after the birth, while still in the delivery room of Central Hospital.

NURSE: You had a boy.

MOTHER: Nurse, how is he?

NURSE [*looking at the baby*]: We'll call the pediatrician and have him examine the child.

MOTHER [*bursting into tears*]: What's wrong with him?

FATHER [*had been standing on the other side of the door but, on hearing his wife crying, entered the room*]: What happened?

MOTHER [*to the father*]: The baby has something wrong with him.

NURSE: Would you like to hold the baby?

MOTHER: No. I don't want to see him ... or hold him. Call the doctor.

The doctor examined the baby and explained to the mother that her child might have Down's syndrome. The mother continued crying, and the father did not react.

MOTHER: When will you have a definite answer?
DOCTOR: Fairly soon.
MOTHER: Take the baby away. Don't show him to us. We're not going to take him home.
FATHER [*after conversing with the mother*]: Yes, we both agree. We're not going to take him home.
MOTHER [*to the father*]: For the time being, don't tell the family that I gave birth ... it's better if we can decide about the child on our own. We don't want them pushing us to make decisions that we don't agree with.
FATHER: O.K.

The father said nothing of his son's birth the entire day. Nevertheless, word spread about and that evening the mother was already surrounded by friends and family. They were also with her when she received the final diagnosis, confirming that her son had Down's syndrome. The women in the family and Marsha's neighbors made it clear to her that "this was God's will," and that "we'll all help care for the child." They did not leave her any possibility of abandoning her child. Three days later the mother was discharged from the hospital. Before leaving she thanked the midwife, adding, "It's the will of God ... I'll take the child home and care for him, ... as if he were normal."

We see that when Marsha and her husband were alone, not surrounded by people from their social network, they were inclined to reject their child, just like many non-religious parents in similar situations. The fact that the parents did not abandon their son stemmed from their not being able to escape the pressures of their social network. Nevertheless, since every decision of an individual living in a close-knit social network is presented as being vested in the values of the network, Marsha also explained the reason for not abandoning her son as being "the will of God." Yosi and Ḥitam also behaved similarly. Even though Yosi, a religious man, renounced his responsibility for his son, as did his non-religious friend Avram, he manipulated the values of the network so as to appear faithful to them. This also pertains to his behavior regarding consulting his extended family. Yosi lived in a religious environment that stressed family values but did not provide assistance within the family. Therefore, knowing that the burden of caring for a crippled child would fall on him and his wife, he did not actually consult his extended family. His imaginary consultation with them enabled him to present his action as being in accord with the values of the network and to reaffirm his belonging to the network and adhering to its values. The behavior of Ḥitam and her husband, who live in a close-knit social network of an Arab village, conveys a similar message. When Ḥitam's husband realized that "something has happened," he saw to it from the outset that he would be outside the network so that he would not have to share his decision-making process with members of the network.[8] Also Ḥitam, despite her attempts at avoiding members of her social network, used the values of the system ("God") in order not to present herself as causing her child's death, on the one hand, and to show her belonging to the system, on the other.

Often, even when a religious family living in a close-knit social network takes home a handicapped child, the family tends to reject the child at one stage or another, giving as the reason some excuse which is based on the network's values and stresses a family orientation, such as infertility (Yosi) or having a defect (such as six fingers) that makes the person unfit for marriage.

In this regard recall Michal, whose parents were also part of the paradoxical game being played here. On the one hand, they spoke of their obligation to maintain the accepted values of the network, one of which was being family-oriented. According to their perception, blood relationships cannot be severed and parents are responsible for the care of the children. On the other hand, Michal was rejected, so her parents maintained, because she did not live up to the rules of the system (she disturbed her parents in their observance of the Sabbath and "desecrated the Sabbath in public").

Thus far I have dwelled on the importance of social networks and their impact on attitudes towards deformed children. Now I must ask, what is the nature of this interconnection? Why is there a connection between one's social network and one's attitude towards one's child? Why do people from close-knit social networks take care of a handicapped child, whereas people from loose-knit social networks reject or abandon such a child? One explanation is based, in our opinion, on the nature of the services supplied by most close-knit social networks.

When I set about investigating these questions I discovered some things which field workers and researchers have ignored. It is indeed true that religious Jews or Arabs who live in close-knit networks relate to handicapped children with good care and devotion. But, for the most part, it is not the parents who care so devotedly for these children, but grandmothers, aunts, sisters, or other family members. In other words, in a loose-knit network, responsibility for a handicapped child is perceived as falling solely on the parents; in a close-knit social network, a handicapped child is perceived as a problem to be addressed by the network, and not by a specific mother or father, and when necessary the network provides welfare assistance, especially insofar as it appoints others to care for the child. Moreover, this is not a matter of reallocation of duties or of support that is purely instrumental, but also a matter of distributing responsibility among relatives. It must be noted that I am not discussing the fact that someone who is not the child's biological parent (a grandmother, stepfather, nurse, etc.) sometimes feels more responsibility towards a baby than his biological parents. I am not asking who feels a sense of responsibility, but who is saddled with the responsibility. In a loose-knit network, when a grandmother or aunt helps in the care of such a child, she does it as a volunteer; a close-knit network, in contrast, is like a manpower pool which does not need volunteers. Sam and Amira's parents, for example, renounced their responsibility for the life of their retarded children, but then the network took the children's lot into its hands by appointing an aunt with cardiac disease, who was ineligible to marry, as the person responsible for their care, and made her the mother in terms of the responsibility placed upon her.

The conclusion which follows from all of the above is that both in close-knit and loose-knit networks, both among religious families and among free-thinkers, parents tend to reject children who are outwardly deformed, and in so doing they define them as "non-persons." However a close-knit network often appoints one of its members to care for the child, according to the network's own considerations; whereas a loose-knit network lets the child be entrusted to the care of state medical and welfare services. In families whose economic position is especially good, the parents see to alternate care within the home, by hiring a nanny (such as Shula's case), or outside the home, in an prestigious institution (as in Gali's case). In these cases, however, it is not the parents, but rather some other person, who takes care of the child. The fact of a person being religious or non-religious has no impact on his or her perception of a handicapped child or on his or her way of relating towards such a child.

Thus far I have explained the importance of the social network on the instrumental plane of providing services. Networks are also important, how-ever, in terms of the support in self-identification that they provide a parent who feels threatened by contact with a handicapped child. Recall Yosi, who knew that the burden for caring for a crippled child would fall on him and his wife. According to his own explicit statement, he refrained from tak-ing his child home since doing so would have meant daily encounter with a person who was a threat to his system of self-image and identification. An aunt has a much easier time caring for a handicapped child than the child's mother, because the child is not perceived as being as part of her as he is perceived as being part of his mother. The boundaries of the self are broad, and that which is around the parents is perceived as an extension of them. It seems that a "non-person" in and of himself does not evoke rejection. What is frightening is the non-human image of the handicapped child mixing with the self-image of the parents. In other words, the attitude of rejection is also directed towards ourselves, insofar as we are part of the non-human in our children.

I conclude this discussion of networks with several words on factions (cf. Shokeid, 1968). In threatening situations the most significant support system does not necessarily include the closest members of the family. In such situations other relatives often feel a threat to their self-identification. They feel attacked, infected, and stress the identification of heredity with contagion and the view that "one weak person cannot help another," as Leah's mother put it. In such circumstances special significance attaches to the assistance of people who are not closely related to the parents, whether the parents were acquainted with them prior to the misfortune (such as Leah's relatives), or whether they met as a result of the misfortune (as in the case of Yosi, Avram and their spouses). As with groups of bereaved parents (Weiss, 1989), support groups for parents of handicapped children also break up when they are no longer needed (as in the faction formed by Avram, Galia, Yosi, and Bracha). Moreover, such factions (comprised of people who are less threatened) are encountered in close-knit social networks more often than in loose-knit networks.

I began this chapter with the statistic that about half of the children born with handicaps are abandoned by their parents. Nevertheless, in the course of the chapter we saw that unwillingness to take a child home does not necessarily indicate a total renunciation of responsibility for the child's life, and that sometimes parents who refuse to care for their children at home undertake one or another type of responsibility for the life or care of their child in a setting outside the home. I found that one must distinguish between two important aspects of parental behavior. One is the degree of intimacy or territorial distance the parents set with respect to their children. The second pertains to the parents' perception of their responsibility towards their children. In the previous chapter I discussed rejection vs. acceptance of a child within the family territory and the degree of intimacy parents have with their children. In this chapter I focused on the type of responsibility parents show towards their children. In the course of the chapter we presented a range of varieties of responsibility that parents accept for handicapped children.

I began with a description of total renunciation of responsibility for a child, coupled with his rejection from the family territory and an expression of a desire for his death. Later I discussed renunciation of responsibility for a child that takes place only in certain settings, as in certain territories (such as the home), or in certain situations (such as when there is a conflict between one's responsibility towards an abnormal child and one's responsibility towards one's own person or one's other children). In other contexts (such as in the hospital), the same parents were found to evince a different sort of responsibility towards their children, as expressed by motherly care, professional nursing care, or supervision of the medical staff supposed to provide such care. In some of these cases I observed how the parents' perception of responsibility towards their child changed with a change in the child's condition, as it appeared to her parents. Lastly, I mentioned the existence of social responsibility without any intimate bond, and of accepting responsibility for the life of a child in any sense whatsoever (including physical and medical care and intimate bonds). We saw that similar manifestations of responsibility, partial or total, exist not only with respect to a baby with which one can form a bond, but also with respect to an aborted fetus or "vegetable."

Behavior was classified as rejective or accepting according to the messages it conveyed. This criteria is most prominent when it comes to viewing a ritual circumcision ceremony (*Brith Milah*) as an expression of responsibility. Some parents do not have circumcision ceremonies performed on their handicapped children, whereas others hold such ceremonies in testimony to their total acceptance of responsibility for their child. Gabi's parents, for example, had their son circumcised and viewed him as "theirs" only after his defect had undergone an aesthetic repair. Mrs. Meshulam, on the other hand, insisted that her son have a circumcision ceremony even though she abandoned him.

We have addressed the question of what accounts for these differences in parental responsibility. The impact of such factors as nationality, ethnicity, education, age, place of residence, sex of the newborn, type of defect or deformity, technical difficulties in establishing a bond with the child, and number of children in the family on parental attitudes towards handicapped children seems quite dubious.[9] These factors cannot account for any substantial difference in attitude towards handicapped children. On the other hand, in our opinion, the type of social network in which the parents live is important in explaining how they actually relate to a handicapped child.

NOTES

1. See Table 1 in Chapter 1.
2. See note 11 in Chapter 1.
3. See note 10 in Chapter 1.
4. On the life support systems to which premature babies are often connected, see Chapter 4, notes 1, 2, and 4.
5. Cleft lip (harelip): a congenital deformity which varies in severity from case to case. Sometimes only a small portion of the upper lip is missing, and sometimes there is a serious disturbance in the structure of the lip and a large part of the nose and its base. The disturbance can occur on one side, usually the left, or it can be bilateral. In severe cases the ala (the expanded lower part of the side of the nose, formed only of skin) may also be affected. The deformity can be repaired by surgery done in several stages, and until

surgery is completed the patient may suffer eating and speech disorders. Bottle feeding is difficult for such children, and they must be fed with a dropper or spoon, using extreme care to avoid entry of food into the lungs. Sometimes feeding can be done in a seated position using narrow nipples with extra large holes.

Cleft palate: a fissure in the hard palate; may occur alone or together with a cleft lip. When only the palate is cleft, the fissure is situated along the center line, is open in the back and closed in front. When it is associated with a cleft lip, the palate is open in back along the center, and as it progresses towards the front it turns towards one of the sides and includes the base of the nose. Sometimes there is a fissure towards both sides. Some infants are given a temporary plate to close the fissure and thus enable almost normal sucking. Babies that suffer only from a cleft lip usually have surgery before they are one or two months old. At age 4 or 5 a surgical repair is made of the first operation, and at puberty a repair is made of the nasal structure. In cases also involving a cleft palate, surgery is postponed until age 18 months or more. When possible, it is recommended to postpone surgery until age 3, and to provide the child a special prosthetic appliance to help the child speak and eat (Brand-Orban, 1979, pp. 47 and 101–102).

6. For example, cf. Begab, 1963; Lobo and Webb, 1970; Farber, 1959; and Boles, 1959.

7. The concept of a social network was introduced into sociological research by Bott (1957). According to Bott in a close-knit social network all its members know one another. One's family are also one's neighbors, one's friends, and one's colleagues at work. In a loose-knit network family, friends, neighbors and work associates do not come into contact with one another. In a study of urban families in London, Bott found that a close-knit network offers a support system to each of the spouses, whereas a loose-knit network does not provide such support and the spouses must rely on each other to bear the burden of the family. In a close-knit network norms are uniform and clear to all and assist in social control; whereas in a loose-knit network such norms are of limited effect.

The term "social network" has gained acceptance in sociological theory and constitutes a factor which can explain many cases (cf. Fisher, 1982; and in Israel, Rubin, 1990). The literature on disability pays almost no attention to the variable of "social network" as a factor in and of itself. In this book the concept of social network as a social and cultural variable contributes to our understanding of patterns of behavior towards handicapped children.

8. In many other cases which I observed, the parents tended to conceal from the network their part in the decision concerning the death of their children and pretended to know about their child's death only after the fact.

9. For example, see the excellent review of the literature in Florian and Katz, 1983.

7

Epilogue

Encountering abnormal children enables us to examine how definitions of a person fit in with the need for cognitive order. What is it that we find threatening in our encounter with an abnormal person?

We have seen that parents feel threatened by the lack of clarity regarding the identity of a child as a "person" and by their sense of a violation of body boundaries. These things make parents fearful that there will be a violation of their own body boundaries as a result of their contracting whatever "pollution" their child suffers. From this it can be concluded that "personhood" is defined in terms of its opposite. The concept of a "nonperson" is needed in order to define a "person."

The tendency to define identity in terms of its opposite has been discussed by various writers and researchers. With regard to Nazism, Packenheim (1978) writes: "The sole meaning of the term 'Aryan' was 'non-Jew'" (p. 92). Sartre also relates to this question in his discussion of the definition of self in terms of a counterimage. In this regard, he says that it is the anti-Semite that makes the Jew (1972B, p. 167); or, as Berger puts it, "one's own shaky identity is guaranteed by the counterimage of the despised group" (Berger, 1963, p. 159). This conclusion ties in with the findings of the anthropologist M. Douglas (1975, p. 17; 1966, p. 53). Her writings imply there is a perception of order that distinguishes between men and women, between husbands and wives, and between mothers and children. This perception is shaken by such things as a man who is also a woman, or a mother who is also the wife of her son, since woman is defined in terms of man and man is defined in terms of woman; a mother is defined by her children's existence, and a child is defined in relationship to his or her mother. Such things as homosexuality or illicit sexual relations create a sense of fear because they violate basic principles of order, they cross the lines of accepted categories, they threaten one's definition of self, and make one feel that if he is not himself, then I am not myself. Hence we feel a need to distance ourselves from entities of uncertain identity.

The threat to a person's identity stems from a cognitive lack of clarity regarding the definition of the other, and relates to a fear of violation of body boundaries as a result of a sort of contagion. Such fears also exist with respect to cancer patients and retarded children, who are perceived as carrying a threat of contamination. Contact with a cancer patient is more threatening, since a person whose abnormality is less evident and whose being conveys an ambivalent message is more difficult to locate cognitively than a person whose abnormality is plain and clear.

In situations such as these relatives feel that their sense of self is being undermined, that their body boundaries are being violated, and that the entity whose identity is uncertain is penetrating into them, infecting them (as one of the women observed said, "The evil has also invaded me").

"Non-Person" and Violence

This book examined attitudes towards abnormalities and the relationship between abnormality and violence. Relationships between parents and deformed or ill children were examined with respect to this issue. The scope of this study was influenced by the anthropological work of Mary Douglas, who investigated how cultures relate to anomalies and how a certain society treats children who are considered abnormal (Douglas, 1966, p. 39). In many societies parent-child relationships are considered to be more intense; cultural guidelines are thought to determine the relationship of a mother to the fruit of her womb and to determine when she will view her child as a "non-person" who is rightly treated as the object of violence. Had I ceased my investigation at the point of establishing the presence of violent behavior towards abnormal children exhibited on the part of strangers, my case would have been far less persuasive, since from the outset the relationship of strangers towards such children is supposedly less strong and positive than that of parents. One might argue that certain parents have not yet formed a parent-child relationship with their newborn abnormal child, and that therefore their relationship resembles the relationship between strangers and such a child. Therefore, I extended my study to include the relationship of parents to children who became abnormal in the wake of an illness, after parent-child relationships had already been formed.

Parent-child relationships are an appropriate setting for examining violence towards the abnormal[1] and for exposing the cultural guidance that determines who shall be shunned from society and who shall be nurtured; who shall live at home, who shall live in isolation, and who shall be condemned to death. The findings of anthropological literature indicate that violence is often viewed as a legitimate solution to the problem of the abnormal child.

Even though the literature does not deal explicitly with legitimized killing, one can infer that every society distinguishes between those situations in which extremely violent behavior, including killing the other, is permitted and those in which it is forbidden. Thus, a person who has human decency is not necessarily someone who does not kill, but rather someone who kills only according to the rules. In this book I was particularly interested in legitimized violence,[2] carried out according to the rules and not considered criminal behavior.

On what is such legitimized killing based? It turns out that labeling a child as beyond the range of human acceptability by defining her as a "non-person" makes it possible, de facto, to remove her from the realm of the human and thus sanctions violence against her. In order for a person who behaves with violence not to be denounced and or feel she is being violent, she must undergo a mental process of transformation, often occurring in a matter of seconds, by which she comes to view the other as a "non-person." Parents who demand or give their consent to the death of a handicapped child justify their actions on the grounds that they are not lending a hand to killing a baby, but rather providing the proper "handling" called for by a "vegetable" or "monster." A similar process occurs among parents who decide to abort a fetus that was discovered to have a defect. Here, too, there is a transition from person to non-person, which in turns gives the stamp of legitimacy to violence: after a fetus is defined as having a defect or being retarded, its right to life is denied.

The behavior of many parents expresses the attitude that a child is defined as their own only if she is normal and does not pose a threat to their social status and existence. If the being born to them is deformed (or becomes deformed in the course of time), she does not resemble a normal human child, and hence is not perceived as being theirs. Even though they know that leaving a child in the hospital, or transferring her to an institution, shortens her life, they do not feel they are being violent or cruel towards her, since they feel their actions are directed at some other, foreign entity.

With respect to maltreatment, one must mention the approach taken by Bakan (1975, p. 73) and Sheleff (1981), who assert the existence of a fundamental element of parental hostility towards children. In discussing the Oedipus complex, these two sociologists claim that Freud disregarded the first part of the Greek myth in that he did not stress that the first aggressive impulse was on the part of the father, Laius, against his son, Oedipus. I have developed these notions in a different direction. While other researchers have focused on proving the existence of fundamental parental hostility towards children, I have taken an interest in determining the guises in which such hostility emerges; for common sense says that even if there really is such fundamental parental hostility towards one's own children, it would not find expression in every time and place.

The basic difference in methodology and scope between my study and the many studies dealing with the battered child syndrome is that the techniques used in other studies stressed correlations and relationships between findings obtained primarily through interviews, and did not take an interest in the ideological self-justification voiced by the child abusers themselves. In contrast, in my study, even when I reported behavior which is considered to be "child abuse," I looked into the ideological justification for such violence.[3]

The study of disabilities associated with "non-persons" and violence is likely to open the way to similar studies in quite different areas; such as the practice of defining others as "non-persons" as a general strategy for removing social "pollutions." This is illustrated by attitudes towards ethnic minorities or communities that are associated with inferior social categories by likening these groups to animals (for example: "They look like animals out of the jungle," or "like pigs").

Human Similarities Prove Greater than Human Differences

One of the obvious conclusions of the present study is that there exist similar patterns of behavior and thought among groups that differ in their national affiliation, ethnic background, economic level, and education. Although it is a commonly held anthropological view that societies close to nature lay great emphasis on the significance attributed to man-animal relationships, this study shows that also Western society, albeit far from nature, attributes crucial significance to the boundary between man and animal. For modern, Western society, too, disability poses a threat due to its violation of this boundary line. We would rather reject those of our children who contradict the accepted definition of "person" than change that definition. As in simple societies, in our society as well a deformed child, who is associated with animal or monster metaphors, is subjected to severe maltreatment on the part of his parents, who often dub him with inhuman names such as "unicorn," "monster," or "snake." Modern society, even though it is not close to nature, uses animal metaphors in relating to the abnormal. This brings us back to the fundamental question of sociology which I wished to address in this book: "what it means to be a man and what it means to be a man in a particular situation" (Berger, 1963, p. 167).

Modern men and women, like their counterparts in simple society, are also strongly influenced particularly by what they see. Hormone level in the blood or the results of mechanized tests carry less weight in their eyes when they must relate to the other as male vs. female or healthy vs. ill.

The similarity between the patterns of thought of simple man/woman and of modern man/woman also finds expression in the importance attributed to hair, shadows, and smells. One's hair symbolizes one's social location, especially one's gender (Adamson, 1972, p. 108); shaving a girl's head indicates a change in her sexual identity. One's first name, shadow, smell, and clothes symbolize the person to whom they belong insofar as they are extensions of the individual (Hallpike, 1978, p. 139).

To sum up the findings of this study, it can be said that human similarities in the realm of parent-child relations towards abnormal children prevail over human differences. Similar patterns of thought were found among people in simple society and modern society, and among people from different age groups, ethnic backgrounds, socio-economic classes and genders.

The Body as a Symbol

In all stages of this study the body was presented as a symbol. The dichotomy between "person" and "non-person" traverses the axis of the body. A child's acceptance or rejection is conditional on the interpretation given his or her body image. This book has dealt with the impact of the distortions that parents have in the body images of their children. This impact spreads over at least four interrelated and interdependent areas, each area representing a specific existential problem or cognitive field. We share cultural categories (that can be interpreted according to the symbols used by the subjects observed) such as body and soul, man-animal, life and death, morality and responsibility. We have seen that the organizing principles of these existential problems are contagion, territory, revealing and concealing, social systems, and power relations. The same holds for the interpretation given life-support systems and the feeling of a violation of body boundaries.

Fathers vs. Mothers

Is there a difference between mothers and fathers in the way they perceive and relate to a handicapped child? In general I did not find any difference. Both mothers and father tended to reject a handicapped child who threatened their definitions of self. Nevertheless, it seems that mothers were more active in implementing the patterns of behavior chosen by both spouses. When children were cared for (in the home or the hospital), it was primarily the mothers who tended them; and when children were abandoned or rejected, the mothers were more firmly decided than the fathers with respect to such abandonment or rejection and with respect to the retreat from such behavior in the course of time. Perhaps the explanation for this lies in a social structure and system of stereotypes in which women have fewer work obligations outside the home and are perceived as responsible for the care of the children. Thus, when dealing with a handicapped child, the woman knows that in the final analysis the burden of caring for the child will fall on her.

Psychoanalytic (Deutsch, 1945) and socio-biological (Wilson, 1977) explanations can also help us understand our findings.

Nevertheless, intergender behavioral differences only account for part of the variations encountered in this study, which variations, it must be remembered, are only in form and not in substance. I discovered certain fundamental patterns of behavior that are common to different ethnic groups, genders, and nationalities. It is hard to isolate gender as a distinct variable. This study was held in a social setting which, from the outset, reserves the role of child-care to the woman. Thus, it is hard to determine whether the attitude towards children stems from an intrinsic feminine quality or from the social role designated for women; whether the behavioral variations observed here were influenced by gender or by other variables related to it.

Religiosity and Willingness to Accept a Handicapped Child

Certain studies report the existence of a connection between religiosity and a person's willingness to accept a handicapped child, but they do not distinguish between a person's religiosity and other variables associated with degree of religiousness that are likely to provide alternative explanations of the relationship that has been found. In this study it was discovered that the tendency of religious people (both Jews and Arabs) not to abandon a deformed child does not stem from a humanitarian world view in which every living being is viewed as one of God's creatures, but from the tendency of religious people to live in close-knit social networks which enable the care for a handicapped child to be entrusted to people other than the parents. The literature dealing directly with attitudes towards handicapped children does not explain the findings in this book, which contradict a large number of its assumptions. In contrast, this study confirms the relevance of other subjects, which in the literature are not clearly associated with parental attitudes toward handicapped children. Thus, the subjects discussed in this book relate to abstract general questions pertaining to the fields of sociology, psychology, and anthropology.

Revealing Patterns of Acceptance and Rejection

Comparing data gathered through observation with data from interviews enables us to ascertain how varied and sensitive the material gathered through observation is in comparison with that obtained through interviews. Occasionally home interviews were conducted with the same parents whose behavior was observed in the hospital. It turned out that when parents were interviewed in a familiar environment and were requested to describe their attitude towards their children verbally, what they said matched the prevailing myth regarding parents' unconditional acceptance of their children. Observation of their actual behavior (such as touching, hugging, etc.), however, revealed a completely different attitude. For example, in an interview in her home, a mother of a child with cancer, whose hair was falling out as a result of chemotherapy, said, "I love this child with all my heart and soul." However, when the very same mother visited her son at the hospital, she maintained physical distance from her child, refrained from touching his bed, and insisted that her other children wash their hands if they had accidentally touched the chair by the sick child's bed. When the nurse asked her to do something that required direct contact with her son, she vomited, cried, and let out the words, "such a disgusting kid." Afterwards she ran off to the washroom, cleaned herself thoroughly, and did not return to her son until the next day. Thus, although the setting of a one-time interview in the parents' own home enables parents to deny their sense of repulsion by their children, observations within the setting of the hospital reveal their actual attitudes.

This research method provided additional data which would have been difficult to obtain any other way. Being able to make observations over a long period of time made it possible to discern changes that took place in parents' behavior towards their children. It could be seen that in many instances acceptance and rejection depend on the context or particular situation. Parents tend to reject their children in certain situations, and to accept them in others. The research method employed made it possible to discern the process of mental and emotional change by which parents' positions and responses switched from a nurturing and possessive attitude towards their children to the opposite extreme of total abandonment, and vice versa. It also disclosed the processes of social control which, when brought into play in the early stages of the process of rejection, are likely to bring about a more socially acceptable solution, such as taking one's child home, even if the result is that the child is isolated within the home. Thus, while general statistical figures indicate a connection between two variables in a specific static situation, observation of cases over time enables analysis of the dynamics of behavioral responses.

Rejection of handicapped children by their parents is the dominant pattern of behavior observed in this book. This finding, however, should not overshadow the fact that some children received devoted parental attention, despite their parents' rejective feelings. Children with cancer generally received unparalleled care and devotion from their mothers, and children with serious internal diseases for the most part received the full attention of their parents, given with a measure self-sacrifice and human effort almost beyond bearing. For 20 percent of the handicapped children in the study we have no evidence of their being isolated within the home, and there was also a minority of parents who attributed a positive image to a Down's syndrome child, at least for some length of time.

Theoretical Reflections

My overall observations indicate a list of external attributes which, once spotted, often result in the child's rejection by his or her parents. This list includes blue skin color, an opening along the spine, a cleft lip, lack of proportion in facial features, being attached to medical apparatus or having openings made in their bodies in unusual places. The list is similar to Scheper-Hughes' (1992, p. 365) indication of physical deformities which lead gradually, but mortally, to the neglect of the child by his/her mother. In the case of modern, Westernized Israel, the mortal neglect so widely practiced in Brazil is replaced by other practices which nevertheless lead to similar results.

Moreover, I found that parents were bothered by external, openly visible impairments more than by internal or disguised defects. These findings cast profound doubt on the "natural" and "regular" process of parent-child attachment called "bonding." Nancy Scheper-Hughes, who found similar types of child neglect among Brazilian mothers, related it to the "struggle of survival" taking place under conditions of high mortality and high fertility. But this kind of materialist explanation is not relevant to the conditions of life in Israel. Alternatively, several possible explanations suggest themselves. I shall proceed to enumerate these explanations, each of which entails its own implicit critique on the myth of bonding.

First, one might suggest that we are dealing here with an ethnically based, specific socio-cultural pattern of behavior, whose grounded in the context of Israeli society. Indeed, other anthropological studies have explored parts of Israeli society as traditional social groups undergoing accelerated processes of modernization; when confronted with modern medical technology, members of these groups reacted apprehensively and were inclined to refuse treatment (for a discussion of the case of impotence, cf. Shokeid and Deshen (1974, p. 151-172)). If this explanation holds, then "bonding"—like its opposite, namely child rejection—must be viewed as an ethnically based and culturally bound phenomenon. "Bonding," as Badinter (1981) and Scheper-Hughes (1992) both argue, must have "sufficient conditions" (namely the bourgeois nuclear family) in order to be successfully employed as a reproductive strategy.

Notwithstanding the possible validity of such a critique of the myth of bonding, such ethnically based cultural explanations would have to be ruled out in our case, since the observed behavior cuts across ethnic, economic, and educational categories. One may still propose that this homogeneity stems from some deeply-rooted characteristic of Israeli society at large, for instance its continuing involvement in an armed conflict with its Arab neighbors; and, according to Douglas (1973), one may be led to conjecture that a society deeply concerned with national boundaries is also deeply concerned with body boundaries. However even such a far-fetched hypothesis is ruled out by the evidence of the wide-spread cross-cultural existence of this phenomenon.

The overwhelming frequency and prevalence of the behavioral pattern observed requires a more general explanation. One such account is readily provided by sociobiology. That offspring must prove themselves "worthwhile" in order to receive parental care is perhaps not surprising to zoologists. Many animal mothers would reject their offspring if the latter failed to communicate some requisite signal—a proper squeak or the red inside of an open mouth (cf. Gould, 1982).

Prehaps sociobiologists would consider this instinctive behavior, and its Darwinian function, as sufficient for explaning the rejection of appearance-impaired children. In this view, "bonding" is seen as the biological outcome of evolution, selected for its function in assisting reproduction. This is indeed the logic of "biological essentialism," mentioned in the preface, which also states that "motherly love" is a by-product of the evolutionary function of bonding. However, this view seems too general to account for the rejection of newborns with only slight external deformities. There is also a "biological" criticism that can be levelled against this theory. With respect to evolution, there are other forms of mothering, some of which are more advantageous to the reproductive success of a group under different conditions. These include forms such as allo-mothering and step-mothering (cf. McKenna, 1979), which do not entail single mother-infant attachment. Why then was the latter type preferred by some human societies? Perhaps because it served the interests of male domination, as some feminists are quick to assert.

The alternative view suggested in this book is that the parents' body image is what determines their reactions toward their appearance-impaired children. Body image, I argued further, is uniquely significant in the very first stages of bonding since no other information concerning the newborn really exists. The image of the body is therefore regarded as being what one might also call the image of the "soul." The overwhelming significance attributed to appearance in the case of the newborn is what can account for the finding that 68.4 percent of the appearance-impaired newborns were abandoned, whereas 93 percent of the newborns suffering from internal defects were "adopted."

This explanation, I believe, is the most far-reaching critique of the theory of bonding, whether biologically or culturally based. It implies that "bonding" is itself a fragile and tentative strategy dependant on our expectations regarding the child's appearance. The "pragmatics of motherhood," then, is a strange blend of aesthetic preferences, body-image conditioning and materialist constraints, not to mention male oppression. Moreover, my findings with regard to child rejection implicate both parents, implying that there is no real difference between the attitudes of mothers and fathers. The assumption concerning the "feminine virtues" of mothers, as opposed to the "cruel and deserting" nature of males, is hence also refuted. One of the most telling examples, in this context, was the observation that non-biological parents of an appearance-impaired foster-child accepted him much more easily and fully than his biological parents.

Bonding, then, becomes an ideology which, like so many other ideologies that pose as social theories, turns the issues of society into the problems of the individual. All of the social ills which concern bonding theorists are reconstructed by bonding theory as problems of women not bonding to their babies. Attention is directed away from fundamental cognitive issues and toward the individual. Women are singled out by calling attention to the possible biological roots of bonding and by arguing that it is only women who possess the biological constitution for solving our social problems.

Feminism Reconsidered: Another Look at Body Image

Adrienne Rich (1977) has argued that women will ultimately achieve liberation and equality only as a result of learning to "think through their body." The feminist argument that women should rediscover themselves through their body has been interpreted in two major directions. First, that rediscovery could take place by touching upon the "biological essence" and the "feminine virtues" of women, presuming that such categories indeed exist. This interpretation, as we saw in the introduction, is derived from the theory of "biological essentialism." Second, the rediscovery of woman's "real" body could take place through unmasking the disguise men had used to conceal and oppress it. This interpretation of the political body, or body politics, characterizes radical, Marxist feminism.

Linda Zerilli (1992) recently compared the teachings of Simone de Beauvoir and Julia Kristeva in a manner reflecting these opposite interpretations of "thinking through the body." Kristeva's writings on maternity reassert the claim that female anatomy is her destiny, and seek to decipher the "female subjectivity" in biological cycles, as well as the duality and alienation of pregnancy (Kristeva 1980; 1986). Thus alluding to biological essentialism, Kristeva's prose was indeed criticized as denying a mother the possibility of questioning female destiny, "either fusing or confusing her with her infant" (Silverman 1988, p. 102) and "understanding the desire to give birth as a species-desire, part of a collective and archaic female libidinal drive that constitutes an ever-recurring metaphysical reality" (Butler 1990, p. 90).

In contrast, Simon De Beauvoir, the mother of second-wave feminism, refers to maternity with an existentialist anxiety about the loss of individual agency and autonomy, suggesting that the maternal body is never a natural body, never a biological referent, but rather part of a (masculine) bio-politic (De Beauvoir, 1949). De Beauvoir's interpretation of maternity suggests that it is engendered both by the biological character of pregnancy and by the common social situation of women, in which they find themselves colluding with men's attempts to make them the "Other." It is therefore a kind of middle road between the two opposing approaches I mention.

This reading of de Beauvoir suggests that the feminist approach of straddling biological essentialism and socialization theory can indeed benefit from such a middle road. My own findings also support this conclusion. My findings refute the biological essentialism of "cultural feminists" by showing that there is no difference between women and men in the rejection of children and by exposing the myth of "motherly love." They do so not through some sort of Marxist criticism of reproduction and the social order, but by demonstrating the significance of body image in acceptance of children.

Body image, itself a rather ambiguously-defined concept demanding more detailed explanation, supposedly belongs to the realm of the theory of biological essentialism. Presumably the universal significance attributed to body image governs social practices—as expressed, for example, both in the materialist hardship and pre-demographic reproductive strategies (see Scheper-Hughes' Brazilian account), as well as in Israeli society, modernized and progressive as it is. Biological images hence become "images of knowledge" which in turn, through social institutions, become both ideology and praxis.

Thus the body encapsulates both opposites—biological essentialism as well as social antagonism. As the case of appearance-impaired children so incisively portrays, the body is the repository of human qualities. Madness, criminality, intelligence, mind, life and a myriad of other qualities—not to mention gender—are assumed to be located "in" bodies. External body insignia such as deformity are hence considered to reflect some essential, "inner" quality. Thus, a "monster-like" child (so perceived because of some external deformity) is nothing short of a "monster" in terms of both outer (appearance) and inner (essence). Similarly, women can be considered "motherly," caring and affectionate, "by their nature," because they are those who were biologically manufactured to carry the baby, as is clearly attested by pregnancy, which is, indeed, a protruding external body insignia. Thus, only through the body can one realize the dialectics of the woman-as-subject and the subjugation of woman. This is the interpretation I offer in this book, in response to Adrienne Rich's "rediscovery of the body."

I therefore call on my colleagues to join in a comparative study which will enable us to see body image as a socio-cultural construct, a collective representation through which bodies are created in different societies (Synnott, 1992) and metaphors of illness are constituted (Turner, 1992).

PERSONAL REFLECTIONS

It is now time, in the very apt words of Zola (1991), for me to bring "my
body and myself back in"—back into the academic account which is all too
often so analytic, as Homans (1964) argued, that it becomes too distant
from those it is trying to study. Nancy Scheper-Hughes, whose book evoked
both my appreciation and disagreement, tells her readers about Mercelinho,
the abandoned infant adopted and reared by her in 1965 (Scheper-Hughes
1992, p. 360). After emotionally trying visits, in which parents willingly
showed me their house, without shame or reluctance letting me observe the
manner in which they treated their appearance-impaired children, I often
found myself crying together with the social workers or medical staff (at
times former students of mine); several times we even appealed jointly to
adopt certain children. In that respect, I identify with Scheper-Hughes'
involvement. However, I cannot share her proclaimed commitment for "establishing some basis for empathy" (1992, p. 340) towards the Brazilian
mothers whose practices of child negligence and rejection she describes. My
ethnography does not, indeed cannot, venture to establish empathy; if there
are any emotional consequences to reading this book, these are probably disturbing and upsetting. It is not the exotic that I had to make familiar (as
Scheper-Hughes seems to have felt), but rather the familiar which I exposed
as bewildering.

The familiar, as I have come to recognize throughout my academic ca-
reer, often conceals tremendous extremes of human tragedy. The greatest
tragedies take place in the most common settings, as Balzac once wrote. I
was working on my Masters degree in sociology when the Yom Kippur War
war broke out, in October 1973. For the next six years, my life (personal
as well as academic) revolved around the subject of bereavement and its
mundane practical implications in the life of Israeli parents. The death of
a son changed the parents' view of life; it made their life unfamiliar, made
them look at it critically, and even gave them social license to restructure
it. The desire to uncover human nature as it lurks behind the familiar and
exposed under extreme conditions also led me to study the Holocaust. I
was especially interested in the German side, in the ordinary people who
could caress their children's heads in the evening and then crack open the
skulls of Jewish children the next morning. I came across transcriptions
of testimonies given by young Nazi soldiers to interrogators from the U.S.
army immediately after the war. They said that while they actually loved
children, the Jewish children did not look like children; what they killed,
they said, was vermin. It was a "process of verminization" whereby the
other is transformed into an insect or beast, and this paves the way for his
or her annihilation.

I was not able to go on with this study; but as I entered an altogether different field—that of the hospital—again I encountered the process of verminization, this time between parents and their children. I lived through several years practically in a state of hypnosis, with hardly any sleep. I have two small children; and in the evening I would cook supper, go out on a round of observations, and return at 6 a.m., before my children awoke. Then I would set off for the university, not feeling any tiredness. For five years I did not leave the ward. I was there, with the parents and their children, doctors and nurses, and myself and my thoughts. What would be, I found myself asking, if it were to happen to me?

Encountering a handicapped child forces us to examine certain very fundamental emotional and value systems, and to shatter certain myths and unverified assumptions. I shall detail several of these unverified assumptions and suggest that the public discuss the questions that they raise and the inferences that follow from them:

The main assumption examined in this study is that of parents' unconditional love for their children. Many studies have not taken an interest in labeling and stigmatization within the family because of their adherence to the unverified assumption regarding the unconditional acceptance of children by their parents.

This assumption was challenged by taking a closer look at the behavior of parents of handicapped children. It turns out that bonding with one's biological child is not spontaneous, automatic, or natural, and that every child undergoes a process of adoption or abandonment, grounded in the child's external appearance and resemblance to the image of a "person." Hence I oppose the approach taken by Parsons (1967, p. 395), who claims, following Helsi, that "By definition, a mother loves her child ... her obligations to her child are diffuse, and affectivity is expected." The findings of this book contradict these assumptions and their underlying myth. The status of a child in the family is also dependent on his/her achievements. It is true that the achievements expected of a child are different from those that will be expected of him/her in his/her place of work; but even in his/her home he/she is not automatically accepted as a member of the family by virtue of simply belonging or having been born into the family, but must attain certain accomplishments and be pleasing to others in order to win their love; if he/she does not, he/she will be rejected. The findings of this study, especially those that point towards a tendency to reject handicapped children, raise a serious question in that they undermine the notion of natural, instinctive, and unconditional parental love; if such love indeed existed, the patterns of rejective behavior which I have noted would not have been possible.

Against this setting of general consensus among researchers regarding the myth of parents' unconditional love for their children and parents "natural guardianship," Harlow's unusual and remarkably original position presents

a refreshing difference: "To a baby all maternal faces are beautiful ...
unfortunately, parents do not seem to follow this rule and to a parent some
babies are more beautiful than others" (Harlow, in Sacket, 1978, pp. 79-80).
Nevertheless, it seems that the shattering of this myth, and the existential
sense of isolation that follows, are hard to live with. As one of the people
whom I observed said, "If we cannot be sure of our parents' love, what can
we be sure of?" Thus, of all the hard things that happen to us, of all the
truths that crumble in the course of our lives, it is most difficult for us to
cope with shattering the myth of parental love of their children; therefore
we tend to oppose any attempt to bring us face to face with the facts that
contradict the myth, or we try, as far as possible, to avoid situations that
will force us to confront this myth and to realize that it does not stand up
to the test of reality.

In this respect, it is interesting to note the highly emotional reactions
elicited by articles in the Israeli press[4] about abandonment of handicapped
children or violence towards them. Clearly the arguments of those people
who were "horrified" are nothing but hot air; the very same people who
raise an outcry about the injustice of children being abandoned by their
parents are capable of preventing a day-care center for Down's syndrome
children from being opened in the building next door. The strength of
their emotional outbursts, however, indicates a tremendous adherence to
the myth even in the face of evidence controverting it in actual fact.

Unwillingness to come to terms with the myth of unconditional parental
love being shattered reminds us of the refusal to recognize the existence
of the battered child syndrome. Only the determined perseverance of researchers and field workers, who toiled indefatigably to bring to the public
awareness facts that the public tried to deny, led to recognition of the syndrome and greater protection of battered children by the system. Similarly,
only the willingness of Israeli society to come to terms with the behavioral
trends mentioned in this chapter will make it possible to locate rejected
children and to care for them. The situation is especially grave precisely
because rejection of children by their parents often occurs within the intimate sphere of the home.

I call on the public to open a bold discussion of the unverified assumption
that parents feel unconditional love for their children. One must also address
such practical implications as the question of the "natural guardianship" of
parents for their children. I observed cases where children were born with
defects requiring surgery immediately after birth. The doctors turned to
the parents of these children, as their natural guardians; and the parents
refused to give their consent for the operations, and their children died.[5] On
what grounds are the parents given the sole right to decide about the death
of their children? Is it the unverified assumption that, when called upon to
decide the fate of their child, their only concern is for the well-being of that

child? Are natural parents really a child's best guardians? Alternatively, we may ask what right does the system have to deliver a child, under police escort, to parents who do not want her? (Here I am looking at the question only from the point of view of the child.) What are the rights of the child as a sick person, as someone who is hospitalized, as a citizen? Let us lay these questions open to public discussion. I believe that the Committee on Sick Person's Rights as well as the Committee for Child Protection ought to address these questions. In my opinion, the law ought to stipulate that cther bodies, in addition to a child's parents, be party to crucial decisions such as refraining from performing an operation to save the child's life. The state must show greater concern for such children. It is unconscionable to leave the care of and decision-making regarding handicapped children solely in the hands of their parents. Israeli society must provide such children fitting care, either within or outside the family setting.

Freedom of Choice to Be a Person

Encountering a handicapped child also forces us to confront the degree of violence that exists in each of us: "He (the deformed child) releases the evil in us," "He draws the demons out of our insides," as several of the people observed commented. Yet contact with a handicapped child puts to the test not only the limits of parental love for their children but also the limits of violence that they are likely to show their children. This encounter also lays bare the parents' need to obtain the stamp of approval for behaving violently towards their children. The decision to reject a deformed child is preceded by a decision to define that child as a "non-person"; relating to a child as a "non-person" is the most important step in the chain of attitudes that eventually leads to violence towards a child, in that it is what provides legitimization for killing the child. The tendency to remove deformed persons from the realm of the human, and thus to sentence them to death legitimately, is not restricted simply to the case of deformed children. Therefore, a public discussion of the matter ought to extend to a general discussion of the tendency to respond to abnormality with violence. A discussion of viewing the other as a "non-person" is especially important, in that so viewing a person encourages and provides justification for violence and cruelty also towards ethnic or national minorities.

We have seen that people in simple societies as well as in various modern societies need a sense of cognitive order and tend to reject whoever violates that order. Their culture provides them guidelines on what falls within the bounds of good order and how to treat those who deviate from this order. The variation noted between the various human categories mentioned pertains solely to the cultural content, to the definitions of order and deviance. Among the Nuer in Africa, as well as in modern Israeli society, a tendency was found to reject someone who is identified as a "non-person"; however, in certain African societies twins might be defined as "non-persons," whereas in Israeli society they are not defined as such. The variation in what different societies dictate to their members as constituting a sense of order is evidence of the relative nature of cultural precepts as binding guidelines for behavior. For example, in a televised discussion of the "legitimate use of arms," Mordechai Gur, then Commander in Chief of the Israel Defense Forces, said:[6] "There are moments when a person must decide, in a split second, whether or not to pull the trigger, . . . and then all the education the person has received must find expression, . . . and he must decide correctly." In other words, the education that a soldier has received is supposed to help him live up to the expectations of his culture and automatically obey its definitions with respect to who has the right to be called human (a prisoner) and who does not have this right (an enemy). According to this line of thought, the "education" that parents receive in Nuer society helps them respond automatically, as it were, and exclude from the realm of the human a child of theirs who, in a different society, might have been given life, simply because their fellow tribesmen have defined that child as a "non-person" (a "hippopotamus"). It is true that in all of these cases there is a ready-made definition that determines who shall be considered a "non-person." But does such a definition indicate that it is "natural" to view someone as a "non-person" and that consequently we must treat such a person in this manner, automatically? Does this public, pre-definition bind us, as individuals, to a certain type of behavior?

I maintain that, as with any cultural precept, it is in the interest of such pre-definition to have most people obey it, and therefore their behavior appears to be automatic. Thus the fact that the same child might be defined as human in another culture shows that the specific type of behavior is not necessarily natural. In Nazi society Jewish children were predefined as "non-persons." Does this mean that every Nazi soldier did not have to decide correctly, lend expression to his education and kill such a child; or should he have "denied his education" and treated such a being as a child, as a "person," as he might treat any other child living in his neighborhood? The same applies to the situation of parents in Nuer society and in our society. One cannot assume that it is natural to kill one's own child, even if the child is deformed. Parents in these societies must make an extremely rapid decision to obey the rules of their culture and to sanction spilling such a child's blood.

A similar line of thought emerges from Berger's remarks (1963) that people are responsible for their actions. Referring to Sartre's concept of "bad faith," Berger describes this as pretending that something follows of necessity when actually it is a matter of free will. Thus the roots of bad faith are the flight from freedom, improperly evading the pain of choice. According to Berger, people's excuse "that they 'have no choice' is the fundamental lie on which all 'bad faith' rests. It is only quantitatively different from the same excuse proffered by the official murderers of the Nazi system of horrors." Sartre describes the anti-Semite as a fearful person. However, it is not the Jew that he fears, but himself, his own consciousness, his own freedom (Sartre, 1972B, p. 161). Moreover, some people decide "incorrectly"; there were Nazi officers who did not obey automatically and did not view a Jewish child as a "non-person." Although it is hardly an equal comparison, there were parents who refused to attribute to their children the image of a "mongoloid" and viewed them for at least some time as normal children with legitimate differences. All this shows that there are alternatives to actions of rejection and that a person goes through a process of decision whether or not to obey an accepted definition of society. The existence of a universal tendency to view certain individuals as "non-persons" and to treat them with violence does not controvert the existence of individual free choice and the moral imperative of pondering over this tendency and perhaps also opposing it.

Sartre's and Berger's remarks, cited above, move me to appeal from the depths of my heart to the parents of handicapped children and to the staff caring for them.

Coping with a handicapped child means coping with ourselves. How many people truly come to terms with themselves? Who is willing to stand, 24 hours a day, opposite a mirror that reflects one's innermost being, one's deepest secrets, all that one has cherished and compressed into one's being through the years of one's life, one's fears and trepidations, one's hates and hardships? After learning for years how to push aside and conceal the darker side of our lives, we are suddenly confronted with a handicapped child, our own child, "lying in wait for us around the corner." The child intrudes into our being and senses our uglier side, and brings out the evil that we tried so hard not to know of. The child is like a blot that arouses in us the part of our being which is "not O.K."; it is our shame, our secret; and it is hard for us to live with our evil bubbling forth; with the "demons in our insides"; with our naked helplessness and our death wishes. It is hard for us to live with ourselves.

The same applies to our need for perfection. For years we have endeavored to surround ourselves with people who enable us to present ourselves as perfect, or who give us hope of reaching greater perfection. All this is wiped out with the stroke of a hand. So too, other aspirations that drag our fictitious defenses along with them are destroyed. All that was sure now stands under question; prior values, our ideal image, put to the test by the evil that comes out of us, by violence and hatred; and we are left alone. We are alone, facing the frailty of our lives. Suddenly we realize that the blows are likely to land on us, too, and that the tragedy has also invaded our territory. Thus, our encounter with an abnormal child threatens the deepest levels of our being: what we experienced in our childhood and youth, on our bodies and souls. Everything is shaken and under attack, nothing inviolate or sure. In this most dangerous situation, we are confronted with two possibilities: one is to follow the "natural," instinctive and universal reaction of rejecting the handicapped child and giving up the battle of coming to terms with ourselves.

The other option holds out a promise of hardship and suffering, but also a chance of growing from this suffering and undergoing a process of development at the end of which we shall feel ourselves free to make the correct choice at the crucial moment. Encountering a handicapped child calls upon us to confront ourselves; I suggest that we try to catch the ball thrown to us, not flee from it. Let us discover the secret, let us put ourselves to the test; let us not be afraid of coping with ourselves, with the sense of chaos, fall, and loss of security; with the question of "who am I," with the evil that bursts forth in us and in our dear ones ("I never knew children could be such sadists"); then we shall know that indeed we are also evil, also sadists. We must talk about these "demons." We must grant legitimacy to the existence of death wishes, violence, insecurity and chaos. Feeling rejection towards a handicapped child is universal. All this should be discussed, without passing judgment. There is no tabu on feelings, there is only tabu on behavior. Only if we try to cope shall we be able to discover the strength that lies alongside our weakness, the good that lies alongside the evil. Only then shall we be capable of choosing whether we shall live with a child in the same territory or not. And every choice that we make is equally good and equally correct.

I am not calling for parent education or preaching morality with the intention of persuading anyone to take a specific action. I wish to help parents listen to themselves and to the members of their family. Many parents give as the reason for removing a handicapped child from the home the fact of their concern that their healthy children "not be adversely affected." Is that indeed true? Have these parents listened to the inner longings of their healthy children? Have they heard their fears that "they will treat me just the same; if I am not healthy and perfect, will they throw me out of the house, too?"

Medical and nursing staffs and paramedics should also be given a deliberate opportunity to face themselves. One must enable the nursing and medical staff to have an awareness of their non-verbal reactions, to unburden themselves of their muffled fears, their magic thoughts, their fear of contagion, their need for symbolic cleansing after contact with cancer patients or retarded children. I am not interested in forcibly preventing specific patterns of behavior. I wish to create an awareness of these behavioral patterns and to put an end to the investment of so much energy in concealing them. Then we shall be able to feel our pain in a supportive atmosphere, and we shall be free to make our own personal choices.

NOTES

1. For this type of proof, see Stinchcombe, 1968, p. 15.

2. Clearly there is sometimes a lack of consensus regarding the definition of decency and legitimacy, such as the disagreements between parents and hospital workers; however, we wish to stress the subjective feeling of the parents that the violence they have shown their children is legitimate.

3. In this sense the present book further develops other directions of thought, primarily anthropological. We have seen that anthropological literature provides evidence that simple societies act with violence towards children who for whatever reason are considered deformed in their parents' eyes. Such violence receives ideological justification. It turns out that a similar manifestation can be found in modern society, as well. Infanticide, deliberate abortions, and, on quite a different level, even genocide, are examples of violence directed at children or adults, examples which receive societal and ideological justification.

4. The public at large, the literature, and a considerable fraction of the professionals in the field deny that there is a tendency to reject and abandon handicapped children. However, if we follow the newspaper reports of such occurrences, we can discover their full scope. For example, cf. Namir, 1982B; Namir, 1984; Rosen, 1984; Tomer, 1987; Balvah, 1984, on abandonment of babies who are "physically handicapped but mentally in perfect health"; and Kampfner, 1987: "They were all abandoned. All the handicapped children born this year in the Kiriyah Hospital were abandoned." Even the ultra-Orthodox population sometimes transfers its handicapped children to institutions or ultra-Orthodox foster families: "Mongoloid babies and children with Downs' Syndrome, ranging in age from one week to three years, were flown this past week to Brooklyn, to ultra-Orthodox foster families who had consented to care for these children for free. The parents of these children included secular and religious families who could not find a suitable institution for their children within Israel" (*Yediot Aḥaronot*, Sept. 15, 1986, p. 12).

5. The parents of these children condemned their children to death. Their guardianship of their children found expression, according to their perception, only in consenting to their death ("the unicorn") and in their readiness to donate parts of their child's body (Victor). It was only due to the efforts of people who were not blood relatives and who prevented the children's deaths that the lives of these children were saved.

6. This discussion was held close to the eve of the Jewish New Year, 1980, and had to do with the trial of Lieutenant Pinto.

Appendix

Introduction

In this study, 1,450 cases were observed. One of the groups observed consisted of the parents of 1,288 children who suffered from one or more of the defects, injuries, or diseases listed in Table 3. In 680 of these cases the parents' behavior was observed at their child's birth or immediately thereafter, and in 608 cases, several months or years after the child's birth.

In addition to these cases, observations were made of 162 women in pregnancy or childbirth; 50 of these women were classified as high risk pregnancies, 100 were women whom we observed delivering normal children, and 12 were women who had stillbirths.

TABLE 1

NUMBER OF NEWBORNS WITH A DISEASE OR DEFECT, WHOSE PARENTS'
BEHAVIOR WAS OBSERVED AT THE CHILD'S BIRTH OR IMMEDIATELY THERE-
AFTER, ACCORDING TO TYPE OF DEFECT, INTERNAL OR EXTERNAL

Type of Internal (Concealed) Defect	Number of Newborns
Turner's syndrome	15
Klinefelter's syndrome	20
Heart defects	20
Blindness	15
Hydrocephaly (not apparent in its early stages)	25
Microcephaly (not immediately apparent in its early stages)	3
Uncertain sex (not immediately apparent)	2
Total internal defects	100

Type of External Defect	Number of Newborns
Anencephaly	15
Spina Bifida	20
Down's syndrome (mongoloidism)	120
Cleft palate	25
Harelip	22
Bone malformation	30
Hemangioma	3
Radically distorted facial features	10
Uncertain sex (with clear external indications)	3
Total children with external defects	250

This table covers 350 (100 + 250) children with impairments, whose parents' behavior was observed at their child's birth or immediately thereafter. It includes only those cases in which the physicians determined that the newborn had a defect. It does not include the cases of newborns suffering from diarrhea, Hirschprung's disease, coma, nor those on life-support systems or premature babies (with the exception of premature neonates with Down's syndrome—cf. Table 3).

TABLE 2

NUMBER OF CASES PRESENTED IN THE BOOK,
ACCORDING TO TYPE OF DEFECT, INJURY OR DISEASE

Type of Case	No. of Cases	Type of Case	No. of Cases
Heart defects	1	Cancer	5
Spina Bifida	6	On life-support systems	3
Burns	3	Distorted facial features	1
Brain abscess	1	Hydrocephaly	1
Down's syndrome	9	Diabetes	2
Colostomy	2	Kidney disease	1
Turner's syndrom	1	Coma	1
Severe disability in the legs	1	Blindness	1
Retardation	1	Lung disease	1
Klinefelter's syndrome	1	Cleft palate	1
External sexual uncertainty	1	Stillbirths	2

Detailed descriptions of 43 cases are presented in this book. Of these, two deal with behavior towards stillborn babies, and 41 describe parental behavior towards live children with impairments or diseases.

Any given case listed in this table was listed only once even if it could apply to two categories, such as a single child who suffered from Hirschprung's disease and also had a colostomy.

TABLE 3

NUMBER OF HANDICAPPED CHILDREN WHOSE PARENTS' BEHAVIOR WAS OBSERVE
ACCORDING TO TYPE OF HANDICAP AND TIME OF OBSERVATION

Type of child's impairment	Observed at birth or soon after	Observed months or years after	Total cases observed
Premature	180	–	250
Uncertain sex	5	–	5
Anencephaly	15	–	15
Microcephaly	5	–	5
Spina Bifida	20	20	40
Hydrocephaly	25	15	40
Down's syndrome	120	120	170
Klinefelter's syndrome	20	–	20
Turner's syndrome	15	–	15
Cleft palate	25	15	40
Harelip	22	10	32
Hirschprung's disease	15	–	15
Bone defects or limping	30	30	60
Heart defects	20	30	50
Hemangioma	3	–	3
Distorted facial features, blindness, or severely impaired vision	15	–	15
Burns	–	40	40
Cancer	–	100	100
Celiac disease	–	3	3
Diabetes	–	20	20
Chronic kidney disease	–	10	10
Tracheostomy (due to illness or automobile accident)	20	50	70
Colostomy	10	20	30
Coma in the wake of an accident or deficient medical care	5	10	15
Diseases or infections such as: diarrhea, tonsilitis, pneumonia, or brain abscess	100	100	200
Total	680	608	1288

Bibliography

Adams, G.R. and A.S. Cohen, "Characteristics of children and teacher expectancy: An extension to the child's social and family life," *Journal of Education Research* 70:87–90 (1976).

Adams, G.R. and J. LaVoie, "Parental expectations of educational and personal-social performance and childrearing patterns as a function of attractiveness, sex and conduct of the child," *Child Study Journal* 5:125–142 (1975).

Adamson, H.E., "Clothing and ornament," in C.C. Hughes (ed.), *Make Men of Them: Introductory Readings for Cultural Anthropology*, Chicago, Rand McNally and Company, 1972.

Ainlay, S., Becker, G. and Coleman, L. (eds.), *The Dilemma of Difference*, New York, Plenum Press, 1986.

Allport, F.H., *Social Psychology*, New York, Johnson Reprint Corp., 1967.

Altman, I. and W.W. Haythorn, "The ecology of isolated groups," *Behavioral Science* 12:169–182 (1967).

Antonovsky, A., "The image of cancer in the eyes of the Israeli public," *Ha-Refuah* 18:464–461. [Hebrew].

Appandurai, A. (ed.), *The Social Life of Things: Commodities in Cultural Perspective*, Cambridge, Cambridge University Press, 1986.

Atzmon, A., "Abortion from a Moral Standpoint," *Hevra u-Revahah* 2 (3):302–310 (1979). [Hebrew].

Bachrach, Ts., *Modern Antisemitism*, Ministry of Defense, 1979. University on the Air [Hebrew].

Badinter, E., *L'amour en Plus*, Paris, Flammarion, 1980.

Bakan, D., *Slaughter of the Innocents: A Study of the Battered Child Phenomenon*, San Francisco, Jossey-Bass, Inc., 1975.

Balvah, E., "'You had a stillbirth,' they told the mother," *Ha'aretz* (July 11, 1984). [Hebrew].

Barr, S., *The relationship between perception of body boundaries and general adjustment among a student population*, Tel Aviv University, 1982. Doctoral dissertation [Hebrew].

Barram, B., "Modern trends in violence," *Reconstructionist* 3:7, 17 (1975).

De Beauvoir, S., *A Very Easy Death*, New York, Pantheon Books, 1965.

Becker, H.S., *Outsiders: Studies in the Sociology of Deviance*, New York, The Free Press, 1963.

Begab, J.M., *The Mentally Retarded Child–A Guide to Services of Social Agencies*, Washington, D.C., Dept. of Health, Education and Welfare; Welfare Administration–Children's Bureau, 1963.

Belfer, M.I., "Discussion: facial plastic surgery in children with Down's Syndrome, by Lemperle, G., and Radu, D.," *Plastic Surgery* 20:343–344 (September, 1980).

Ben-Sira, Z., "The structure and dynamics of the image of diseases," *Journal of Chronic Diseases* 30 (12):831–842 (1977b).

Benedek, T., "Organization of the reproductive drive," *International Journal of Psychoanalysis* 41 (January-February, 1960).

Berger, P.L., *Invitation to Sociology: A Humanistic Perspective*, New York, Anchor Books, 1963.

Berger, P.L. and Luckman, T., *The Social Construction of Reality: A Treatise in the Sociology of Knowledge*, London, Penguin Books, 1966.

Berry, J.O. and W.W. Zimmerman, "The stage model revisited," *Rehabilitation Literature* 44:275–277 (September-October, 1983).

Berscheid, E. and E. Walster, "Physical attractiveness," in L. Gerkowitz (ed.), *Advances in Experimental Social Psychology*, Vol. 7, New York, Academic Press, 1974.

Beuf, A.H., *Beauty is the Beast: Appearance-Impaired Children in America*, Philadelphia, University of Pennsylvania Press, 1990.

Binger, C.M., A.R. Albin, R.C. Feuerstein, J.H. Kushner, S. Zoger and C. Mikelsen, "Childhood leukemia, emotional impact on patient and the family," *New England Journal of Medicine* 20:414–418 (February, 1969).

Blake, F.G. and F.H. Wright, *Essentials of Pediatric Nursing*, Philadelphis, J.B. Lippincott Company (7th ed.), 1963.

Boles, G., "Personality factors in mothers of cerebral palsied children," *Genetic Psychology Monographs* 59:159–218 (1959).

Bolkenius, M., R. Daum, and E. Heinrich, "Pediatric Surgical Principles in the Management of Children with Intersex," *Progressive Pediatric Surgery* (17):33–38 (1984).

Book, W.E., "Judgement of intelligence from photographs," *Journal of Abnormal and Social Psychology* 34 (4):384–389 (1939).

Bott, E., *Family and Social Network*, London, Tavistok, 1957.

Brand-Orban, A., *Pediatric Medicine*, Jerusalem, Kolek and Sons, 1979. [Hebrew].

Brauer, P.H., "When cancer is diagnosed," *Medical Insight* 21:20–25 (1970).

Brenner, D. and Hinsdale, G., "Body build stereotypes and self identification in three age groups of females," *Adolescence* 20:551–562 (1978).

Brinker, M., "History of Beauty in the West," in Yannai, Ts. (ed.), *Ideas*, IBM publaddr Tel Aviv, 1990. [Hebrew].

Bruckner, L.S., *Triumph of Love*, New York, Simon and Schuster, 1954.

Campbell, J.K., *Honour, Family, and Patronage: a Study of Institutions and Moral Values in a Greek Mountain Community*, Oxford, Clarendon, 1964.

Casell, W.A., "A projective index of body interior awareness," *Psychosomatic Medicine* 26:172–177 (1964).

Castro-Magana, M., M. Angulo and P.J. Collipp, "Management of the Child with Ambiguous Genitalia," *Medical Aspects of Human Sexuality* (18):172–188 (1984).

Centers, L. and R. Centers, "Peer group attitudes toward the amputee child," *Journal of Social Psychology* 61:127–132 (1973).

Chodorow, N., *The Reproduction of Mothering*, Berkeley, University of California Press, 1978.

Clifford, M., "Physical attractiveness and academic performance," *Child Study Journal* 5:201–209 (1975).

Clifford, M. and E. Walster, "The effect of physical attractiveness on teacher expectations," *Sociology of Education* 46:248–258 (1973).

Cohen, E., "The Study of Touristic Images of Native People," paper presented at the 1991 Biannual Seminar of the International Academy for the Study of Tourism, Calgary, Alberta, Canada, 1991.

*Combating Stigma Resulting from Deformity and Disease,*seminar held on November 6, 1969. Leonard Wood Memorial for the Eradication of Leprosy, New York, 1969.

Cook, S.W., "Judgement of Intelligence from photographs," *Journal of Abnormal and Social Psychology* 34 (3):384–389 (1939).

Cooper, C., "The house as symbol of self," Working Paper No. 20, Institute of Urban and Regional Development, University of California, Berkeley, May, 1971.

Corter, C., S. Trehub, C. Boukydis, L. Ford, L. Celhoffer and I. Minde, "Nurses' judgments of the attractiveness of premature infants," *Infant Behavior and Development* 1:373–380 (1978).

Cross, J.F. and J. Cross, "Age, sex, race, and the perception of facial beauty," *Developmental Psychology* 5:433–439 (1971).

Csikszentmihalyi, M. and Rocherg-Halton, *The Meaning of Things*, Cambridge, Cambridge University Press, 1981.

Cumming, J. and E. Cumming, "Mental health education in a Canadian community," in B.D. Paul (ed.), *Health, Culture and Community*, New York, Russel Sage Foundation, 1955.

Daniels, L.L. and C. Berg, "The crisis of birth and adaptive patterns of parents of amputee children," *Clinical Proceedings Children's Hospital* 24 (4):108–117 (1968).

Davison, R.L., "Opinion of nurses on cancer, its treatment and curability," *British Journal of Preventive and Social Medicine* 19:24–29 (1965).

Dennis, S., *Internal organ images of patients with an affective syndrome and schizophrenics*, Tel Aviv, 1980. Doctoral dissertation in medicine [Hebrew]

Deutsch, H., "The Psychology of Women," in *Motherhood*, Vol. 2, New York, Grune and Stratton, 1945.

Dion, K., "The incentive value of physical attractiveness for young children," *Personality and Social Psychology Bulletin* 3:67–70 (1977).

Dion, K., "Children's physical attractiveness and sex as determinants of adult punitiveness," *Developmental Psychology* 10:772–778 (1974).

Dion, K., "Young children's stereotyping of facial attractiveness," *Developmental Psychology* 9:183–188 (1973).

Dion, K., "Physical attractiveness and evaluation of children's transgressions," *Journal of Personality and Social Psychology* 24:207–213 (1972).

Dion, K., "What is Beautiful is Good," *Journal of Personality and Social Psychology* 24:215–20 (1972b).

Doe, "Still hounding Mr. and Mrs. Doe," *The New York Times* (March 13, 1984).

Douglas, M., *Implicit Meanings*, London, Routledge and Kegan Paul, 1975.

Douglas, M., *Purity and Danger*, London, Routledge and Kegan Paul, 1966.

Douglas, M., *Natural Symbols*, New York, Pantheon Books, 1970.

Douglas, M. and Calvez, M., "The self as risk taker: a cultural theory of contagion in relation to AIDS," *The Sociological Review* 38 (13):465–483 (1990).

Ebbin, A.J., "Discussion: facial plastic surgery in children with Down's Syndrome," *Plastic Surgery*:343 (September, 1980).

Eco, U., *A Theory of Semiotics*, Indiana University Press, 1979.

Edgerton, R.G., *Deviance: A Cross Cultural Perspective*, Menlo Park, California, The Benjamin-Cummings Publishing Company, 1976.

Edgerton, R.G., "Pokot intersexuality: An East African example of sexual incongruity," *American Anthropologist* 66:1288–1299 (1964).

Efran, M., "The effect of physical appearance on the judgement of guilt, interpersonal attraction, and severity of recommended punishment in simulated jury task," *Journal of Research in Personality* 8:45–54 (1974).

Engel, G.L., "Is grief a disease? A challenge for medical research," *Psychosomatic Medicine* 23:18–22 (1961a).

Engel, G.L., "Grief and grieving," *American Journal of Nursing* 1:93–98 (September, 1961b).

Engler, G., "Physics and Beauty," in Yannai, Ts. (ed.), *Ideas*, Tel Aviv, IBM, 1990. [Hebrew].

English, R.W., "Correlates of stigma towards physically disabled persons," *Rehabilitation Research and Practice Review* 2 (4):1–17 (1971).

English, R., and D.A. Pallo, "Attitudes towards a photograph of a mildly and severely mentally retarded child," *Training School Bulletin* 68:55–63 (1971).

Erikson, K.T., "Notes on the sociology of deviance," in H. Becker (ed.), *The Other Side*, New York, The Free Press, 1964.

Evans-Pritchard, E.E., *Nuer Religion*, London, Oxford University Press, 1956.

Farber, B., "Effects of severely mentally retarded child on family integration," *Monographs of the Society for Research in Child Development*, 24 (2):5–107 (1959).

Farber, B., *Mental Retardation: Its Social Context and Social Consequences*, Boston, Houghton Mifflin, 1968.

Feifel, H., "Dealing with death," in A. Davis (ed.), *The Meaning of Dying in American Society*, California, University of Southern California, 1973.

Feuerstein, R., Y. Rand, Y. Mintzker, "Plastic and reconstructive surgery," unpublished paper, 1984.

Firth, R., *Symbols: Public and Private*, London, Allen and Unwin, 1973.

Fischer, H. Th., "The clothes of the naked Nuer," in T. Polhemus (ed.), *Social Aspects of the Human Body*, New York, Penguin Books, 1978.

Fisher, S., "Body image in neurotic and schizophrenic patients," *Archives of General Psychiatry* 15:90–101 (1966).

Fisher, S., "Body Image," in T. Polhemus (ed.), *Social Aspects of the Human Body*, New York, Penguin Books, 1978.

Fisher, S. and S.E. Cleveland, *Body Image and Personality*, Princeton, New Jersey, Van Nostrand, 1958.

Fleming, M.Z., B.R. MacGowan, L. Robinson, J. Spitz, and P. Salt, "The body image of the postoperative female-to-male transsexual," *Journal Consulting and Clinical Psychology* 50:461–462 (1982).

Florian, V. and E. Shurka, "Jewish and Arab parents' coping patterns with their disabled child in Israel," *International Journal of Rehabilitation Research* 4 (2):201–204 (1981).

Florian, V. and S. Katz, "The impact of cultural, ethnic, and national variables on attitudes towards the disabled in Israel," *International Journal of Intercultural Relations* 7:167–179 (1983).

Foucault, M., *The Birth of the Clinic*, London, Tavistock, 1973.

Franck, K.A., "Social construction of the physical environment: the case of gender," *Sociological Focus* 18 (2):143–159 (1985).

Frank, A.W., "For a sociology of the body: an analytical review," in M. Featherstone, M. Hepworth and B.S. Turner (eds.), *The Body: Social Process and Cultural Theory*, London, Sage Publications, 1991.

Frankl, Y. Y., "A Fetus is Also a Living Being," *Yediot Aharonot* (Dec. 17, 1979). [Hebrew].

Frazer, S.G., *The Golden Bough*, abridged edition, New York, Macmillan, 1922.

Freud, S., "On narcissism: An introduction," in J. Rickman (ed.), *A General Selection from the Works of Sigmund Freud*, London, Hogarth Press, 1937b.

Freud, S., "Mourning and melancholia," in J. Rickman (ed.), *A General Selection from the Works of Sigmund Freud*, London, Hogarth Press, 1937a.

Friedman, M., "Life tradition and book tradition in ultra orthodox judaism," in H. Goldberg (ed.), *Judaism From Within and Without: Anthropological Studies*, New York, State University of New York Press, 1987.

Futterman, E.H. and I.H. Hoffman, "Crisis and adaptation in the families of fatally-ill children," in E.J. Anthony and C. Koupernik (eds.), *The Child and His Family*, New York, John Wiley and Sons, 1973.

Gardner, G.E., "The psychiatric considerations underlying parental concern for handicapped children," in *Helping Parents of Handicapped Children: Group Approaches*, Boston, Children's Medical Center Child Study Association of America, 1959.

Geertz, C., "The impact of the concept of culture on the concept of man," in J. Platt (ed.), *New Views on Human Nature*, Chicago, University of Chicago Press, 1965.

Gellert, E., "Children's conception of the content and functions of the human body," *Genetic Monographs* 65:293–405 (1962).

Gergen, K.J. and M. Gergen, *Social Psychology*, New York, Harcourt Brace Janovich, Inc., 1981.

Gilligan, C., *In a Different Voice*, Cambridge, Mass., Harvard University Press, 1982.

Glaser, B.G. and A.L. Strauss, "Awareness contexts and social interactions," *American Sociological Review*, 29 (5):669–679 (1964).

Glassberg, K.I., "Gender Assignment in Newborn Male Pseudohermaphrodites," *Urologic Clinics of North America* 7:409–421 (1980).

Goffman, E.S., *Stigma: Notes on the Management of Spoiled Identity*, New Jersey, Prentice Hall, 1963.

Goodman, R.M. and R.J. Gorlin, *The Malformed Infant and Child*, New York, Oxford University Press, 1983.

Gould, J.L., *Ethnology.*, New York, W.W. Norton, 1982.

Gourevitch, M., "A survey of family reactions to disease and death in a family member," in J.E. Anthony and C. Koupernik (eds.), *The Child and His Family*, New York, John Wiley and Sons, 1973.

Greenblat, S., *Reconstructing Individualism*, in T.C. Heller, M. Sosna and D.E. Wellbery,, Stanford, Stanford University Press, 1986.

Greenlee, D., *Peirce's Concept of the Sign*, The Hague, Moulton, 1973.

Guy, R.F., B.A. Rankin and N.S. Norvell, "The relation of sex-role stereotyping to body-image," *Journal of Psychology* 105 (2):167–173 (1980).

Hallpike, C.R., "Social hair," in T. Polhemus (ed.), *Social Aspects of the Human Body*, New York, Penguin Books, 1978.

Halsey, A.H., "The sociology of education," in N.J. Smelser (ed.), *Sociology: An Introduction*, New York, John Wiley and Sons, 1967.

Harlap, S., "A time-series analysis of the incidence of Down's Syndrome in West Jerusalem," *American Journal of Epidemiology* 99 (3):210–217 (1974).

Harlap, S., A.M. Davies, M. Haber, H. Rossman, R. Prywes and N. Samueloff, "Congenital malformation in the Jerusalem perinatal study," *Israel Journal of Medical Sciences* 7:1520 (1971).

Harris, M., *Cannibals and Kings*, New York, Random House, 1977.

Hastrup, K. and P. Elsass, "Anthropological advocacy: A contradiction in terms," *Current Anthropology* 31:301–308 (1990).

Herzfeld, M., "Meaning and morality: a semiotic approach to evil eye accusation in a Greek village," *American Ethnologist* 8:560–574 (1981).

Herzfeld, M., "Closure as cure: Tropes in the exploration of bodily and social disorder," *Current Anthropology* 27 (2):107–120 (1986).

Hildebrandt, K.A. and H.E. Fitzgerald, "Adults' perceptions of infant sex and cuteness," *Sex Roles* 5:471–481 (1979).

Hildebrandt, K.A. and H.E. Fitzgerald, "Adults' responses to infants varying in perceived cuteness," *Behavioral Processes* 3:159–172 (1978).

Hildebrandt, K.A. and H.E. Fitzgerald, "Mothers' responses to infant physical appearance," *Infant Mental Health Journal* 2:56–61 (1981).

Hildebrandt, K.A., "The Role of physical appearance in infant and child development," in E. Fitzgerald, B.M. Lester and M.W. Yongman, *Theory and Research in Behavioral Pediatrics*, New York, Plenum Press, 1982.

Hill, W.W., "The status of the hermaphrodite and transvestite in Navaho culture," *American Anthropologist* 37:273–279 (1935).

Hjorth, C.W. and M. Harway, "Body image of physically abused and normal adolescents," *Journal of Clinical Psychology* 37:863–866 (1981).

Hoebel, A.E., *The Cheyennes: Indians of the Great Plains*, New York, Holt, Rinehart, and Winston, 1960.

Holland, J.C.B., "Coping with cancer: a challenge to the behavioral sciences," in J.W. Cullen et al., *Cancer, The Behavioral Dimensions*, New York, Raven Press, 1976.

Holt, K.S., "The influence of a retarded child upon family limitations," *Journal of Mental Deficiency Research* 2:28–34 (1958).

Honkasalo, M.L., "Medical symptoms: a challenge for semiotic research," *Semiotica* 87 (3/4):251–268 (1991).

Horn, D. and S. Waingrow, "What changes are occurring in public opinion survey," *American Journal of Public Health* 54:431–440 (1964).

Hospers, J., *Introductory Readings in Aesthetics*, New York, Macmillan, 1960.

Hunter, R., N. Kilstrom, E. Krybill and F. Loda, "Antecedents of child abuse and neglect in premature infants," *Pediatrics* 61:629 (1978).

Idler, E.L., "Definitions of health and illness and medical sociology," *Social Science and Medicine* 13A:723–731 (1979).

Iwawaki, S. and R.M. Lerner, "Cross-cultural analyses of body behavior relations: Developmental intra- and inter-cultural factor congruence in the body build stereotypes of Japanese and American males and females," *Psychologia* 19:67–76 (1976).

Iwawaki, S. and R.M. Lerner, "Cross cultural analyses of body behavior relations: A comparison of body build stereotypes of Japanese and American males and females," *Psychologia* 17:75–81 (1974).

Jenkins, C.D. and S.J. Zyzanski, "Dimensions of belief and feeling concerning three diseases, poliomyelitis, cancer and mental illness: A factor analytic study," *Behavioral Science* 13:372–381 (1968).

Jolland, J.C.B., "Coping with cancer: A challenge to the behavioral sciences," in J.W. Cullen et al., *Cancer, The Behavioral Dimensions*, New York, Raven Press, 1976.

Jones, E.J. et al., *Social Stigma: The Psychology of Marked Relationships*, New York, Freeman, 1984.

Junod, H.A., *The Life of a South African Tribe*, London, Macmillan, 1927.

Kalir, E., *National Registry of Children with Congenital Defects*, Israel Ministry of Health, Child-Care Department. [Hebrew].

Kamfner, M., "All were abandoned. All the deformed children born this year in the Kiryah Hospital were abandoned. What happens to these children? Who is responsible for them? Who pays the bill?," *Yediot Aharonot, Tel Aviv Weekend Magazine* (April 30, 1987). [Hebrew].

Kaplan, D.M., A. Smith and R. Groberstein, "School management of the seriously ill child," *The Journal of School Health* 44:250–257 (1974).

Kaplan, D.M. and E.A. Mason, "Maternal reaction to premature birth viewed as an acute emotional disorder," in H.J. Parad (ed.), *Crisis Intervention*, New York, Family Service Association of America, 1965.

Katz, J., *Gay American History: Lesbians and Gay men in the U.S.A.*, New York, Crowell, 1976.

Katz, R.B, *Recreating Motherhood*, New York, Norton, 1989.

Katz, S. and E. Shurka, "The influence of contextual variables on evaluations of the physically disabled by the nondisabled," *Rehabilitation Literature* 38 (2):369–373 (1977).

Kehle, T.J., W.J. Bramble and J. Mason, "Teachers' expectations: Ratings of student performance as biased by student characteristics," *Journal of Experimental Education* 43:54–60 (1974).

Kellerman, J. (ed.), *Psychological Aspects of Childhood Cancer*, Springfield, Ill., Charles C. Thomas, 1980.

Kennell, H.J., H. Slyter and H.M. Klaus, "The mourning response of parents to the death of a newborn infant," *New England Journal of Medicine* 13:283, 344–349 (1970).

Kessler, S.J., "The Medical construction of gender: case management of intersexed infants," *Signs* 16 (11):3–27 (1990).

Klaus, M.H. and J.H. Kennel, *Maternal-infant Bonding*, St. Louis, C.V. Mosby Co., 1976.

Klein, M. and L. Stern, "Low birth weight and the battered child syndrome," *American Journal of Disabilities in Childhood* 122:15–18 (July, 1971).

Klingberg, M.A., R. Chen, C.M. Paier, S. Chemke and G. Amizur, "Parental age and Down Syndrome," *Congenital Anomalies* 22 (1):1–6 (1982).

Korolick, E., *Personality variables and organization of body image after amputation of a limb*, Tel Aviv University, 1972. Thesis for Master of Arts [Hebrew]

Kroeber, A.L., *Handbook of the Indians of California*, U.S. BAE Bulletin, Vol. 78, Washington, D.C., U.S. GPO, 1925.

Kurti, L., "Home/body: anatomy of the Hungarian house," paper presented at the 112th Annual Spring Meeting of the American Ethnological Society: The Body in Society and Culture, held jointly with the 25th Annual Meeting of the Southern Anthropological Society: African-American in the South. Atlanta, Georgia, April 26–28, 1990.

Langolis, J.H. and C. Stephan, "Effects of physical attractiveness and ethnicity on children's behavioral attributions and peer preferences," *Child Development* 48:1694–1698 (1977).

LaVoie, J.C. and G.R. Adams, "Teacher expectancy and its relation to physical and interpersonal characteristics of the child," *Alberta Journal of Education Research* 20:122–132 (1974).

Leach, E.R., "Magical Hair," *Journal of the Royal Anthropological Institute* 88:147–164 (1958).

Leach, E.R., *Culture and Communication*, Cambridge, Cambridge University Press, 1976.

Lemperle, G. and D. Radu, "Facial plastic surgery in children with Down's Syndrome," paper presented at the Annual Meeting of the Association of German Plastic Surgeons. Cologne, Germany, October, 1978.

Lennard, S.H.C. and H.L. Lennard, "Architecture: Effect of territory, boundary and orientation of family functioning," *Family Process* 16 (1):49–66 (1977).

Lerner, R.M. and S.J. Korn, "The development of body build stereotypes in males," *Child Development* 43:908–920 (1972).

Lerner, R.M., "The development of stereotyped expectancies of body build-behavior relations," *Child Development* 40:137–141 (1969).

Lerner, R.M. and S. Iwawaki, "Cross-cultural analysis of body behavior relations: Factor structure of body build stereotypes of Japanese and American adolescents," *Psychologia* 18:83–91 (1975).

Levy, R., *Tahitians: Mind and Experience in the Society Islands*, Chicago, University of Chicago Press, 1973.

Linton, R., *The Study of Man*, New York, Appleton-Century Crofts, 1936.

Lobo, E.D. and A. Webb, "Parental reactions to their mongol baby," *The Practitioner* 204:412–415 (March, 1970).

Longacre, J.J., *Rehabilitation of Facially Disfigured*, Springfield, Ill., Charles C. Thomas, 1973.

Lorber, J., *Paradoxes of Gender*, New Haven, Yale University Press, 1993.

Lukianowicz, C., "Body image disturbances in personal disorders," *British Journal of Psychiatry* 113:31–47 (1967).

MacGregor, F.C., *Transformation and Identity: The Face and Plastic Surgery*, New York, Times Book Company, 1974.

MacGregor, F.C., *Transformations and Identity: The Face and Plastic Surgery*, Oak Grove, Ill, Eterna Press, 1980.

MacGregor, F.C., Abel, T., Bryt, A., Laner, E., and Weismann, S., *Facial Deformities and Plastic Surgery*, Springfield Ill., Charles C. Thomas, 1953.

Mandelbaum, A. and M.E. Wheeler, "The meaning of a defective child to parents," *Social Casework* 41 (7):360–367 (1960).

Marwit, K.L., S.J. Marwit and E. Walker, "Effects of student race and physical attractiveness on teacher's judgements of transgressions," *Journal of Educational Psychology* 70:911–915 (1978).

Matza, P., *Becoming Deviant*, Englewood Cliffs, New Jersey, Prentice-Hall, 1969.

Meggitt, M.J., *Desert People*, Sydney, Angus and Robertson, 1962.

Middlebrook, P.N., *Social Psychology and Modern Life*, 2nd edition, New York, Knopf, 1980.

Mintzker, Y., "Facial surgery on children and adolescents with Down's Syndrome: Reactions of children (patients), parents and environment," paper presented at the Fourth International Congress of the European Association for Special Education, Tel-Aviv, July, 1983.

Morris, D., *Manwatching*, New York, Harry N. Abrams, 1977.

Morris, W. (ed.), *The American Heritage Dictionary of the English Language*, New York, Heritage Publishing Company and Houghton-Mifflin Company, 1969.

Munroe, R., Whiting, J., and D. Hally, "Institutionalized Male Transvestism and Sex Distinctions," *American Anthropologist* 71:87–91 (1969).

Nagy, M.H., "Conception of some bodily functions," *Journal of Genetic Psychology* 83:99–216 (1953).

Namir, D., "Dozens of handicapped children abandoned in the hospital last year," *Yediot Aharonot* (March 10, 1982). [Hebrew].

Namir, D., "The Gur Rebbe permitted a young ultra-Orthodox couple to abandon their retarded child," *Yediot Aharonot* (April 11, 1984). [Hebrew].

Nanda, S., *Neither Man nor Women, the Hijras of India*, Belmont, Cal., Wadsworth Publishing Co., 1990.

Oberman, C.E., *A History of Vocational Rehabilitation in America*, Minneapolis, T.S. Denison and Co., 1968.

Offord, D.R. and J.F. Aponte, "Distortion of disability and effect on family life," *Journal of the American Academy of Child Psychiatry* 6:499–511 (July, 1967).

Opler, M, "A Letter to the Editor," *American Anthropologist* 62 (3):505–511 (1960).

Packenheim, A.L., "Human Condition after Auschwitz," *Yissum Mehkarim* 25:85–100 (1978). [Hebrew].

Padilla, G., "Second Quarterly Project Report to the American Cancer Society," California Division, (January, 1972).

Palgi, P., "Attitudes towards the disabled among immigrants from Middle Eastern countries," *Public Health* 56:16–17 (1962).

Peirce, Charles Sanders (1931-1935), *Collected Papers*, Vol. 2, Cambridge, Mass., Harvard University Press.

Peres, Y., "Questions in Sociobiology," paper delivered at a sociobiology conference in Haifa, 1983.

Pfuhk, E., *The Deviance Process*, New York, Van Nostrand, 1980.

Phoenix, A., Woollett, A. and Lloyd, E. (eds.), *Motherhood, Meanings, Practices and Ideologies*, London, Sage Publications, 1991.

Polunin, I., "The Body as an indicator of Health and Disease," in J. Blacking (ed.), *The Anthropology of the Body*, London, Academic Press, 1977.

Postal, S., "Body image and identity: A comparison of Kwakiutl and Hope," in T. Polhemus (ed.), *Social Aspects of the Human Body*, New York, Penguin Books, 1978.

Proschansky, H.M., W.H. Ittelson and L.G. Rivlin, "Freedom of choice and behavior in physical setting," in H.M. Proshansky, W.H. Ittelson, L.G. Rivlin (eds.), *Environmental Psychology: Man and his Physical Setting*, New York, Holt, Rinehart and Winston, 1967.

Quint, J.S., "Institutionalized practices of information control," *Psychiatry* 28:119–132 (1965).

Rae, W.A., "Body image of children and adolescents during physical illness and hospitalization," *Psychiatric Anals* 12 (12):1065 (1982).

Richardson, S.A., L. Ronald and R.E. Kleck, "The social status of handicapped boys in a camp setting," *Journal of Special Education* 8:143–152 (1974).

Richardson, S.A., N. Goodman, A.H. Hastorf and S.M. Dornbush, "Cultural uniformity in reaction to physical disabilities," *American Sociological Review* 26:241–247 (1961).

Rofe, H., Almagor, M. and Y. Yafe, "Relationship of ethnic origin and belonging to a group of handicapped persons and attitudes towards them," *Megamot* 25 (4):488–493. [Hebrew].

Rosen, E., "Lost Children," *Ma'ariv Weekend Magazine* (July 6,1984). [Hebrew].

Rosenblat, P.C. and L.G. Budd, "Territoriality and privacy in married and unmarried couples," *Journal of Social Psychology* 97:67–76 (1975).

Ross, A.O., *The Exceptional Child in the Family*, New York, London, Grune and Stratton, 1964.

Ross, M.B. and J. Salvia, "Attractiveness as a biasing factor in teacher judgments," *American Journal of Mental Deficiency* 80:96–98 (1975).

Roth, J.S., "Ritual and magic in the control of contagion," *American Sociological Review* 22:310–314 (1957).

Roumeguère-Eberhardt, J., "La notion de vie, base de la structure sociale Venda," *Journal del la Societe des Africanists* 27:2 (1957).

Rubin, J., F.J. Provenzano, and Z. Luria, "The Eye of the beholder: parents' views on sex of newborns," *American Journal of Orthopsychiatry* 44 (4):512–519 (1974).

Rubin, N., "Social networks and mourning: A comparative approach," *Omega* 21:113–127 (1990).

Rubin, N., C. Shmilovitz and M. Weiss, "From fat to thin: informal rites affirming identity change," *Symbolic Interaction* 16 (1) (1993).

Ruddick, S., *Maternal Thinking: Towards a Politics of Peace*, London, The Women's Press, 1989.

Sackett, G.P. (ed.), *Observing Behavior*, Vol. 1, Baltimore, University Park Press, 1978.

Sadan, H., "Statistics and Abortion," *Yediot Aharonot* (March 15, 1982). [Hebrew].

Salyer, M., A. Jensen and C. Borden, "Effects of facial deformities and physical attractiveness on mother-infant bonding," in *Craniofacial Surgery*, Proceedings of the First International Society of Cranio-Mexillo-Facial Surgery, 1985.

Salvia, J., J.B. Sheare and B. Algozzine, "Facial attractiveness and personal-social development," *Journal of Abnormal Child Psychology* 3:171–178 (1975).

Sartre, J.P., *The Wall and Other Stories*, Lloyd Alexander (trans.), New York, New Directions Publishing Co., 1948.

Schalit, B., *Forming body image and adjusting to pressure situations*, Hebrew University, 1971. Doctoral dissertation [Hebrew]

Scheff, T.J., *Being Mentally Ill*, Chicago, Aldine Publishing Company, 1966.

Scheffler, H., *Choiseul Island Social Structure*, Berkeley, University of California Press, 1965.

Scheper-Hughes, N., *Death Without Weeping: The Violence of Everyday Life in Brazil*, Berkeley, University of California Press, 1992.

Schilder, P., *Psychoanalysis, Man and Society*, New York, Norton, 1951.

Schilder, P., *The image and appearance of the human body*, Psychological Monographs No. 4, London, K. Paul, Trench, Trubner and Company, 1935.

Schneider, D.E., "The image of the heart and the synergic principle in psychoanalysis," *Psychoanalytic Review* 41:197–215 (1954).

Schonfeld, W.A., "Body image in adolescents: A psychiatric concept for the pediatrician," *Pediatrics*:845–854 (1963).

Schur, E., *The Politics of Deviance*, Engelwood Cliffs, New Jersey, Prentice Hall, 1980.

Schwartz, C.G., "Perspectives on deviance: Wives' definitions of their husbands mental illness," *Psychiatry* 20:275–291 (1957).

Schwartz, J., and S. Abramonitz, "Effects of female client physical attractiveness on clinical judgement," *Psychotherapy: Theory, Research and Practice* 15:251–257 (1978).

Sebba, R. and A. Churchman, "The uniqueness of the home," *Architecture and Behavior* 3 (1):7–24 (1986).

Severino, S.K., "Body image changes in hemodialysis and rental transplant," *Psychosomatics* 21 (6):509 (1980).

Shainess, N., "The psychologic experience of labor," *New York State Journal of Medicine* 63:2924 (October, 1963).

Shalinsky, A. and A. Glascock, "Killing infants and the aged in non-industrial societies: Removing the liminal," *The Social Science Journal* 25 (3):277–287 (1988).

Shamgar-Handelman, L. and R. Belkin, "They won't stay home forever: Pattern of home space allocation," *Urban Anthropology* 13 (1):117–144 (1984).

Shamgar-Handelman, L. and R. Belkin, "Patterns of space allocation in living quarters," in L. Shamgar-Handelman and R. Bar-Yosef (eds.), *Families in Israel*, Jerusalem, Akademon, Hebrew University, 1991. [Hebrew].

Sharma, S.K., *Hijras: the Labelled Deviants*, New Delhi, Gian Publishing House, 1989.

Sheldon, W.H., *The Varieties of Human Physique*, New York, Harper, 1940.

Sheldon, W.H., *The Varieties of Temperament*, New York, Harper, 1942.

Sheleff, L., *Generations Apart*, New York, McGraw-Hill Book Company, 1981.

Shinfeld, Y., *Cancer: Important Information*, Tel Aviv, Yediot Aharonot, 1980. [Hebrew].

Shneidman, E.S., *Death: Current Perspectives*, California, Mayfield Publishing Company, 1976.

Shokeid, M., and Deshen, S., *The Predicament of Homecoming: Cultural and Social Life of North African Immigrants in Israel*, Ithaca, Cornell University Press, 1974.

Shurka, E. and V. Florian, "A study of Israeli Jewish and Arab parental perceptions of their disabled children," *Journal of Comparative Family Studies* 14:367–376 (1983).

Silberford, M. and S. Greer, "Psychological concomitants of cancer: Clinical aspects," *American Journal of Psychotherapy* 36:470–478 (1982).

Smith, E., *Psychosocial Aspects of Cancer Patient Care*, New York, McGraw-Hill Book Co., 1976.

Sontag, S., *Illness as Metaphor*, New York, Vintage Books, 1978.

Spinetta, J.J., "The dying child's awareness of death: A review," *Psychological Bulletin* 52:256–260 (1974).

Spock, B., *Baby and Child Care*, New York, Pocket Books, 1968.

Staffieri, J.R., "Body image stereotypes of mentally retarded," *American Journal of Mental Deficiency* 72:841–843 (1968).

Staffieri, J.R., "Body build and behavioral expediencies in young females," *Developmental Psychology* 6:125–127 (1972).

Staiano, K., "Medical semiotics: Redefining an ancient craft," *Semiotica* 38 (3/4):319–346 (1982).

Stinchcombe, A.L., "The logic of scientific inference," in A.L. Stinchcombe (ed.), *Constructing Social Theories*, New York, Harcourt, 1968.

Stone, G.P., "Appearance and the self," in A.M. Rose (ed.), *Human Behavior and Social Process*, Boston, Houghton-Mifflin, 1962.

Styczynski, E. and J. Langolis, "The effects of familiarity on behavioral stereotypes associated with physical attractiveness in young children," *Child Development* 48:1137–1141 (1977).

Synnott, A., "Tomb, temple, machine and self: the social construction of the body," *British Journal of Sociology* 43 (1):79–110 (1992).

Tewari, A.S., "A Review of Sharma (1989)," *Eastern Anthropologist* 43 (1):103–105 (1990).

Thalidomide, "Rehabilitation of Thalidomide-deformed children," *Canadian Medical Association Journal* 88:488–489 (1963).

Tisza, V.B., "Management of the parents of the chronically ill child," *American Journal of Orthopsychiatry* 32 (1):53–59 (1962).

Tisza, V.B. and E. Gompertz, "The parents reaction to the birth and early care of children with cleft palate," *Pediatrics* 30 (1):86–90 (1962).

Tomer, Y., "Parents abandon 30 children in the hospital every year," *Yediot Aharonot* (Nov. 12, 1987). [Hebrew].

Trnavsky, P.A. and R. Bakeman, "Physical attractiveness: Stereotype and social behavior in preschool children," paper presented at the meeting of the American Psychological Association. Washington, D.C., 1976.

Tudor, M.J., "Family habilitation: A child with birth defect," in D.P. Hymovich and M.U. Barnard (eds.) 2nd ed., *Family Health Care*, Vol. 2, New York, McGraw-Hill Book Company, 1979.

Turner, B.S., "Review article: missing bodies—towards a sociology of embodiment," *Sociology of Health and Illness* 13 (2):265–272 (1991).

Van-Gennep, A., *The Rites of Passage*, Chicago, University of Chicago Press, 1960.

Weiss, M., *Disability and Identity*, Tel Aviv University, 1985. Doctoral dissertation [Hebrew].

Weiss, M., "The Metaphor of AIDS," Presented at the 19th meetings of the Israel Sociological Association. Ben Gurion University, Beer Sheba, 1988.

Weiss, M., "The bereaved parent's position: aspects of life review and self fulfillment," *Current Perspectives on Aging and Life Cycle* 3:269–280 (1989).

Weiss, M., *Conditional Love: Parental Relations Towards Handicapped Children*, Tel Aviv, Sifriat Hapoalim, 1991. [Hebrew].

Weiss, M., "Of Man and beast: defining the child as a non-person paves the way to his/fer rejection," *Semiotica* (1993a). [to appear].

Weiss, M., "'Non-person' and 'Non-home': territorial seclusion of appearance-impaired children," *Journal of Contemporary Ethnography* 22 (4) (1994). [to appear].

Wexler, M.R., Y. Mintzker, Y. Peled, Y. Rand, M. Sela, and R. Feuerstein, "Rehabilitative plastic surgery in Down's Syndrome," *Ha-Refuah* 113:3–4 (1986). [Hebrew].

Wilson, E., *On Human Nature*, Cambridge, Mass., Harvard University Press, 1977.

Winnicott, D.W., *Holding and Interpretation*, New York, Grove Press, 1987.

Weller, L., H. Costeff, B. Cohen and D. Rahman, "Social variables in the perception and acceptance of retardation," *American Journal of Mental Deficiency* 9 (3):274–278 (1974).

Williams, W.L., *The Spirit and the Flesh: Sexual Diversity in American Indian Culture*, Boston, Beacon Press, 1986.

Woollett, A. and Phoenix, A., "Psychological views of mothering," in Phoenix, A., Woollett, A. and Lloyd, E. (eds.), *Motherhood, Meanings, Practices and Ideologies*, London, Sage Publications, 1991.

Wright, B.A., *Physical Disability: A Psychological Approach*, New York, Harper and Row, 1960.

Yannai, Ts., "On the biological foundation of beauty," in Yannai, Ts. (ed.), *Ideas*, IBM publaddr Tel Aviv, 1990. [Hebrew].

Yavsam, A., "Hair," *Yediot Aharonot Weekend Magazine* (May 6, 1983). [Hebrew].

Yarrow, M.R., C.G. Schwartz, H.S. Murphy and L.C. Deasy, "The psychological meaning of mental illness in the family," *Journal of Social Issues* 11:12–24 (1955).

Young, J.C., "The idea of God in northern Nayasaland," in E.W. Smith (ed.), *African Ideas of God*, London, Edinburgh House Press, 1950.

Young R.D. and A. Avdzej, "Effects of obedience-disobedience and obese-nonobese body type on social acceptance by peers," *The Journal of Genetic Psychology* 134:43–51 (1979).

Yuchtman, A. and Y. Ram, "Impact of improvements in living conditions on family welfare," in *Yissum Mehkarim*, Tel Aviv, 1975. [Hebrew].

Zeidel, A., "Problems of emotional adjustment in juvenile diabetes," in J.E. Anthony and C. Koupernik (eds.), *The Child and His Family*, New York, John Wiley and Sons, 1973.

Zeider, Y. and A. Marom, "How families cope with accepting an exceptional child," *Hevra u-Revahah* 3 (4):405–394 (1980). [Hebrew].

Zeman, J., "Peirce's Theory of Signs," in T.A. Sebeok, *A Perfusion of Signs*, Bloomington, Indiana University Press, 1977.

Index

Acknowledgments

This book was written with the assistance of many fine people, who stood by my side along the way, from beginning to end.

I wish to thank Moshe Shokeid and Shlomo Deshen. We traveled a long road together, and I am greatful for the wonderful good fortune I had in being able to benefit from their talent and outlook on research. I owe a great debt to Haim Hazan, who lent a willing ear and stood by my side through a long and difficult period. He was sensitive to the data which I gathered and assisted in sorting and categorizing it. Thanks to Leonard Weller, Aron Weller, and Sonia Weller, and to Rivka Bergman and Tamar Krulik, who encouraged me from the start and accompanied this endeavor, step by step.

In the final shaping of the book I was helped much by the late Victor Turner, by Judith Lorber, Yochanan Peres, Judith Shuval, Lea Shamgar-Handelman, Victor Azarya, Baruch Kimmerling, Harvey Goldberg, Sasha Whitman, Dafna Izraeli, Susan Sered, and Abraham and Sima Yogev. I also wish to thank Emanuel Marx, Leon Sheleff, Nissan Rubin, Victor Florian, and Penina Klein.

I am grateful to The Rosita and Esteban Herzeg Program on Sex Difference in Society, the Shaine Center for Research in Social Sciences, The Levi Eshkol Institute for Economic, Social, and Political Research, and The Israel Foundations Trustees for providing me grants that helped in the production of this book.

I also wish to thank the translator, Rachel Rowen, for rendering the book into English and typesetting it. I am also grateful to Lynn Flint and Jay Williams of Greenwood Press for making production of this book an enjoyable experience.

Special thanks go to my students, and to the nurses and doctors who let me glimpse into their world and share the dramas that take place in their work every day. Unfortunately, ethical constraints prevent me from mentioning by name the doctors, nurses, and social workers who shared their professional and personal experiences with me. Their help was inestimable.

To my family—Shraga, Tami, and Shay—who shared my sorrows and joys, I extend my love.

Last but not least, I wish to thank the sick children and their families, who permitted me to peer into their world. I wish them all good health and long life.

About the Author

MEIRA WEISS is a lecturer in the Department of Sociology and Anthropology at the Hebrew University of Jerusalem. Her Hebrew edition of *Conditional Love* has received wide acclaim. Dr. Weiss has worked extensively in the medical profession in Israel and is a certified Gestalt therapist as well as a sociologist.